593 Country-Style Recipes Right at Your Fingertips

IT'S no surprise that the *Taste of Home Annual Recipes* cookbook continues to be our best-selling book year after year. After all, it was readers themselves who asked us to gather an entire year's worth of recipes from *Taste of Home*—the most popular food magazine in North America—into one convenient, thoroughly indexed book.

Like the previous editions, we think this *1999 Taste of Home Annual Recipes* collection will become a valued reference in your kitchen for a number of reasons:

1. Its 324 pages are organized into 16 handy chapters for easy reference. Between its covers, you have at hand every single *Taste of Home* recipe we published in 1998.
2. Plus we've included *dozens* of bonus recipes—47 to be exact! So you'll have a whole group of new home-style recipes to try.
3. Finding all of the 593 recipes is a snap with this book's *three different indexes*— one indexes dishes by food category, one tells you which issue of *Taste of Home* it originally appeared in, and one designates every recipe that includes Nutritional Analysis and Diabetic Exchanges. These handy indexes can be found on pages 306-318.
4. The full-color pictures in this cookbook are *bigger* than ever so you can plainly see what many of these dishes will look like before you begin preparing them.
5. We've used larger print for easy reading while cooking. And each recipe is presented "all-on-a-page", so you never have to turn back and forth while cooking.
6. This volume is printed on the highest quality coated paper to make the foods more attractive and appealing. More importantly, it lets you wipe away spatters easily.
7. The book lies open and *stays open* as you cook. Its durable hard cover will give you *years* of use (you'll never have to worry about dog-earring your magazine collection again).

But the real proof of this volume's value is in the tasting. Your family will *rave* at the results of these recipes, all of which are favorites of other families.

Tight on time? Rely on the fast-to-fix recipes in our "Meals in Minutes" chapter. Each complete meal goes from stovetop to tabletop in 30 minutes or less.

On a budget? You need just *92¢ a plate* to serve your family "Garlic Swiss Steak", "Simple White Bread" and "Lemon-Glazed Carrots". (You'll find this flavorful feast on page 284.)

Family picnic? The 41 "Potluck Pleasers" recipes fill the bill when you need to feed 10, 100 or any number in between!

Planning a special supper? For 12 delectable menus that come straight from the kitchens of fellow country cooks, turn to the "My Mom's Best Meal" and "Editors' Meals" chapters.

With 593 down-home dishes, this taste treasury sets the table for delicious dining in your home year after year!

1999 Taste of Home Annual Recipes

Editor: Julie Schnittka
Art Director: Linda Dzik
Food Editor: Coleen Martin
Associate Editor: Kristine Krueger
Assistant Art Director:
Stephanie Marchese
Production: Ellen Lloyd, Claudia Wardius
Cover Photography: Scott Anderson

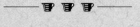

Executive Editor: Kathy Pohl
Food Editor: Coleen Martin
Associate Food Editor: Corinne Willkomm
Senior Recipe Editor: Sue A. Jurack
Senior Editor: Bob Ottum
Managing Editor: Ann Kaiser
Assistant Managing Editor: Faithann Stoner
Associate Editors: Henry de Fiebre,
Kristine Krueger, Sharon Selz
Test Kitchen Home Economist:
Sue Draheim
Test Kitchen Assistants: Judith Scholovich,
Sherry Smalley, Sue Hampton
Editorial Assistants: Barb Czysz,
Mary Ann Koebernik
Design Director: Jim Sibilski
Art Director: Vicky Marie Moseley
Food Photography: Scott Anderson,
Glenn Thiesenhusen
Food Photography Artist: Stephanie Marchese
Photo Studio Manager: Anne Schimmel
Production: Ellen Lloyd,
Claudia Wardius
Publisher: Roy Reiman

Taste of Home Books
©1998 Reiman Publications, L.P.
5400 S. 60th St., Greendale WI 53129

International Standard Book Number:
0-89821-239-1
International Standard Serial Number:
1094-3463

PICTURED AT RIGHT. Clockwise from upper left: Little Dixie Pound Cake, Vegetable Ramekins and Beef Tenderloin in Mushroom Sauce (pp. 206 and 207); Chocolate Marvel Cake (p. 152); Mom's Vegetable Medley (p. 228); Stuffed Crown Roast of Pork (p. 242).

Taste of Home 1999 Annual Recipes

PICTURED ON FRONT COVER. Top to bottom: Sour Cream Chocolate Cake (p. 154), Paprika Pork Roast (p. 81), Harvest Sweet Potato Soup (p. 50).

PICTURED ON BACK COVER. Clockwise from upper left: Creamy Lime Sherbet (p. 171), Marble Chiffon Cake (p. 158), White Chocolate Fruit Tart (p. 178).

Photo Contributor: Mike Huibregste (pp. 38, 70, 71, 72, 73, 105, 122)

FOR ADDITIONAL COPIES of this book or information on other books, write: *Taste of Home* Books, P.O. Box 990, Greendale WI 53129. **Credit card orders call toll-free 1-800/558-1013.**

Snacks & Beverages

Whether you're looking for a satisfying opener to a meal,
a light midday snack or a thirst-quenching beverage, you'll uncover
a mouth-watering assortment on the pages that follow.

HEARTY STARTERS. Clockwise from upper left: Sausage Quiche Squares (p. 20), Mocha Punch (p. 8), Garlic Pepper Toast (p. 18), Tropical Fruit Dip (p. 19), Championship Bean Dip (p. 9) and Stuffed Cuke Snacks (p. 20).

Onion Cheese Ball

My husband and I and our friends from church love to dig into this creamy, savory cheese ball. It's an appealing addition to any snack buffet. —Shelby Finger
Hickory, North Carolina

☑ Nutritional Analysis included

> 1 package (8 ounces) fat-free cream cheese, softened
> 8 slices (3/4 ounce *each*) fat-free sharp cheddar cheese, cut into thin strips
> 1 small onion, diced
> 1 tablespoon Worcestershire sauce
> 1 teaspoon garlic powder
> Dash hot pepper sauce
> 1/2 cup minced fully cooked low-fat ham
> Fresh vegetables *or* reduced-fat crackers

In a mixing bowl, beat the cheeses. Add onion, Worcestershire sauce, garlic powder and hot pepper sauce; mix well. Shape into a ball and roll in ham. Cover and refrigerate for at least 1 hour. Serve with vegetables or crackers. **Yield:** 1-1/2 cups.
Nutritional Analysis: One 2-tablespoon serving (calculated without crackers or vegetables) equals 24 calories, 198 mg sodium, 2 mg cholesterol, 2 gm carbohydrate, 4 gm protein, trace fat. **Diabetic Exchange:** 1/2 lean meat.

Chicken Meatball Appetizers

These nicely seasoned chicken meatballs are a crowd-pleasing change of pace on the appetizer tray. They're great plain or dipped in mustard.
—Norma Snider, Chambersburg, Pennsylvania

☑ Nutritional Analysis included

> 2-1/2 cups minced cooked chicken breast
> 3 tablespoons finely chopped onion
> 3 tablespoons finely chopped celery
> 2 tablespoons finely chopped carrot
> 2 tablespoons dry bread crumbs
> 1 egg white
> 1/2 teaspoon poultry seasoning
> Pinch pepper

In a bowl, combine all ingredients; mix well. Shape into 3/4-in. balls; place on a baking sheet that has been coated with nonstick cooking spray. Bake at 400° for 8-10 minutes or until lightly browned.
Yield: about 2-1/2 dozen. **Nutritional Analysis:** One serving (3 meatballs) equals 42 calories, 23 mg sodium, 21 mg cholesterol, 2 gm carbohydrate, 6 gm protein, 1 gm fat. **Diabetic Exchange:** 1 very lean meat.

Mocha Punch

(Pictured above)

I first tried this smooth, creamy punch at a friend's Christmas open house. It was so special and distinctive I didn't leave until I had the recipe. Having a frosty glass of this chocolate punch is like sipping a chocolate shake. —Yvonne Hatfield, Norman, Oklahoma

> 1-1/2 quarts water
> 1/2 cup instant chocolate drink mix
> 1/2 cup sugar
> 1/4 cup instant coffee granules
> 1/2 gallon vanilla ice cream
> 1/2 gallon chocolate ice cream
> 1 cup whipped cream, whipped
> Chocolate curls, optional

In a large saucepan, bring the water to a boil. Remove from the heat. Add drink mix, sugar and coffee; stir until dissolved. Cover and refrigerate for 4 hours or overnight. About 30 minutes before serving, pour into a punch bowl. Add ice cream by scoopfuls; stir until partially melted. Garnish with dollops of whipped cream and chocolate curls if desired. **Yield:** 20-25 servings (about 5 quarts).

Zesty Beef Spread

Green olives and dried beef are a flavorful combination in this spread. I really like the fact that I can make these logs in advance. —Rosa Martin
Bridgewater, Virginia

- 1 package (8 ounces) cream cheese, softened
- 1/4 cup grated Parmesan cheese
- 1/3 cup chopped stuffed olives
- 2 tablespoons prepared horseradish
- 1 teaspoon chopped green onion *or* chives, optional
- 2 packages (2-1/2 ounces *each*) sliced dried beef, chopped, *divided*

Sliced stuffed olives, optional
Assorted crackers

In a mixing bowl, combine the first five ingredients. Mix in 1 cup of beef. Shape into two logs, about 6 in. each. Press remaining beef onto each log. Garnish with olives if desired. Chill for at least 1 hour. Serve with crackers. **Yield:** about 2 cups.

Creamy Horseradish Dip

In this simple-to-prepare vegetable dip, horseradish shines through without being too overpowering. —Barbara Coleman, Dunbar, West Virginia

✓ Nutritional Analysis included

- 1 cup mayonnaise
- 2 tablespoons prepared horseradish
- 1 teaspoon cider *or* white wine vinegar
- 1/2 teaspoon curry powder
- 1/2 teaspoon garlic salt *or* 1/4 teaspoon garlic powder
- 1/2 teaspoon ground mustard

Assorted fresh vegetables

In a bowl, combine the first six ingredients. Cover and chill for at least 1 hour. Serve with vegetables. **Yield:** about 1 cup. **Nutritional Analysis:** One 2-tablespoon serving (prepared with fat-free mayonnaise and garlic powder) equals 23 calories, 214 mg sodium, 0 cholesterol, 5 gm carbohydrate, trace protein, trace fat. **Diabetic Exchange:** 1 vegetable.

Championship Bean Dip

(Pictured at right)

My friends and neighbors expect me to bring this irresistible dip to every gathering. When I arrive, they ask, "You brought your bean dip, didn't you?" If there are any leftovers, we use them to make bean and cheese burritos the next day. I've given out this recipe a hundred times. —Wendi Wavrin Law
Omaha, Nebraska

- 1 can (16 ounces) refried beans
- 1 cup picante sauce
- 1 cup (4 ounces) shredded Monterey Jack cheese
- 1 cup (4 ounces) shredded cheddar cheese
- 3/4 cup sour cream
- 1 package (3 ounces) cream cheese, softened
- 1 tablespoon chili powder
- 1/4 teaspoon ground cumin

Tortilla chips and salsa

In a bowl, combine the first eight ingredients; transfer to a slow cooker. Cover and cook on high for 2 hours or until heated through, stirring once or twice. Serve with tortilla chips and salsa. **Yield:** 4-1/2 cups.

Popcorn's a Perfect Snack

MOVE OVER, salt and butter! Popcorn can be topped and combined in lots of fun and deliciously different ways, as these recipes prove. Give them a try—compliments are sure to pop up!

Lemon Cloud Popcorn

(Pictured below)

I love the unexpected lemony flavor of this light snack. I'm sure your family will, too! —Trudie Hagen
Roggen, Colorado

4-1/2 quarts popped popcorn
    2 cups sugar
1/2 cup light corn syrup
1/2 cup water
    1 tablespoon lemon extract
1/2 teaspoon baking soda
1-1/2 teaspoons grated lemon peel

Place popcorn in two greased 15-in. x 10-in. x 1-in. baking pans. Keep warm in a 225° oven. Meanwhile, in a heavy saucepan, combine sugar, corn syrup and water; bring to a boil over medium heat. Stir occasionally until mixture reaches 290° on a candy thermometer (soft-crack stage). Remove

KERNEL OF TRUTH. Snacks like crisp Lemon Cloud Popcorn and Ribbon-o-Fudge Popcorn Bars (shown above, top to bottom) are made for munching.

from the heat; quickly stir in extract and baking soda. Pour over warm popcorn. Sprinkle with lemon peel; stir until well coated. Store in an airtight container. **Yield:** 5 quarts.

Ribbon-o-Fudge Popcorn Bars

(Pictured below left)

Two sweet layers of butterscotch- and marshmallow-coated popcorn are held together with chocolate in these scrumptious snack bars. —Flo Burtnett
Gage, Oklahoma

> 2 cups (12 ounces) semisweet chocolate chips
> 2 tablespoons shortening
> 3 tablespoons butter *or* margarine
> 4 cups miniature marshmallows
> 1 cup butterscotch chips
> 3 quarts popped popcorn

In a microwave or double boiler, melt chocolate chips and shortening. Chill for 15-20 minutes or until thickened. Meanwhile, line a 9-in. square baking pan with foil; grease the foil and set pan aside. In a heavy saucepan over low heat, melt butter. Stir in marshmallows and butterscotch chips until melted and smooth. Place the popcorn in a large bowl; add marshmallow mixture and toss until coated. Firmly press half of the popcorn mixture into prepared pan. Spread chocolate mixture evenly over popcorn. Firmly press remaining popcorn mixture over chocolate. Chill for 30 minutes. Lift out of pan, using foil edges. Remove foil; cut into bars. **Yield:** 2 dozen.

Popcorn Snack Mix

With steak sauce, curry and garlic powder, this snack mix has an appealing bold, spicy taste.
—Heidi Harrington, Steuben, Maine

> 3 quarts popped popcorn
> 2-1/3 cups salted peanuts
> 2 cups pretzel sticks
> 2 cups miniature cheese crackers
> 1/3 cup butter *or* margarine, melted
> 3/4 teaspoon salt
> 3/4 teaspoon *each* curry powder, garlic powder and onion powder
> 3/4 teaspoon steak sauce

In a large bowl, combine popcorn, peanuts, pretzels and crackers. Combine remaining ingredients. Pour over popcorn mixture; toss to coat. Place in

two ungreased 15-in. x 10-in. x 1-in. baking pans. Bake, uncovered, at 250° for 1 hour, stirring every 15 minutes. Store in an airtight container. **Yield:** about 4 quarts.

Cinnamon Graham Popcorn

Flavors usually found in cookies or spice cake dress up popcorn for a treat that's always a hit.
—Mary Ellen Agnew, Dundalk, Ontario

> 2-1/2 quarts popped popcorn
> 2 cups Golden Grahams cereal
> 1-1/2 cups golden raisins
> 1 cup chopped dates
> 1 cup miniature marshmallows
> 1/3 cup butter *or* margarine, melted
> 1/4 cup packed brown sugar
> 2 teaspoons ground cinnamon
> 1/2 teaspoon ground ginger
> 1/2 teaspoon ground nutmeg

In a large bowl, combine popcorn, cereal, raisins, dates and marshmallows. Combine remaining ingredients. Pour over popcorn mixture and toss to coat. Place in two greased 15-in. x 10-in. x 1-in. baking pans. Bake, uncovered, at 250° for 20 minutes; stir once. Store in an airtight container. **Yield:** about 3 quarts.

Nacho Popcorn

We like to munch this while watching TV. The nacho flavoring is a zesty alternative to butter and salt.
—Linda Boehme, Fairmont, Minnesota

> 5 quarts popped popcorn
> 1/2 cup butter *or* margarine, melted
> 2 tablespoons grated Parmesan cheese
> 2 tablespoons dried parsley flakes
> 1 teaspoon garlic salt
> 1 teaspoon chili powder
> 4 to 6 drops hot pepper sauce

Place popcorn in a large bowl. Combine the remaining ingredients; drizzle over popcorn and toss until well coated. **Yield:** 5 quarts.

Popcorn Pointer

1/2 cup of unpopped kernels equals about 4 cups of popped popcorn.

Seafood Delight

The addition of extra horseradish to prepared seafood sauce gives this spread a little more zip that friends and family rave about. —*Sandra Pacak*
Indianapolis, Indiana

> 1 package (8 ounces) cream cheese, softened
> 1 can (6 ounces) crabmeat, drained, flaked and cartilage removed
> 1/2 cup seafood sauce
> 1/4 cup prepared horseradish
> 1 teaspoon lemon juice
> Assorted crackers

In a mixing bowl, beat cream cheese until smooth. Spread onto a 10-in. serving plate. Combine crab, seafood sauce, horseradish and lemon juice; mix well. Spread over cream cheese. Serve with crackers. **Yield:** about 2 cups.

Tortilla Pizzas

(Pictured below)

These cheesy tortilla slices are gobbled up fast whenever I serve them. The spread keeps well in the fridge, so it's simple to whip up these snacks for unexpected guests. Plus, you can easily substitute some ingredients to cut calories and fat...without cutting flavor.
—*Gillian Capps, Downers Grove, Illinois*

☑ Nutritional Analysis included

> 3/4 cup mayonnaise
> 1/2 cup grated Parmesan cheese
> 1/2 cup shredded mozzarella cheese

> 1/2 cup minced red onion
> 1/4 cup minced green pepper
> 1/4 cup minced sweet red pepper
> 3 garlic cloves, minced
> 2 teaspoons dried basil
> 1/4 teaspoon salt
> 1/8 teaspoon pepper
> 4 flour tortillas (7 inches)

In a bowl, combine the first 10 ingredients; mix well. Place the tortillas on greased baking sheets; spread with cheese mixture. Bake at 400° for 8-10 minutes or until golden. Cut into wedges. **Yield:** 8 servings. **Nutritional Analysis:** One serving (prepared with light mayonnaise, reduced-fat mozzarella and fat-free tortillas) equals 146 calories, 424 mg sodium, 16 mg cholesterol, 16 gm carbohydrate, 6 gm protein, 8 gm fat. **Diabetic Exchanges:** 1 starch, 1 fat, 1/2 meat.

Honeycomb Goodies

This snack has a sweet peanutty flavor that makes it a satisfying treat for kids of all ages.
—*Opal Blackmer, Rockford, Illinois*

> 1 package (14-1/2 ounces) Honeycomb cereal
> 1 pound white confectionery coating*
> 2/3 cup creamy peanut butter

Place cereal in a large bowl and set aside. In a saucepan over low heat, stir confectionery coating and peanut butter until smooth, about 10 minutes. Pour over cereal and stir until well coated. Immediately spread onto two greased baking sheets. Cool completely. Store in an airtight container. **Yield:** about 20 cups. ***Editor's Note:** White confectionery coating is found in the baking section of most grocery stores. It is sometimes labeled "almond bark" or "candy coating" and is often sold in bulk packages of 1 to 1-1/2 pounds.

Creole-Cajun Wings

These chicken wings make a delightfully zippy appetizer. I've received lots of compliments on this simple dish. —*Ron Treadaway, Acworth, Georgia*

> Oil for deep-fat frying
> 1 package (4 pounds) frozen separated chicken wings, thawed
> 1 can (8 ounces) tomato sauce
> 1/2 cup butter *or* margarine, melted
> 1/4 cup hot pepper sauce

In an electric skillet or deep-fat fryer, heat oil to 350°. Fry chicken wings, a few at a time, for 10-12 minutes or until the juices run clear. Drain on paper towels. Combine tomato sauce, butter and hot pepper sauce in a large bowl; add wings and toss to coat. Let stand for 15 minutes. Remove wings from sauce. Cover and refrigerate for 8 hours or overnight. Place wings in a greased 13-in. x 9-in. x 2-in. baking dish. Cover and bake at 350° for 25-30 minutes or until heated through. Uncover and bake 5 minutes longer. Baste wings with pan drippings; serve immediately. If desired, serve with Blue Cheese Garlic Dip (recipe below). **Yield:** 12-14 servings.

Blue Cheese Garlic Dip

This creamy dip is great alongside my spicy Creole-Cajun Wings (below left) or as a vegetable dip. If you like, you can substitute crab for the shrimp—it makes an excellent variation. —Ron Treadaway

    1 jar (12 ounces) refrigerated blue cheese
      dressing
    1 can (4-1/2 ounces) tiny shrimp, rinsed
      and chopped
    4 green onions, thinly sliced
    1 to 2 garlic cloves, minced
  1/4 teaspoon celery seed
  1/4 teaspoon dried thyme
  1/8 to 1/4 teaspoon cayenne pepper
  1/8 to 1/4 teaspoon ground mustard
  1/8 to 1/4 teaspoon white pepper
  1/8 to 1/4 teaspoon hot pepper sauce

In a bowl, combine all of the ingredients; mix well. Cover and chill for at least 2 hours. Serve with vegetables, crackers or chicken wings. **Yield:** about 2 cups.

Herbed Cheese Wafers

These bite-size snacks are rich, buttery and full of flavor. You can either serve them alone or for dipping.
                —Mildred Sherrer, Bay City, Texas

  3/4 cup butter *or* margarine, softened
  1/2 cup shredded cheddar cheese
  1/3 cup crumbled blue cheese
    1 tablespoon minced fresh tarragon *or*
      1 teaspoon dried tarragon
  1/2 teaspoon dried oregano
    1 small garlic clove, minced
    2 cups all-purpose flour

In a mixing bowl, beat butter, cheeses, tarragon, oregano and garlic until well mixed. Beat in flour (the dough will be crumbly). Shape into a 14-in. roll. Wrap tightly with plastic wrap. Refrigerate for 4 hours or overnight. Cut into 1/4-in. slices; place on ungreased baking sheets. Bake at 375° for 10-12 minutes or until golden brown. Cool on wire racks. **Yield:** about 4-1/2 dozen.

Snack Mix Squares

(Pictured above)

A fun snack mix pressed into chewy bars, this treat is popular wherever I take it. Someone is always asking me for this quick-and-easy recipe. Folks seem to enjoy the combination of sweet and salty flavors.
                —Lisa Byler, Millersburg, Indiana

2-1/2 cups halved pretzel sticks
    2 cups Corn Chex
1-1/2 cups M&M's
  1/2 cup butter *or* margarine
  1/3 cup creamy peanut butter
    5 cups miniature marshmallows

In a large bowl, combine the pretzels, cereal and M&M's. In a large saucepan over low heat, melt butter and peanut butter. Add marshmallows; cook and stir until marshmallows are melted and mixture is smooth. Pour over pretzel mixture; stir to coat. Press into a greased 13-in. x 9-in. x 2-in. baking pan. Cool until firm; cut into squares. **Yield:** about 3 dozen.

1/4 teaspoon Worcestershire sauce
1/8 teaspoon garlic powder
1/4 cup bread crumbs
Assorted crackers *or* fresh vegetables

In a bowl, combine the first 10 ingredients; stir until smooth. Spread in a 9-in. pie plate. Sprinkle with bread crumbs. Cover and bake at 350° for 20 minutes or until bubbly. Uncover and bake 5 minutes more. Serve with crackers or vegetables. **Yield:** 6-8 servings.

Chili Cheese Dip

This hearty and tasty dip is easy to prepare and is always a big hit, especially when you want something more than ordinary chips and salsa.
—Miriam Hershberger, Holmesville, Ohio

1 package (8 ounces) cream cheese, softened
1 can (15 ounces) chili con carne
1 can (4 ounces) chopped green chilies
1/2 cup salsa
1 cup (4 ounces) shredded cheddar cheese
Tortilla chips

Spread the cream cheese in an 8-in. square baking dish. Layer with chili, green chilies and salsa. Sprinkle with cheese. Bake at 350° for 5 minutes or until cheese is melted and dip is warmed. Serve with tortilla chips. **Yield:** 8-10 servings.

Halloween Party Mix

This colorful snack mix has a light, crisp coating that makes it perfect to take to such gatherings as hayrides and card parties.
—Jeanette Urbom
Overland Park, Kansas

1 package (11 ounces) pretzels
1 package (10-1/2 ounces) miniature peanut butter filled butter-flavored crackers
1 cup dry roasted peanuts
1 cup sugar
1/2 cup butter *or* margarine
1/2 cup light corn syrup
2 tablespoons vanilla extract
1 teaspoon baking soda
1 package (10 ounces) M&M's
1 package (18-1/2 ounces) candy corn

In a large bowl, combine pretzels, crackers and peanuts. In a large saucepan, combine sugar, butter and corn syrup. Bring to a boil over medium heat; boil for 5 minutes. Remove from the heat; stir

Sugar-Coated Pecans

(Pictured above)

It's impossible to stop snacking on these crispy nuts, so I make several batches in order to keep a supply on hand. —Carol Crowley, West Haven, Connecticut

1 tablespoon egg white
2 cups pecan halves
1/4 cup sugar
2 teaspoons ground cinnamon

In a bowl, beat egg white until foamy. Add pecans and toss until well coated. Combine the sugar and cinnamon; sprinkle over the pecans and toss to coat. Spread in a single layer on an ungreased baking sheet. Bake at 300° for 30 minutes or until browned. Cool on waxed paper. **Yield:** 3 cups.

Seafood Dip

I got this recipe from my sister-in-law, who's an excellent cook. She makes this dip every Christmas Eve for our annual "appetizer meal". Everyone looks forward to it. —Marilyn Dick, Centralia, Missouri

1 cup (6 ounces) flaked imitation crabmeat
1/2 cup shredded cheddar cheese
1/4 cup cream cheese, softened
1/4 cup mayonnaise
1/4 cup sour cream
1/4 cup grated Parmesan cheese
1/4 cup sliced green onions
1 teaspoon lemon juice

in vanilla and baking soda (mixture will foam). Pour over pretzel mixture and stir until coated. Pour into a greased 15-in. x 10-in. x 1-in. baking pan. Bake at 250° for 45 minutes, stirring every 10-15 minutes. Break apart while warm. Toss with M&M's and candy corn. Cool completely. Store in airtight containers. **Yield:** 16 cups.

———— 🐚 🐚 🐚 ————

Homemade Pretzels

These pretzels are crisp on the outside and chewy inside. They rival many of the hot pretzels found in stores. —*Suzanne McKinley, Lyons, Georgia*

> 2 packages (1/4 ounce *each*) active dry yeast
> 1-1/2 cups warm water (110° to 115°)
> 4-1/2 cups all-purpose flour
> 1/2 teaspoon salt
> 4 teaspoons baking soda
> 1/2 cup cold water
> Coarse salt

In a large bowl, dissolve the yeast in warm water. Add flour and salt; stir to form a soft dough. Turn onto a floured surface; knead 4-5 times. Cover and let rise in a warm place for 15 minutes. Punch the dough down and divide into 20 equal pieces. On a lightly floured surface, roll each piece into a 15-in.-long strip; twist into a pretzel shape. Combine baking soda and cold water; brush over pretzels. Sprinkle with coarse salt. Place on greased baking sheets. Bake at 450° for 15-20 minutes or until golden brown. **Yield:** 20 pretzels.

———— 🐚 🐚 🐚 ————

Apricot Leather

Since it's not sticky, this is a tasty, nutritious snack that's perfect to take along on whatever trail you travel. In pioneer days, fruit leather was made by thinly rolling fruit and drying it in the sun.
—*Patsy Faye Steenbock, Riverton, Wyoming*

> 8 ounces dried apricots
> 1/4 cup sugar
> 1 drop almond extract
> Vegetable oil
> Confectioners' sugar

Place apricots in a saucepan. Add water to cover by 1 in.; bring to a boil. Reduce heat; simmer for 30 minutes or until soft. Drain and discard liquid. Place the apricots in a blender or food processor; cover and puree. Return to the pan; stir in sugar. Simmer for 5 minutes, stirring constantly. Remove from the heat; stir in extract. Cover two baking sheets with foil; brush generously with oil. Spoon fruit mixture onto baking sheets and spread evenly into two 12-in. x 8-in. rectangles. Bake at 200° for 2 hours or until dry to the touch (fruit will be very dark). When cool enough to handle, dust with confectioners' sugar. Invert and peel off foil; dust again with sugar. With a sharp knife or pizza cutter, cut into 1/2-in. x 8-in. strips; roll up. Store in an airtight container in a cool dry place for up to 1 month. **Yield:** 4 dozen pieces. **Editor's Note:** If baked fruit sticks to the knife, air-dry for 15-30 minutes, then slice and roll.

———— 🐚 🐚 🐚 ————

Savory Party Bread

(Pictured below)

It's impossible to stop nibbling on warm pieces of this cheesy, oniony bread. The sliced loaf fans out for a fun presentation. —*Kay Daly, Raleigh, North Carolina*

> 1 unsliced round loaf (1 pound) sourdough bread
> 1 pound Monterey Jack cheese, sliced
> 1/2 cup butter *or* margarine, melted
> 1/2 cup chopped green onions
> 2 to 3 teaspoons poppy seeds

Cut the bread lengthwise and crosswise without cutting through the bottom crust. Insert cheese between cuts. Combine butter, onions and poppy seeds; drizzle over the bread. Wrap in foil; place on a baking sheet. Bake at 350° for 15 minutes. Uncover; bake 10 minutes longer or until the cheese is melted. **Yield:** 6-8 servings.

Hawaiian Chicken Wings

(Pictured below)

The slightly sweet sauce in this recipe makes it hard to stop munching these golden chicken wings.
—*Carol Jones, Oregon City, Oregon*

   4 pounds whole chicken wings
   1 cup all-purpose flour
1-1/2 teaspoons salt
Oil for deep-fat frying
   1/3 cup sugar
   1/4 cup soy sauce
   1 garlic clove, minced
   1 green onion, thinly sliced
   1 teaspoon finely chopped jalapeno pepper*

Cut chicken wings into three sections; discard wing tips. In a large plastic bag or shallow bowl, combine flour and salt. Add wings in small batches; toss to coat. In an electric skillet or deep-fat fryer, heat oil to 350°. Fry wings, a few at a time, until juices run clear, about 9 minutes. Drain on paper towels. In a bowl, combine sugar, soy sauce, garlic, onion and jalapeno. Dip fried wings in sauce; serve immediately. **Yield:** 12-16 servings. ***Editor's Note:** When cutting or seeding hot peppers, use rubber or plastic gloves to protect your hands. Avoid touching your face or eyes.

Frothy Apricot Drink

Four simple ingredients make this drink as refreshing as it is pretty. It's a great treat to sip a glass on a hot day. —*Diane Hixon, Niceville, Florida*

   1 can (15-1/4 ounces) apricot halves, undrained
   1/2 cup milk
   1/4 cup orange juice concentrate
   1 pint lemon sherbet

In a blender, place apricot halves with juice, milk and orange juice concentrate. Cover and process until smooth. Add sherbet; cover and process just until combined. Pour into glasses; serve immediately. **Yield:** 4 cups.

Snack Rye Pizzas

This hearty snack is much like a sloppy joe sandwich, so it could be a meal in itself. Have knives and forks handy for folks to dig into these! —*Margaret Allen Abingdon, Virginia*

   1 pound ground beef
   1 medium onion, chopped
   1/2 cup chopped green pepper
   1 garlic clove, minced
   1 can (6 ounces) tomato paste
   3/4 cup water
4-1/2 teaspoons minced fresh oregano *or* 1-1/2 teaspoons dried oregano
1-1/2 teaspoons minced fresh thyme *or* 1/2 teaspoon dried thyme
   1/2 teaspoon fennel seed
   1/2 to 1 teaspoon garlic salt
   36 slices snack rye bread
Grated Parmesan cheese

In a skillet, brown beef, onion, green pepper and garlic; drain. Add tomato paste, water and seasonings; cook over low heat until thickened and heated through, about 10 minutes. Spread 1 tablespoonful on each slice of bread. Place on ungreased baking sheets; sprinkle with cheese. Bake at 350° for 8-10 minutes or until heated through. Serve immediately. **Yield:** 3 dozen.

Roasted Vegetables with Dip

These colorful vegetables and zippy dip taste so good it never occurs to my family and guests that they're eating something nutritious and low in fat.
—*Melinda Sheridan, Pittsburg, Kansas*

✓ Nutritional Analysis included

   1/2 cup mayonnaise
   1/4 cup sour cream
   2 tablespoons salsa

1 garlic clove, minced
12 fresh mushrooms
1 medium sweet red pepper, cut into
    1-1/2-inch pieces
1 medium green pepper, cut into 1-1/2-inch
    pieces
1 medium red onion, cut into wedges
1 medium yellow summer squash, cut into
    1-1/2-inch pieces
1 tablespoon olive *or* vegetable oil

For dip, combine the first four ingredients in a small bowl; refrigerate for 30 minutes or overnight. Toss vegetables with oil; place in a single layer in an ungreased 15-in. x 10-in. x 1-in. baking pan. Bake, uncovered, at 450° for 10 minutes or until crisp-tender. Serve with dip. **Yield:** 8 servings (1 cup dip). **Nutritional Analysis:** 1 cup of vegetables with 2 tablespoons of dip (prepared with fat-free mayonnaise and nonfat sour cream) equals 65 calories, 140 mg sodium, 1 mg cholesterol, 10 gm carbohydrate, 2 gm protein, 2 gm fat. **Diabetic Exchange:** 2 vegetable.

desired. Cool. Store in a covered container. **Yield:** about 3 cups.

Honey Granola

I'm always interested in finding new ways to put fiber into my kids' diets. This granola makes a sweet, healthy treat with only a small amount of sugar. It's one snack I encourage them to eat! —Sharon Mensing
Greenfield, Iowa

1/4 cup honey
1/4 cup butter *or* margarine, melted
1 tablespoon brown sugar
1/4 teaspoon ground cinnamon
2 cups rolled oats
1/2 cup unprocessed bran
1/2 cup raisins, optional

In a 9-in. square baking pan, combine honey, butter, brown sugar and cinnamon. Stir in oats and bran. Bake at 350° for 25-30 minutes, stirring occasionally, until golden brown. Stir in the raisins if

Handy Meat Pies
(Pictured above)

These pies are a favorite snack around our house. But they also make a great entree when time is short. —Amy Stumpf, Hampton, Virginia

3/4 pound ground beef
3/4 pound bulk pork sausage
1 medium onion, chopped
1/3 cup chopped green onions
1 garlic clove, minced
2 tablespoons minced fresh parsley
1 tablespoon water
2 teaspoons all-purpose flour
1/2 teaspoon baking powder
1/2 teaspoon salt
1/4 teaspoon pepper
2 tubes (12 ounces *each*) buttermilk biscuits

In a skillet over medium heat, brown the beef and sausage; drain. Add onions and garlic; cook until tender. Add parsley, water, flour, baking powder, salt and pepper; mix well. Heat through. Cover and refrigerate for at least 1 hour. On a floured surface, pat 10 biscuits into 4-in. circles. Top each with about 1/3 cup of the meat mixture. Pat remaining biscuits into 5-in. circles and place over filling; seal edges with water. Press edges together with a fork dipped in flour; pierce the top. Place on an ungreased baking sheet. Bake at 375° for 12-14 minutes or until golden brown and filling is hot. **Yield:** 10 servings.

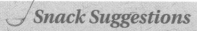

Snack Suggestions

You can perk up regular microwave popcorn by sprinkling in a bit of cayenne pepper. Then refold the bag and shake well to distribute the flavor.

If you're making deviled eggs for a crowd, mix the yolks and other ingredients in your food processor, then pipe the mixture into the whites using a pastry bag. You'll have fancy eggs fast.

Black Bean Pizza

(Pictured above)

Tomatoes and cheese give this bean pizza traditional pizza flavor. A refrigerated crust makes fast work of this snack.   —Janet Miller, Pittsburgh, Pennsylvania

   1 tube (10 ounces) refrigerated pizza dough
   1 medium onion, chopped
   1 garlic clove, minced
   1 tablespoon vegetable oil
   1/2 cup finely chopped zucchini
   1 can (15 ounces) black beans, rinsed and drained
   1 can (14-1/2 ounces) Italian diced tomatoes, undrained
1-1/2 cups (6 ounces) shredded Mexican-blend cheeses,* *divided*

Press dough into a greased 15-in. x 10-in. x 1-in. baking pan. Bake at 425° for 4-6 minutes or until crust just begins to brown. Meanwhile, in a skillet, saute the onion and garlic in oil until tender. Add zucchini; cook and stir for 1 minute. Add the beans and tomatoes; bring to a boil. Boil, uncovered, for 2 minutes; drain. Sprinkle 2/3 cup of cheese over crust. Top with bean mixture and remaining cheese. Bake 8-10 minutes longer or until crust is browned and cheese is melted. **Yield:** 15-20 servings. ***Editor's Note:** A combination of Monterey Jack and cheddar cheeses may be substituted for the Mexican-blend cheeses.

———— 🦃 🦃 🦃 ————

Cinnamon Pastry Wedges

Pie crust is turned into a treat of its own in this simple recipe. Friends and family will have a hard time eating just one of these delightfully seasoned flaky strips.   —Debra Benjamin, New Plymouth, Idaho

Pastry for double-crust pie (9 inches)
   1 tablespoon butter *or* margarine, melted
   2 tablespoons honey
   2 tablespoons sugar
   1 teaspoon ground cinnamon, divided
   1/4 cup finely chopped pecans

Divide pastry in half; roll each half into a 10-in. circle. Transfer to two ungreased 12-in. pizza pans. Using a pizza cutter or sharp knife, score pastry into wedges (do not cut through). Brush one pastry with butter and the other with honey. Combine sugar and 1/2 teaspoon cinnamon; sprinkle over butter. Combine the pecans and remaining cinnamon; sprinkle over honey. Bake at 350° for 15-18 minutes or until edges are golden brown. Cut along scored lines; immediately remove from pan. Serve warm. **Yield:** 2 dozen.

———— 🦃 🦃 🦃 ————

Graham Coconut Treats

To satisfy a sweet tooth, try these deliciously different bars. A fun variety of flavors and textures assures these treats don't last long.   —Renee Schwebach Dumont, Minnesota

   3 eggs, lightly beaten
1-1/2 cups sugar
   1 cup butter *or* margarine
   4 cups miniature marshmallows
   3 cups graham cracker crumbs (about 48 squares)
   3/4 cup flaked coconut
   3/4 cup chopped pecans
1-1/2 teaspoons vanilla extract

In a double boiler, combine eggs, sugar and butter. Cook and stir over boiling water until the mixture thickens and reaches 160°. Remove from the heat; cool. Add remaining ingredients; mix well. Spoon into a greased 13-in. x 9-in. x 2-in. pan. Refrigerate for at least 2 hours. Cut into squares. **Yield:** 3 dozen.

———— 🦃 🦃 🦃 ————

Garlic Pepper Toast

(Pictured on page 6)

So pretty and colorful, this is one of my favorites. It's also nice as an appetizer or alongside soup or salad.   —Mary Detweiler, West Farmington, Ohio

   1 cup sliced onion
   1 *each* small green, sweet red and yellow pepper, julienned
   3 garlic cloves, minced

    5 tablespoons vegetable oil, *divided*
1-1/2 teaspoons minced fresh basil *or*
     1/2 teaspoon dried basil
   1/2 teaspoon garlic salt
     1 loaf (1 pound) French bread
     1 cup (4 ounces) shredded mozzarella
     cheese

In a skillet, saute onion, peppers and garlic in 2 tablespoons of oil until tender. Add basil and garlic salt; set aside. Cut bread into 1-in. slices. Place on an ungreased baking sheet. Broil each side for 1-2 minutes or until lightly browned. Brush remaining oil on one side of bread. Top with pepper mixture and cheese. Broil for 2-3 minutes or until cheese is bubbly. **Yield:** 1 to 1-1/2 dozen appetizers.

Baked Potato Skins

I combined two separate recipes to come up with this delightfully seasoned baked snack, which my family requests often. —*Trish Perrin, Keizer, Oregon*

    4 large baking potatoes, baked
    3 tablespoons vegetable oil
    1 tablespoon grated Parmesan cheese
  1/2 teaspoon salt
  1/4 teaspoon garlic powder
  1/4 teaspoon paprika
  1/8 teaspoon pepper
    8 bacon strips, cooked and crumbled
1-1/2 cups (6 ounces) shredded cheddar cheese
  1/2 cup sour cream
    4 green onions, sliced

Cut potatoes in half lengthwise; scoop out pulp, leaving a 1/4-in. shell (save pulp for another use). Place potato skins on a greased baking sheet. Combine the oil, Parmesan cheese, salt, garlic powder, paprika and pepper; brush over both sides of skins. Bake at 475° for 7 minutes; turn. Bake until crisp, about 7 minutes. Sprinkle the bacon and cheddar cheese inside skins. Bake 2 minutes longer or until cheese is melted. Top with sour cream and onions. Serve immediately. **Yield:** 8 servings.

Tater Nuggets

We enjoy snacking on these homemade tater treats after a long day of hard work on our farm. The addition of ham and cheese is a pleasant surprise. –*Shelley Mitchell, Baldur, Manitoba*

    2 cups hot mashed potatoes (without added
     milk or butter)
    1 cup ground fully cooked ham

    1 cup (4 ounces) shredded cheddar cheese
  1/4 cup mayonnaise
    2 eggs, beaten
  1/4 cup finely chopped onion
    1 teaspoon prepared mustard
  1/2 teaspoon salt
  1/4 teaspoon pepper
1-1/2 cups crushed cornflakes

Combine potatoes, ham, cheese, mayonnaise, eggs, onion, mustard, salt and pepper; shape into 1-in. balls. Roll in cornflakes. Place on greased baking sheets. Bake at 350° for 15 minutes or until golden brown. **Yield:** about 4 dozen.

Tropical Fruit Dip

(Pictured below)

This is a refreshing and light summer snack. I love coconut and use any excuse to make this yummy dip. —*Suzanne Strocsher, Bothell, Washington*

    1 carton (16 ounces) cottage cheese
  1/4 cup lemon yogurt *or* flavor of your choice
    3 to 4 tablespoons honey
    1 teaspoon grated orange peel
    2 tablespoons flaked coconut, toasted
Assorted fresh fruit

Place the cottage cheese and yogurt in a blender; cover and process until smooth. Stir in honey and orange peel. Pour into a serving dish. Cover and refrigerate for at least 1 hour. Sprinkle with coconut. Serve with fruit. **Yield:** about 1-1/2 cups.

Sausage Quiche Squares

(Pictured below)

Having done some catering, I especially appreciate interesting, appetizing finger foods. I'm constantly asked to make these popular bites for parties.
—Linda Wheeler, Middleburg, Florida

      1 **pound bulk pork sausage**
      1 **cup (4 ounces) shredded cheddar cheese**
      1 **cup (4 ounces) shredded Monterey Jack cheese**
  1/2 **cup finely chopped onion**
      1 **can (4 ounces) chopped green chilies**
      1 **tablespoon minced jalapeno pepper,* optional**
    10 **eggs**
      1 **teaspoon chili powder**
      1 **teaspoon ground cumin**
      1 **teaspoon salt**
  1/2 **teaspoon garlic powder**
  1/2 **teaspoon pepper**

In a large skillet, cook sausage until no longer pink; drain. Place in a greased 13-in. x 9-in. x 2-in. baking dish. Layer with cheeses, onion, chilies and jalapeno if desired. In a bowl, beat eggs and seasonings. Pour over cheese. Bake, uncovered, at 375° for 18-22 minutes or until a knife inserted near the center comes out clean. Cool for 10 minutes; cut into 1-in. squares. **Yield:** about 8 dozen. ***Editor's Note:** When cutting or seeding hot peppers, use rubber or plastic gloves to protect your hands. Avoid touching your face or eyes.

Stuffed Cuke Snacks

(Pictured on page 6)

Looking for a refreshing snack? Try these crunchy cucumber slices with a creamy filling. They look so pretty on an appetizer plate.
—Dorothy Pritchett
Wills Point, Texas

      1 **large cucumber**
      1 **package (3 ounces) cream cheese, softened**
      1 **tablespoon crumbled blue cheese**
      2 **teaspoons minced fresh parsley**
      1 **teaspoon minced fresh dill**
      1 **teaspoon grated onion**
    20 to 26 **pimiento strips**
Additional dill sprigs

Run the tines of a fork lengthwise down the cucumber. Cut a 1-in. slice from each end. Cut cucumber in half lengthwise; remove and discard seeds. Place cucumber cut side down on paper towel for 10 minutes. Combine cheeses, parsley, dill and onion; spoon into cucumber halves. Put halves back together; wrap in plastic wrap. Refrigerate for 3-4 hours. Cut into 1/2-in. slices; garnish with pimiento and dill. **Yield:** about 1-1/2 dozen.

Cranberry Appetizer Meatballs

For a memorable meatball party snack with a tangy non-traditional sauce, I suggest this recipe. The meatballs are mouth-watering.
—Jim Ulberg
Elk Rapids, Michigan

      2 **eggs, beaten**
      1 **cup dry bread crumbs**
  1/3 **cup minced fresh parsley**
  1/3 **cup ketchup**
      2 **tablespoons finely chopped onion**
      2 **tablespoons soy sauce**
      2 **garlic cloves, minced**
  1/2 **teaspoon salt**
  1/4 **teaspoon pepper**
      2 **pounds ground beef**
SAUCE:
      1 **can (16 ounces) whole-berry cranberry sauce**
      1 **bottle (12 ounces) chili sauce**
      1 **tablespoon brown sugar**
      1 **tablespoon prepared mustard**
      1 **tablespoon lemon juice**
      2 **garlic cloves, minced**

In a bowl, combine the first nine ingredients. Add beef and mix well. Shape into 1-in. balls. Place in an ungreased 15-in. x 10-in. x 1-in. baking pan.

Bake, uncovered, at 450° for 8-10 minutes or until no longer pink. Transfer with a slotted spoon to a slow cooker or chafing dish. Combine sauce ingredients in a saucepan; simmer for 10 minutes, stirring occasionally. Pour over meatballs. Serve warm. **Yield:** about 7 dozen.

Mock Guacamole

This tempting mixture is a light alternative to traditional guacamole. No one will guess that peas are the secret ingredient. —*Diane Molberg*
Emerald Park, Saskatchewan

✓ Nutritional Analysis included

1-1/2 cups frozen peas
    2 tablespoons water
    1/3 cup sour cream
    2 tablespoons mashed ripe avocado
    1 tablespoon lemon juice
    1 garlic clove, minced
    1/2 teaspoon ground cumin
Dash hot pepper sauce
    1/2 cup chopped tomato
    2 tablespoons finely chopped onion
Raw vegetables *or* baked tortilla chips

Place peas and water in a saucepan; cook for 2 minutes or until heated through. Drain; place the peas in a food processor or blender. Add sour cream, avocado, lemon juice, garlic, cumin and hot pepper sauce; cover and process until smooth. Stir in tomato and onion. Cover and refrigerate for 1 hour. Serve with vegetables or tortilla chips. **Yield:** 1-2/3 cups. **Nutritional Analysis:** 2 tablespoons of dip (prepared with nonfat sour cream) equals 25 calories, 25 mg sodium, trace cholesterol, 4 gm carbohydrate, 1 gm protein, trace fat. **Diabetic Exchange:** 1 vegetable.

Fruit Kabobs

(Pictured above right)

This treat looks like you worked hard on it, even though you don't. Fresh fruit is great with the special dip.
—*Cheryl Ollis, Matthews, North Carolina*

✓ Nutritional Analysis included

    1 medium tart apple, cut into 1-inch chunks
    1 medium pear, cut into 1-inch chunks
    1 tablespoon lemon juice
    1 can (8 ounces) pineapple chunks, drained
24 grapes (about 1/4 pound)

    24 fresh strawberries
COCONUT DIP:
1-1/2 cups vanilla yogurt
4-1/2 teaspoons flaked coconut
4-1/2 teaspoons orange marmalade

Toss apple and pear with lemon juice. Divide fruit into 12 portions and thread onto wooden skewers. Combine dip ingredients in a small bowl; serve with kabobs. **Yield:** 12 kabobs. **Nutritional Analysis:** One kabob with 1 tablespoon of dip (prepared with unsweetened pineapple, nonfat yogurt and reduced-sugar marmalade) equals 52 calories, 10 mg sodium, trace cholesterol, 12 gm carbohydrate, 1 gm protein, trace fat. **Diabetic Exchange:** 1 fruit.

Meatball Mania

To make 1-inch meatballs of equal size, pat the meat mixture into a 1-inch-thick rectangle. Cut the rectangle into the same number of squares as meatballs in the recipe. Gently roll each square into a ball.

To prepare meatballs without having to stand over the stove turning each one, arrange meatballs on a greased broiler pan; bake at 350° for 20-25 minutes. They'll brown on all sides.

1 cup mixed nuts
1/2 cup butter *or* margarine, melted
1 tablespoon dried parsley flakes
1 teaspoon celery salt
1 teaspoon garlic powder
1/4 to 1/2 teaspoon cayenne pepper
1/4 teaspoon hot pepper sauce

Combine the cereals, pretzels and nuts. Pour into an ungreased 15-in. x 10-in. x 1-in. baking pan. Mix remaining ingredients; pour over the cereal mixture and stir to coat. Bake at 250° for 40-60 minutes, stirring every 15 minutes. Store in airtight containers. **Yield:** 8 cups.

Peanut Nuggets

This crisp, sweet and chewy snack is one of my favorites. It's quick and simple to make and can be served anytime. —Pamela Steward, Rochester, Minnesota

1/3 cup peanut butter
1/4 cup butter *or* margarine
3 cups miniature marshmallows
4 cups Life cereal
3/4 cup dry roasted peanuts

In a large saucepan over low heat, melt peanut butter and butter. Add marshmallows; cook and stir until melted. Remove from the heat. Stir in the cereal and peanuts; mix well. Spread onto a greased baking sheet. Cool. Break into bite-size pieces. Chill for at least 1 hour. Store in the refrigerator. **Yield:** 8 cups.

Reuben Roll-Ups

(Pictured above)

This recipe turns the popular Reuben sandwich into an interesting and hearty snack. We love these roll-ups at our house. —Patty Kile, Greentown, Pennsylvania

1 tube (10 ounces) refrigerated pizza dough
1 cup sauerkraut, well drained
1 tablespoon Thousand Island salad dressing
4 slices corned beef, halved
4 slices Swiss cheese, halved

Roll dough into a 12-in. x 9-in. rectangle. Cut into eight 3-in. x 4-1/2-in. rectangles. Combine sauerkraut and salad dressing. Place a slice of beef on each rectangle. Top with about 2 tablespoons of the sauerkraut mixture and a slice of cheese. Roll up. Place with seam side down on a greased baking sheet. Bake at 425° for 12-14 minutes or until golden. **Yield:** 8 roll-ups.

Cajun Party Mix

This crisp snack has just the right amount of "punch". Once you get started eating it, it's hard to stop.
—Miriam Hershberger, Holmesville, Ohio

2-1/2 cups Corn Chex cereal
2 cups Rice Chex cereal
2 cups Crispix cereal
1 cup mini pretzels

Quick Turkey Nachos

My husband is one of the biggest snackers around. I keep the ingredients for this on hand so I can whip them up "pronto". They're hearty and filling, so I sometimes serve them alone as a light supper.
—Kathy Faulk, East Hartford, Connecticut

1 pound ground turkey
1 envelope taco seasoning
3/4 cup water
Tortilla chips
1/2 cup sour cream
1/2 cup salsa
1/2 cup shredded Monterey Jack cheese
1/2 cup shredded cheddar cheese
Shredded lettuce, chopped tomatoes *and/or* green onions, optional

In a skillet, brown the turkey; drain. Add taco seasoning and water; simmer for 15 minutes. Place the tortilla chips on a greased baking sheet. Layer with turkey, sour cream and salsa. Sprinkle with the cheeses. Microwave or broil for a few minutes or until cheese is melted. Top with lettuce, tomatoes and/or onions if desired. **Yield:** 6-8 servings. **Editor's Note:** Ground beef can be substituted for the turkey.

Holiday Wassail

Warm and fruity, this richly colored beverage is perfect for Christmas and is very easy to prepare. We love to sip this when our merry group gathers.
—Lucy Meyring, Walden, Colorado

  1 **quart hot tea**
  1 **cup sugar**
  1 **bottle (32 ounces) cranberry juice**
  1 **bottle (32 ounces) apple juice**
  2 **cups orange juice**
3/4 **cup lemon juice**
  2 **cinnamon sticks (3 inches)**
24 **whole cloves,** *divided*
  1 **orange, sliced**

In a large kettle, combine tea and sugar. Add juices, cinnamon sticks and 12 of the cloves. Bring to a boil and boil for 2 minutes. Remove from the heat. Serve warm or cool. Garnish punch bowl with orange slices studded with remaining cloves. **Yield:** 12-16 servings (1 gallon).

Hot Apple Cider

A few years back, friends and I threw a bridal shower and incorporated a "You're the Apple of Our Eye" theme. This aromatic cider was one of the recipes.
—Marlys Benning, Wellsburg, Iowa

2/3 **cup packed brown sugar**
  1 **teaspoon whole cloves**
  1 **teaspoon ground allspice**
  3 **cinnamon sticks (3 inches), broken**
  1 **gallon apple cider**

Fill the filter-lined basket of a large automatic percolator with the brown sugar, cloves, allspice and cinnamon sticks. Prepare as you would coffee according to manufacturer's directions, but substitute cider for water. **Yield:** 16-20 servings. **Editor's Note:** Do not use a drip-style coffeemaker for this recipe.

Pepper Poppers
(Pictured below)

These creamy and zippy stuffed jalapenos are the most popular appetizer I make. My husband and co-workers are always hinting that I should prepare a batch.
—Lisa Byington, Port Crane, New York

  1 **package (8 ounces) cream cheese, softened**
  1 **cup (4 ounces) shredded sharp cheddar cheese**
  1 **cup (4 ounces) shredded Monterey Jack cheese**
  6 **bacon strips, cooked and crumbled**
1/4 **teaspoon salt**
1/4 **teaspoon chili powder**
1/4 **teaspoon garlic powder**
  1 **pound fresh jalapenos, halved lengthwise and seeded***
1/2 **cup dry bread crumbs**
Sour cream, onion dip *or* **ranch salad dressing**

In a mixing bowl, combine cheeses, bacon and seasonings; mix well. Spoon about 2 tablespoonfuls into each pepper half. Roll in bread crumbs. Place in a greased 15-in. x 10-in. x 1-in. baking pan. Bake, uncovered, at 300° for 20 minutes for spicy flavor, 30 minutes for medium and 40 minutes for mild. Serve with sour cream, dip or dressing. **Yield:** about 2 dozen. ***Editor's Note:** When cutting or seeding hot peppers, use rubber or plastic gloves to protect your hands. Avoid touching your face or eyes.

Salads

Toss together these salads for enticing meal accompaniments.

SUPERB SALADS. Clockwise from upper left: Rosy Rhubarb Mold (p. 28), Buffalo Steak Salad (p. 34), Spinach Salad with Rhubarb Dressing (p. 29) and Oriental Asparagus Salad (p. 27).

Company Fruit Salad

(Pictured above)

We first tried a salad like this at a local deli. Since I couldn't get that recipe, I starting mixing up different dressings until I hit on this one. Now I make this refreshing delightful salad for every picnic and get-together. It can be a snack, side dish or dessert.
—Connie Osterhout, Napoleon, Ohio

  4 medium Golden Delicious apples, diced
  4 medium Red Delicious apples, diced
  2 cups seedless green grapes, halved
  2 cups seedless red grapes, halved
  1 can (20 ounces) pineapple chunks, drained
  1 can (11 ounces) mandarin oranges, drained
DRESSING:
  1 package (3 ounces) cream cheese, softened
  1/2 cup sour cream
  1/2 cup mayonnaise
  1/2 cup sugar

Combine all the fruit in a large bowl. In a mixing bowl, beat the dressing ingredients until smooth. Pour over fruit; toss gently to coat. Serve immediately. **Yield:** 16-20 servings.

— ▼ ▼ ▼ —

Gelatin Fruit Salad

This gorgeous salad is so refreshing and bursting with flavor that you won't think of it as sugar-free. A diabetic friend shared the delicious recipe with me.
—Eleanor Mielke, Snohomish, Washington

☑ Nutritional Analysis included

  1 cup unsweetened applesauce
  1 package (.6 ounce) sugar-free cherry gelatin
  1 can (12 ounces) *or* 1-1/2 cups diet ginger ale
  1 can (8 ounces) unsweetened crushed pineapple, undrained
Apple slices and fresh mint, optional

In a saucepan, bring the applesauce to a boil; remove from the heat. Stir in gelatin until dissolved. Slowly add ginger ale and pineapple. Pour into a 2-qt. serving bowl. Chill until set. Garnish with apples and mint if desired. **Yield:** 8 servings. **Nutritional Analysis:** One serving equals 30 calories, 53 mg sodium, 0 cholesterol, 7 gm carbohydrate, 1 gm protein, trace fat. **Diabetic Exchange:** 1/2 fruit.

Shortcut Worth Sharing

When making gelatin, stir the powder and hot liquid with a slotted spoon. This keeps the clumps of powder from sticking to the sides of the dish.

Curried Rice Salad

This is a refreshing alternative to potato salad. I rely on dishes like this often for open houses or entertaining friends. —Pat Medley, Fayetteville, Arkansas

☑ Nutritional Analysis included

2-1/4 cups water
  1 cup uncooked long grain rice
  1 tablespoon butter *or* margarine
  1 teaspoon salt, optional
  1 cup frozen peas, partially cooked
  1 cup thinly sliced celery
  4 green onions, sliced
  1/2 cup mayonnaise
  1/2 cup prepared chutney
  1 teaspoon curry powder
Lettuce leaves, optional

In a saucepan, combine water, rice, butter and salt if desired; bring to a boil. Reduce heat; cover and simmer for 20-25 minutes or until rice is tender. Cool. Add peas, celery and onions. In a small bowl, combine mayonnaise, chutney and curry powder; add to rice mixture and stir well. Serve in a lettuce-lined bowl if desired. **Yield:** 10 servings. **Nutritional Analysis:** One 1/2-cup serving (prepared with margarine and fat-free mayonnaise and without salt) equals 129 calories, 155 mg sodium, 0 cholesterol, 26 gm carbohydrate, 3 gm protein, 1 gm fat. **Diabetic Exchanges:** 1-1/2 starch, 1 vegetable.

Spinach Salad with Dates

Dates are a sweet surprise in this recipe. I hope you try this unusual salad soon. —Donna Higbee
Woodruff, Utah

- 1/3 cup vegetable oil
- 1/4 cup cider *or* red wine vinegar
- 2 tablespoons sugar
- 1-1/2 teaspoons diced onion
- 1 teaspoon poppy seeds
- 1/2 teaspoon salt
- 1/4 teaspoon ground mustard
- 10 cups torn fresh spinach
- 3 cups torn iceberg lettuce
- 1/2 pound fresh mushrooms, sliced
- 1 cup (8 ounces) cottage cheese, drained
- 1 cup (4 ounces) shredded Swiss cheese
- 1 cup chopped dates
- 1/2 large red onion, sliced into rings
- 2 hard-cooked eggs, sliced *or* chopped

Combine the first seven ingredients in a blender; cover and process for 30 seconds. Pour into a jar with a tight-fitting lid; refrigerate for 2-3 hours. In a large bowl, toss remaining ingredients. Just before serving, shake dressing and pour over salad. **Yield:** 14 servings.

Salad with Oil-Free Dressing

This dressing is a treat for anyone who likes a refreshing salad topper with a big herb flavor. Even without oil, it's thick and satisfying. —Ellen Benninger
Stoneboro, Pennsylvania

✓ Nutritional Analysis included

- 1 tablespoon powdered fruit pectin
- 1/4 teaspoon dried herb (oregano, basil, thyme, tarragon, savory *or* dill weed)
- Artificial sweetener equivalent to 2 teaspoons sugar
- 1/8 teaspoon ground mustard
- 1/8 teaspoon salt
- 1/8 teaspoon pepper
- 1/4 cup water
- 2 teaspoons vinegar
- 1 garlic clove, minced
- Salad greens, tomatoes, cucumbers and carrots *or* vegetables of your choice

In a small bowl, combine pectin, herb of choice, sweetener, mustard, salt and pepper. Stir in water, vinegar and garlic. Chill. Serve over greens and vegetables of your choice. Refrigerate leftovers. **Yield:** 1/3 cup. **Nutritional Analysis:** 1 tablespoon of dressing equals 13 calories, 60 mg sodium, 0 cholesterol, 3 gm carbohydrate, trace protein, trace fat. **Diabetic Exchange:** Free.

Oriental Asparagus Salad
(Pictured below)

A delightful change of pace from hot vegetable side dishes, this lovely asparagus salad gets an Oriental twist with a simple marinade and sesame seeds. Once you try it, you'll serve it time and again.
—Linda Hutton, Hayden, Idaho

- 1 pound asparagus, cut into 2-inch pieces
- 2 tablespoons soy sauce
- 1 tablespoon vegetable oil
- 1 tablespoon vinegar
- 1-1/2 teaspoons sugar
- 1 teaspoon sesame seeds, toasted
- 1/4 to 1/2 teaspoon ground ginger
- 1/4 teaspoon ground cumin

In a saucepan, cook the asparagus in a small amount of water until crisp-tender, about 3-4 minutes. Drain well and place in a large bowl. Combine the soy sauce, oil, vinegar, sugar, sesame seeds, ginger and cumin; pour over asparagus and toss to coat. Cover and chill for 1 hour. Drain before serving. **Yield:** 4 servings.

Rosy Rhubarb Mold

(Pictured below)

Any meal benefits from this ruby-colored salad—it's always a refreshing accompaniment. I never have leftovers, since the combination of sweet, tangy and crunchy ingredients is so irresistible.
—*Regina Albright, Southhaven, Mississippi*

✓ Nutritional Analysis included

    4 cups chopped fresh *or* frozen rhubarb
    1 cup water
  2/3 cup sugar
  1/4 teaspoon salt
    1 package (6 ounces) strawberry gelatin
1-1/2 cups cold water
  1/4 cup lemon juice
    2 cans (11 ounces *each*) mandarin oranges, drained
    1 cup chopped celery
Optional garnishes: lettuce leaves, sliced strawberries, green grapes, sour cream and ground nutmeg

In a saucepan, combine rhubarb, water, sugar and salt; bring to a boil over medium heat. Boil for 1-2 minutes or until the rhubarb is tender; remove from the heat. Stir in gelatin until dissolved. Stir in cold water and lemon juice. Chill until partially set. Fold in oranges and celery. Pour into a 6-cup mold or an 8-in. square dish that has been coated with nonstick cooking spray. Chill until set. Unmold onto lettuce leaves or cut into squares. If desired, garnish with fruit and serve with sour cream sprinkled with nutmeg. **Yield:** 12 servings. **Nutritional Analysis:** One 1/2-cup serving (prepared with sugar-free gelatin; calculated without garnishes) equals 79 calories, 98 mg sodium, 0 cholesterol, 19 gm carbohydrate, 2 gm protein, trace fat. **Diabetic Exchange:** 1 fruit.

Maple Salad Dressing

Once sap is made into syrup, it can be used in a variety of recipes, including this super salad topper. I hope you enjoy its light yet sweet flavor. —*Laurie Couture St. Albans, Vermont*

✓ Nutritional Analysis included

    1 cup pure maple syrup
    2 tablespoons vegetable oil
    1 tablespoon lemon juice
  1/2 teaspoon paprika
  1/4 teaspoon celery seed
  1/4 teaspoon salt
  1/4 teaspoon onion powder
  1/4 teaspoon ground mustard

Combine all ingredients in a jar with tight-fitting lid; shake well. Serve over salad greens. **Yield:** about 1 cup. **Nutritional Analysis:** One serving (2 tablespoons) equals 137 calories, 76 mg sodium, 0 cholesterol, 27 gm carbohydrate, trace protein, 4 gm fat. **Diabetic Exchanges:** 2 fruit, 1/2 fat.

Tarragon Vegetable Salad

You'll surely receive compliments when this pretty colorful salad appears on the table. The fresh-tasting tarragon dressing is just delicious. —*Margaret Slocum Ridgefield, Washington*

✓ Nutritional Analysis included

    1 pound turnips, peeled and cut into 1/2-inch cubes
    1 pound small red potatoes, cut into 1/2-inch cubes and cooked
    1 pound fresh green beans, cut into 1-inch pieces and cooked
    1 package (16 ounces) frozen peas and carrots, thawed
  1/2 cup olive *or* vegetable oil
    3 tablespoons cider *or* white wine vinegar
  1/4 cup sliced green onions

3 to 4 teaspoons minced fresh tarragon *or*
   1-1/4 teaspoons dried tarragon
1 tablespoon minced fresh parsley
2 teaspoons Dijon mustard
1 teaspoon salt, optional
1/2 teaspoon pepper
Lettuce leaves and tomato wedges, optional

Cook the turnips in boiling water for 8-10 minutes or until tender; drain. Place in a large bowl; add potatoes, beans, peas and carrots. In a small bowl, whisk oil, vinegar, onions, tarragon, parsley, mustard, salt if desired and pepper; pour over vegetables and toss to coat. Cover and refrigerate for 1 hour. If desired, serve on lettuce and top with a tomato wedge. **Yield:** 16 servings. **Nutritional Analysis:** One 1/2-cup serving (calculated with cider vinegar and without salt, lettuce and tomato) equals 108 calories, 54 mg sodium, 0 cholesterol, 10 gm carbohydrate, 2 gm protein, 7 gm fat. **Diabetic Exchanges:** 1-1/2 fat, 1/2 vegetable, 1/2 starch.

Popcorn Salad

I make this unique change-of-pace salad all the time… much to the delight of my family and friends!
    —Rebecca Parker, Franklin, New Hampshire

3/4 cup mayonnaise
1 cup diced celery
1-1/4 cups (5 ounces) shredded cheddar cheese, *divided*
1 can (8 ounces) sliced water chestnuts, drained
3/4 cup crumbled cooked bacon, *divided*
1/4 cup shredded carrots
2 tablespoons minced chives
6 cups popped popcorn*

In a large bowl, combine the mayonnaise, celery, 1 cup cheese, water chestnuts, 1/2 cup bacon, carrots and chives; mix well. Add popcorn; stir to coat. Spoon into a lettuce-lined bowl. Top with the remaining cheese and bacon. Serve immediately. **Yield:** 10-12 servings. *****Editor's Note:** 3/4 cup of unpopped kernels equals about 6 cups popped popcorn.

Spinach Salad with Rhubarb Dressing

(Pictured above right)

Spinach salad is excellent with this tangy topping. It really perks it up. A friend shared a similar salad

dressing recipe with me, which I modified a bit. The rhubarb adds rosy color and mouth-watering flavor.
    —Twila Mitchell, Lindsborg, Kansas

2 cups chopped fresh *or* frozen rhubarb
1/2 cup sugar
1/4 cup vinegar
3/4 cup vegetable oil
3 tablespoons grated onion
1-1/2 teaspoons Worcestershire sauce
1/2 teaspoon salt
SALAD:
6 cups torn fresh spinach
6 bacon strips, cooked and crumbled
1/2 cup fresh bean sprouts
1/2 cup shredded cheddar cheese
1 to 2 hard-cooked eggs, chopped

In a saucepan, combine rhubarb, sugar and vinegar; cook over medium heat until the rhubarb is tender, about 6 minutes. Drain, reserving about 6 tablespoons juice; discard pulp. Pour juice into a jar with tight-fitting lid; add the oil, onion, Worcestershire sauce and salt. Shake well. Refrigerate for at least 1 hour. Just before serving, combine salad ingredients in a large bowl. Add the dressing and toss to coat. **Yield:** 6-8 servings.

toss gently. Add celery and set aside. In a saucepan, cook asparagus in a small amount of water until crisp-tender, about 3-4 minutes; drain. Immerse in ice water; drain well. Add to the potato mixture. In a small bowl, combine sour cream, mustard, thyme, tarragon and remaining lemon juice; fold into salad. Serve immediately or refrigerate. **Yield:** 12 servings. **Nutritional Analysis:** One 1/2-cup serving (prepared with nonfat sour cream and without salt) equals 80 calories, 83 mg sodium, 1 mg cholesterol, 11 gm carbohydrate, 3 gm protein, 3 gm fat. **Diabetic Exchanges:** 1 vegetable, 1/2 starch, 1/2 fat.

Springtime Pea Salad

Celery, cauliflower, bacon and sunflower kernels add crunch to this bright blend. —Donna Brockett
Kingfisher, Oklahoma

    1 package (10 ounces) frozen peas, thawed
    2 celery ribs, thinly sliced
    1 cup small cauliflowerets
    3 green onions, thinly sliced
1/2 cup ranch salad dressing
1/4 cup sour cream
    4 bacon strips, cooked and crumbled
1/4 cup sunflower kernels

In a large bowl, combine peas, celery, cauliflower and onions. Combine dressing and sour cream; pour over salad and mix well. Cover and refrigerate for 1 hour. Just before serving, stir in bacon and sunflower kernels. **Yield:** 6-8 servings.

Tomatoes with Thyme Dressing

When my garden harvest yields an abundance of tomatoes, I appreciate this easy-to-assemble side dish.
—Margaret Allen, Abingdon, Virginia

    1 cup (8 ounces) sour cream
    2 tablespoons cider *or* red wine vinegar
1-1/2 teaspoons minced fresh thyme
        or 1/2 teaspoon dried thyme
    1 teaspoon sugar
1/2 teaspoon salt
1/4 teaspoon celery seed
Dash pepper
    4 medium tomatoes, cut into wedges

In a small bowl, combine the sour cream, vinegar and seasonings; mix well. Cover and refrigerate for 1 hour. Drizzle 1/3 to 1/2 cup over tomatoes. Store the remaining dressing in the refrigerator. **Yield:** 4-6 servings.

West Coast Potato Salad

(Pictured above)

This potato salad incorporates tender asparagus and the tongue-tingling tang of herbs and lemon juice. Here in the San Francisco Bay area, which is close to the state's primary asparagus-growing region, we look forward to spring and fresh asparagus.
—Phyllis Lee Ciardo, Albany, California

✓ Nutritional Analysis included

1-1/2 pounds medium red potatoes, cooked and peeled
1/4 cup chopped green onions
    4 tablespoons lemon juice, *divided*
    2 tablespoons vegetable oil
    2 tablespoons minced fresh parsley
1/2 teaspoon salt, optional
1/4 teaspoon pepper
3/4 cup thinly sliced celery
    1 pound fresh asparagus, cut into 3/4-inch pieces
1/2 cup sour cream
    2 tablespoons Dijon mustard
    1 teaspoon dried thyme
    1 teaspoon dried tarragon

Place potatoes in a large bowl and set aside. In a jar with tight-fitting lid, combine onions, 3 tablespoons of lemon juice, oil, parsley, salt if desired and pepper; shake well. Pour over potatoes and

Fruit-Filled Melons

Fresh summer fruit is extra appealing served in a melon half and topped with a light yogurt dressing.
—*Tamie Foley, Pasadena, California*

✓ Nutritional Analysis included

    2 large cantaloupe melons, halved and
      seeded
    1 medium orange, peeled and sectioned
    1 medium apple, cubed
    1 medium peach, sliced
    1 teaspoon lemon juice
    1 cup fresh blueberries
  1/2 cup halved fresh strawberries
    1 carton (6 ounces) nonfat pineapple,
      lemon *or* vanilla yogurt
    2 tablespoons unsweetened applesauce
    1 teaspoon honey
  1/4 teaspoon ground ginger
    4 large lettuce leaves

With a melon baller, scoop out 2 cups of cantaloupe balls and set aside. Cut out and reserve remaining cantaloupe for another use, leaving 1/2-in. thick shells. In a large bowl, combine orange, apple and peach. Sprinkle with lemon juice; toss gently. Stir in cantaloupe balls, blueberries and strawberries. In a small bowl, combine the yogurt, applesauce, honey and ginger. Line melon shells with lettuce; add fruit. Top with yogurt mixture. **Yield:** 4 servings. **Nutritional Analysis:** One serving equals 216 calories, 57 mg sodium, 1 mg cholesterol, 51 gm carbohydrate, 6 gm protein, 1 gm fat. **Diabetic Exchanges:** 3 fruit, 1/2 skim milk.

Minted Pea Salad

In this unique and refreshing recipe, fresh mint complements the peas' sweet flavor. —*Inez Orsburn*
Demotte, Indiana

  1/2 cup mayonnaise
  1/4 cup sour cream
  1/4 cup minced fresh mint
  3/4 teaspoon salt
  1/4 teaspoon Dijon mustard
Dash pepper
    3 cups frozen peas*, thawed
    1 small onion, finely chopped

In a bowl, combine the first six ingredients; mix well. Add peas and onion; toss to coat. Cover and refrigerate for 1 hour. **Yield:** 4-6 servings. ***Editor's Note:** 3 pounds of fresh peas, shelled and cooked for 3-5 minutes, may be substituted for the frozen peas.

Nutty Apple Salad

(Pictured below)

Peanut butter in the dressing and interesting ingredients like marshmallows and mixed nuts give Waldorf salad a tasty twist. I've tried versions without the peanut butter and this is my favorite.
—*Maryellen Hays, Fort Wayne, Indiana*

    2 cups cubed tart apples
    2 cups thinly sliced celery
    2 cups halved seedless grapes
    1 cup miniature marshmallows
  1/3 cup cold evaporated milk
  1/2 teaspoon sugar
  1/4 teaspoon vanilla extract
    3 tablespoons mayonnaise
    3 tablespoons peanut butter
  1/2 cup mixed nuts, optional

In a large bowl, combine apples, celery, grapes and marshmallows. In a chilled mixing bowl, beat milk until frothy. Add sugar and vanilla. Beat in mayonnaise and peanut butter. Pour over apple mixture; stir until coated. Cover and refrigerate. Just before serving, stir in nuts if desired. **Yield:** 12-14 servings.

Picnic-Perfect Potato Salads

WHETHER you're planning a picnic or headed to the backyard for a barbecue, make potato salad part of the menu.

— 🍴 🍴 🍴 —

Fiesta Potato Salad

(Pictured below)

With Mexican foods so popular, this salad has plenty of appeal. For a low-fat version, substitute fat-free ranch dressing and reduced-fat cheese.
—Marlene Muckenhirn, Delano, Minnesota

    6 cups cooked cubed peeled potatoes
1-1/2 cups (6 ounces) shredded cheddar cheese
   2/3 cup black beans, rinsed and drained
   2/3 cup chopped sweet red pepper
   1/2 cup thinly sliced celery
   1/3 cup thinly sliced green onions
     1 to 2 tablespoons minced fresh cilantro *or*
       parsley
   3/4 cup ranch salad dressing
   1/2 cup chunky salsa
   1/2 teaspoon salt
Lettuce leaves, optional

A BRIMMING BOWL of Fiesta Potato Salad, Low-Fat Potato Salad or German Potato Salad (shown above, clockwise from top) is prime picnic fare.

In a large bowl, combine the potatoes, cheese, beans, red pepper, celery, onions and cilantro. In a small bowl, combine salad dressing, salsa and salt; pour over potato mixture and toss to coat. Cover and refrigerate for at least 1 hour. Serve in a lettuce-lined bowl if desired. **Yield:** 12-16 servings.

German Potato Salad

(Pictured below left)

Lemon-lime soda is the secret ingredient in this recipe, which was given to me years ago by my mother.
—Aljene Wendling, Seattle, Washington

  6 **bacon strips, diced**
1/2 **cup chopped onion**
1/2 **cup chopped green pepper**
  1 **tablespoon all-purpose flour**
  1 **to 2 teaspoons salt**
1/2 **teaspoon ground mustard**
Pinch pepper
  1 **cup lemon-lime soda**
1/3 **cup vinegar**
  3 **pounds potatoes, peeled, cooked and sliced**

In a large skillet, cook bacon until crisp; remove with a slotted spoon and set aside. Drain, reserving 3 tablespoons drippings. In the drippings, saute onion and green pepper until tender. Stir in flour, salt, mustard and pepper. Add soda and vinegar. Bring to a boil, stirring constantly; boil and stir for 1 minute. Gently stir in potatoes and bacon; heat through. **Yield:** 12-14 servings.

Low-Fat Potato Salad

(Pictured at left)

We make this favorite chunky salad the day before to let the flavors mellow.   *—Jesse and Anne Foust*
Bluefield, West Virginia

 Nutritional Analysis included

  2 **pounds red potatoes, cubed**
1/2 **cup Italian salad dressing**
  1 **cup chopped celery**
1/2 **cup chopped green pepper**
1/2 **cup chopped red onion**
1/2 **cup thinly sliced radishes**
1/4 **cup minced fresh parsley**
  1 **teaspoon salt, optional**
1/2 **teaspoon pepper**

1/2 **cup mayonnaise**
1-1/2 **teaspoons Dijon mustard**
1/4 **teaspoon sugar**

Cook potatoes in boiling water until tender, about 15-20 minutes; drain thoroughly. Place in a bowl; cool slightly. Pour salad dressing over warm potatoes; toss to coat. Add celery, green pepper, onion, radishes, parsley, salt if desired and pepper; mix well. Combine mayonnaise, mustard and sugar; pour over potato mixture and toss to coat. Cover and refrigerate for at least 2 hours. **Yield:** 14 servings. **Nutritional Analysis:** One 1/2-cup serving (prepared with fat-free salad dressing and mayonnaise and without salt) equals 55 calories, 147 mg sodium, 0 cholesterol, 11 gm carbohydrate, 2 gm protein, trace fat. **Diabetic Exchanges:** 1 vegetable, 1/2 starch.

Old-Fashioned Potato Salad

This traditional recipe has been passed down through several generations in my mother's family.
—Kathy Anderson, Wallkill, New York

  5 **pounds red potatoes**
  1 **cup sugar**
  1 **tablespoon all-purpose flour**
  1 **teaspoon salt**
1/2 **teaspoon ground mustard**
1/4 **teaspoon pepper**
3/4 **cup vinegar**
1/4 **cup water**
  3 **eggs, lightly beaten**
  1 **cup thinly sliced green onions**
1-1/2 **cups (12 ounces) sour cream**

Cook potatoes in boiling water until tender; drain and cool. Meanwhile, in a saucepan, combine sugar, flour, salt, mustard and pepper. Add vinegar and water; bring to a boil. Boil and stir for 2 minutes. Add a small amount to eggs; return all to the pan. Cook and stir for 1-1/2 to 2 minutes or until mixture is thickened and a thermometer reads 160°. Refrigerate until cooled. Peel potatoes if desired; slice and place in a large bowl. Add onions. Stir sour cream into dressing; pour over potato mixture and toss to coat. **Yield:** 16-18 servings.

Make Store-Bought Better

Quickly pep up potato salad from the deli by stirring in finely chopped green or sweet red pepper, shredded cheddar cheese or herbs such as basil, dill or parsley.

Buffalo Steak Salad

(Pictured below)

We raise buffalo on our ranch, so I cook plenty of buffalo steak as well as other cuts. During the warmer months, this cool salad is a refreshing change of pace from the heavier meals I feed my crew other times of the year. The meat is tender, and the dressing is mouth-watering. —Burt Guenin, Chappell, Nebraska

> 1/3 cup olive *or* vegetable oil
> 2 tablespoons cider *or* red wine vinegar
> 1 tablespoon lemon juice
> 1 garlic clove, minced
> 1/2 teaspoon salt
> 1/8 teaspoon pepper
> Dash Worcestershire sauce
> 1/2 cup crumbled blue cheese
> 2 buffalo sirloin *or* rib eye steaks (about 8 ounces *each*)
> 6 cups torn salad greens
> 1 medium tomato, thinly sliced
> 1 small carrot, thinly sliced
> 1/2 cup thinly sliced onion
> 1/4 cup sliced stuffed olives

In a small bowl, combine the first seven ingredients; mix well. Stir in blue cheese. Cover and refrigerate. Grill steaks, uncovered, over medium-hot heat for 6-10 minutes on each side or until meat reaches desired doneness (for rare, a meat thermometer should read 140°; medium, 160°; well-done, 170°). Thinly slice meat. On a serving platter or individual salad plates, arrange lettuce, tomato, carrot, onion and olives. Top with steak and dressing. **Yield:** 4 servings.

Raspberry Gelatin Salad

We had an annual potluck at work. Wonderful recipes came out of that meal—this cool, tart gelatin salad is one. I'm diabetic, and when I'm asked to share a dish, this is what I take. —Pat Squire Alexandria, Virginia

☑ Nutritional Analysis included

> 3 packages (.3 ounce *each*) sugar-free raspberry gelatin
> 1-1/2 cups boiling water
> 1 package (12 ounces) frozen unsweetened raspberries
> 1 can (20 ounces) unsweetened pineapple, undrained
> 2 medium ripe bananas, mashed
> 1 cup (8 ounces) nonfat sour cream

In a bowl, dissolve gelatin in water. Stir in raspberries, pineapple and bananas. Pour half into an 11-in. x 7-in. x 2-in. dish; refrigerate for 30 minutes or until firm. Set aside the remaining gelatin mixture at room temperature. Spread sour cream over gelatin in pan; top with the remaining gelatin mixture. Refrigerate for 1 hour or until firm. **Yield:** 15 servings. **Nutritional Analysis:** One serving equals 63 calories, 50 mg sodium, 1 mg cholesterol, 14 gm carbohydrate, 2 gm protein, trace fat. **Diabetic Exchange:** 1 fruit.

Spinach Pasta Salad

Since we grow and harvest our own spinach, we use it in lots of dishes. One of our favorite ways to enjoy it is in this pasta salad. —Ruby Pyles Myersville, Maryland

> 4 cups torn fresh spinach
> 4 cups cooked spiral pasta
> 4 cups cubed cooked chicken
> 2-1/2 cups sliced celery
> 2 cups green grapes, halved
> 1 cup fresh snow peas
> 1 medium tomato, chopped
> 3 green onions, sliced
> DRESSING:
> 1/2 cup vegetable oil

1/4 cup sugar
2 tablespoons vinegar
2 tablespoons minced fresh parsley
1 teaspoon salt
1 teaspoon lemon juice
1/2 teaspoon finely chopped onion

In a large bowl, combine the first eight ingredients. In a small bowl, whisk together dressing ingredients; pour over salad and toss to coat. Serve immediately. **Yield:** 12-16 servings.

—— 🍷 🍷 🍷 ——

Spaghetti Squash Salad

I've tried other spaghetti squash recipes, but I like this one since it's so crisp, colorful and fun. Plus, it can be a side dish or a relish. —*Patricia Aurand*
Arcadia, Ohio

1 spaghetti squash (about 2-1/2 pounds)
1 large onion, finely chopped
1 cup sugar
1 cup diced celery
1/2 cup chopped sweet red pepper
1/2 cup chopped green pepper
1/2 cup vegetable oil
1/4 cup vinegar
1/2 teaspoon salt

Cut squash in half lengthwise; scoop out seeds. Place squash, cut side down, in a 13-in. x 9-in. x 2-in. baking pan. Fill pan with hot water to a depth of 1/2 in. Bake, uncovered, at 350° for 30-40 minutes or until tender. When cool enough to handle, scoop out the squash, separating strands with a fork. Combine remaining ingredients in a bowl; add squash and stir well. Cover and refrigerate for at least 2 hours. Serve with a slotted spoon as a salad or as a relish with burgers and hot dogs. Store in the refrigerator. **Yield:** 8 servings.

—— 🍷 🍷 🍷 ——

Kielbasa Summer Salad

(Pictured above right)

The unexpected combination of flavors and textures in this cool salad really sparks taste buds. It can be a main course for a luncheon or a side dish at a dinner or a barbecue. I've received many compliments sharing it as a potluck dish. —*Sara Primarolo*
Sauquoit, New York

 Nutritional Analysis included

1 pound fully cooked smoked kielbasa *or* Polish sausage

1 can (15-1/2 ounces) black-eyed peas, rinsed and drained
2 medium tart apples, cut into 1/2-inch chunks
1 medium green pepper, chopped
4 large green onions, thinly sliced
DRESSING:
1/3 cup vegetable oil
3 tablespoons cider vinegar
1 tablespoon Dijon mustard
2 teaspoons sugar
1/2 to 1 teaspoon pepper

Halve the sausage lengthwise and cut into 1/4-in. slices. In a nonstick skillet, brown sausage. Drain on paper towels. In a bowl, combine peas, apples, green pepper, onions and sausage. Combine dressing ingredients in a small bowl; mix well. Pour over sausage mixture and toss to coat. Cover and refrigerate for 4 hours or overnight. **Yield:** 10 servings. **Nutritional Analysis:** One 1-cup serving (prepared with low-fat smoked turkey sausage) equals 192 calories, 561 mg sodium, 28 mg cholesterol, 14 gm carbohydrate, 9 gm protein, 12 gm fat. **Diabetic Exchanges:** 1 starch, 1 meat, 1 fat.

Polish Potato Salad

(Pictured above)

When my in-laws from Poland visited, I made this dish for them, knowing their fondness for sausage and potatoes. They liked it enough to ask for the recipe, and I gained the reputation of a good cook.
—Odette Dallaire, Los Alamos, New Mexico

    8 to 10 small red potatoes
    2 fresh bratwurst links
    1 fresh kielbasa *or* Polish sausage link
    2 tablespoons butter *or* margarine
    5 teaspoons sugar
    4 teaspoons all-purpose flour
    1 teaspoon salt
    1 teaspoon ground mustard
  1/2 teaspoon celery seed
  3/4 cup chicken broth
  1/3 cup cider *or* white wine vinegar
    1 small red onion, sliced
  1/2 cup sliced celery
  1/4 cup minced fresh parsley

Cook potatoes just until tender; drain. When cool, peel and slice potatoes; set aside. In a large skillet, cook sausage until no longer pink. Remove and cut into 1/4-in. slices; set aside. Add butter, sugar, flour, salt, mustard and celery seed to the skillet. Cook and stir over medium heat until mixture is hot and bubbly. Gradually add broth and vinegar; bring to a boil. Cook and stir until thickened. Gently stir in onion, celery, parsley, potatoes and sausage; heat through. **Yield:** 6-8 servings.

Sweet Potato Slaw

I grew up in a small Louisiana town, and we ate lots of sweet potatoes. With their crispness and color, they look almost like shredded carrots in this delightful salad. —Brenda Sharon, Channing, Michigan

  1/2 cup mayonnaise
  1/2 cup sour cream
    2 tablespoons honey
    2 tablespoons lemon juice
    1 teaspoon grated lemon peel
  1/2 teaspoon salt
  1/4 teaspoon pepper
    3 cups shredded peeled uncooked sweet potatoes
    1 medium apple, peeled and chopped
    1 can (8 ounces) pineapple tidbits, drained
  1/2 cup chopped pecans

In a bowl, combine the first seven ingredients; blend until smooth. In a large bowl, combine potatoes, apple, pineapple and pecans. Add dressing and toss to coat. Cover and refrigerate for at least 1 hour. **Yield:** 6-8 servings.

Chicken Fruit Salad

I love the challenge of finding creative new ways to serve foods. So putting peaches in chicken salad seems only natural. My husband and I enjoy this hearty cool salad on hot summer evenings. —Elizabeth Waden Timmonsville, South Carolina

✓ Nutritional Analysis included

    3 cups cooked elbow macaroni
    3 cups cubed cooked chicken
    2 cups cubed peeled fresh peaches
    1 cup sliced celery
    1 cup halved strawberries
    1 can (11 ounces) mandarin oranges, drained
    1 can (8 ounces) pineapple tidbits, drained
    1 can (8 ounces) sliced water chestnuts, drained
  1/2 cup chopped apple
  1/2 cup golden raisins
  1/2 cup chopped pecans
    1 cup mayonnaise
  1/4 cup orange juice
    2 tablespoons sugar
  1/2 teaspoon ground ginger
  1/8 teaspoon pepper
Shredded lettuce

In a large bowl, combine the first 11 ingredients. In a small bowl, combine the mayonnaise, orange juice, sugar, ginger and pepper; pour over salad and toss to coat. Serve on a bed of lettuce. **Yield:** 12 servings. **Nutritional Analysis:** One 1-cup serving (prepared with fat-free mayonnaise) equals 207 calories, 157 mg sodium, 21 mg cholesterol, 34 gm carbohydrate, 9 gm protein, 5 gm fat. **Diabetic Exchanges:** 1 starch, 1 fruit, 1 meat.

Bell Pepper Slaw

Try this recipe when you want to round out a small-serving meal with a crisp, creamy slaw without a week's worth of leftovers. —*Angela Andrews Whitby, Ontario*

      2 **teaspoons butter** *or* **margarine, melted**
      2 **teaspoons all-purpose flour**
  1/3 **cup half-and-half cream**
      1 **egg yolk**
      2 **teaspoons vinegar**
      1 **teaspoon sugar**
  1/4 **to 1/2 teaspoon ground mustard**
  1/8 **teaspoon salt**
  1/8 **teaspoon pepper**
      1 **cup finely shredded cabbage**
      2 **tablespoons** *each* **diced sweet red pepper, green pepper and celery**

In a saucepan, whisk butter and flour until smooth. In a bowl, whisk cream and egg yolk; gradually add to butter mixture. Add vinegar, sugar, mustard, salt and pepper. Bring to a boil, stirring constantly until thickened and bubbly (the dressing will be very thick). In a bowl, combine the cabbage, peppers and celery. Add warm dressing and toss to coat. Cover and refrigerate for at least 2 hours. **Yield:** 2 servings.

Savory Sweet Potato Salad

Give any meal a special twist with this creamy, distinctive make-ahead salad. It's especially good alongside ham. —*Marlene Schott, Devine, Texas*

      3 **pounds sweet potatoes, cooked, peeled and cubed**
      1 **cup chopped sweet red pepper**
  1/2 **cup chopped onion**
1-1/4 **cups mayonnaise**
      1 **teaspoon salt**
  1/4 **teaspoon pepper**
  1/8 **to 1/4 teaspoon hot pepper sauce**

In a large bowl, combine potatoes, red pepper and onion. In a small bowl, blend mayonnaise,

salt, pepper and hot pepper sauce. Pour over potato mixture and toss to coat. Cover and refrigerate for at least 1 hour. **Yield:** 6-8 servings.

'I Wish I Had That Recipe...'

"WHILE VISITING Watts Bar Resort in Watts Bar Dam, Tennessee, I enjoyed wonderful Grapefruit Gelatin," writes Ruth Jeffers of Brandon, Mississippi. "It was such a refreshing side dish that I'd like to make it at home."

Resort owner Joyce Probst was happy to comply. She relates, "Grapefruit Gelatin was included in a collection of recipes for the restaurant when we bought Watts Bar Resort in 1977.

"We have no idea where the recipe originated, but this unique salad is always well received. It's a popular choice with a sandwich for our luncheon combinations and is also served as a dinner side dish. Many people prefer it to a tossed salad."

Located between Knoxville and Chattanooga on the shore of 38,000-acre Watts Bar Lake, the restaurant is open April through October from 7:30 a.m. to 8:30 p.m. daily. Reservations are suggested, especially on weekends. 1-800/365-9598.

Grapefruit Gelatin

      8 **jars (16 ounces** *each***) grapefruit sections**
      1 **cup water**
      8 **envelopes unflavored gelatin**
      2 **cups sugar**
      2 **to 3 teaspoons salt**
  1/3 **cup lemon juice**

Drain grapefruit, reserving 6 cups of juice; set fruit and 4 cups of juice aside. In a saucepan, combine 2 cups juice, water and gelatin; let stand for 1 minute. Cook and stir over low heat until gelatin is dissolved. Remove from the heat. Add sugar and salt; stir until dissolved. Add lemon juice and reserved grapefruit and juice. Pour into two 13-in. x 9-in. x 2-in. pans. Cover and refrigerate until set. **Yield:** 30 servings.

Strawberry Onion Salad

The color and sweetness fresh berries add to this lovely salad make it perfect for company. When strawberries are out of season, use fresh orange sections instead. —Ruth Benning, Hamburg, New York

    1 bunch romaine, torn
    1 pint fresh strawberries, sliced
    1 small red onion, thinly sliced
    1 cup salad dressing *or* mayonnaise
1/3 cup sugar
1/4 cup milk
    2 tablespoons cider vinegar
    1 tablespoon poppy seeds

In a large salad bowl, toss the romaine, strawberries and onion. Combine all remaining ingredients in a small bowl or a jar with tight-fitting lid; mix well. Pour over salad and toss lightly. Serve immediately. **Yield:** 6-8 servings.

— 🛒 🛒 🛒 —

Frozen Cranberry Banana Salad

(Pictured below)

A luscious combination of sweet and tangy, crunchy and creamy, this pretty salad makes a great side dish or dessert. Its light pink color and delicate banana flavor make it perfect for a bridal shower or ladies' luncheon. —Phylis Hoffmann, Conway, Arkansas

    1 can (20 ounces) pineapple tidbits
    5 medium firm bananas, halved lengthwise
      and sliced
    1 can (16 ounces) whole-berry cranberry
      sauce
1/2 cup sugar
    1 carton (12 ounces) frozen whipped
      topping, thawed
1/2 cup chopped walnuts

Drain pineapple juice into a medium bowl; set the pineapple aside. Add bananas to the juice. In a large bowl, combine cranberry sauce and sugar. Remove bananas, discarding juice, and add to the cranberry mixture. Stir in pineapple, whipped topping and nuts. Pour into a 13-in. x 9-in. x 2-in. dish. Freeze until solid. Remove from the freezer 15 minutes before cutting. **Yield:** 12-16 servings.

— 🛒 🛒 🛒 —

Herbed Salad Dressing

Nothing adds tasty flavor to foods like fresh herbs. In this recipe, a blend of herbs quickly combine for an unforgettable dressing. —Marge Clarke
West Lebanon, Indiana

       1 to 1-1/3 cups tarragon vinegar
       1 cup vegetable oil
   2/3 cup olive oil
       4 teaspoons mayonnaise
       3 garlic cloves, minced
       1 tablespoon minced fresh thyme *or* 1
         teaspoon dried thyme
       2 teaspoons Dijon mustard
1-1/2 teaspoons minced fresh tarragon *or* 1/2
         teaspoon dried tarragon
       1 teaspoon brown sugar
       1 teaspoon salt
Salad greens and vegetables of choice

In a jar with tight-fitting lid, combine the first 10 ingredients; shake well. Refrigerate. Serve over salad. **Yield:** 3 cups.

— 🛒 🛒 🛒 —

Tropical Chicken Salad

Over the years, my husband and I have moved to different areas, and I've collected recipes from all over the United States. This flavorful salad recipe comes from New York. I've served it for luncheons for many years, and it's one of my husband's very favorites. —Linda Wheatley, Garland, Texas

    2 cups cubed cooked chicken
    1 cup chopped celery

1 cup mayonnaise
1/2 to 1 teaspoon curry powder
1 can (20 ounces) chunk pineapple, drained
2 large firm bananas, sliced
1 can (11 ounces) mandarin oranges,
  drained
1/2 cup flaked coconut
Salad greens, optional
3/4 cup salted peanuts *or* cashew halves

Place chicken and celery in a large bowl. Combine mayonnaise and curry powder; add to chicken mixture and mix well. Cover and chill for at least 30 minutes. Before serving, add the pineapple, bananas, oranges and coconut; toss gently. Serve on salad greens if desired. Sprinkle with nuts. **Yield:** 4-6 servings.

— ♟ ♟ ♟ —

Orange Blossom Salad

This salad is wonderful year-round—both for every-day and entertaining. It fits nicely into a "hurry-up" meal. —*Dorothy Anderson, Ottawa, Kansas*

☑ Nutritional Analysis included

3 oranges, peeled and sectioned
2 cups cauliflowerets
1/4 cup chopped green pepper
2 cups torn fresh spinach
DRESSING:
1 can (12 ounces) evaporated skim milk
1 can (6 ounces) frozen orange juice
  concentrate, thawed

In a large salad bowl, combine orange segments, cauliflower, green pepper and spinach. Place dressing ingredients in a jar with a tight-fitting lid; shake until well mixed. Add desired amount of dressing to salad and toss. Refrigerate leftover dressing. **Yield:** 6 servings (2 cups dressing). **Nutritional Analysis:** One serving (with 1 tablespoon of dressing) equals 62 calories, 47 mg sodium, trace cholesterol, 13 gm carbohydrate, 3 gm protein, trace fat. **Diabetic Exchanges:** 1 vegetable, 1/2 fruit.

— ♟ ♟ ♟ —

Chicken Salad Puffs

(Pictured above right)

For a unique way to serve chicken salad, these puffs can't be beat! The tasty filling gets color and crunch from the olives and celery. Guests have told me they are delicious and satisfying. —*Marlys Benning Wellsburg, Iowa*

CREAM PUFFS:
1/2 cup water
1/4 cup butter *or* margarine
1/2 cup all-purpose flour
Dash salt
2 eggs, room temperature
FILLING:
2 cups diced cooked chicken
3/4 cup chopped celery
1 can (2-1/4 ounces) sliced ripe olives,
  drained
1/3 cup mayonnaise *or* salad dressing
1 tablespoon lemon juice
1 teaspoon grated onion
1/4 teaspoon Worcestershire sauce
1/8 teaspoon pepper
Salt to taste

In a medium saucepan, bring water and butter to a boil. Add flour and salt all at once; stir until a smooth ball forms. Remove from the heat; let stand for 5 minutes. Add eggs, one at a time, beating well after each addition. Continue to beat until the dough is well blended. Drop by rounded tablespoonfuls onto a greased baking sheet, making six mounds 3 in. apart. Bake at 400° for 30-35 minutes or until golden brown and dry and firm to the touch. Transfer to a wire rack. Immediately split puffs open; remove tops and set aside. Discard soft dough from inside. Cool puffs. For filling, combine the chicken, celery and olives in a large bowl. In a small bowl, combine remaining ingredients; stir into chicken mixture. Fill the cream puffs just before serving. **Yield:** 6 servings.

Soups & Sandwiches

**Looking to warm body and soul on a chilly day?
Dig into a big bowl brimming with soup, chili or chowder and
a pretty platter stacked with savory sandwiches.**

DYNAMITE DUOS. Clockwise from upper left:
Super Sandwich (p. 48), Sausage Cabbage Soup
(p. 53), Surprise Sausage Bundles (p. 51) and
Texican Chili (p. 44).

1-cup serving equals 192 calories, 801 mg sodium, 51 mg cholesterol, 22 gm carbohydrate, 18 gm protein, 4 gm fat. **Diabetic Exchanges:** 2 lean meat, 1 starch, 1 vegetable.

Friendship Soup Mix

I layer this pretty, delicious soup mix in glass jars to give as gifts. With a few additional ingredients, folks can have soup simmering on the stove in minutes.
—Wendy Taylor, Mason City, Iowa

✓ Nutritional Analysis included

- **1/2 cup dry split peas**
- **1/3 cup beef bouillon granules**
- **1/4 cup pearl barley**
- **1/2 cup dry lentils**
- **1/4 cup dried minced onion**
- **2 teaspoons Italian seasoning**
- **1/2 cup uncooked long grain rice**
- **1/2 cup alphabet macaroni *or* other small macaroni**

ADDITIONAL INGREDIENTS:
- **1 pound ground beef**
- **3 quarts water**
- **1 can (28 ounces) diced tomatoes, undrained**

In a 1-1/2-pint jar, layer the first eight ingredients in the order listed. Seal tightly. **Yield:** 1 batch. **To prepare soup:** Carefully remove macaroni from top of jar and set aside. In a large saucepan or Dutch oven, brown beef; drain. Add the water, tomatoes and soup mix; bring to a boil. Reduce heat; cover and simmer for 45 minutes. Add the reserved macaroni; cover and simmer for 15-20 minutes or until macaroni, peas, lentils and barley are tender. **Yield:** 16 servings (4 quarts) per batch. **Nutritional Analysis:** One 1-cup serving (prepared with low-sodium bouillon and lean ground beef) equals 165 calories, 106 mg sodium, 19 mg cholesterol, 21 gm carbohydrate, 12 gm protein, 4 gm fat. **Diabetic Exchanges:** 1-1/2 starch, 1 meat.

Venison Vegetable Soup

(Pictured above)

We always seem to have venison in the freezer, so I came up with the recipe for this delicious soup as a different way to use some of that meat. —Susette Reif
Liberty, Pennsylvania

✓ Nutritional Analysis included

- **3/4 pound venison, cubed**
- **1 tablespoon vegetable oil**
- **1 cup diced onion**
- **1 package (16 ounces) frozen mixed vegetables**
- **2 cans (14-1/2 ounces *each*) diced tomatoes, undrained**
- **2 cups cubed peeled potatoes**
- **2 cups water**
- **1 tablespoon sugar**
- **2 teaspoons beef bouillon granules**
- **1 teaspoon salt**
- **1/2 teaspoon pepper**
- **1/2 teaspoon garlic powder**
- **1/4 teaspoon hot pepper sauce**

In a Dutch oven or large saucepan, brown venison in oil. Add onion; cover and simmer for 10 minutes or until tender. Add remaining ingredients; cover and simmer 1 hour longer or until meat is tender. **Yield:** 8 servings. **Nutritional Analysis:** One

---

Tender Turkey Burgers

These juicy, tender patties make a wholesome, satisfying sandwich. We especially like to grill them.
—Sherry Hulsman, Louisville, Kentucky

✓ Nutritional Analysis included

- **2/3 cup soft whole wheat bread crumbs**
- **1/2 cup finely chopped celery**

1/4 cup finely chopped onion
Egg substitute equivalent to 1 egg
  1 tablespoon minced fresh parsley
  1 teaspoon Worcestershire sauce
  1 teaspoon dried oregano
1/2 teaspoon salt
1/4 teaspoon pepper
1-1/4 pounds ground turkey breast
  6 whole wheat hamburger buns, split

In a bowl, combine the first nine ingredients. Add turkey and mix well. Shape into six patties. Pan-fry, grill or broil until no longer pink. Serve on buns. **Yield:** 6 servings. **Nutritional Analysis:** One burger (calculated without bun) equals 163 calories, 398 mg sodium, 47 mg cholesterol, 10 gm carbohydrate, 26 gm protein, 2 gm fat. **Diabetic Exchanges:** 3 very lean meat, 1/2 starch, 1/2 vegetable.

Asparagus Cheese Soup

Thyme has a sweet, savory flavor that really enhances a variety of dishes, including this creamy soup.
    —Elizabeth Montgomery, Taylorville, Illinois

1/4 cup butter *or* margarine
1/4 cup all-purpose flour
  2 teaspoons salt
1/8 teaspoon pepper
  6 cups milk
  4 cups cut fresh asparagus (1-inch pieces), cooked and drained *or* 2 packages (10 ounces *each*) frozen cut asparagus, thawed
  3 cups (12 ounces) shredded cheddar cheese
  4 teaspoons minced fresh thyme *or* 1-1/2 teaspoons dried thyme
1/8 teaspoon ground nutmeg
Additional shredded cheddar cheese, optional

In a 3-qt. saucepan, melt the butter. Stir in flour, salt and pepper until smooth. Gradually add milk and bring to a boil. Boil and stir for 2 minutes. Add asparagus and heat through. Add the cheese, thyme and nutmeg. Cook until cheese is melted, stirring frequently (do not boil). Garnish with additional cheese if desired. **Yield:** 6-8 servings (2 quarts).

Teriyaki Sandwiches

(Pictured at right)

The meat for these sandwiches comes out of the slow cooker tender and flavorful. Living as we do in the foothills of the Cascades, we frequently have deer and elk in the freezer. I sometimes substitute that in this recipe, and it never tastes like game.
    —Bernice Muilenburg, Molalla, Oregon

  2 pounds boneless chuck steak
1/4 cup soy sauce
  1 tablespoon brown sugar
  1 teaspoon ground ginger
  1 garlic clove, minced
  4 teaspoons cornstarch
  2 tablespoons water
  8 French rolls, split
1/4 cup butter *or* margarine, melted
Pineapple rings
Chopped green onions

Cut steak into thin bite-size slices. In a slow cooker, combine soy sauce, sugar, ginger and garlic. Add steak. Cover and cook on low for 7-9 hours or until meat is tender. Remove meat with a slotted spoon; set aside. Carefully pour liquid into a 2-cup measuring cup; skim fat. Add water to liquid to measure 1-1/2 cups. Pour into a large saucepan. Combine cornstarch and water until smooth; add to pan. Cook and stir until thick and bubbly, about 2 minutes. Add meat and heat through. Brush rolls with butter; broil 4-5 in. from the heat for 2-3 minutes or until lightly toasted. Fill with meat, pineapple and green onions. **Yield:** 8 servings.

Broccoli Cheese Soup

I love cheese and cook with it as often as possible. This soup is creamy and comforting with lots of noodles.
—Nick Welty, Smithville, Ohio

- 1/3 cup chopped onion
- 1 tablespoon butter *or* margarine
- 5 cups chicken broth
- 1 package (8 ounces) fine egg noodles
- 1 package (10 ounces) frozen chopped broccoli
- 1 garlic clove, minced
- 4 cups milk
- 3/4 pound process American cheese, cubed

In a large saucepan over medium heat, saute onion in butter until tender. Add broth; bring to a boil. Add noodles; reduce heat and cook for 3 minutes. Stir in broccoli and garlic; cook for 4 minutes. Add milk and cheese. Cook over low heat until cheese is melted. **Yield:** 12 servings (about 3 quarts). **Editor's Note:** 3/4 cup shredded zucchini may be substituted for the broccoli.

Texican Chili

(Pictured below)

This is a great way to serve a crowd without last-minute preparation. I got the idea from my mother, who used her slow cooker often for soups and stews.
—Stacy Law, Cornish, Utah

✓ Nutritional Analysis included

- 8 bacon strips, diced
- 2-1/2 pounds beef stew meat, cut into 1/2-inch cubes
- 2 cans (one 28 ounces, one 14-1/2 ounces) stewed tomatoes
- 2 cans (8 ounces *each*) tomato sauce
- 1 can (16 ounces) kidney beans, rinsed and drained
- 2 cups sliced carrots
- 1 medium onion, chopped
- 1 cup chopped celery
- 1/2 cup chopped green pepper
- 1/4 cup minced fresh parsley
- 1 tablespoon chili powder
- 1 teaspoon salt, optional
- 1/2 teaspoon ground cumin
- 1/4 teaspoon pepper

In a skillet, cook bacon until crisp. Remove to paper towel to drain. Brown beef in the drippings over medium heat; drain. Transfer to a 5-qt. slow cooker; add bacon and remaining ingredients. Cover and cook on low for 9-10 hours or until the meat is tender, stirring occasionally. **Yield:** 16-18 servings. **Nutritional Analysis:** One 1-cup serving (prepared with turkey bacon, no-salt-added stewed tomatoes and tomato sauce and without salt) equals 163 calories, 242 mg sodium, 44 mg cholesterol, 12 gm carbohydrate, 16 gm protein, 6 gm fat. **Diabetic Exchanges:** 2 lean meat, 1 starch.

Cajun Burgers

Experimentation is what makes cooking fun and exciting. I'm especially proud of the original recipe for these burgers. —Ron Treadaway, Acworth, Georgia

- 1 large green pepper, chopped
- 1 large onion, chopped
- 6 green onions, thinly sliced
- 6 garlic cloves, minced
- 1 egg
- 2 tablespoons Worcestershire sauce
- 1 tablespoon soy sauce
- 1 tablespoon dry bread crumbs
- 1 tablespoon cream cheese, softened
- 1/4 teaspoon cornstarch
- 1/4 teaspoon seasoned salt
- 1/4 teaspoon salt
- 1/4 teaspoon pepper
- 1/4 teaspoon dried thyme
- 1/4 teaspoon ground mustard
- 1/4 teaspoon hot pepper sauce
- 2 pounds ground beef
- 8 hamburger buns, split

In a bowl, combine the first 16 ingredients. Add beef and mix well. Shape into eight patties. Pan-fry, grill or broil until no longer pink. Serve on buns. **Yield:** 8 servings.

Ham Pecan Pitas

For a delightfully different twist on ham salad, try this hearty variation. —Bea John, Dixon, Illinois

- 1 cup diced fully cooked ham
- 1 hard-cooked egg, chopped
- 1/2 cup shredded sharp cheddar cheese
- 1/2 cup chopped pecans
- 2/3 cup sour cream
- 2 tablespoons chopped green onions
- 4 pita breads, halved

Combine the first six ingredients. Spoon into pita bread. **Yield:** 4 servings.

Morel Mushroom Soup

Some years, we have an abundance of morel mushrooms growing wild on our farm. So, I came up with this recipe. This rich, flavorful soup is a great way to use these rare mushrooms. —Geraldine Davenport, Madison, Wisconsin

- 1 pound fresh morel *or* other mushrooms, sliced
- 2 tablespoons lemon juice
- 1 large onion, chopped
- 3 tablespoons butter *or* margarine
- 2 tablespoons all-purpose flour
- 1 quart milk
- 3 chicken bouillon cubes
- 1/2 teaspoon dried thyme
- 1/2 teaspoon salt
- 1/8 teaspoon pepper

Sprinkle the mushrooms with lemon juice. In a saucepan, saute mushrooms and onion in butter until tender. Sprinkle with flour; stir well. Gradually add milk, bouillon, thyme, salt and pepper. Bring to a boil; boil and stir for 2 minutes. Reduce heat; simmer for 10-15 minutes. **Yield:** 6 servings.

Sausage Calzones

(Pictured above right)

My husband, Tom, and I both enjoy cooking Italian food. We took the filling we usually use for ravioli and wrapped it in a dough to make these excellent calzone sandwiches. Italian sausage blends so beautifully with the ricotta, Parmesan and spinach. —Janine Colasurdo, Chesapeake, Virginia

- 1 package (1/4 ounce) active dry yeast
- 1/2 cup warm water (110° to 115°)
- 3/4 cup warm milk (110° to 115°)

- 2 tablespoons olive *or* vegetable oil
- 1-1/2 teaspoons salt
- 1 teaspoon sugar
- 3 to 3-1/4 cups all-purpose flour
- 1 pound bulk Italian sausage
- 1 package (10 ounces) frozen chopped spinach, thawed and well drained
- 1 carton (15 ounces) ricotta cheese
- 1/2 cup grated Parmesan cheese
- 1 tablespoon minced fresh parsley
- 1/8 teaspoon pepper
- 2 tablespoons cornmeal
- Additional oil
- 1/2 teaspoon garlic salt
- 1-1/2 cups pizza sauce, warmed

In a mixing bowl, dissolve yeast in water. Add milk, oil, salt, sugar and 2 cups flour; beat until smooth. Add enough remaining flour to form a soft dough. Turn onto a floured surface; knead until smooth and elastic, about 6-8 minutes. Place in a greased bowl, turning once to grease top. Cover and let rise in a warm place until doubled, about 1 hour. Meanwhile, in a skillet, cook the sausage until no longer pink; remove from the heat. Drain. Add spinach, cheeses, parsley and pepper; mix well. Punch dough down. Divide into six pieces. On a floured surface, roll each piece into an 8-in. circle. Top each with 2/3 cup filling. Fold dough over filling; pinch edges to seal. Place on greased baking sheets that have been sprinkled with cornmeal. Brush tops lightly with oil; sprinkle with garlic salt. Bake at 400° for 20-25 minutes or until golden brown. Serve with pizza sauce. Store leftovers in the refrigerator. **Yield:** 6 servings.

Super Soups for Summer

SOUP is not just for winter. Summer is the perfect time to enjoy fruits and vegetables in a refreshing mixture.

— 🍶 🍶 🍶 —

Summer Fruit Soup

(Pictured below)

I've served this delightful medley for about 37 years, and it has never failed to elicit raves from those eating it. —Gladys De Boer, Castleford, Idaho

1/2 cup sugar
3 tablespoons quick-cooking tapioca

2-1/2 cups water, *divided*
  1 can (6 ounces) frozen orange juice concentrate
  1 package (10 ounces) frozen sliced sweetened strawberries, thawed
  2 cups fresh *or* frozen sliced peaches, thawed and cut into bite-size pieces
  1 can (11 ounces) mandarin oranges, drained
  2 medium ripe bananas, sliced
  1 pint lime sherbet, optional

In a saucepan, combine sugar, tapioca and 1-1/2 cups water. Cook over medium heat for 5-6 min-

EVEN ON A WARM DAY, serving soup can be delightful if you ladle up Summer Fruit Soup, Pretty Peach Soup or Garden Chowder (shown above, clockwise from bottom).

utes or until thickened and clear. Remove from the heat; stir in orange juice concentrate and remaining water until the concentrate is thawed. Stir in strawberries, peaches and oranges. Cover and refrigerate for 2 hours. Just before serving, stir in the bananas. Top each serving with a scoop of sherbet if desired. **Yield:** 6 servings.

— 🍴 🍴 🍴 —

Garden Chowder

(Pictured below left)

This creamy blend is chock-full of fresh, savory ingredients straight from the garden. —*Darlene Markel Sublimity, Oregon*

    1/2 cup chopped green pepper
    1/2 cup chopped onion
    1/4 cup butter *or* margarine
      1 cup *each* diced potato, celery, cauliflower,
        carrot and broccoli
      3 cups water
      3 chicken bouillon cubes
      1 teaspoon salt
    1/4 teaspoon pepper
    1/2 cup all-purpose flour
      2 cups milk
      1 tablespoon minced fresh parsley
      3 cups (12 ounces) shredded cheddar
        cheese

In a Dutch oven or soup kettle, saute green pepper and onion in butter until tender. Add vegetables, water, bouillon, salt and pepper; bring to a boil. Reduce heat; cover and simmer for 20 minutes or until the vegetables are tender. Combine flour and milk until smooth; stir into pan. Bring to a boil; cook and stir for 2 minutes. Add the parsley. Just before serving, stir in the cheese until melted. **Yield:** 6-8 servings (2 quarts).

— 🍴 🍴 🍴 —

Pretty Peach Soup

(Pictured at left)

A delightful change of pace, this cool, fruity soup is always the hit of a dinner party. It's simple yet impressive. —*Laura Stoltzfus, New Holland, Pennsylvania*

✓ Nutritional Analysis included

      1 cup fresh *or* frozen raspberries, thawed
      3 cups fresh *or* frozen peaches, thawed
      3 tablespoons lemon juice
      1 cup peach nectar
      1 cup (8 ounces) plain yogurt

    1/4 cup sugar, optional
      1 teaspoon almond extract

Place raspberries in a blender; cover and process until smooth. Strain and discard seeds. Cover and refrigerate puree. Place peaches and lemon juice in the blender; cover and process until smooth. Transfer to a bowl; stir in nectar, yogurt, sugar if needed (if fruit is tart) and extract. Cover and refrigerate for 2 hours. To garnish as shown in the photo, drizzle 1 tablespoon raspberry puree in a 3-in. circle on top of each serving. Use a toothpick to draw six lines toward the center of circle, forming a flower. **Yield:** 4 servings. **Nutritional Analysis:** One 1-cup serving (prepared with nonfat yogurt) equals 129 calories, 42 mg sodium, 1 mg cholesterol, 31 gm carbohydrate, 3 gm protein, 1 gm fat. **Diabetic Exchanges:** 1-1/2 fruit, 1/2 skim milk.

— 🍴 🍴 🍴 —

Easy Sausage Chowder

This super soup, flavored with fresh basil, makes a hearty summer lunch or tempting first course. —*Suzanne Ververka, White Cloud, Michigan*

      1 pound fully cooked smoked sausage,
        halved and thinly sliced
      1 medium onion, quartered and thinly
        sliced
      4 cups diced potatoes
      3 cups water
      2 tablespoons minced fresh parsley *or* 2
        teaspoons dried parsley flakes
      1 tablespoon minced fresh basil *or* 1
        teaspoon dried basil
      1 teaspoon salt
    1/8 teaspoon pepper
      1 can (15-1/4 ounces) whole kernel corn,
        drained
      1 can (14-3/4 ounces) cream-style corn
      1 can (12 ounces) evaporated milk

In a soup kettle or Dutch oven over medium heat, brown the sausage and onion. Slowly add the potatoes, water, parsley, basil, salt and pepper; bring to a boil. Reduce heat; cover and simmer for 15-20 minutes or until potatoes are tender. Add remaining ingredients; cook 5-10 minutes longer or until heated through. **Yield:** 12 servings (about 3 quarts).

✐ Sneak in Some Zucchini

When your zucchini crop is booming, grate some and freeze in small bags. Toss in a bagful or two when making vegetable soup in fall.

fourth of the ham, salami, pork and cheeses inside the shell. Top with a third of the vegetable mixture. Repeat layers, ending with meat and cheeses, gently pressing down to flatten as needed. Replace bread top; wrap tightly in plastic wrap. Refrigerate until serving. **Yield:** 8 servings. **Editor's Note:** This recipe may be made a day ahead.

Cream of Pea Soup

This creamy soup is nice for supper on a chilly night. It's so simple to make with canned peas.
—Edie Despain, Logan, Utah

```
    1  can (15 ounces) peas
    2  tablespoons chopped onion
  1/4  cup butter or margarine
  1/4  cup all-purpose flour
    1  teaspoon sugar
  1/2  teaspoon salt
  1/8  teaspoon pepper
  1/8  teaspoon rubbed sage
    2  cups water
    1  can (12 ounces) evaporated milk
    4  bacon strips, cooked and crumbled
```

Drain peas, reserving 1/3 cup of liquid. Place the peas and liquid in a blender or food processor; cover and puree until smooth. Set aside. In a saucepan, saute the onion in butter until tender. Stir in the flour, sugar, salt, pepper and sage until smooth. Gradually add water; bring to a boil. Boil and stir for 2 minutes. Stir in milk and pureed peas; heat through. Garnish with bacon. **Yield:** 4-5 servings.

Low-Fat Broccoli Soup

This delicious soup is a great way to eat a nutritious vegetable. It has a wonderful fresh flavor.
—Kay Fairley, Charleston, Illinois

☑ Nutritional Analysis included

```
    2  cups chopped fresh or frozen broccoli
  1/2  cup chopped onion
    1  can (14-1/2 ounces) low-sodium chicken
       broth
    2  tablespoons cornstarch
    1  can (12 ounces) evaporated skim milk
```

In a saucepan, combine broccoli, onion and broth; simmer for 10-15 minutes or until vegetables are tender. Puree half of the mixture in a blender; return to the saucepan. In a small bowl, whisk cornstarch and 3 tablespoons of milk until smooth.

Super Sandwich

(Pictured above)

This big meaty sandwich is one I've made many times when I knew I'd be feeding a hungry bunch. Everyone remarks on the tasty olive salad tucked between slices of meat and cheese.
—Patrice Barker
Tampa, Florida

```
    1  medium cucumber, peeled, seeded and
       chopped
    1  medium tomato, seeded and chopped
    1  small onion, chopped
  1/2  cup pitted ripe olives, chopped
  1/2  cup stuffed olives, chopped
  1/4  cup Italian salad dressing
    1  unsliced round loaf (1-1/2 pounds)
       sourdough, white or whole wheat bread
  1/2  pound sliced fully cooked ham
  1/4  pound sliced salami
  1/4  pound sliced cooked pork
  1/2  pound sliced Swiss cheese
  1/2  pound sliced Muenster cheese
```

In a bowl, combine the cucumber, tomato, onion, olives and salad dressing; set aside. Cut 1 in. off the top of the bread; set aside. Carefully hollow out top and bottom of loaf, leaving a 1/2-in. shell. (Discard removed bread or save for another use.) Layer a

Gradually add remaining milk. Stir into the broccoli mixture. Bring to a boil; boil and stir for 2 minutes. **Yield:** 4 servings. **Nutritional Analysis:** One 3/4-cup serving equals 112 calories, 157 mg sodium, 5 mg cholesterol, 18 gm carbohydrate, 9 gm protein, 1 gm fat. **Diabetic Exchanges:** 2 vegetable, 1/2 skim milk.

Dressed-Up Dogs

These tasty sandwiches are great for lunches since they reheat well in the microwave. —Roseann Loker
Vicksburg, Michigan

    2 cups all-purpose flour
    1 tablespoon baking powder
1/2 teaspoon salt
1/2 cup shortening
3/4 cup milk
    1 tablespoon butter *or* margarine, melted
    2 tablespoons grated Parmesan cheese
    1 tablespoon minced fresh parsley *or*
    1 teaspoon dried parsley flakes
   12 hot dogs

In a bowl, combine flour, baking powder and salt. Cut in shortening until the mixture resembles coarse crumbs. Stir in milk just until moistened. Turn onto a floured surface; knead 10-12 times. Roll into a 13-in. circle. Brush with butter; sprinkle with cheese and parsley. Cut into 12 wedges. Place hot dogs at wide end of wedges and roll up. Place on an ungreased baking sheet with point down. Bake at 425° for 25 minutes or until golden brown. **Yield:** 12 servings.

Turkey Minestrone

(Pictured at right)

I love serving this savory soup to lunch guests. Italian turkey sausage gives the broth just the right spice. Great recipes like this can make anyone a good cook.
—Betty Christensen, Victoria, British Columbia

✓ Nutritional Analysis included

2/3 cup chopped onion
    2 tablespoons vegetable oil
1/2 pound ground turkey
1/2 pound hot Italian turkey sausage links, casings removed
1/2 cup minced fresh parsley
    2 garlic cloves, minced
    1 teaspoon dried oregano

    1 teaspoon dried basil
    2 cans (14-1/2 ounces *each*) Italian stewed tomatoes
    6 cups chicken broth
    1 medium zucchini, sliced
    1 package (10 ounces) frozen mixed vegetables
    1 can (16 ounces) kidney beans, rinsed and drained
1-1/2 cups cooked elbow macaroni
    2 tablespoons cider vinegar
1/2 teaspoon salt, optional
Pinch pepper

In a large kettle over medium heat, saute onion in oil until tender, about 4 minutes. Add the next six ingredients; cook until meat is no longer pink. Add tomatoes, broth, zucchini and mixed vegetables; cover and cook on low heat for 5 minutes. Add beans, macaroni, vinegar, salt if desired and pepper; simmer for 3-4 minutes or until heated through. **Yield:** 16 servings (4 quarts). **Nutritional Analysis:** One 1-cup serving (prepared with low-sodium broth and without salt) equals 170 calories, 208 mg sodium, 23 mg cholesterol, 21 gm carbohydrate, 10 gm protein, 5 gm fat. **Diabetic Exchanges:** 1 starch, 1 meat, 1 vegetable.

Harvest Sweet Potato Soup

(Pictured below and on front cover)

I always double this recipe whenever I make it since we love to have leftovers. This is the easiest soup I've ever made. We prefer it warm, but it can also be served chilled. —*Gayle Becker, Mt. Clemens, Michigan*

✓ Nutritional Analysis included

    1 cup chopped celery
1/2 cup chopped onion
    1 tablespoon vegetable oil
    3 medium sweet potatoes (about 1 pound), peeled and cubed
    3 cups chicken broth
    1 bay leaf
1/2 teaspoon dried basil
1/4 teaspoon salt, optional

In a Dutch oven or soup kettle, saute celery and onion in oil until tender. Add remaining ingredients; bring to a boil over medium heat. Reduce heat; simmer for 25-30 minutes or until tender. Discard bay leaf. Cool slightly. In a blender or food processor, process soup in batches until smooth. Return all to pan and heat through. **Yield:** 4 servings. **Nutritional Analysis:** One 1-cup serving (prepared with low-sodium broth and without salt) equals 133 calories, 116 mg sodium, 4 mg cholesterol, 20 gm carbohydrate, 4 gm protein, 5 gm fat. **Diabetic Exchanges:** 1 starch, 1 vegetable, 1 fat.

Speedy Vegetable Soup

This fresh-tasting soup is packed with colorful nutritious vegetables. I've recommended it to my friends for years. —*Vera Bathurst, Rogue River, Oregon*

✓ Nutritional Analysis included

    2 cans (one 49 ounces, one 14-1/2 ounces) low-sodium chicken broth
    2 celery ribs, thinly sliced
    1 medium green pepper, chopped
    1 medium onion, chopped
    2 medium carrots, chopped
    1 envelope onion soup mix
    1 bay leaf
1/4 teaspoon garlic powder
1/4 teaspoon pepper
    1 can (14-1/2 ounces) diced tomatoes, undrained

In a saucepan, combine the first nine ingredients; bring to a boil over medium heat. Reduce heat; cover and simmer for 15-20 minutes or until vegetables are tender. Add tomatoes; heat through. Remove bay leaf. **Yield:** 11 servings (about 3 quarts). **Nutritional Analysis:** One 1-cup serving equals 38 calories, 195 mg sodium, 3 mg cholesterol, 5 gm carbohydrate, 3 gm protein, 1 gm fat. **Diabetic Exchange:** 1 vegetable.

Leek Soup

When leeks are perfect for picking in my area, I start making this hearty soup. We pick as many wild leeks as we can find, and I freeze what we don't use immediately to try and stretch the season.
—*Cecilia Chynoweth, Hamilton, Ontario*

        6 wild leeks
        1 medium onion, thinly sliced
    1/4 cup butter *or* margarine
        6 medium potatoes, peeled and sliced
        6 cups chicken broth
    1/2 cup minced fresh parsley
        1 egg yolk, beaten
    1-1/2 teaspoons salt
    1/4 teaspoon pepper
Pinch ground nutmeg
        2 cups half-and-half cream
        4 bacon strips, cooked and crumbled

Cut leeks into thin slices. In a skillet, saute leeks and onion in butter until tender but not browned. Transfer to a soup kettle or Dutch oven. Add potatoes, broth and parsley; cover and simmer until the vegetables are tender. Strain; set broth aside. Puree vegetables in a blender or food processor. Return puree and broth to pan. Stir a small amount of pureed mixture into egg yolk; return to pan. Add salt, pepper and nutmeg. Cook over medium heat until a thermometer reads 160°, stirring occasionally. Add the cream; heat through but do not boil. Garnish with bacon. **Yield:** 12 servings (3 quarts).

Marjoram Mushroom Soup

This creamy soup features fresh mushrooms and the pleasant flavoring of marjoram.
—Michele Odstrcilek, Lemont, Illinois

 1 large potato, peeled and diced
 1 large leek (white portion only), chopped
 1 medium onion, diced
 2 tablespoons vegetable oil
 1/2 pound fresh mushrooms, sliced
 4 cups chicken broth
 1 tablespoon minced fresh marjoram *or* 1
   teaspoon dried marjoram, *divided*
 1 cup (8 ounces) sour cream
 2 tablespoons butter *or* margarine
Salt and pepper to taste

In a Dutch oven or soup kettle, saute potato, leek and onion in oil for 4 minutes. Add mushrooms and cook for 2 minutes. Stir in broth and half of the marjoram. Cover and simmer for 10 minutes or until potato is tender. Cool slightly. Puree in small batches in a blender; return all to the pan. Whisk in sour cream and butter. Season with salt and pepper. Heat through but do not boil. Sprinkle with the remaining marjoram just before serving. **Yield:** 6 servings.

Surprise Sausage Bundles

(Pictured above right)

Kielbasa and sauerkraut star in a tasty filling for these scrumptious stuffed rolls, which are great for dinner with soup or salad. Leftovers right out of the refrigerator make a quick lunch. —*Barb Ruis*
Grandville, Michigan

 6 bacon strips, diced
 1 cup chopped onion
 1 can (16 ounces) sauerkraut, drained
 1/2 pound fully cooked smoked kielbasa *or*
   Polish sausage, coarsely chopped
 2 tablespoons brown sugar
 1/2 teaspoon garlic salt
 1/4 teaspoon caraway seeds
 1/8 teaspoon pepper
DOUGH:
 1 package (16 ounces) hot roll mix
 1 egg, beaten
 1 cup warm water (120° to 130°)
 2 tablespoons butter *or* margarine, softened
TOPPING:
 1 egg, beaten
Poppy seeds

In a skillet, cook bacon until crisp; remove to paper towels to drain. Reserve 2 tablespoons drippings. Saute onion in drippings until tender. Stir in sauerkraut, sausage, brown sugar, garlic salt, caraway and pepper. Cook and stir for 5 minutes. Remove from the heat; add bacon. Set aside to cool. In a bowl, combine contents of hot roll mix. Stir in egg, water and butter to form a soft dough. Turn onto a floured surface; knead until smooth and elastic, about 5 minutes. Cover the dough with a large bowl; let stand for 5 minutes. Divide dough into 16 pieces. On a floured surface, roll out each piece into a 4-in. circle. Top each with 1/4 cup filling. Fold dough around filling, forming a ball; pinch edges to seal. Place seam side down on greased baking sheets. Cover loosely with plastic wrap that has been coated with nonstick cooking spray. Let rise in a warm place for 15 minutes. Brush with egg. Sprinkle with poppy seeds. Bake at 350° for 16-17 minutes or until golden brown. Serve warm. **Yield:** 16 servings.

Tuna Schooners

(Pictured above)

Instead of plain tuna salad sandwiches, I fix this creamy tuna mixture, which includes crunchy apples. Then I put it on a crisp English muffin half with triangle tortilla chips sticking out to look like the sails of a ship. —Judy Archuleta, Escalon, California

   1 can (6 ounces) tuna, drained and flaked
1/2 cup chopped apple
1/4 cup mayonnaise
1/4 teaspoon salt
   4 lettuce leaves
   2 English muffins, split and toasted
   8 tortilla chips

In a bowl, combine tuna, apple, mayonnaise and salt; mix well. Place lettuce on muffin halves; top with tuna mixture. Place tortilla chips in tuna mixture to resemble sails. **Yield:** 2-4 servings.

Chicken Rice Soup

Our granddaughters have been making this soup for years...all the kids loved it—despite the chopped onion! —Dee Berube, Hampton, Virginia

   8 cups chicken broth
   3 celery ribs, sliced
   1 small onion, chopped
Salt and pepper to taste
   2 cups cubed cooked chicken
   1 cup uncooked long grain rice

In a large saucepan, combine broth, celery, onion, salt and pepper; bring to a boil. Reduce heat; cover and simmer for 10 minutes. Add chicken and rice; bring to a boil. Reduce heat; cover and simmer for 20-25 minutes or until the rice is tender. **Yield:** 8-10 servings (2-1/2 quarts).

Southwestern Hot Dogs

Plain hot dogs are dressed up with an appealing Tex-Mex flavor. I made these stuffed hot dogs for my kids when they were young and later for my grandchildren, too. —Marion Stanley, Joseph, Oregon

   1 cup (4 ounces) finely shredded cheddar
     cheese
1/2 cup crushed tortilla chips
   2 green onions, thinly sliced
   3 tablespoons salsa
   2 tablespoons mayonnaise
1/2 teaspoon chili powder
 10 hot dogs
 10 hot dog buns, split

In a bowl, combine the first six ingredients. Cut a 1/2-in.-deep lengthwise slit in each hot dog. Spoon about 2 tablespoons cheese mixture into each. Broil for 2-3 minutes or until cheese is melted. Serve on buns. **Yield:** 10 servings.

Corn Chowder

On cool fall days, this creamy chowder really hits the spot as an appetizer or light lunch. —Nancy Johnson, Connersville, Indiana

☑ Nutritional Analysis included

   1 medium onion, chopped
   6 cups fresh *or* frozen corn, *divided*
   3 cups chicken broth, *divided*
1/2 cup chopped sweet red pepper
1/2 teaspoon dried rosemary, crushed
1/2 teaspoon dried thyme
1/8 teaspoon pepper
Dash cayenne pepper

Coat the bottom of a saucepan with nonstick cooking spray. Add onion; cook and stir over medium heat until tender, about 4 minutes. Add 4 cups corn; cook and stir until softened, about 5 minutes. Add 2 cups broth; bring to a boil. Reduce heat; cover and simmer for 10 minutes or until corn is tender. Cool slightly. Puree in a blender or food processor until smooth; return to pan. Add red pepper, rosemary, thyme, pepper, cayenne, and remaining corn and broth; cook and stir for 10 minutes or until corn is cooked. **Yield:** 4-6 servings (about 1-1/2 quarts). **Nutritional Analysis:** One 1-cup serving (prepared with low-sodium broth) equals 171 calories, 61 mg sodium, 3 mg cholesterol, 38 gm carbohydrate, 7 gm protein, 2 gm fat. **Diabetic Exchanges:** 2 starch, 1 vegetable.

Tortilla Club

These sandwiches don't get soggy or fall apart by lunch time. My husband and teenagers tell me these are the best sandwiches I've ever created.
—Judy Armstrong, Norwell, Massachusetts

- **2 tablespoons mayonnaise**
- **2 teaspoons prepared mustard**
- **2 flour tortillas (8 inches)**
- **1 ounce** *each* **thinly sliced fully cooked ham, roast beef and turkey**
- **2 slices process American cheese**
- **4 thin slices sweet red pepper**
- **4 thin slices onion**
- **1/4 cup alfalfa sprouts**

Combine mayonnaise and mustard; spread over tortillas. Layer with remaining ingredients. Roll up and wrap in plastic wrap. **Yield:** 2 sandwiches. **Editor's Note:** Dijon-mayonnaise blend may be substituted for the mayonnaise and mustard.

Sausage Cabbage Soup

(Pictured at right)

My family often requests this satisfying soup. I've served it to guests for lunch and as a cold-weather Sunday supper. It's really good with a green salad and a loaf of bread. —Stella Garrett, Orlando, Florida

- **1 medium onion, chopped**
- **1 tablespoon vegetable oil**
- **1 tablespoon butter** *or* **margarine**
- **2 medium carrots, thinly sliced and halved**
- **1 celery rib, thinly sliced**
- **1 teaspoon caraway seeds**
- **2 cups water**
- **2 cups chopped cabbage**

- **1/2 pound fully cooked smoked kielbasa** *or* **Polish sausage, halved and cut into 1/4-inch slices**
- **1 can (14-1/2 ounces) diced tomatoes, undrained**
- **1 tablespoon brown sugar**
- **1 can (15 ounces) white kidney beans, rinsed and drained**
- **1 tablespoon vinegar**
- **1 teaspoon salt**
- **1/4 teaspoon pepper**

Minced fresh parsley

In a 3-qt. saucepan, saute onion in oil and butter until tender. Add carrots and celery; saute for 3 minutes. Add caraway; cook and stir 1 minute longer. Add water, cabbage, sausage, tomatoes and brown sugar; bring to a boil. Reduce heat; cover and simmer for 15-20 minutes or until vegetables are tender. Add the beans, vinegar, salt and pepper. Simmer, uncovered, 5-10 minutes more or until heated through. Sprinkle with parsley. **Yield:** 6 servings.

Sausage Cheese Olive Loaves

(Pictured below)

A friend once brought us one of these attractive rings, and it was so good I asked for the recipe. I make this hearty bread to serve for special breakfasts. It's perfect for any occasion. —Shana Bailey, Tulia, Texas

> 3 loaves (1 pound *each*) frozen bread dough
> 1 pound bulk hot pork sausage
> 1 pound bulk mild pork sausage
> 1 pound bulk sage pork sausage
> 1 pound fully cooked smoked kielbasa *or* Polish sausage, cut into 1/2-inch pieces
> 2 cups (8 ounces) shredded cheddar cheese
> 2 cups (8 ounces) shredded mozzarella cheese
> 1 cup grated Parmesan cheese
> 1 can (6 ounces) ripe olives, drained and sliced
> 1 jar (5-3/4 ounces) stuffed olives, drained and sliced
> 3 tablespoons butter *or* margarine, melted

Thaw bread dough on a greased baking sheet according to package directions; let rise until nearly doubled. Meanwhile, in a large skillet, cook pork sausages until no longer pink; drain. Place in a large bowl. Add kielbasa, cheeses and olives; set aside. Roll each loaf of bread into a 17-in. x 9-in. rectangle. Spread a third of the sausage mixture on each rectangle to within 1 in. of edges. Roll up jelly-roll style, starting with a long side. Pinch seams; place seam side down on greased baking sheets. Form each into a circle; pinch ends to seal. Bake at 375° for 25-30 minutes or until golden brown. Brush with butter while warm. Store in the refrigerator or freezer. **Yield:** 3 loaves. **Editor's Note:** Baked loaves may be frozen when cooled. Thaw at room temperature for 2 hours. Bake at 350° for 30-40 minutes or until heated through.

Chicken Apricot Bundles

My husband regularly requests these unusual sandwiches for his lunch. The sweet-tart flavor of the apricots is excellent with chicken, cheese and pecans. —Brenda Lawson, Jefferson City, Missouri

> 2 tubes (8 ounces *each*) refrigerated crescent rolls
> 1 can (10 ounces) chunk chicken, drained and chopped
> 1/2 cup shredded cheddar cheese
> 1 package (3 ounces) cream cheese, softened
> 1/4 cup chopped dried apricots
> 1/4 cup chopped pecans
> 1/4 teaspoon celery seed

Unroll crescent roll dough and separate into eight rectangles. Place on an ungreased baking sheet and press perforations together. Combine remaining ingredients; spoon 1/4 cupful onto the center of each rectangle. Bring edges to the center; pinch to seal. Bake at 375° for 12-15 minutes or until golden. **Yield:** 8 servings.

Caraway Sour Cream Soup

A small bowl of this rich soup goes a long way. It's delicious served with crusty French bread. —Kim Gilliland, Simi Valley, California

> 2 medium onions, diced
> 1 cup diced celery
> 1 cup diced carrots
> 1 tablespoon caraway seeds
> 3 tablespoons butter *or* margarine
> 1/2 cup all-purpose flour
> 4 cups chicken broth
> 1 cup (8 ounces) sour cream
> 1/2 cup milk
> Salt and pepper to taste

In a large saucepan, saute onions, celery, carrots and caraway in butter until vegetables are tender. Remove from the heat; stir in flour until well blended. Gradually stir in broth. Return to the heat; bring to a boil. Cook and stir for 2 minutes. Reduce heat;

simmer for 10 minutes. Combine sour cream and milk; add about 1 cup broth mixture. Return all to the pan; heat through (do not boil). Season with salt and pepper. **Yield:** 6-8 servings.

Avocado Bacon Sandwiches

Since we grow avocadoes, I slice or cube them and toss them in to whatever I'm cooking. These open-faced sandwiches are one of our favorite light meals or snacks. —Alva Snider, Fallbrook, California

  1 **pound sliced bacon, halved**
  2 **medium ripe avocados, sliced**
Salt and pepper to taste
  1/3 **cup mayonnaise**
  1 **tablespoon lemon juice**
  8 **slices whole wheat bread, toasted**

Cook bacon until crisp; drain on paper towels. Gently toss avocados with salt and pepper. Combine mayonnaise and lemon juice; spread over toast. Top with avocado and bacon. Serve immediately. **Yield:** 8 sandwiches.

Creamy Potato Soup

This is one of my favorite recipes that uses wholesome milk—an important product we produce on our dairy farm. It's rich and delicious…even the kids gobble it up! —Janis Plagerman, Lynden, Washington

  7 **medium potatoes, peeled and cubed**
  2 **celery ribs, diced**
  1 **medium onion, chopped**
  1 **quart water**
  4 **teaspoons chicken bouillon granules**
  1/4 **cup butter**
  1/4 **cup all-purpose flour**
  2 **teaspoons salt**
  1/2 **teaspoon pepper**
  1 **quart milk**
Sour cream and shredded cheddar cheese,
  optional

In a Dutch oven or soup kettle, combine potatoes, celery, onion, water and bouillon; bring to a boil. Reduce heat; cover and simmer for 20-25 minutes or until potatoes are tender. Cool slightly. Place half of the potato mixture in a blender; cover and puree. Repeat with remaining potato mixture; set aside. In the same kettle, melt butter. Stir in flour, salt and pepper until smooth. Gradually add milk; bring to a boil. Boil and stir for 2 minutes. Return potato puree to the pan and heat through. Garnish indi-

vidual servings with sour cream and cheese if desired. **Yield:** 8-10 servings (2-3/4 quarts).

Trout Chowder
(Pictured above)

This hearty chowder cooks conveniently in a slow cooker so I can spend more time fishing and less in the kitchen. Broccoli adds fresh taste and lively color to the rich cheesy broth. —Linda Kesselring
Corning, New York

  1 **medium onion, chopped**
  1 **tablespoon butter** *or* **margarine**
  2 **cups milk**
  1 **cup ranch salad dressing**
  1 **pound boneless trout fillets, skin removed**
  1 **package (10 ounces) frozen broccoli cuts,**
    thawed
  1 **cup cubed** *or* **shredded cheddar cheese**
  1 **cup cubed** *or* **shredded Monterey Jack**
    cheese
  1/4 **teaspoon garlic powder**
Paprika, optional

In a skillet, saute onion in butter until tender. Transfer to a slow cooker; add milk, salad dressing, fish, broccoli, cheeses and garlic powder. Cover and cook on high for 1-1/2 to 2 hours or until soup is bubbly and fish flakes easily with a fork. Sprinkle with paprika if desired. **Yield:** 6 servings.

Peasant Soup

(Pictured above)

You'll agree this soup is anything but meager! The hearty vegetable broth really satisfies, and it's inexpensive as well.
—Bertha McClung
Summersville, West Virginia

☑ Nutritional Analysis included

> 1 **pound dry great northern beans**
> 3 **carrots, sliced**
> 3 **celery ribs, sliced**
> 2 **medium onions, chopped**
> 2 **garlic cloves, minced**
> 2 **bay leaves**
> 1 **can (14-1/2 ounces) tomatoes, undrained and chopped**
> 1 **teaspoon dried basil**
> 1/2 **teaspoon pepper**
> 2 **tablespoons olive *or* vegetable oil**

Place the beans in a Dutch oven and cover with water; bring to a boil. Boil for 2 minutes. Remove from the heat; cover and let stand for 1 hour. Drain and rinse beans; return to the Dutch oven. Add 6 cups of water, carrots, celery, onions, garlic, bay leaves, tomatoes, basil and pepper; bring to a boil. Reduce heat; cover and simmer for 1-1/2 hours or until the beans are tender. Discard the bay leaves. Add oil and heat through. **Yield:** 12 servings (3 quarts). **Nutritional Analysis:** One 1-cup serving equals 140 calories, 73 mg sodium, 0 cholesterol, 22 gm carbohydrate, 8 gm protein, 3 gm fat. **Diabetic Exchanges:** 1 vegetable, 1 starch, 1/2 lean meat, 1/2 fat.

"Forgotten" Minestrone

I'm a free-lance writer, so I appreciate no-fuss recipes. I can compose an article while this full-flavored soup is simmering. I like to sprinkle servings with Parmesan cheese.
—Marsha Ransom
South Haven, Michigan

☑ Nutritional Analysis included

> 1 **pound lean beef stew meat**
> 6 **cups water**
> 1 **can (28 ounces) tomatoes, undrained and chopped**
> 1 **beef bouillon cube**
> 1 **medium onion, chopped**
> 2 **tablespoons dried parsley flakes**
> 2-1/2 **teaspoons salt, optional**
> 1-1/2 **teaspoons ground thyme**
> 1/2 **teaspoon pepper**
> 1 **medium zucchini, thinly sliced**
> 2 **cups finely chopped cabbage**
> 1 **can (16 ounces) garbanzo beans, drained**
> 1 **cup uncooked small elbow *or* shell macaroni**
> 1/4 **cup grated Parmesan cheese, optional**

In a slow cooker, combine beef, water, tomatoes, bouillon, onion, parsley, salt if desired, thyme and pepper. Cover and cook on low for 7-9 hours or until meat is tender. Add zucchini, cabbage, beans and macaroni; cook on high, covered, for 30-45 minutes or until the vegetables are tender. Garnish with Parmesan cheese if desired. **Yield:** 8 servings. **Nutritional Analysis:** One serving (prepared without salt and Parmesan cheese) equals 246 calories, 453 mg sodium, 33 mg cholesterol, 30 gm carbohydrate, 19 gm protein, 6 gm fat. **Diabetic Exchanges:** 2 vegetable, 1-1/2 starch, 1 meat.

Turkey Reuben

This single-serving sandwich combines a nice medley of flavors for a delicious Reuben taste even without the corned beef.
—Patricia Rutherford
Winchester, Illinois

> 1 **slice white bread, toasted**
> 1 **teaspoon prepared mustard**
> 2 **ounces thinly sliced cooked turkey breast**
> 1/8 **teaspoon caraway seeds**
> 1/2 **cup sauerkraut**
> 1 **slice Swiss cheese**
> **Green pepper rings, optional**

Place the toast on an ungreased baking sheet; spread the top with mustard. Arrange turkey over mustard. Sprinkle with caraway; top with the sauerkraut and cheese. Broil about 4 in. from the heat for 3 minutes or until cheese is bubbly and lightly browned. Top with pepper rings if desired. **Yield:** 1 serving.

—🏺 🏺 🏺—

Lunchbox "Handwiches"

These unique sandwich pockets are filled with ingredients kids like. I always keep some in the freezer ready to reheat. —Callie Myers, Rockport, Texas

>   1 loaf (1 pound) frozen bread dough, thawed
> 2-1/2 cups finely chopped fully cooked ham
>   1 cup (4 ounces) shredded Swiss cheese
>   1 egg yolk
>   1 tablespoon water

Allow dough to rise according to package directions. Punch down; divide into 10 equal pieces. Roll each piece into a 5-in. circle. Place about 1/4 cup ham and 2 tablespoons cheese on each circle; press filling to flatten. Beat egg yolk and water; brush on edges of circles. Fold into semicircles and pinch edges to seal. Brush tops with egg yolk mixture. Place on a greased baking sheet. Bake at 375° for 15-20 minutes or until golden brown. Serve warm or cold. If desired, cool and freeze. **Yield:** 10 sandwiches.

—🏺 🏺 🏺—

Hearty Ham Chowder

Corn adds wonderful appeal to this recipe I got from my sister. It's satisfying on a chilly winter day. —Muriel Lerdal, Humboldt, Iowa

> 3/4 cup chopped onion
>   2 tablespoons butter *or* margarine
>   1 cup diced cooked peeled potatoes
>   1 cup diced fully cooked ham
>   2 cups fresh, frozen *or* canned sweet corn
>   1 cup cream-style corn
>   1 can (10-3/4 ounces) condensed cream of mushroom soup, undiluted
> 2-1/2 cups milk
> Salt and pepper to taste
>   1 tablespoon chopped fresh parsley

Creative Chili Choices

To enhance the flavor of your homemade chili, stir in a jar of bacon bits and a can of mushrooms. Or sprinkle some grated or shredded Parmesan cheese on top of each serving.

In a heavy saucepan, saute the onion in butter until tender. Add remaining ingredients; bring to a boil. Reduce heat; simmer, uncovered, for 20-30 minutes. **Yield:** 6-8 servings (2 quarts).

—🏺 🏺 🏺—

East Coast Tomato Soup

(Pictured below)

I put the elements of two recipes together to come up with this tasty seafood soup. I'm not always able to get fresh shellfish on short notice, so I keep a supply of canned fish and shellfish on hand. —Eleanor Henderson, Brick, New Jersey

>   3 tablespoons finely chopped onion
>   1 garlic clove, minced
> 1/4 cup butter *or* margarine
> 1/4 cup all-purpose flour
> 1/2 teaspoon salt
> 1/8 teaspoon pepper
> 2-1/2 cups half-and-half cream
>   2 cups tomato juice
> 1/4 teaspoon Worcestershire sauce
> 1/4 teaspoon ground savory
> Dash hot pepper sauce
>   2 cans (6 ounces *each*) lump crabmeat, rinsed and drained
> Sour cream and minced fresh parsley, optional

In a 2-qt. saucepan, saute the onion and garlic in butter until onion is tender. Stir in the flour, salt and pepper until bubbly. Gradually add the cream, tomato juice, Worcestershire sauce, savory and hot pepper sauce; bring to a boil, stirring constantly. Add crab; heat through. Garnish servings with sour cream and parsley if desired. **Yield:** 4-5 servings.

Side Dishes

*From vegetables and pasta to beans and grains,
these delightful dishes are a wonderful way to
round out your mouth-watering menus.*

COUNTRY COMPLEMENTS. Clockwise from upper left: Partytime Beans (p. 60), Mushroom Stuffing (p. 63), Zucchini and Corn Saute (p. 62) and Campfire Potatoes (p. 70).

mix well. Add the beans and peas; mix well. Cover and cook on low for 5-7 hours or until onion and peppers are tender. Remove bay leaves. **Yield:** 14-16 servings. **Nutritional Analysis:** One 1/2-cup serving (prepared with no-salt-added ketchup) equals 211 calories, 138 mg sodium, 0 cholesterol, 32 gm carbohydrate, 11 gm protein, 5 gm fat. **Diabetic Exchanges:** 2 starch, 1 meat.

Creamy Asparagus Casserole

Unlike most kids, my son doesn't consider asparagus "yucky". He loves it...especially in this dish. Whenever I serve this creamy combination, there's never any left. —Teresa Kachermeyer, Frederick, Maryland

> 1 can (10-3/4 ounces) condensed creamy chicken mushroom soup, undiluted
> 1/2 cup milk
> 1 package (10 ounces) frozen cut green beans, thawed
> 1 package (8 ounces) frozen asparagus cuts and tips, thawed and drained
> 1 can (4 ounces) mushroom stems and pieces, drained
> 2 cups cubed day-old bread
> 2 tablespoons sliced almonds
> 2 tablespoons butter *or* margarine, melted

In a large bowl, combine soup and milk. Add the beans, asparagus and mushrooms; mix well. Pour into a greased 8-in. square baking dish. Cover and bake at 350° for 20 minutes. Toss bread cubes, almonds and butter; sprinkle over the casserole. Bake, uncovered, 15-20 minutes longer or until bubbly. **Yield:** 6-8 servings.

Dilly Green Beans

My family eats a lot of vegetables. I credit this to creative seasonings like the combination on these green beans. They don't last long on the buffet. —Anne Mitchell, Mesa, Arizona

☑ Nutritional Analysis included

> 1 pound fresh *or* frozen cut green beans
> 1 teaspoon margarine
> 1/2 teaspoon dill weed

Place beans in a saucepan and cover with water. Bring to a boil; cook until tender. Drain all but 2 tablespoons of the liquid. Add margarine and dill; stir to coat. **Yield:** 6 servings. **Nutritional Analysis:** One 1/2-cup serving equals 29 calories, 9 mg sodium,

Partytime Beans

(Pictured above)

A friend brought this colorful bean dish to my house for a church circle potluck dinner. As soon as I tasted these slightly sweet baked beans, I had to have the recipe. —Jean Cantner, Boston, Virginia

☑ Nutritional Analysis included

> 1-1/2 cups ketchup
> 1 medium onion, chopped
> 1 medium green pepper, chopped
> 1 medium sweet red pepper, chopped
> 1/2 cup water
> 1/2 cup packed brown sugar
> 2 bay leaves
> 2 to 3 teaspoons cider vinegar
> 1 teaspoon ground mustard
> 1/8 teaspoon pepper
> 1 can (16 ounces) kidney beans, rinsed and drained
> 1 can (15-1/2 ounces) great northern beans, rinsed and drained
> 1 can (15 ounces) lima beans, rinsed and drained
> 1 can (15 ounces) black beans, rinsed and drained
> 1 can (15-1/2 ounces) black-eyed peas, rinsed and drained

In a slow cooker, combine the first 10 ingredients;

0 cholesterol, 5 gm carbohydrate, 1 gm protein, 1 gm fat. **Diabetic Exchange:** 1 vegetable.

— 🍷 🍷 🍷 —

Colorful Vegetable Casserole

With its eye-opening zippy flavor, horseradish gives this vegetable casserole a "root" awakening!
—Precious Owens, Elizabethtown, Kentucky

- 3 cups cauliflowerets
- 3 cups sliced carrots
- 3 cups broccoli florets
- 1 cup mayonnaise
- 1/4 cup finely chopped onion
- 3 tablespoons prepared horseradish
- 1/4 teaspoon salt
- 1/8 teaspoon pepper
- 1/3 cup dry bread crumbs
- 2 tablespoons butter *or* margarine, melted
- 1/8 teaspoon paprika

Place cauliflower and carrots in a large saucepan; add a small amount of water. Cover and cook for 3 minutes. Add broccoli; cook 4-6 minutes longer or until all the vegetables are crisp-tender. Drain. Combine mayonnaise, onion, horseradish, salt and pepper; add vegetables and mix well. Pour into a greased 2-qt. baking dish. Combine bread crumbs, butter and paprika; sprinkle over vegetables. Bake, uncovered, at 350° for 25-30 minutes or until heated through. **Yield:** 12-14 servings.

— 🍷 🍷 🍷 —

Scalloped Potatoes

This creamy, stick-to-your-ribs casserole is especially great alongside a roast. I've always enjoyed cooking foods that are down-to-earth and practical.
—Wendell Obermeier, Charles City, Iowa

- 8 medium potatoes, peeled and diced
- 1 tablespoon all-purpose flour
- 1-1/2 teaspoons salt
- 1/4 to 1/2 teaspoon pepper
- 1 medium onion, finely chopped
- 1 can (10-3/4 ounces) condensed cream of mushroom soup, undiluted
- 1 cup milk *or* half-and-half cream
- 1/2 cup dry bread crumbs
- 3 tablespoons butter *or* margarine, melted

In a greased 2-qt. baking dish, layer a third of the potatoes. Combine flour, salt and pepper; sprinkle a third over potatoes. Top with a third of the onion. Combine soup and milk; pour a third over onion.

Repeat layers twice. Combine bread crumbs and butter; sprinkle over top. Cover and bake at 350° for 1 hour. Uncover and bake 30 minutes more. **Yield:** 8 servings.

— 🍷 🍷 🍷 —

Rhubarb Corn Bread Stuffing
(Pictured below)

I'm a rhubarb fan, so I couldn't wait to try my friend's recipe for this distinctive stuffing. It's awesome along-side ham or poultry. When I serve this, my guests are usually curious about my special ingredient...and they love it! —Kathy Petrullo, Long Island City, New York

- 5 cups chopped fresh *or* frozen rhubarb (1/2-inch pieces), thawed
- 1/2 cup sugar
- 1 medium onion, chopped
- 1/2 cup butter *or* margarine, *divided*
- 3 cups corn bread stuffing
- 1/2 cup chopped walnuts

In a large bowl, toss rhubarb and sugar; set aside. In a skillet over medium heat, saute onion in 2 tablespoons butter until tender; add to rhubarb mixture. Stir in stuffing and walnuts. Melt the remaining butter; pour over the stuffing mixture and toss lightly. Spoon into a greased 2-qt. shallow baking dish. Bake, uncovered, at 325° for 40-45 minutes or until stuffing is heated through and top is lightly browned. Serve warm. **Yield:** 6-8 servings.

Zucchini and Corn Saute

(Pictured below)

I fix this vegetable side dish often to put a big crop of zucchini to good use. Corn and bell peppers add color and flair. It goes great with any summer meal.
—*Vera Reid, Laramie, Wyoming*

✓ Nutritional Analysis included

- 2 **medium zucchini, thinly sliced**
- 1 **medium green pepper, thinly sliced**
- 1 **medium sweet red pepper, thinly sliced**
- 2 **to 3 tablespoons vegetable oil, optional**
- 2 **cups fresh *or* frozen corn**
- 1 **teaspoon garlic salt, optional**
- 1/2 **teaspoon Italian seasoning**

In a large skillet, saute zucchini and peppers in oil until crisp-tender, about 4 minutes. Add remaining ingredients; saute 3-4 minutes longer or until the corn is tender. **Yield:** 10 servings. **Nutritional Analysis:** One 1/2-cup serving (prepared with non-stick cooking spray instead of oil and without salt) equals 48 calories, 7 mg sodium, 0 cholesterol, 11 gm carbohydrate, 2 gm protein, 1 gm fat. **Diabetic Exchange:** 2 vegetable.

Creamy Green Beans

This satisfying side-dish casserole has a slightly sweet-and-sour flavor. It's a favorite around my house for the holidays and anytime. —*Lynn Hansen*
North Liberty, Iowa

✓ Nutritional Analysis included

- 2 **cups frozen French-style green beans**
- 1 **tablespoon chopped onion**
- 1 **tablespoon butter *or* margarine**
- 1 **tablespoon all-purpose flour**
- 1/2 **cup plain yogurt**
- **Pepper to taste**
- 1/4 **cup shredded process American cheese**

Place beans in a microwave-safe baking dish; microwave on high for 4-5 minutes or until tender. Set aside. In a saucepan, saute onion in butter for 1 minute. Stir in flour until smooth; cook and stir for 1 minute. Stir in yogurt. Add beans and pepper. Top with cheese; let stand until melted. **Yield:** 4 servings. **Nutritional Analysis:** One 1/2-cup serving (prepared with reduced-fat margarine, nonfat yogurt and light process American cheese) equals 70 calories, 162 mg sodium, 4 mg cholesterol, 8 gm carbohydrate, 4 gm protein, 3 gm fat. **Diabetic Exchanges:** 1-1/2 vegetable, 1/2 fat. **Editor's Note:** This recipe was tested in a 700-watt microwave.

Pizza-Style Tomatoes

While my husband eats tomatoes just about any way I fix them, our daughter would only eat tomato sauce. This recipe came about when I experimented with an old recipe for fried tomatoes. Now our daughter requests these often!
—*Dawn Booth*
Somers Point, New Jersey

- 1/2 **cup all-purpose flour**
- 1-1/4 **teaspoons dried basil**
- 1-1/4 **teaspoons dried oregano**
- 1/2 **teaspoon salt**
- 1/4 **teaspoon pepper**
- 2 **medium firm red tomatoes, sliced 1/2 inch thick**
- **Vegetable oil**
- **Chopped green pepper, optional**
- 3/4 **cup shredded mozzarella cheese**

In a bowl, combine the flour, basil, oregano, salt and pepper. Dip tomatoes in flour mixture. In a skillet, fry tomatoes in oil, a few at a time, until golden on both sides. Sprinkle with green pepper if desired. Top with cheese; cook until the cheese is melted. Drain on paper towels; serve warm. **Yield:** 4-6 servings.

Instant Stuffing Mix

I use dry bread for this recipe, which costs just a fraction of the price of a store-bought mix.
—Darlene Markel, Sublimity, Oregon

✓ Nutritional Analysis included

3-1/2 cups unseasoned toasted bread cubes
3 tablespoons dried celery flakes
1 tablespoon dried parsley flakes
2 teaspoons dried minced onion
2 teaspoons chicken bouillon granules
1/4 teaspoon poultry seasoning
1/4 teaspoon rubbed sage
ADDITIONAL INGREDIENTS:
1 cup water
2 tablespoons butter *or* margarine

Place bread cubes in a jar or resealable plastic bag. In a small plastic bag, combine the celery flakes, parsley flakes, onion, bouillon, poultry seasoning and sage; mix well. Tie bag shut and attach to jar or bag of bread cubes. **Yield:** 1 batch. **To prepare stuffing:** In a saucepan over medium heat, bring water, butter and contents of seasoning packet to a boil. Reduce heat; cover and simmer for 10 minutes. Remove from the heat; add bread cubes and mix gently. Cover and let stand for 5 minutes. Toss with a fork before serving. **Yield:** 6 servings per batch. **Nutritional Analysis:** One 1/2-cup serving (prepared with margarine and low-sodium bouillon) equals 122 calories, 162 mg sodium, trace cholesterol, 15 gm carbohydrate, 3 gm protein, 6 gm fat. **Diabetic Exchanges:** 1 starch, 1 fat.

Peas Amandine

This is a favorite vegetable dish when the "Kidds" come home to visit!
—Shirley Kidd
New London, Minnesota

1 package (16 ounces) frozen peas
1/4 cup slivered almonds
3 tablespoons butter *or* margarine
1 jar (4-1/2 ounces) sliced mushrooms, drained
1/4 cup chopped onion
1/4 teaspoon salt
1/8 teaspoon pepper

Cook peas according to package directions; drain. Set aside and keep warm. In a skillet, saute almonds in butter until lightly browned. Remove with a slotted spoon; add to peas. In the same skillet, saute mushrooms and onion until tender; add to peas. Season with salt and pepper. **Yield:** 8 servings.

Mushroom Stuffing

(Pictured above)

I first tried this stuffing a few years ago. The hearty corn bread mix has plenty of mushroom and bacon accents.
—Kathy Traetow, Waverly, Iowa

4 bacon strips, diced
4 celery ribs, chopped
1 medium onion, chopped
1 pound fresh mushrooms, chopped
1 teaspoon rubbed sage
1/2 teaspoon salt
1/4 teaspoon pepper
1 package (16 ounces) corn bread stuffing
1/2 cup chopped celery leaves
2 tablespoons minced fresh parsley
4 eggs, beaten
2-1/2 cups chicken broth
1 tablespoon butter *or* margarine

In a large skillet, cook bacon until crisp; remove with a slotted spoon to paper towel. Drain, reserving 2 tablespoons drippings. Saute celery and onion in drippings until tender. Add mushrooms, sage, salt and pepper; cook and stir for 5 minutes. Remove from the heat; stir in stuffing, celery leaves, parsley and bacon; mix well. Combine eggs and broth; add to stuffing mixture and mix well. Spread into a greased 13-in. x 9-in. x 2-in. baking dish (dish will be full). Dot with butter. Cover and bake at 350° for 30 minutes. Uncover; bake 10 minutes longer or until lightly browned. **Yield:** 13 cups (enough to stuff one 16- to 18-pound turkey or three 5- to 7-pound roasting chickens).

Down-Home Dumplings

HIGH on most everyone's list of "comfort foods", dumplings bring to mind fond memories of meals with Mom or Grandma. Here, fellow cooks share traditional favorites and newer variations.

Spinach Dumplings

(Pictured below)

I've been making these green dumplings—called gnocchi verdi in Italian—since the 1970's. They are a great side dish for almost any meal.
—Gail Sykora, Menomonee Falls, Wisconsin

1 tablespoon finely chopped onion
6 tablespoons butter *or* margarine
3 packages (10 ounces *each*) frozen chopped spinach, thawed and drained
1 cup ricotta cheese
1-1/2 cups all-purpose flour, *divided*
1/2 cup grated Parmesan cheese
3/4 teaspoon garlic salt
2 eggs, beaten
3 quarts water
3 tablespoons chicken bouillon granules
TOPPING:
1/4 cup butter *or* margarine, melted
1/2 cup grated Parmesan cheese

OLD-FASHIONED FARE like Spinach Dumplings, Cheddar Tomato Dumplings and Baked Cornmeal Dumplings (shown above, clockwise from top) makes for memorable meals.

In a skillet, saute onion in butter until tender. Add spinach; cook and stir over medium heat until liquid has evaporated, about 5 minutes. Stir in ricotta; cook and stir for 3 minutes. Transfer to a large bowl. Add 3/4 cup flour, Parmesan and garlic salt. Cool for 5 minutes. Stir in eggs; mix well. Place remaining flour in a bowl. Drop batter by tablespoonfuls into flour; roll gently to coat and shape each into an oval. In a large saucepan, bring water and bouillon to a boil. Reduce heat. Add a third of the dumplings at a time; simmer, uncovered, for 8-10 minutes or until a toothpick inserted in a dumpling comes out clean. Remove with a slotted spoon; keep warm. Drizzle with butter; sprinkle with Parmesan. **Yield:** 12 servings.

Baked Cornmeal Dumplings

(Pictured at left)

These big golden dumplings are delicious with stew or any type of dish with gravy. —*Grace Yaskovic Branchville, New Jersey*

  2/3 **cup all-purpose flour**
  2/3 **cup cornmeal**
    3 **tablespoons grated Parmesan cheese**
    2 **teaspoons baking powder**
    1 **tablespoon minced fresh parsley *or* 1 teaspoon dried parsley flakes**
  1/4 **teaspoon salt**
  1/2 **cup milk**
  1/4 **cup vegetable oil**
    1 **quart chicken broth**
Additional minced fresh parsley, optional

In a bowl, combine the first six ingredients. Combine milk and oil; stir into dry ingredients. Bring broth to a boil; carefully transfer to a 2-1/2-qt. round baking dish. Drop batter in six mounds onto broth. Cover and bake at 400° for 20-25 minutes or until a toothpick inserted in a dumpling comes out clean (do not lift the cover while baking). Garnish with parsley if desired. **Yield:** 6 servings.

Cheddar Tomato Dumplings

(Pictured at left)

Simmered in tomato sauce, these fluffy dumplings with cheddar cheese in the dough make a satisfying side dish as well as a delicious, economical meatless meal. —*Marie Hattrup, The Dalles, Oregon*

    2 **tablespoons finely chopped onion**
    1 **tablespoon finely chopped green pepper**
    2 **tablespoons vegetable oil**
    2 **tablespoons all-purpose flour**
    1 **can (28 ounces) diced tomatoes, undrained**
    1 **tablespoon minced celery leaves**
    1 **teaspoon sugar**
  1/2 **teaspoon salt**
  1/4 **teaspoon pepper**
DUMPLINGS:
    1 **cup all-purpose flour**
    2 **teaspoons baking powder**
  1/2 **teaspoon salt**
    2 **tablespoons shortening**
  1/2 **cup shredded cheddar cheese**
  1/2 **cup milk**

In a large skillet, saute onion and green pepper in oil until tender. Add flour; stir well. Gradually blend in tomatoes. Add celery leaves, sugar, salt and pepper; bring to a boil over medium heat. Cook and stir for 2 minutes. Reduce heat; cover and simmer for 5 minutes. Meanwhile, for dumplings, combine flour, baking powder and salt in a bowl; cut in shortening until crumbly. Add cheese. Stir in milk just until moistened. Drop by tablespoonfuls onto simmering tomato sauce. Cover and simmer for 20 minutes or until a toothpick inserted in a dumpling comes out clean (do not lift the cover while simmering). **Yield:** 4-5 servings.

Chicken Dumpling Strips

I've shared this recipe with many people, and all agree—it never fails. The light, tender dumplings are cut into strips like wide noodles. —*Gay Nell Nicholas Henderson, Texas*

1-1/4 **cups all-purpose flour**
  1/2 **teaspoon salt**
  1/4 **teaspoon poultry seasoning**
  1/4 **cup shortening**
    1 **egg, beaten**
  1/4 **cup milk**
    3 **cups chicken broth**
    1 **cup cubed cooked chicken**

In a bowl, combine flour, salt and poultry seasoning; cut in shortening until crumbly. Combine egg and milk; stir into flour mixture just until combined. On a heavily floured surface, roll dough to 1/4-in. thickness. Cut into 1-in. strips; cut strips into 2-in. lengths. In a large saucepan, bring broth to a boil. Add chicken. Reduce heat; drop dumplings onto simmering broth. Cover and simmer for 15-20 minutes or until a toothpick inserted in a dumpling comes out clean (do not lift the cover while simmering). **Yield:** 4 servings.

Sweet Potatoes Au Gratin

(Pictured above)

There's no end to the delicious and diverse ways to use sweet potatoes. I recommend this rich, cheesy casserole, which is a standby in our home.
—Patti Kirchhoff, Lake Geneva, Wisconsin

  2 **large uncooked sweet potatoes, peeled and sliced 1/4 inch thick**
  1 **egg**
  2 **cups whipping cream**
3/4 **teaspoon salt**
1/8 **teaspoon ground nutmeg**
Pinch pepper
  3 **tablespoons grated Parmesan cheese**

Place potatoes in a greased 8-in. square baking dish. In a bowl, beat egg. Add cream, salt, nutmeg and pepper; mix well. Pour over potatoes. Sprinkle with cheese. Bake, uncovered, at 375° for 40-45 minutes or until potatoes are tender. **Yield:** 6-8 servings.

Herbed Rice Mix

For Christmas gifts, I fill pint-size plastic zipper bags with this savory blend. I include the cooking directions on a holiday label.
—Emily Chaney
Penobscot, Maine

  1 **package (3 pounds) long grain rice**
  2 **cups dried celery flakes**
2/3 **cup dried minced onion**
1/2 **cup dried parsley flakes**
  2 **tablespoons dried chives**
  1 **tablespoon dried tarragon**
  3 **to 4 teaspoons salt**
  2 **teaspoons pepper**

ADDITIONAL INGREDIENTS:
2/3 **cup water**
  1 **teaspoon butter** *or* **margarine**

Combine the first eight ingredients; mix well. Store in airtight containers. **Yield:** 40 batches (10 cups total). **To prepare one serving of rice:** In a saucepan over medium heat, bring water and butter to a boil. Add 1/4 cup rice mixture. Reduce heat; cover and simmer for 20 minutes. Remove from the heat; let stand for 5 minutes or until liquid is absorbed. Fluff with a fork. **Yield:** 1 serving per batch. **Editor's Note:** To prepare more than 1 serving, multiply the rice mix, water and butter by the total number of desired servings and cook as directed.

Baked Onion Rings

My family loves the flavor of these homemade onion rings. The coating is delightfully seasoned.
—Peggy Burdick, Burlington, Michigan

☑ Nutritional Analysis included

1-1/2 **cups crushed cornflakes**
  2 **teaspoons sugar**
  1 **teaspoon paprika**
1/4 **teaspoon seasoned salt**
1/4 **teaspoon garlic salt**
  2 **large sweet onions**
Egg substitute equivalent to 2 eggs

In a large bowl, combine the first five ingredients; set aside. Cut onions into 1/2-in.-thick slices. Separate into rings, reserving the small rings for another use. In a small mixing bowl, beat egg substitute until frothy. Dip onion rings into egg, then into crumb mixture, coating well. Place in a single layer on baking sheets that have been coated with nonstick cooking spray. Bake at 375° for 15-20 minutes or until onions are tender and coating is crispy. **Yield:** about 6 servings. **Nutritional Analysis:** One serving (four onion rings) equals 143 calories, 442 mg sodium, trace cholesterol, 30 gm carbohydrate, 5 gm protein, 1 gm fat. **Diabetic Exchange:** 2 starch.

Green Beans with Thyme

Chopped onion, thyme and other seasonings give fresh green beans great flavor.
—Doris Dibert
Everett, Pennsylvania

  1 **pound fresh green beans, cut into 2-inch pieces**
1/2 **cup water**

1/2 teaspoon salt
1/4 cup finely chopped onion
  2 tablespoons butter *or* margarine
  1 tablespoon minced fresh parsley
  1 tablespoon lemon juice
3/4 teaspoon minced fresh thyme *or*
    1/4 teaspoon dried thyme
1/8 teaspoon paprika

In a 3-qt. saucepan, combine beans, water and salt; bring to a boil. Reduce heat; cover and simmer for 15 minutes or until tender. Meanwhile, in a small saucepan, saute the onion in butter until tender. Add parsley, lemon juice, thyme and paprika. Drain beans; add butter mixture and toss to coat. **Yield:** 6 servings.

Potato Packets

I usually fire up our grill four or five times a week. In addition to entrees, it's so easy to grill side dishes like this. —*Stanley Pichon, Slidell, Louisiana*

  2 medium potatoes, peeled and diced
  1 cup chopped onion
  2 tablespoons butter *or* margarine
1/2 teaspoon salt
1/4 teaspoon white pepper

On two pieces of heavy-duty foil (about 18 in. x 18 in.), divide potatoes, onion, butter, salt and pepper. Fold foil around potato mixture; seal tightly. Cook on a covered grill over medium heat for 20-30 minutes or until potatoes are tender. **Yield:** 4 servings.

Surprise Stuffing

Squash is well camouflaged in this recipe...even the name doesn't give away the secret ingredient! —*Frances Tanner, Milledgeville, Georgia*

  2 cups chopped yellow summer squash
  1 medium onion, chopped
1/4 cup butter *or* margarine
  4 cups crumbled corn bread
  1 can (10-3/4 ounces) condensed cream of chicken soup, undiluted
  3 eggs, beaten
1/4 teaspoon salt
Dash pepper

In a large skillet, saute the squash and onion in butter until tender. Remove from the heat; stir in remaining ingredients. Transfer to a greased 1-qt. baking dish. Bake, uncovered, at 350° for 40 minutes. **Yield:** 6 servings.

'I Wish I Had That Recipe...'

"ONCE you've tasted the corn fritters at The Old Tavern restaurant in Unionville, Ohio, you'll go back again and again," raves Don Ritter from Madison, Ohio.

Don requested *Taste of Home's* help in pursuing the how-to on these famed fritters.

We contacted Laura Lagasse, banquet manager at The Old Tavern. "Two co-workers who also subscribe to *Taste of Home* helped me convince owners Gary and Ralph Haskins to give out the recipe," Laura relates. "It's been a secret for nearly 200 years!

"The Old Tavern was built in 1798 as a rest stop for travelers. In 1818, it was expanded from the original 12-foot by 15-foot cabin to its present saltbox design. Up to 30 stagecoaches a day would disembark passengers under the enclosed archway."

Located on Route 84 at County Line Road, The Old Tavern opens at 11:30 a.m. Tuesday through Saturday for lunch and dinner. Sunday brunch begins at 9 a.m. 1-800/7-TAVERN (782-8376).

Old Tavern Corn Fritters

  1 cup all-purpose flour
1-1/2 teaspoons baking powder
  2 eggs
1/3 cup milk
  1 can (15-1/4 ounces) whole kernel corn, drained
  1 tablespoon butter *or* margarine, melted
Oil for deep-fat frying
Confectioners' sugar
Maple syrup, warmed

In a bowl, combine flour and baking powder; set aside. In another bowl, beat the eggs and milk; stir in corn and butter. Stir into dry ingredients just until blended. In a deep-fat fryer or electric skillet, heat oil to 375°. Drop batter by heaping teaspoonfuls into hot oil; fry for 2-3 minutes or until golden brown. Drain on paper towels. Dust with confectioners' sugar. Serve with syrup. **Yield:** about 2 dozen.

Spinach-Stuffed Tomatoes

I refused to try spinach for many years. Then one day I found this interesting recipe and decided to give it a whirl. It convinced my taste buds that spinach can be delicious! —Wendy Furie, Frederick, Maryland

> 6 medium tomatoes
> 4 tablespoons butter *or* margarine, *divided*
> 1 package (10 ounces) frozen chopped spinach, thawed and drained
> 3/4 cup dry bread crumbs
> 1 teaspoon Italian seasoning
> 1/2 cup shredded mozzarella cheese
> 1/8 teaspoon garlic salt
> 1/8 teaspoon pepper

Cut a thin slice off the top of each tomato. Scoop out pulp, leaving a 1/2-in.-thick shell. Invert the tomatoes onto paper towels to drain. Meanwhile, melt 2 tablespoons butter in a skillet. Add spinach; cook and stir for 7 minutes. In a bowl, combine bread crumbs and Italian seasoning. Set aside 1/4 cup for topping. Add spinach and cheese to remaining crumb mixture. Sprinkle tomato shells with garlic salt and pepper; stuff with spinach mixture. Place in a greased 13-in. x 9-in. x 2-in. baking dish. Melt remaining butter; toss with reserved crumbs. Sprinkle over tomatoes. Bake, uncovered, at 375° for 20-25 minutes or until crumbs are lightly browned. **Yield:** 6 servings.

Oregano Potato Casserole

Seasonings, cottage cheese, sour cream and eggs dress up ordinary mashed potatoes. These are fluffy and light and pair well with any meaty main dish.
—Barbara Stewart, Portland, Connecticut

> 2-1/2 cups mashed potatoes (with milk)
> 1 cup cream-style cottage cheese
> 1/2 cup sour cream
> 3 eggs, *separated*
> 2 tablespoons minced fresh oregano *or* 2 teaspoons dried oregano
> 2 tablespoons minced fresh parsley *or* 2 teaspoons dried parsley flakes
> 1/2 teaspoon seasoned salt
> 2 tablespoons butter *or* margarine

In a large bowl, combine potatoes, cottage cheese, sour cream, egg yolks, oregano, parsley and seasoned salt. In a mixing bowl, beat egg whites until stiff peaks form; fold into potato mixture. Transfer to a lightly greased 2-1/2-qt. baking dish. Dot with butter. Bake, uncovered, at 350° for 1 hour or until lightly browned. **Yield:** 6-8 servings.

Veggie Pancakes

These taste like potato pancakes but have a fun colorful look from nutritious carrots, zucchini, peas and corn. It's a surefire way to get your kids to eat a variety of vegetables. —Colleen Schneider
Johnsonburg, Pennsylvania

> 2 to 3 medium zucchini, coarsely grated (about 2 cups)
> 1 medium carrot, grated
> 1 medium potato, peeled and grated
> 1/3 cup frozen peas
> 1/3 cup frozen corn
> 2 eggs
> 1/4 cup all-purpose flour
> 1/4 cup grated Parmesan cheese
> 1/4 teaspoon *each* salt, pepper, garlic powder and celery seed
> Vegetable oil for frying

In a sieve or colander, drain zucchini, squeezing to remove excess liquid. Combine zucchini, carrot, potato, peas and corn in a bowl. Stir in the eggs, flour, cheese and seasonings; mix well. In a skillet, heat 1/4 in. of oil over medium heat. Drop batter by 1/4 cupfuls; press lightly to flatten. Fry until golden brown, about 3 minutes on each side. Serve warm. **Yield:** 1 dozen.

Herbed Pecan Stuffing

I've updated a basic stuffing recipe by using wholesome multi-grain bread in place of customary white bread. It adds a hearty, crunchy taste.
—Edie Despain, Logan, Utah

> 8 cups day-old multi-grain bread cubes
> 3/4 cup golden raisins
> 1/2 cup apple juice
> 4 celery ribs, diced
> 1 large onion, chopped
> 3 garlic cloves, minced
> 1/4 cup olive *or* vegetable oil
> 1 cup minced fresh parsley
> 1-1/2 teaspoons salt
> 1-1/2 teaspoons rubbed sage
> 3/4 teaspoon dried thyme
> 1/2 teaspoon fennel seeds, crushed
> 1/4 teaspoon pepper
> 1 egg
> 1-1/2 to 2 cups chicken broth
> 1-1/2 cups coarsely chopped pecans, toasted

Place bread cubes in a single layer on an ungreased baking sheet. Bake at 225° for 30-40 minutes, tossing occasionally, until partially dried. Meanwhile, combine raisins and apple juice in a saucepan;

bring to a boil. Remove from the heat; let stand for 15 minutes. In a large skillet or Dutch oven, saute celery, onion and garlic in oil until tender. Add parsley, salt, sage, thyme, fennel seeds and pepper; mix well. Remove from the heat. Beat egg and broth; add to vegetable mixture with bread cubes and raisin mixture. Toss well. Stir in pecans. Transfer to a greased 13-in. x 9-in. x 2-in. baking dish. Cover and bake at 325° for 30 minutes. Uncover; bake 15-20 minutes longer or until lightly browned. **Yield:** 10-12 servings.

Corn Dumplings

Cornmeal and kernel corn give a double dose of harvest flavor to the soft dumplings. I serve them with chicken and gravy. —Pat Habiger
Spearville, Kansas

   1 **cup cornmeal**
   2 **teaspoons salt**
   2 **cups water**
 3/4 **cup chopped whole kernel corn**
   2 **tablespoons butter *or* margarine**
   1 **teaspoon finely chopped onion**
 1/8 **teaspoon pepper**
   1 **egg, beaten**
1-1/4 **cups all-purpose flour, *divided***
2-1/2 **teaspoons baking powder**
   2 **quarts chicken broth**

In a saucepan, combine cornmeal, salt and water; bring to a boil over medium-high heat, stirring constantly. Cook and stir until very thick. Reduce heat; cook and stir for 3 minutes. Remove from the heat. Stir in corn, butter, onion and pepper; let stand for 3 minutes. Add egg; mix well. In a bowl, combine 3/4 cup flour and baking powder. Add to cornmeal mixture; beat well. Shape into 1-1/2-in. balls; roll in remaining flour to lightly coat. In a Dutch oven or kettle, bring broth to a boil. Add dumplings. Cover and simmer for 15 minutes or until a toothpick inserted in a dumpling comes out clean (do not lift the cover while simmering). **Yield:** 8-9 servings.

Stuffed Butternut Squash

(Pictured above)

I enjoy experimenting with new recipes and that's how I came up with this meal-in-one squash idea. Ham, mustard, apples and brown sugar go so well with butternut squash. —Bev Spain, Bellville, Ohio

   3 **small butternut squash (about 1-1/2**
      pounds *each*)
   2 **cups cubed fully cooked ham**
   1 **cup soft bread crumbs**
 1/2 **cup shredded tart apple**
 1/4 **cup packed brown sugar**
   2 **tablespoons prepared mustard**

Cut squash in half lengthwise; discard seeds. Place squash, cut side down, in a 15-in. x 10-in. x 1-in. baking pan. Fill pan with hot water to a depth of 1/2 in. Bake, uncovered, at 350° for 30 minutes. Combine remaining ingredients. Turn squash cut side up; stuff with ham mixture. Cover stem end with foil to prevent drying. Bake at 350° for 30 minutes or until squash is tender. **Yield:** 6 servings.

Campfire Potatoes

(Pictured above)

Potatoes, onion, cheddar cheese and Worcestershire sauce combine to make a super side dish for any grilled meat. —JoAnn Dettbarn, Brainerd, Minnesota

5 medium potatoes, peeled and thinly sliced
1 medium onion, sliced
6 tablespoons butter *or* margarine
1/3 cup shredded cheddar cheese
2 tablespoons minced fresh parsley
1 tablespoon Worcestershire sauce
Salt and pepper to taste
1/3 cup chicken broth

Place the potatoes and onion on a large piece of heavy-duty foil (about 20 in. x 20 in.); dot with butter. Combine the cheese, parsley, Worcestershire sauce, salt and pepper; sprinkle over potatoes. Fold foil up around potatoes and add broth. Seal the edges of foil tightly. Grill, covered, over medium coals for 35-40 minutes or until the potatoes are tender. **Yield:** 4-6 servings.

Apple Almond Pilaf

This pilaf is packed with a delightful mix of tastes and textures.   —Mary Patterson, Bethel, Connecticut

✓ Nutritional Analysis included

2 teaspoons butter *or* margarine
1/4 cup sliced blanched almonds
2 large pitted prunes, cut into strips
2 tablespoons raisins
4 dried apple slices, halved

1-1/2 cups water
1/2 cup uncooked long grain rice
2 teaspoons honey

Melt butter in a nonstick saucepan. Add almonds; cook and stir over medium heat until lightly browned. Stir in prunes, raisins and apple slices; cook and stir for 1 minute. Add remaining ingredients; bring to a boil. Reduce heat; cover and simmer until rice is tender, about 20 minutes. **Yield:** 4 servings. **Nutritional Analysis:** One 1/2-cup serving (prepared with margarine) equals 203 calories, 28 mg sodium, 0 cholesterol, 33 gm carbohydrate, 4 gm protein, 6 gm fat. **Diabetic Exchanges:** 1 starch, 1 fruit, 1 fat.

Light Scalloped Potatoes

Even with lighter ingredients, this is a comforting potato dish.   —Tamie Foley, Pasadena, California

✓ Nutritional Analysis included

6 medium potatoes, peeled and thinly sliced
3 cups water
4 chicken bouillon cubes
1 garlic clove, minced
1/2 cup grated Parmesan cheese
Minced fresh parsley, optional

Place potatoes in a greased 2-qt. baking dish. In a saucepan, heat water, bouillon and garlic until bouillon is dissolved; pour over potatoes. Sprinkle with Parmesan cheese. Bake, uncovered, at 350° for 1-1/4 to 1-1/2 hours or until tender. Let stand 10 minutes before serving. Sprinkle with parsley if desired. Serve with a slotted spoon. **Yield:** 6 servings. **Nutritional Analysis:** One 1/2-cup serving (prepared with low-sodium bouillon) equals 175 calories, 168 mg sodium, 7 mg cholesterol, 32 gm carbohydrate, 3 gm protein, 3 gm fat. **Diabetic Exchanges:** 2 starch, 1/2 fat.

Cranberry-Stuffed Acorn Squash

I combine two of fall's best foods in this recipe. The pretty, fresh-tasting filling makes this an extra-special side dish.   —Jim Ulberg, Elk Rapids, Michigan

4 medium acorn squash
1 cup fresh *or* frozen cranberries, coarsely chopped
1 medium tart apple, coarsely chopped
1 medium orange, peeled and diced
2/3 cup packed brown sugar
1/4 cup chopped walnuts

1/4 cup butter *or* margarine, melted
1 teaspoon grated orange peel
Pinch salt

Cut squash in half; discard seeds. Place squash, cut side down, in a 15-in. x 10-in. x 1-in. baking pan. Fill pan with hot water to a depth of 1/2 in. Bake, uncovered, at 350° for 30 minutes. Meanwhile, combine cranberries, apple, orange, brown sugar, walnuts, butter and orange peel. Drain water from pan; turn squash cut side up. Sprinkle with salt. Stuff with the cranberry mixture. Bake 25 minutes longer or until squash is tender. **Yield:** 8 servings.

Wild Rice Stuffing Bake

If you prefer, you can stuff this mixture loosely into a bird to bake rather than in a separate dish.
—*Frances Poste, Wall, South Dakota*

1/2 cup chopped celery
1/3 cup chopped onion
3 tablespoons butter *or* margarine
1 egg
1 can (10-3/4 ounces) condensed cream of chicken soup, undiluted
1/2 cup chicken broth
1 tablespoon minced fresh parsley
1/2 teaspoon poultry seasoning
1/4 teaspoon salt
1/8 teaspoon pepper
3 cups day-old bread cubes
1-1/2 cups cooked wild rice

In a skillet, saute celery and onion in butter until tender. Combine egg, soup, broth, parsley, poultry seasoning, salt and pepper. Add celery mixture, bread cubes and rice; mix well. Spoon into a greased 1-1/2-qt. baking dish. Cover and bake at 350° for 20 minutes. Uncover; bake 10-15 minutes longer or until set. **Yield:** 6-8 servings.

Hearty Poultry Stuffing

This was my mother's recipe and is now a tradition at my house, too. My mother-in-law even preferred it to her own stuffing!
—*Phyllis Hickey*
Bedford, New Hampshire

1/2 pound ground beef
1 medium onion, chopped
1 garlic clove, minced
11 slices day-old bread, cut into 1/2-inch cubes
1/2 to 2/3 cup seasoned bread crumbs

2 tablespoons grated Romano cheese
1/2 teaspoon Italian seasoning
1/2 teaspoon salt
Dash pepper
3 tablespoons butter *or* margarine, melted
1 egg
1/2 to 3/4 cup water
1/2 cup raisins
1/2 cup chopped walnuts

In a saucepan, cook beef, onion and garlic until meat is no longer pink; drain and set aside. In a bowl, combine bread cubes and crumbs, cheese, Italian seasoning, salt and pepper. Add butter; toss to coat. Beat egg and water; add to bread mixture. Add beef mixture, raisins and walnuts. Spoon into a greased 13-in. x 9-in. x 2-in. baking dish. Cover and bake at 350° for 30 minutes. Uncover; bake 10 minutes longer or until browned. **Yield:** 10-12 servings.

Grilled Mushrooms
(Pictured below)

Mushrooms cooked over hot coals always taste good, but this easy recipe makes the mushrooms taste fantastic. —*Melanie Knoll, Marshalltown, Iowa*

1/2 pound whole fresh mushrooms (medium size work best)
1/4 cup butter *or* margarine, melted
1/2 teaspoon dill weed
1/2 teaspoon garlic salt

Thread mushrooms on skewers. Combine butter, dill and garlic salt; brush over mushrooms. Grill over hot coals for 10-15 minutes, basting and turning every 5 minutes. **Yield:** 4 servings.

Low-Fat Refried Beans

A local Mexican restaurant shared this recipe with me. It's so simple and tasty you'll never go back to canned refried beans. —Kitty Shelton, Ketchum, Idaho

☑ Nutritional Analysis included

- 1 package (16 ounces) dry pinto *or* red beans
- 1 large onion, quartered
- 3 garlic cloves
- 1/2 teaspoon ground cumin
- 3 to 4 drops hot pepper sauce

Place beans in a Dutch oven; add water to cover by 2 in. Bring to a boil; boil for 2 minutes. Remove from the heat; cover and let stand for 1 hour. Drain beans; discard liquid. Return beans to pan; add water to cover. Add onion and garlic; bring to a boil. Cover and cook over low heat for 2 hours or until beans are very tender, adding water to keep covered if needed. Discard onion and garlic. Mash beans with a potato masher, leaving some beans whole. Stir in cumin and hot pepper sauce. **Yield:** 9 servings. **Nutritional Analysis:** One 1/2-cup serving equals 180 calories, 6 mg sodium, 0 cholesterol, 34 gm carbohydrate, 11 gm protein, 1 gm fat. **Diabetic Exchanges:** 2 starch, 1 vegetable.

———— 🦃 🦃 🦃 ————

Orange-Kissed Beets

(Pictured below)

This is an original recipe I developed some years ago. Now it's my husband's favorite. The sweet, tangy sauce nicely complements the beets.
— Bonnie Baumgardner, Sylva, North Carolina

- 1/3 cup orange juice
- 2 tablespoons light brown sugar
- 1 tablespoon butter *or* margarine

- 1/2 teaspoon cornstarch
- 1/8 teaspoon ground ginger
- 1/8 teaspoon salt
- 1/8 teaspoon pepper
- 1 can (8-1/4 ounces) sliced beets, drained
- 2 tablespoons golden raisins

Strips of orange peel

In a saucepan over medium heat, cook and stir orange juice, brown sugar, butter, cornstarch, ginger, salt and pepper until thick. Add the beets and raisins; heat through. Garnish with orange peel. **Yield:** 2 servings.

———— 🦃 🦃 🦃 ————

Creamy Squash Casserole

This is so easy to prepare. With squash, carrots and stuffing mix, it's an excellent holiday side dish.
—Sue Moore, Columbiana, Ohio

- 2 pounds acorn *or* butternut squash
- 1 can (10-3/4 ounces) condensed cream of chicken soup, undiluted
- 1 cup (8 ounces) sour cream
- 1/3 cup butter *or* margarine, melted
- 2 medium carrots, shredded
- 1/2 cup finely chopped onion
- 2-1/4 cups herb-seasoned stuffing mix, *divided*

Cut squash in half; remove and discard peel and seeds. Cut squash into 1/2-in. cubes. Cook squash in a small amount of water for 3 minutes; drain and set aside. In a bowl, combine soup, sour cream, butter, carrots and onion; stir in 2 cups stuffing mix. Fold in squash. Transfer to a greased 11-in. x 7-in. x 2-in. baking dish. Sprinkle with remaining stuffing mix. Bake, uncovered, at 350° for 25 minutes or until squash is tender. **Yield:** 12 servings.

———— 🦃 🦃 🦃 ————

Scalloped Spinach

I treat friends to this dish whenever I attend a potluck or gathering. The crumbled bacon on top is so appealing...and brings people back for seconds!
—Patricia Bassler, Ellicott City, Maryland

- 6 bacon strips, diced
- 1/4 cup chopped onion
- 1 package (10 ounces) fresh spinach, chopped
- 2 cups soft bread crumbs, *divided*
- 2 cups milk
- 2 eggs, beaten
- 1/4 cup butter *or* margarine, melted
- 1/2 teaspoon salt
- 1/8 teaspoon pepper

In a skillet, cook bacon until crisp. Remove to paper towels to drain. Saute onion in the drippings until tender. Place spinach and a small amount of water in a saucepan; cover and cook until tender, about 8 minutes. Drain well; place in a large bowl. Add onion, 1-1/2 cups bread crumbs, milk, eggs, butter, salt and pepper. Pour into a greased 2-qt. baking dish. Top with the bacon and remaining crumbs. Bake, uncovered, at 350° for 50-60 minutes or until a knife inserted near the center comes out clean. **Yield:** 6-8 servings.

Grilled Onion

This side dish may be simple, but it always gets a terrific reaction, even from folks who typically don't care for onions. —*Stanley Pichon, Slidell, Louisiana*

> **1 large onion, peeled**
> **1 tablespoon butter *or* margarine**
> **1 teaspoon beef bouillon granules**

Hollow center of onion to a depth of 1 in.; chop removed onion. Place butter and bouillon in center of onion; top with the chopped onion. Wrap tightly in heavy-duty foil. Cook on a covered grill over medium heat for 25-30 minutes or until tender. Cut into wedges. **Yield:** 4 servings.

Flavorful Sugar Snap Peas

Our family enjoys the first peas from our garden stir-fried as a fresh, crisp treat. I serve them with grilled burgers. —*Connie Moore, Medway, Ohio*

 Nutritional Analysis included

> **1 pound fresh sugar snap *or* snow peas**
> **1 tablespoon vegetable oil**
> **1/2 cup finely chopped fully cooked ham**
> **1 garlic clove, minced**
> **1/2 teaspoon dried thyme**
> **1/8 teaspoon salt**
> **1/8 teaspoon pepper**

Cook peas in small amount of water until crisp-tender, about 3-4 minutes. Heat oil in a large skillet; add ham, garlic and thyme. Cook and stir for 2 minutes. Drain peas; add to skillet and saute for 2 minutes. Season with salt and pepper. **Yield:** 8 servings. **Nutritional Analysis:** One 1/2-cup serving (prepared with low-fat ham) equals 53 calories, 167 mg sodium, 4 mg cholesterol, 5 gm carbohydrate, 3 gm protein, 2 gm fat. **Diabetic Exchanges:** 1 vegetable, 1/2 fat.

Broccoli Rice Casserole

(Pictured above)

This hearty casserole is my favorite dish to make for a potluck. With the green of the broccoli and the rich cheese sauce, it's pretty to serve, and it makes a tasty side dish for almost any kind of meat.
—*Margaret Mayes, La Mesa, California*

> **1 small onion, chopped**
> **1/2 cup chopped celery**
> **1 package (10 ounces) frozen chopped broccoli, thawed**
> **1 tablespoon butter *or* margarine**
> **1 jar (8 ounces) process cheese spread**
> **1 can (10-3/4 ounces) condensed cream of mushroom soup, undiluted**
> **1 can (5 ounces) evaporated milk**
> **3 cups cooked rice**

In a large skillet over medium heat, saute onion, celery and broccoli in butter for 3-5 minutes. Stir in cheese, soup and milk until smooth. Place rice in a greased 8-in. square baking dish. Pour cheese mixture over rice; do not stir. Bake, uncovered, at 325° for 25-30 minutes or until hot and bubbly. **Yield:** 8-10 servings.

Mashed Potato Makeover

Combine leftover mashed potatoes with chopped onion and shredded cheese, then bake. It tastes like twice-baked potatoes without the work.

Main Dishes

Satisfy hunger around the clock with oven meals, slow-cooker creations, skillets and more. Don't forget the complementary condiments!

— 🛒 🛒 🛒 —

DOWN-HOME DISHES. Clockwise from upper left: Southwestern Hash (p. 90), Cranberry Spareribs (p. 78), Savory Meat Pie (p. 99) and Beef Barley Stew (p. 101).

Nutritional Analysis: One serving (prepared with low-sodium broth) equals 162 calories, 92 mg sodium, 50 mg cholesterol, 5 gm carbohydrate, 19 gm protein, 7 gm fat. **Diabetic Exchanges:** 3 lean meat, 1/2 fruit.

Gooseberry Chutney

My husband is especially fond of this chutney with our holiday ham—it has a wonderful zesty flavor he enjoys. —Jane Larter, Hallock, Minnesota

> 1 cup packed brown sugar
> 1 cup sugar
> 1 cup cider vinegar
> 1/4 teaspoon ground nutmeg
> 1 cinnamon stick (3 inches)
> 4 whole cloves
> 4 whole allspice
> 4 cups canned, fresh *or* frozen gooseberries

In a saucepan, combine sugars, vinegar and nutmeg. Place the cinnamon, cloves and allspice in a cheesecloth bag; place in saucepan. Simmer until sugar is dissolved. Add gooseberries; simmer, uncovered, for 20-30 minutes or until mixture is very thick, stirring occasionally. Remove and discard spice bag. Serve the chutney with pork or ham. Store in the refrigerator. **Yield:** 2-1/4 cups.

Festive Pork

(Pictured above)

Slices of tender pork are dressed up in a tangy sauce in this quick recipe. It has a mouth-watering Yuletide touch. —Marilyn Paradis, Woodburn, Oregon

☑ Nutritional Analysis included

> 1 pork tenderloin (3/4 pound), trimmed
> 1 tablespoon olive *or* vegetable oil
> 1/2 cup beef broth, *divided*
> 2 tablespoons dried cranberries
> 1-1/2 teaspoons Dijon mustard
> 1 tablespoon orange juice concentrate
> 1 teaspoon cornstarch

Cut tenderloin into 12 slices; flatten to 1/4-in. thickness. Brown in oil in a skillet over medium heat. Add 1/4 cup of beef broth; cover and simmer for 5-10 minutes or until meat is no longer pink. Remove meat to a serving dish and keep warm. Add cranberries, mustard and remaining broth to skillet. Combine orange juice concentrate and cornstarch until smooth; gradually add to broth mixture, stirring constantly. Bring to a boil; cook and stir for 1-2 minutes. Pour over pork. **Yield:** 4 servings.

Kids Love It Casserole

I haven't found any child yet who doesn't gobble up this dish. It combines spaghetti-like ingredients plus nutritious spinach—which they never detect! —Lou Monger, Richmond, Virginia

> 1-1/2 pounds ground beef
> 1 cup chopped onion
> 1 garlic clove, minced
> 1 jar (14 ounces) spaghetti sauce with mushrooms
> 1 can (8 ounces) tomato sauce
> 1 can (6 ounces) tomato paste
> 3/4 cup water
> 1 teaspoon Italian seasoning
> 1/2 teaspoon salt
> Dash pepper
> 1 package (7 ounces) macaroni shells, cooked and drained
> 1 package (10 ounces) frozen chopped spinach, thawed and drained
> 2 eggs, beaten
> 1 cup (4 ounces) shredded sharp cheddar cheese

1/2 cup soft bread crumbs
1/4 cup grated Parmesan cheese

In a saucepan over medium heat, cook beef, onion and garlic until meat is no longer pink and vegetables are tender; drain. Add the next seven ingredients; bring to a boil. Reduce heat; cover and simmer for 10 minutes. Stir in macaroni, spinach, eggs, cheese and bread crumbs. Transfer to a greased 13-in. x 9-in. x 2-in. baking dish. Sprinkle with Parmesan cheese. Cover and bake at 350° for 30-35 minutes or until bubbly. Let stand for 10 minutes before serving. **Yield:** 10-12 servings.

Maple Country Ribs

I brought this recipe with me from Quebec after my husband and I were married. The rich maple flavor impressed my in-laws the first time I made dinner for them. —Anne-Marie Fortin, Swanton, Vermont

3 pounds country-style pork ribs
1 cup pure maple syrup
1/2 cup applesauce
1/4 cup ketchup
3 tablespoons lemon juice
1/4 teaspoon *each* salt, pepper, paprika, garlic powder and ground cinnamon

Place ribs in a large kettle or Dutch oven. Cover with water; bring to a boil. Reduce heat and simmer for 10 minutes. Drain. Place ribs in a greased 13-in. x 9-in. x 2-in. baking pan. Combine remaining ingredients; pour half over the ribs. Bake, uncovered, at 325° for 1-1/2 hours or until the meat is tender, basting often with remaining sauce. **Yield:** 4 servings.

Oven Fish 'n' Chips

(Pictured at right)

Enjoy moist, flavorful fish with a coating that's as crunchy and golden as the deep-fried variety...plus, crisp, irresistible "fries". —Janice Mitchell Aurora, Colorado

☑ Nutritional Analysis included

2 tablespoons olive *or* vegetable oil
1/4 teaspoon pepper
4 medium baking potatoes (1 pound), peeled
FISH:
1/3 cup all-purpose flour
1/4 teaspoon pepper
1 egg *or* egg substitute equivalent

2 tablespoons water
2/3 cup crushed cornflakes
1 tablespoon grated Parmesan cheese
1/8 teaspoon cayenne pepper
1 pound frozen haddock fillets, thawed
Tartar sauce, optional

In a medium bowl, combine oil and pepper. Cut potatoes lengthwise into 1/2-in. strips. Add to oil mixture; toss to coat. Place on a greased 15-in. x 10-in. x 1-in. baking pan. Bake, uncovered, at 425° for 25-30 minutes or until golden brown and crisp. Meanwhile, combine flour and pepper in a shallow dish. In a second dish, beat egg and water. In a third dish, combine the cornflakes, cheese and cayenne. Dredge fish in flour, then dip in egg mixture and coat with crumb mixture. Place on a greased baking sheet. Bake at 425° for 10-15 minutes or until fish flakes easily with a fork. Serve with chips and tartar sauce if desired. **Yield:** 4 servings. **Nutritional Analysis for fish:** One 4-ounce serving (prepared with egg substitute; calculated without tartar sauce) equals 243 calories, 328 mg sodium, 67 mg cholesterol, 28 gm carbohydrate, 27 gm protein, 2 gm fat. **Diabetic Exchanges:** 3 very lean meat, 2 starch. **Nutritional Analysis for chips:** One 4-ounce serving equals 137 calories, 4 mg sodium, 0 cholesterol, 18 gm carbohydrate, 2 gm protein, 7 gm fat. **Diabetic Exchanges:** 1-1/2 fat, 1 starch.

Creole Seasoning Mix

I make up this zippy blend to have on hand when a recipe calls for Creole or Cajun seasoning.
—*Marian Platt, Sequim, Washington*

2 tablespoons plus 1-1/2 teaspoons paprika
2 tablespoons garlic powder
1 tablespoon salt
1 tablespoon onion powder
1 tablespoon dried oregano
1 tablespoon dried thyme
1 tablespoon cayenne pepper
1 tablespoon pepper

Combine all ingredients. Store in an airtight container. Use to season chicken, seafood, steaks or vegetables. **Yield:** 1 batch (about 1/2 cup).

Slow-Cooked Oriental Chicken

(Pictured below)

Extremely tender chicken is smothered in a flavorful, dark gravy in this easy and elegant entree. It's so nice to find another tantalizing way to serve chicken. Sprinkled with almonds, this is a dish I proudly serve to family or guests. —*Ruth Seitz,*
Columbus Junction, Iowa

1 broiler-fryer chicken (3-1/2 to 4 pounds), cut up
2 tablespoons vegetable oil
1/3 cup soy sauce
2 tablespoons brown sugar
2 tablespoons water

1 garlic clove, minced
1 teaspoon ground ginger
1/4 cup slivered almonds

In a large skillet over medium heat, brown the chicken in oil on both sides. Transfer to a slow cooker. Combine the soy sauce, brown sugar, water, garlic and ginger; pour over chicken. Cover and cook on high for 1 hour. Reduce heat to low; cook 4-5 hours longer or until the meat juices run clear. Remove chicken to a serving platter; sprinkle with almonds. Spoon juices over chicken or thicken if desired. **Yield:** 4-6 servings.

Cranberry Spareribs

(Pictured on page 74)

This may seem like an odd combination of ingredients, but the result is absolutely delicious. My mom made this main dish when we five kids were growing up. At the end of the meal, the table was surrounded by satisfied smiles and piled high with bare rib bones.
—*Leslie Picard, Salmon Arm, British Columbia*

4 pounds spareribs
1 can (16 ounces) whole-berry cranberry sauce
1 can (10 ounces) beef gravy
1/2 cup orange marmalade
1/4 cup lemon juice
1/8 teaspoon ground cinnamon
1 teaspoon vinegar

Cut ribs into serving-size pieces; place in a Dutch oven or large kettle. Cover with water; bring to a boil. Reduce heat; cover and simmer for 45 minutes. Meanwhile, in a medium saucepan, combine cranberry sauce, gravy, marmalade, lemon juice and cinnamon; bring to a boil. Reduce heat; simmer for 10-15 minutes or until thickened, stirring occasionally. Remove from the heat; stir in vinegar. Drain ribs; place with meat side up in a greased 13-in. x 9-in. x 2-in. baking dish. Pour 2-1/2 cups of sauce over ribs. Cover and bake at 400° for 20 minutes. Uncover and bake 15-20 minutes longer or until meat is tender, basting every 5 minutes with remaining sauce. **Yield:** 6 servings.

Egg and Broccoli Casserole

For years, I've prepared this filling egg casserole—which is delicious for brunch—in my slow cooker. It's an unusual recipe for this appliance but is welcomed wherever I serve it. Folks always go back for seconds. —*Janet Sliter, Kennewick, Washington*

1 carton (24 ounces) small-curd cottage
  cheese
1 package (10 ounces) frozen chopped
  broccoli, thawed and drained
2 cups (8 ounces) shredded cheddar cheese
6 eggs, beaten
1/3 cup all-purpose flour
1/4 cup butter *or* margarine, melted
3 tablespoons finely chopped onion
1/2 teaspoon salt
Additional shredded cheddar cheese, optional

In a large bowl, combine the first eight ingredients. Pour into a greased slow cooker. Cover and cook on high for 1 hour. Stir. Reduce heat to low; cover and cook 2-1/2 to 3 hours longer or until a thermometer placed in the center reads 160° and the eggs are set. Sprinkle with cheese if desired. **Yield:** 6 servings.

Sesame Pork Ribs

No one ever believes how little effort it takes to make these tender, juicy ribs. The flavor of the lightly sweet and tangy sauce penetrates through the meat as the ribs simmer in the slow cooker. —Sandy Alexander
Fayetteville, North Carolina

3/4 cup packed brown sugar
1/2 cup soy sauce
1/2 cup ketchup
1/4 cup honey
2 tablespoons cider *or* white wine vinegar
3 garlic cloves, minced
1 teaspoon ground ginger
1 teaspoon salt
1/4 to 1/2 teaspoon crushed red pepper flakes
5 pounds country-style pork ribs
1 medium onion, sliced
2 tablespoons sesame seeds, toasted
2 tablespoons chopped green onions

In a large bowl, combine the first nine ingredients. Add ribs and turn to coat. Place the onion in a 5-qt. slow cooker; arrange ribs on top. Cover and cook on low for 5-6 hours or until a meat thermometer reads 160°-170°. Place ribs on a serving platter; sprinkle with sesame seeds and green onions. **Yield:** 6 servings.

Slow-Cooker Enchiladas

(Pictured above right)

As a busy wife and mother of two young sons, I rely on this handy recipe. I layer enchilada ingredients in the slow cooker, turn it on and forget about it. With a bit of spice, these hearty enchiladas are especially nice during the colder months. —Mary Luebbert
Benton, Kansas

1 pound ground beef
1 cup chopped onion
1/2 cup chopped green pepper
1 can (16 ounces) pinto *or* kidney beans,
  rinsed and drained
1 can (15 ounces) black beans, rinsed and
  drained
1 can (10 ounces) diced tomatoes and green
  chilies, undrained
1/3 cup water
1 teaspoon chili powder
1/2 teaspoon ground cumin
1/2 teaspoon salt
1/4 teaspoon pepper
1 cup (4 ounces) shredded sharp cheddar
  cheese
1 cup (4 ounces) shredded Monterey Jack
  cheese
6 flour tortillas (6 or 7 inches)

In a skillet, cook beef, onion and green pepper until beef is browned and vegetables are tender; drain. Add the next eight ingredients; bring to a boil. Reduce heat; cover and simmer for 10 minutes. Combine cheeses. In a 5-qt. slow cooker, layer about 3/4 cup beef mixture, one tortilla and about 1/3 cup cheese. Repeat layers. Cover and cook on low for 5-7 hours or until heated through. **Yield:** 4 servings.

Hot cooked white *or* brown rice
1 medium tomato, cut into eight wedges

Lightly coat a large skillet or wok with nonstick cooking spray. Add turkey; stir-fry over medium-high heat until no longer pink, about 5 minutes. Remove and keep warm. Stir-fry asparagus, carrots, onions, mushrooms, garlic and ginger until vegetables are crisp-tender, about 5 minutes. Combine water, soy sauce and cornstarch; add to skillet with water chestnuts. Cook and stir until thickened and bubbly. Return turkey to the skillet and heat through. Serve over rice; garnish with tomato. **Yield:** 5 servings. **Nutritional Analysis:** One 1-cup serving (prepared with light soy sauce; calculated without rice) equals 148 calories, 355 mg sodium, 55 mg cholesterol, 13 gm carbohydrate, 22 gm protein, 1 gm fat. **Diabetic Exchanges:** 3 vegetable, 2 very lean meat.

Chicken Rice Casserole

We love rice, so I serve it at almost every meal. This is a stand-by in our home. —Donna Tyler
Rivervale, Arkansas

> 1 **broiler-fryer chicken (3 to 3-1/2 pounds), cut up**
> 2 **quarts water**
> 2 **teaspoons salt**
> 3 **garlic cloves, minced**
> 1/4 **teaspoon dried thyme**
> 3 **cups uncooked long grain rice**
> 1 **can (10-3/4 ounces) condensed cream of chicken soup, undiluted**
> 1 **can (10-3/4 ounces) condensed cream of mushroom soup, undiluted**
> 3 **celery ribs, diced**
> 2 **medium onions, diced**
> 1 **medium carrot, grated**

Place chicken, water, salt, garlic and thyme in a Dutch oven. Cover and cook until chicken is tender, about 1-1/4 hours. Remove chicken; cool. Debone and cut into chunks. Skim fat from broth. Place 3 cups of broth in a bowl (save remaining broth for another use); add chicken and remaining ingredients. Place in a greased 13-in. x 9-in. x 2-in. baking dish. Cover and bake at 350° for 35-40 minutes or until rice is tender. **Yield:** 6-8 servings.

Turkey Asparagus Stir-Fry

(Pictured above)

Mild turkey picks up delightful flavor in this colorful stir-fry. My husband, who never cared for asparagus, enjoys it in this entree. —Darlene Kennedy
Plymouth, Ohio

☑ Nutritional Analysis included

> 1 **pound uncooked boneless turkey breast, cut into strips**
> 1 **pound fresh asparagus, cut into 1-inch pieces**
> 2 **medium carrots, quartered lengthwise and cut into 1-inch pieces**
> 4 **green onions, cut into 1-inch pieces**
> 4 **ounces fresh mushrooms, sliced**
> 2 **garlic cloves, minced**
> 1/2 **teaspoon ground ginger**
> 2/3 **cup water**
> 2 **tablespoons soy sauce**
> 1 **tablespoon plus 1 teaspoon cornstarch**
> 1 **can (8 ounces) sliced water chestnuts, drained**

Whiter Rice

Adding a little lemon juice to the water when cooking rice keeps the grains white and separated.

Spicy Rice Skillet

Rice is nutritious, economical and easy to prepare. This zippy main dish is both delicious and satisfying. I've served it to countless guests.
—Katherine Cruthis, Roe, Arkansas

    2 pounds ground beef
    1 large onion, chopped
    1 large green pepper, chopped
    1 can (10 ounces) diced tomatoes and green chilies, undrained
    1 can (4 ounces) chopped green chilies
    1 cup beef broth
    2 tablespoons Worcestershire sauce
    1 to 2 tablespoons chili powder
    2 teaspoons salt
    1 teaspoon pepper
  1/4 teaspoon hot pepper sauce
    4 cups cooked long grain rice
    2 cups (16 ounces) sour cream
    2 cups (8 ounces) shredded cheddar cheese
Corn chips

In a large skillet, brown beef, onion and green pepper until the meat is no longer pink; drain. Add the next eight ingredients. Simmer, uncovered, for 10 minutes. Add rice, sour cream and cheese; cook over low heat until cheese is melted, about 6-8 minutes, stirring occasionally (do not boil). Serve over corn chips. **Yield:** 8-10 servings.

Turkey Manicotti

My teenage daughter enjoys making this main course. It's one of my favorites since it uses ground turkey and garlic. —Connie Nelson-Smith
Sugar Land, Texas

    2 slices bread
1-1/2 pounds ground turkey
  1/4 cup chopped onion
    2 garlic cloves, minced
  1/2 teaspoon salt
  1/4 teaspoon pepper
    1 cup (4 ounces) shredded mozzarella cheese
  1/2 cup grated Parmesan cheese
   14 manicotti shells (8 ounces), cooked and drained
    1 jar (30 ounces) spaghetti sauce

Soak bread in water; squeeze to remove excess water. Tear into small pieces; set aside. In a skillet, cook the turkey, onion, garlic, salt and pepper until meat is no longer pink and onion is tender; drain. Stir in the bread and cheeses; mix well. Spoon into manicotti shells. Pour half of the spaghetti sauce

into a greased 13-in. x 9-in. x 2-in. baking dish. Arrange shells over sauce; top with the remaining sauce. Cover and bake at 350° for 25-30 minutes or until heated through. **Yield:** 6-8 servings.

Paprika Pork Roast

(Pictured below and on front cover)

I like to experiment with flavors. For a dinner party, I came up with this spectacular-looking yet simple recipe. My guests were so impressed when I sliced the roast thin and served it with steamed vegetables.
—Jonnie Faye Thompson, Raleigh, North Carolina

    2 teaspoons garlic salt
    1 teaspoon ground ginger
    1 teaspoon pepper
    1 teaspoon paprika
    1 boneless rolled pork loin roast (4 to 4-1/2 pounds)
    1 to 2 medium onions, sliced
    1 cup water

Combine garlic salt, ginger, pepper and paprika; rub over the entire roast. Place roast with fat side up on a greased rack in a roasting pan. Top with onion. Pour water into pan. Bake, uncovered, at 325° for 2 to 2-1/2 hours or until a meat thermometer reads 160°-170°. Let stand for 10-15 minutes before slicing. **Yield:** 8-10 servings.

Lip-Smacking Lamb from Locals

SAMPLE these lambs dishes from Wyoming cooks and see just how versatile this flavorful meat can be.

— ❦ ❦ ❦ —

Lamb Fajitas

(Pictured below)

This is a tasty alternative to beef or chicken. I got this recipe from a friend. —Bonnie Hiller, Powell, Wyoming

    1 **boneless leg of lamb** *or* **lamb shoulder (3 to 4 pounds)**
1/2 **cup vegetable oil**
1/2 **cup lemon juice**
1/3 **cup soy sauce**
1/3 **cup packed brown sugar**
1/4 **cup vinegar**
    3 **tablespoons Worcestershire sauce**
    1 **tablespoon ground mustard**
1/2 **teaspoon pepper**
    1 **large green pepper, sliced**
    1 **large sweet red pepper, sliced**
    1 **large onion, sliced**
  16 **flour tortillas (7 inches), warmed**
Chopped tomato and cucumber, optional

Cut the meat into thin bite-size strips. Combine the next eight ingredients; pour into a large resealable plastic bag or shallow glass container. Add meat; seal or cover and refrigerate for 3 hours, turning occasionally. Place the meat and marinade in a Dutch oven or large saucepan; bring to a boil. Reduce heat; cover and simmer for 8-10 minutes or until meat is tender. Add peppers and onion; cook until vegetables are crisp-tender, about 4 minutes. Using a slotted spoon, place meat and vegetables on

A PALATE-PLEASING PART of everyday menus, lamb satisfies in Wyoming Lamb Stew, Cheesy Lamb Cups and Lamb Fajitas (shown above, clockwise from top).

tortillas; top with tomato and cucumber if desired. Fold in sides of tortilla and serve immediately. **Yield:** 8 servings.

Cheesy Lamb Cups

(Pictured below left)

I first made this special main dish for a 4-H demonstration, and it won an award. Now it's a winner with my family.   —Pat Horton, Riverton, Wyoming

  1 envelope onion soup mix
1/3 cup dry bread crumbs
  1 cup evaporated milk
  2 pounds ground lamb
  4 ounces cheddar cheese, cut into 12 cubes
  1 can (10-3/4 ounces) condensed cheddar cheese soup, undiluted
1/2 cup milk
  1 teaspoon Worcestershire sauce

In a bowl, combine soup mix, bread crumbs and evaporated milk. Add lamb and mix well. Press half of the mixture into 12 greased muffin cups, filling each half full. Press one cube of cheese into the center of each cup. Cover with the remaining lamb mixture, mounding each slightly. Bake at 375° for 20-25 minutes or until a meat thermometer reads 160°. Meanwhile, combine the soup, milk and Worcestershire sauce in a small saucepan; heat through, stirring until smooth. Serve over lamb cups. **Yield:** 6 servings.

Wyoming Lamb Stew

(Pictured at left)

I often make a big batch of this satisfying stew. Leftovers come in handy around our busy house.
   —Sandra Ramsey, Elk Mountain, Wyoming

  5 bacon strips, diced
1/4 cup all-purpose flour
  1 teaspoon salt
1/2 teaspoon pepper
  6 lamb shanks (about 6 pounds)
  1 can (28 ounces) diced tomatoes, undrained
  1 can (14-1/2 ounces) beef broth
  1 can (8 ounces) tomato sauce
  2 cans (4 ounces _each_) mushroom stems and pieces, undrained
  2 medium onions, chopped
  1 cup chopped celery
1/2 cup minced fresh parsley

  2 tablespoons prepared horseradish
  1 tablespoon cider vinegar
  2 teaspoons Worcestershire sauce
  1 garlic clove, minced

In a Dutch oven, cook bacon until crisp; remove and set aside. Combine flour, salt and pepper in a large resealable plastic bag; add lamb shanks and shake to coat. Brown shanks on all sides in the bacon drippings; drain. Add remaining ingredients. Bring to a simmer. Cover and bake at 325° for 4 hours or until the meat is very tender; skim fat. Garnish with bacon. **Yield:** 6 servings.

Minty Lamb Pie

Mint—a traditional partner with lamb—gets a special twist in this recipe's unique pastry crust.
   —Vera Reid, Laramie, Wyoming

MINT CRUST:
1-1/2 cups all-purpose flour
  1/2 teaspoon salt
  2/3 cup shortening
  1/4 cup finely chopped fresh mint
    2 to 3 tablespoons cold water
FILLING:
    1 pound lamb stew meat, cut into 1-inch cubes
    2 tablespoons shortening
    1 teaspoon salt
  1/2 teaspoon pepper
1-1/4 cups water, _divided_
    1 cup sliced fresh mushrooms
    2 cups fresh or frozen peas
    3 medium carrots, sliced
    8 pearl onions
  1/4 cup all-purpose flour

In a bowl, combine flour and salt; cut in shortening until the mixture resembles coarse crumbs. Add mint. Add water, 1 tablespoon at a time, until the mixture can be formed into a ball. On a lightly floured surface, roll dough to fit a 9-in. pie plate. Bake at 425° for 12 minutes; set aside. In a large skillet, brown lamb in shortening; sprinkle with salt and pepper. Add 1 cup of water and mushrooms; cover and simmer for 45-60 minutes or until meat is tender. Meanwhile, place the peas, carrots and onions in a large saucepan; cover with water. Cover and cook until tender; drain. Spoon into the crust. Using a slotted spoon, remove lamb and mushrooms from skillet and place over vegetables. Combine flour and remaining water until smooth; stir into pan drippings. Cook and stir until thick and bubbly. Pour over lamb mixture. Serve with a spoon. **Yield:** 6-8 servings.

until golden brown. Cool for 5-10 minutes. Spread sour cream over the top; sprinkle with lettuce, tomato, green pepper, onions and cheese. Serve immediately. **Yield:** 8 servings.

Stuffed Green Peppers

My family grows 200 acres of green peppers. We think one of the best ways to enjoy this fresh vegetable is in the classic recipe. —Marlene Karnemaat
Fremont, Michigan

 6 medium green peppers
1-1/2 pounds uncooked lean ground beef
 1 cup cooked long grain rice
 1/2 cup chopped onion
 1/2 cup chopped celery
 1 small tomato, seeded and chopped
 1 garlic clove, minced
 1 teaspoon salt
 1/4 teaspoon pepper
 1 can (10-3/4 ounces) condensed tomato
  soup, undiluted
 1/2 teaspoon dried basil
 1/2 cup shredded sharp cheddar cheese

Cut tops off peppers and remove seeds. In a large kettle, cook peppers in boiling water for 3 minutes. Drain and rinse in cold water; set aside. In a bowl, combine the next eight ingredients. Spoon into peppers. Place in a greased 13-in. x 9-in. x 2-in. baking dish. Combine soup and basil; spoon over peppers. Cover and bake at 350° for 55-60 minutes or until the beef is no longer pink. Sprinkle with cheese; return to the oven for 5 minutes or until the cheese is melted. **Yield:** 6 servings.

Colorful Kabobs

This is a perfect recipe for kids old enough to carefully handle skewers. It's not too messy, and the kabobs cook up in a snap and taste wonderful.
—Janell Aguda, Joelton, Tennessee

 12 cherry tomatoes
 1 pound fully cooked smoked turkey
  sausage, cut into 1/2-inch chunks
 2 medium green peppers, cut into 1-inch
  pieces
 1 medium onion, cut into wedges
Hot cooked rice

Thread a cherry tomato onto six metal or soaked wooden skewers. Alternate the sausage, green pepper and onion pieces on skewers, ending with an-

Taco Quiche

(Pictured above)

This is the dish I often take to potluck suppers, and my pan always comes home empty. That's probably because this stick-to-your-ribs casserole has the appeal of tacos. Fortunately it's not tricky to whip up, since it's a popular supper at home, too. —Kim Stoller
Smithville, Ohio

 2 pounds ground beef
 2 envelopes taco seasoning
 4 eggs
 3/4 cup milk
1-1/4 cups biscuit/baking mix
Dash pepper
 1/2 cup sour cream
 2 to 3 cups chopped lettuce
 3/4 cup chopped tomato
 1/4 cup chopped green pepper
 1/4 cup chopped green onions
 2 cups (8 ounces) shredded cheddar cheese

In a skillet, brown beef; drain. Add taco seasoning and prepare according to the package directions. Spoon meat into a greased 13-in. x 9-in. x 2-in. baking dish. In a bowl, beat eggs and milk. Add biscuit mix and pepper; mix well. Pour over the meat. Bake, uncovered, at 400° for 20-25 minutes or

other tomato. Grill, uncovered, over medium-hot heat for 10-15 minutes or until meat is heated through and vegetables are tender. Remove meat and vegetables from skewers and serve over rice. **Yield:** 6 servings.

— 🍴 🍴 🍴 —

Baked Beef Patties

This simple recipe turns ordinary burgers into an attractive tasty meal. You can make them ahead and bake when ready for dinner. —*Diane Hixon*
Niceville, Florida

4-1/2 teaspoons minced fresh thyme *or* 1-1/2 teaspoons dried thyme, *divided*
  3 tablespoons water
1/2 teaspoon garlic salt
1/2 teaspoon dried oregano
Dash paprika
Dash pepper
1-1/4 pounds lean ground beef
1/4 cup all-purpose flour
  1 egg, beaten
1/4 cup seasoned bread crumbs
  2 tablespoons butter *or* margarine
  1 cup spaghetti sauce, *divided*
3/4 cup shredded cheddar cheese
  2 tablespoons grated Parmesan cheese
  4 to 6 hamburger buns, split, optional

In a large bowl, combine 1-1/2 teaspoons of fresh thyme (or 1/2 teaspoon dried), water, garlic salt, oregano, paprika and pepper. Add beef; mix well. Shape into four to six patties. Coat patties with flour; dip into egg and then crumbs. In a skillet, brown patties in butter. Arrange in a greased shallow baking dish. Pour half of the spaghetti sauce over patties. Sprinkle with cheeses; top with remaining sauce. Bake at 400° for 25 minutes or until meat is no longer pink. Sprinkle with remaining thyme. Serve patties and sauce on buns if desired. **Yield:** 4-6 servings.

— 🍴 🍴 🍴 —

Stuffed Chicken Rolls

(Pictured at right)

The wonderful aroma of this moist, delicious chicken cooking sparks our appetites. The ham and cheese rolled inside is a tasty surprise. When I prepared this impressive main dish for a church luncheon, I received lots of compliments. The rolls are especially nice served over rice or pasta. —*Jean Sherwood*
Kenneth City, Florida

  6 large boneless skinless chicken breast halves
  6 slices fully cooked ham
  6 slices Swiss cheese
1/4 cup all-purpose flour
1/4 cup grated Parmesan cheese
1/2 teaspoon rubbed sage
1/4 teaspoon paprika
1/4 teaspoon pepper
1/4 cup vegetable oil
  1 can (10-3/4 ounces) condensed cream of chicken soup, undiluted
1/2 cup chicken broth
Chopped fresh parsley, optional

Flatten chicken to 1/8-in. thickness. Place ham and cheese on each breast. Roll up and tuck in ends; secure with a toothpick. Combine the flour, Parmesan cheese, sage, paprika and pepper; coat chicken on all sides. Cover and refrigerate for 1 hour. In a large skillet, brown chicken in oil over medium-high heat. Transfer to a 5-qt. slow cooker. Combine soup and broth; pour over the chicken. Cover and cook on low for 4-5 hours. Remove toothpicks. Garnish with parsley if desired. **Yield:** 6 servings.

Bluegill Parmesan

(Pictured below)

All the fishermen at your house will be pleased to turn over their catch for this tasty recipe. The seasoned crumb mixture produces a crispy coating.
—*Margaret Garbers, Van Horne, Iowa*

> 1/4 cup butter *or* margarine, melted
> 1/2 cup dry bread crumbs
> 1/3 cup grated Parmesan cheese
> 2 tablespoons minced fresh parsley
> 1 teaspoon salt
> 1/2 teaspoon paprika
> 1/4 teaspoon dried oregano
> 1/4 teaspoon dried basil
> 1/4 teaspoon pepper
> 1 pound fresh *or* frozen bluegill fillets,* thawed

Place butter in a shallow dish. In another shallow dish, combine bread crumbs, Parmesan cheese and seasonings. Dip fillets in butter, then coat with crumb mixture. Place in a greased 15-in. x 10-in. x 1-in. baking pan. Bake, uncovered, at 350° for 20 minutes or until fish flakes easily with a fork. **Yield:** 4 servings. ***Editor's Note:** Perch or crappie may be substituted for the bluegill.

Scotch Braised Beef

On a trip to Scotland, I fell in love with this meal and brought the recipe home with me. Since then, it's risen to the top of my family's list of favorite foods.
—*Celia Collier, Stillwater, Oklahoma*

> 4 bacon strips, diced
> 1 medium carrot, diced
> 1 small turnip, peeled and diced
> 1 small onion, diced
> 2 tablespoons butter *or* margarine
> 1-1/2 pounds top round roast
> 2 cans (14-1/2 ounces *each*) beef broth
> 10 whole peppercorns
> 1 tablespoon minced fresh parsley *or* 1 teaspoon dried parsley flakes
> 1-1/2 teaspoons minced fresh marjoram *or* 1/2 teaspoon dried marjoram
> 1/2 teaspoon ground mace
> 1/2 teaspoon ground allspice

In a Dutch oven, saute bacon, carrot, turnip and onion in butter for 3 minutes. Remove vegetables with a slotted spoon; set aside. Add roast; brown on all sides. Return vegetables to the pan. Add broth. Place peppercorns on a double thickness of cheesecloth; bring up corners and tie with string to form a bag. Add to the pan with the other seasonings. Cover and simmer for 2 hours or until meat is tender. Remove roast; discard spice bag. Thicken pan drippings if desired to serve with the roast. **Yield:** 4 servings.

Oven-Fried Chicken

My mother, who is diabetic, often relies on this simple recipe. The meat is lightly seasoned and stays moist.
—*Suzanne McKinley, Lyons, Georgia*

✓ Nutritional Analysis included

> 1-1/2 cups instant nonfat dry milk powder
> 1 tablespoon paprika
> 2 teaspoons poultry seasoning
> 1/4 teaspoon pepper
> 4 boneless skinless chicken breast halves* (1 pound)

Combine the first four ingredients in a large resealable plastic bag. Add chicken, one piece at a time, and shake to coat. Place in an 8-in. square baking pan that has been coated with nonstick cooking spray. Bake, uncovered, at 350° for 30 minutes or until juices run clear. **Yield:** 4 servings. **Nutritional Analysis:** One serving equals 240 calories, 204 mg sodium, 78 mg cholesterol, 15 gm carbohydrate, 36 gm protein, 4 gm fat. **Diabetic Ex-**

changes: 4 very lean meat, 1 starch. **Editor's Note:** Pork chops may be substituted for the chicken. Bake for 1 hour or until a meat thermometer reads 160°-170°.

—— ☕ ☕ ☕ ——

Rice-Crust Spinach Quiche

Everyone will want to try this microwave quiche. The rice crust is an interesting and tasty alternative to a pastry crust. —*Laurie Zenner, Norwood, Ontario*

☑ Nutritional Analysis included

1-1/2 cups cooked brown rice
   1 cup (4 ounces) shredded reduced-fat Swiss cheese, *divided*
 3/4 cup egg substitute, *divided*
 1/4 teaspoon curry powder
   1 package (10 ounces) frozen chopped spinach, thawed and well drained
 3/4 cup evaporated skim milk
 1/2 cup sliced fresh mushrooms
   2 tablespoons chopped onion
 1/4 teaspoon garlic powder
 1/8 to 1/4 teaspoon pepper

Combine rice, 1/2 cup cheese, 1/4 cup egg substitute and curry powder. Press onto the bottom and up the sides of a microwave-safe 9-in. pie plate. Microwave on high for 4-5 minutes or until firm. Combine the spinach, milk, mushrooms, onion, garlic powder, pepper, and remaining cheese and egg substitute; pour into the crust. Microwave on 50% power for 20 minutes, rotating a quarter turn every 5 minutes, or until a knife inserted near the center comes out clean. **Yield:** 8 servings. **Nutritional Analysis:** One serving equals 116 calories, 135 mg sodium, 6 mg cholesterol, 14 gm carbohydrate, 11 gm protein, 2 gm fat. **Diabetic Exchanges:** 1 starch, 1 lean meat. **Editor's Note:** This recipe was tested in a 700-watt microwave.

—— ☕ ☕ ☕ ——

Hearty New England Dinner

(Pictured above right)

This favorite slow-cooker recipe came from a friend. At first, my husband was a bit skeptical about a roast that wasn't fixed in the oven, but he loves the old-fashioned goodness of this version with zesty gravy. —*Claire McCombs, San Diego, California*

   2 medium carrots, sliced
   1 medium onion, sliced
   1 celery rib, sliced
   1 boneless chuck roast (about 3 pounds)

   1 teaspoon salt, *divided*
 1/4 teaspoon pepper
   1 envelope onion soup mix
   2 cups water
   1 tablespoon vinegar
   1 bay leaf
 1/2 small head cabbage, cut into wedges
   3 tablespoons butter *or* margarine
   2 tablespoons all-purpose flour
   1 tablespoon dried minced onion
   2 tablespoons prepared horseradish

Place carrots, onion and celery in a 5-qt. slow cooker. Place the roast on top; sprinkle with 1/2 teaspoon salt and pepper. Add soup mix, water, vinegar and bay leaf. Cover and cook on low for 7-9 hours or until beef is tender. Remove beef and keep warm; discard bay leaf. Add cabbage. Cover and cook on high for 30-40 minutes or until cabbage is tender. Meanwhile, melt butter in a small saucepan; stir in flour and minced onion. Add 1-1/2 cups cooking liquid from the slow cooker. Stir in horseradish and remaining salt; bring to a boil. Cook and stir over low heat until thick and smooth, about 2 minutes. Serve with roast and vegetables. **Yield:** 6-8 servings.

thickened. Serve over rice if desired. **Yield:** 4 servings. **Nutritional Analysis:** One serving (prepared with low-sodium bouillon and no-salt-added stewed tomatoes and ketchup; without salt and rice) equals 227 calories, 183 mg sodium, 37 mg cholesterol, 34 gm carbohydrate, 16 gm protein, 4 gm fat. **Diabetic Exchanges:** 2 lean meat, 2 vegetable, 1 starch.

Dijon Chicken Kabobs

People are always asking for the recipe for these tangy, juicy chicken kabobs. It's a fun and festive way to bake chicken. —Earleen Lillegard, Prescott, Arizona

✓ Nutritional Analysis included

  1/2 cup Dijon mustard
    1 tablespoon finely chopped green onion
    2 cups fresh bread crumbs
  1/4 cup minced fresh parsley
1-1/4 pounds boneless skinless chicken breasts, cut into 3/4-inch chunks

In a bowl, combine mustard and onion. In another bowl, combine bread crumbs and parsley. Toss chicken in the mustard mixture, then coat evenly with crumb mixture. Line a baking sheet with foil; coat the foil with nonstick cooking spray. Thread chicken onto metal or soaked wooden skewers, leaving a small space between chunks. Place on the prepared baking sheet. Bake, uncovered, at 450° for 6-8 minutes or until juices run clear. **Yield:** 5 servings. **Nutritional Analysis:** One serving equals 222 calories, 762 mg sodium, 73 mg cholesterol, 12 gm carbohydrate, 30 gm protein, 6 gm fat. **Diabetic Exchanges:** 4 very lean meat, 1 starch.

Tangy Pork Chops

(Pictured above)

Fancy enough for company, these mouth-watering pork chops also make a great family meal. I usually have all the ingredients on hand. This recipe is so convenient. —Karol Hines, Kitty Hawk, North Carolina

✓ Nutritional Analysis included

    4 pork chops (1/2 inch thick)
  1/2 teaspoon salt, optional
  1/8 teaspoon pepper
    2 medium onions, chopped
    2 celery ribs, chopped
    1 large green pepper, sliced
    1 can (14-1/2 ounces) stewed tomatoes
  1/2 cup ketchup
    2 tablespoons cider vinegar
    2 tablespoons brown sugar
    2 tablespoons Worcestershire sauce
    1 tablespoon lemon juice
    1 beef bouillon cube
    2 tablespoons cornstarch
    2 tablespoons water
Hot cooked rice, optional

Place chops in a slow cooker; sprinkle with salt if desired and pepper. Add the onions, celery, green pepper and tomatoes. Combine ketchup, vinegar, brown sugar, Worcestershire sauce, lemon juice and bouillon; pour over vegetables. Cover and cook on low for 5-6 hours. Mix cornstarch and water until smooth; stir into liquid in slow cooker. Cover and cook on high for 30 minutes or until

Spinach Meat Roll

We love the spinach, ham and cheese swirled in every slice. Sometimes I serve it with spaghetti sauce and pasta. —Gail Buss, Westminster, Maryland

    2 eggs
  3/4 cup seasoned bread crumbs
  1/3 cup ketchup
  1/4 cup milk
    1 teaspoon salt, *divided*
  1/4 teaspoon pepper
  1/4 teaspoon dried oregano
    2 pounds ground beef
    1 package (10 ounces) frozen leaf spinach, thawed and drained

1/2 pound thinly sliced fully cooked ham
2 cups (8 ounces) shredded mozzarella
   cheese, *divided*

In a bowl, lightly beat the eggs; add bread crumbs, ketchup, milk, 1/2 teaspoon of salt, pepper and oregano. Add beef and mix well. On a large piece of heavy-duty foil, pat beef mixture into a 12-in. x 10-in. rectangle. Cover with spinach to within 1/2 in. of edges. Sprinkle with remaining salt. Top with ham and 1-1/2 cups cheese. Roll up jelly-roll style, starting with a short side and peeling foil away while rolling. Seal seam and ends; place with seam side down in a greased 15-in. x 10-in. x 1-in. baking pan. Bake, uncovered, at 350° for 1 hour and 10 minutes. Top with remaining cheese; bake 5 minutes longer or until cheese is melted. **Yield:** 8 servings.

Turkey Sausage Patties

Everybody who samples my breakfast sausage enjoys the taste and is amazed to learn it's made of turkey.
—Sally Brassfield, California, Maryland

☑ Nutritional Analysis included

2 to 3 teaspoons rubbed sage
1 teaspoon brown sugar
1/4 teaspoon crushed red pepper flakes
1/4 teaspoon ground nutmeg
1/4 teaspoon pepper
Pinch allspice
1 pound ground turkey breast

In a bowl, combine the first six ingredients. Add turkey; mix until combined. Shape into six patties. Lightly coat a skillet with nonstick cooking spray. Cook the patties over medium heat until browned on both sides and the meat is no longer pink, about 15-20 minutes. **Yield:** 6 servings. **Nutritional Analysis:** One serving equals 86 calories, 51 mg sodium, 37 mg cholesterol, 1 gm carbohydrate, 18 gm protein, 1 gm fat. **Diabetic Exchange:** 2-1/2 very lean meat.

Cider Beef Stew

(Pictured at right)

It's especially nice to use this recipe in fall when the weather gets crisp and Nebraska's apple orchards start selling fresh apple cider. This entree's subtle sweetness is a welcome change from other savory stews.
—Joyce Glaesemann, Lincoln, Nebraska

☑ Nutritional Analysis included

2 pounds beef stew meat, cut into
   1-inch cubes
2 tablespoons vegetable oil
3 cups apple cider
2 tablespoons cider vinegar
2 teaspoons salt, optional
1/4 to 1/2 teaspoon dried thyme
1/4 teaspoon pepper
3 medium potatoes, peeled and cubed
4 medium carrots, cut into 3/4-inch pieces
3 celery ribs, cut into 3/4-inch pieces
2 medium onions, cut into wedges
1/4 cup all-purpose flour
1/4 cup water

In a Dutch oven, brown beef in oil; drain. Add cider, vinegar, salt if desired, thyme and pepper; bring to a boil. Reduce heat; cover and simmer for 1-1/4 hours. Add potatoes, carrots, celery and onions; return to a boil. Reduce heat; cover and simmer for 30-35 minutes or until beef and vegetables are tender. Combine flour and water until smooth; stir into stew. Bring to a boil; boil and stir for 2 minutes. **Yield:** 8 servings. **Nutritional Analysis:** One 1-cup serving (prepared without salt) equals 315 calories, 238 mg sodium, 70 mg cholesterol, 29 gm carbohydrate, 24 gm protein, 12 gm fat. **Diabetic Exchanges:** 3 lean meat, 1 starch, 1 vegetable.

Southwestern Hash

(Pictured at left)

I had a similar dish at a restaurant in Arizona. I enjoyed it so much I tried re-creating it at home. It's a special way to serve eggs. —Marilyn Paradis
Woodburn, Oregon

 8 **bacon strips, diced**
1/2 **cup chopped onion**
 1 **garlic clove, minced**
 4 **cups frozen cubed hash brown potatoes**
 1 **can (4 ounces) chopped green chilies**
 1 **medium tomato, diced**
 4 **eggs, poached**
Salsa

In a skillet, cook bacon until crisp. Drain, reserving 2 tablespoons of drippings; set the bacon aside. In the drippings, saute onion and garlic until tender. Stir in the hash browns and chilies. Cook and stir over low heat for 20 minutes or until lightly browned and heated through. Just before serving, add tomato. Spoon onto plates; top with eggs and bacon. Serve with salsa. **Yield:** 4 servings.

DASH to the kitchen and whip up some hash when hunger hits. Try favorites like Southwestern Hash (above) and Sausage Hash (below).

Sausage Hash

(Pictured below left)

We always have plenty of pork sausage around, so when I need a quick supper, I use this handy recipe. The colorful vegetables give this dish a perky look to match its flavor. —Virginia Krites, Cridersville, Ohio

 1 **pound bulk pork sausage**
 1 **medium onion, chopped**
 2 **medium carrots, grated**
 1 **medium green pepper, chopped**
 3 **cups diced cooked potatoes**
1/2 **teaspoon salt**
1/4 **teaspoon pepper**

In a skillet over medium heat, brown the sausage. Add onion, carrots and green pepper; cook until tender. Stir in potatoes, salt and pepper. Reduce heat; cook and stir for 20 minutes or until lightly browned and heated through. **Yield:** 6 servings.

Turkey Hash

I recommend this recipe for mild-tasting hash. It's a deliciously different use for leftover turkey.
—Edna Hoffman, Hebron, Indiana

✓ Nutritional Analysis included

1 medium onion, chopped
1/2 cup chopped green pepper
1/2 cup chopped sweet red pepper
2 tablespoons butter *or* margarine
6 cups diced cooked potatoes
2 cups cubed cooked turkey
1/2 teaspoon salt, optional
1/8 teaspoon cayenne pepper
1/8 teaspoon ground nutmeg

In a skillet, saute onion and peppers in butter until tender. Add the potatoes, turkey, salt if desired, cayenne and nutmeg. Cook and stir over low heat for 20 minutes or until lightly browned and heated through. **Yield:** 8 servings. **Nutritional Analysis:** One 1-cup serving (prepared with margarine and without salt) equals 187 calories, 66 mg sodium, 27 mg cholesterol, 23 gm carbohydrate, 13 gm protein, 5 gm fat. **Diabetic Exchanges:** 1 starch, 1 meat, 1 vegetable.

Hash in a Flash

I cook more roast beef than we need for one meal so that we'll have leftovers for this homey hash. We look forward to this satisfying supper. —Wendy Masters
Grand Valley, Ontario

1 medium onion, chopped
2 tablespoons vegetable oil
3 cups frozen hash brown potatoes
3 cups finely chopped cooked roast beef
1/2 cup beef gravy
2 tablespoons ketchup
1 teaspoon salt
1/2 teaspoon ground mustard
1/8 teaspoon pepper

In a skillet, saute onion in oil until tender. Stir in the remaining ingredients. Cook over medium heat without stirring until browned, about 10 minutes. Turn and brown the other side. **Yield:** 4 servings.

Oven Beef Hash

With just the two of us, we usually have leftovers of some sort, so hash is a regular menu item at our house. It's nice to have a hash that I can pop in the oven.
—Dorothy Pritchett, Wills Point, Texas

3 cups diced cooked potatoes
1-1/2 cups cubed cooked roast beef
1 can (5 ounces) evaporated milk
1/4 cup minced fresh parsley
1/4 cup finely chopped onion

2 teaspoons Worcestershire sauce
1/2 teaspoon salt
1/8 teaspoon pepper
1/3 cup crushed saltines
1 tablespoon butter *or* margarine, melted

In a bowl, combine the first eight ingredients. Spoon into a greased 1-1/2-qt. baking dish. Combine saltines and butter; sprinkle over top. Bake, uncovered, at 350° for 30 minutes or until heated through. **Yield:** 4 servings.

Italian Omelet

Garden vegetables and herbs give a savory zing to this fresh-tasting omelet. This is a flavorful meal with a salad and bread. —Dixie Terry, Marion, Illinois

1 cup sliced fresh mushrooms
1 cup sliced zucchini
3 tablespoons butter *or* margarine, *divided*
4 eggs
3 tablespoons water
1/4 teaspoon salt
1/4 teaspoon pepper
1/2 cup shredded mozzarella cheese
SAUCE:
1 tablespoon butter *or* margarine
1 medium tomato, chopped
2 tablespoons minced fresh parsley
1 garlic clove, minced
1/2 teaspoon dried basil
1/8 teaspoon salt

In an 8-in. nonstick skillet, saute mushrooms and zucchini in 2 tablespoons butter until tender; remove and keep warm. In the same skillet, melt remaining butter. In a bowl, beat eggs, water, salt and pepper. Pour into the skillet; cook over medium heat. As eggs set, lift edges, letting uncooked portion flow underneath. When eggs are nearly set, spoon vegetable mixture over half of the omelet; sprinkle with cheese. Fold omelet in half over filling. Cover and cook for 1-2 minutes or until cheese is melted. Meanwhile, for sauce, melt butter in a small saucepan over medium heat. Add remaining ingredients. Cook and stir for 5 minutes or until heated through. Serve over omelet. **Yield:** 1-2 servings.

Fry 'Em Up in a Pan

To make sure your scrambled eggs come out tender and light every time, use an electric fry pan. Its controlled heat keeps eggs from becoming tough.

Marinated Rib Eyes

(Pictured below)

We have these tempting steaks weekly. Whenever I suggest a change in the recipe, my husband reminds me, "Don't fix it if it's not broken." Everyone enjoys the savory marinade.
—Rosalie Usry
Flaxton, North Dakota

1/3 cup hot water
3 tablespoons finely chopped onion
2 tablespoons cider *or* red wine vinegar
2 tablespoons olive *or* vegetable oil
2 tablespoons soy sauce
1 teaspoon beef bouillon granules
1 garlic clove, minced
1/2 teaspoon paprika
1/2 teaspoon coarsely ground pepper
2 beef rib eye steaks (about 1 inch thick and 12 ounces *each*)

In a bowl, combine the first nine ingredients. Remove 1/2 cup of marinade and refrigerate. Pierce steaks several times on both sides with a fork; place in an 11-in. x 7-in. x 2-in. glass dish. Pour remaining marinade over steaks; turn to coat. Cover and refrigerate overnight. Remove steaks, discarding marinade. Grill, uncovered, over medium-hot heat for 4-8 minutes on each side or until the meat reaches desired donness (for rare, a meat thermometer should read 140°; medium, 160°; well-done, 170°). Warm reserved marinade and serve with steaks. **Yield:** 2 servings.

Garden Lasagna

As soon as we have tomatoes and zucchini in the garden, my family asks for this dish. —Harriet Stichter
Milford, Indiana

3-1/2 cups spaghetti sauce
1 can (6 ounces) tomato paste
1 cup sliced fresh mushrooms
2 tablespoons vegetable oil
3 cups cream-style cottage cheese
1 cup grated Parmesan cheese
2 eggs, beaten
1 to 2 tablespoons minced fresh oregano *or* 1 to 2 teaspoons dried oregano
1 tablespoon minced fresh basil *or* 1 teaspoon dried basil
1-1/2 teaspoons minced fresh parsley *or* 1/2 teaspoon dried parsley flakes
1 garlic clove, minced
1/2 teaspoon seasoned salt
1/2 teaspoon lemon-pepper seasoning
10 lasagna noodles, cooked and drained
2 medium zucchini, shredded, *divided*
3 cups (12 ounces) shredded mozzarella cheese
3 large tomatoes, cut into 1/2-inch slices

In a saucepan, combine spaghetti sauce, tomato paste, mushrooms and oil. Simmer, uncovered, for 20 minutes. In a bowl, combine the next nine ingredients. In a greased 13-in. x 9-in. x 2-in. baking dish, layer half of the noodles and cheese mixture. Top with 2-1/2 cups of zucchini. Layer with a third of the spaghetti sauce and half of the mozzarella. Repeat layers of noodles, cheese mixture and sauce. Top with tomato slices and remaining sauce and mozzarella. Cover and bake at 350° for 35-40 minutes. Uncover and bake 10 minutes longer. Sprinkle with remaining zucchini. Let stand for 20 minutes before cutting. **Yield:** 8-10 servings.

Herbed Pasta Sauce

I rely on this garden-fresh pasta sauce instead of any store-bought variety. This is a stand-by all summer long. —Dorothy Angley, Carver, Massachusetts

1 medium onion, chopped
3 to 4 celery ribs, chopped
2 tablespoons olive *or* vegetable oil

2 cups chopped fresh tomatoes
2 garlic cloves, minced
2 tablespoons minced fresh parsley *or* 2
   teaspoons dried parsley flakes
1 tablespoon minced fresh oregano *or* 1
   teaspoon dried oregano
1 to 3 teaspoons minced fresh cilantro
   or 1/4 to 1 teaspoon dried cilantro
1 teaspoon sugar
Salt and pepper to taste
Hot cooked pasta

In a large saucepan, saute onion and celery in oil until tender. Stir in tomatoes, garlic, parsley, oregano, cilantro, sugar, salt and pepper. Simmer, uncovered, for 5 minutes. Serve over pasta. **Yield:** about 3 servings (2-1/2 cups sauce).

—— 🚩 🚩 🚩 ——

Swiss Oven Omelet

Mellow onions and Swiss cheese are a mouth-watering medley in this favorite egg dish, a favorite of my family. —Dorothy Smith, El Dorado, Arkansas

2 cups chopped red onion
2 teaspoons sugar
1 tablespoon olive *or* vegetable oil
1/4 cup chopped green onions
2 teaspoons Dijon mustard
1/2 teaspoon dried thyme
6 eggs
1/4 cup water
1/4 teaspoon salt
1/4 teaspoon pepper
1 cup (4 ounces) shredded Swiss cheese,
   divided

In a 10-in. ovenproof skillet, cook and stir red onion and sugar in oil over medium heat for 10-12 minutes or until golden brown. Remove 1/4 cup; set aside. To the skillet, add green onions, mustard and thyme; mix well. Remove from the heat. In a bowl, beat eggs, water, salt and pepper. Pour into skillet; sprinkle with 1/4 cup cheese. Bake, uncovered, at 375° for 10-15 minutes or until a knife inserted near the center comes out clean. Top with reserved onion mixture and remaining cheese. Cut into wedges. **Yield:** 4-6 servings.

No-Fuss Lasagna

When preparing lasagna, place the cheese mixture in a resealable plastic bag with one corner snipped off. Then squeeze out the mixture evenly onto the noodles. There's no mess or big clumps of cheese.

Barbecued Short Ribs

(Pictured above)

This is a very popular recipe for short ribs in our area. The meat is fork-tender and the sauce is wonderfully tangy. We raised beef for many years and still use this recipe. —Margery Bryan, Royal City, Washington

3-1/2 to 4 pounds beef short ribs
1-1/2 cups water
1 medium onion, sliced
1 tablespoon vinegar
SAUCE:
1/2 cup ketchup
1/4 cup chopped onion
2 tablespoons lemon juice
2 garlic cloves, minced
1 teaspoon sugar
1/2 teaspoon salt
1/8 teaspoon pepper

In a Dutch oven, combine ribs, water, onion and vinegar; bring to a boil. Reduce heat; cover and simmer for 1 hour, turning ribs occasionally. Drain. Place ribs in a single layer in an ungreased 13-in. x 9-in. x 2-in. baking dish. Combine sauce ingredients; spoon over ribs. Cover and bake at 325° for 1-1/4 hours or until the meat is tender. **Yield:** 4-6 servings.

Cranberry Pot Roast

I had heard a local restaurant was selling pot roast with cranberry gravy. One day I had some leftover cranberry barbecue sauce and decided to try it over pot roast. It turned out tender, flavorful and delicious! —*Jim Ulberg, Elk Rapids, Michigan*

> 2 tablespoons all-purpose flour
> 1 teaspoon salt
> 1/2 teaspoon pepper
> 1 chuck roast (4 to 5 pounds)
> 2 tablespoons shortening
> 1 medium onion
> 6 whole cloves
> 1 cup water
> 1 medium carrot, shredded
> 2 cinnamon sticks (3 inches)
> 1 can (16 ounces) whole-berry cranberry sauce
> 2 tablespoons cider vinegar

Combine flour, salt and pepper; rub over roast. In a Dutch oven, brown roast in shortening. Cut onion in half; stick cloves into onion. Add onion, water, carrot and cinnamon sticks to pan. Bring to a boil. Reduce heat; cover and simmer for 2-1/2 hours. Add additional water if needed. Spoon off fat. Combine cranberry sauce and vinegar; pour over roast. Cover and simmer 45 minutes longer or until meat is tender. Discard onion, cloves and cinnamon. **Yield:** 10-12 servings.

Winter Squash Quiche

I always get compliments when I serve this quiche to my hungry crew. Our grandchildren especially love it for breakfast. The sweet flavor of the Swiss cheese and squash really comes through. —*Mary Detweiler, West Farmington, Ohio*

> 2 tablespoons chopped onion
> 2 teaspoons vegetable oil
> 2 cups (8 ounces) shredded Swiss cheese
> 1-1/2 cups milk
> 1 cup mashed cooked winter squash
> 3 eggs
> 1/4 teaspoon salt
> 1/8 teaspoon pepper
> 1/8 teaspoon ground nutmeg

In a skillet, saute onion in oil until tender. Transfer to a greased 9-in. pie plate. Sprinkle with cheese. In a bowl, whisk milk, squash, eggs, salt, pepper and nutmeg until smooth; pour over cheese. Bake at 325° for 50-60 minutes or until a knife inserted near the center comes out clean. **Yield:** 6 servings.

Moose Steak

(Pictured above)

Our family really enjoys this tender moose main dish in the fall and winter when an oven meal truly satisfies. The seasonings cover the game flavor wonderfully. —*Chris Mountain, Innisfail, Alberta*

> 1 boneless moose *or* buffalo sirloin steak (about 1 inch thick and 1-1/2 pounds)
> 1/4 cup cornstarch
> 1 tablespoon ground mustard
> 1 teaspoon salt
> 1/2 teaspoon pepper
> 2 tablespoons vegetable oil
> 1 can (14-1/2 ounces) diced tomatoes, undrained
> 1 medium onion, thinly sliced
> 1 medium carrot, diced
> Hot cooked noodles, optional

Cut steak into serving-size pieces. Combine cornstarch, mustard, salt and pepper; rub half over steak. Pound with a meat mallet to tenderize. Rub with remaining cornstarch mixture; pound on both sides with the mallet. In a skillet, brown steak in oil. Transfer to a greased 2-1/2-qt. baking dish. Top with tomatoes, onion and carrot. Cover and bake at 350° for 1-1/4 to 1-1/2 hours or until meat is tender. Serve over noodles if desired. **Yield:** 4-6 servings.

Lingonberry Horseradish Sauce

I grew up eating lots of wild game and other wild foods. We'd prepare a batch of this zippy sauce to serve alongside venison or elk. It can also be made with cranberries and used to give beef a tasty new twist.
—*Kathie Hardy, Springfield, Oregon*

1 cup fresh *or* frozen lingonberries
1/2 cup sugar
1 tablespoon water
1/2 cup sour cream
2 teaspoons prepared horseradish

In a saucepan over medium heat, combine berries, sugar and water; bring to a boil. Boil and stir for 5 minutes. Cool. Stir in sour cream and horseradish. Serve as an accompaniment to meat. Store in the refrigerator. **Yield:** about 1 cup. **Editor's Note:** Cranberries may be substituted for the lingonberries.

— 🍴 🍴 🍴 —

Apricot Salsa Chicken

In an unusual but tongue-tingling combination, apricots and salsa in this recipe smother golden pieces of chicken with a sweet and spicy sauce.
—*Grace Yaskovic, Branchville, New Jersey*

1/2 cup all-purpose flour
1 teaspoon salt
1/4 teaspoon pepper
1/4 teaspoon paprika
6 boneless skinless chicken breast halves
(about 1-1/2 pounds)
3 tablespoons vegetable oil
1 jar (16 ounces) salsa
1 jar (12 ounces) apricot preserves
1/2 cup apricot nectar
Hot cooked rice

In a shallow bowl, combine the first four ingredients. Add chicken; turn to coat. In a skillet, brown chicken in oil; drain. Stir in salsa, preserves and nectar; bring to a boil. Reduce heat; simmer, uncovered, for 15 minutes or until sauce thickens and meat juices run clear. Serve over rice. **Yield:** 6 servings.

— 🍴 🍴 🍴 —

Stan's Smoky Ribs

You can't stop eating these tender, saucy ribs. When folks smell them cooking, they come running!
—*Stanley Pichon, Slidell, Louisiana*

3 pounds country-style spareribs
1/2 teaspoon garlic salt
1/2 teaspoon pepper

1 cup ketchup
1/2 cup packed brown sugar
1/2 cup molasses
1/4 cup spicy brown mustard
2 tablespoons Worcestershire sauce
1 tablespoon liquid smoke, optional
1/8 teaspoon cayenne pepper

Place ribs in a 5-qt. Dutch oven; cover with water. Add garlic salt and pepper; bring to a boil over medium heat. Reduce heat; cover and simmer for 1 hour. Meanwhile, combine remaining ingredients; set aside. Drain ribs. Cook on an uncovered grill over medium heat for 8-10 minutes or until meat is tender, basting several times with sauce. Serve remaining sauce with ribs. **Yield:** 4 servings.

— 🍴 🍴 🍴 —

Breakfast Patties

(Pictured below)

This homemade sausage is terrific because it's so lean, holds together well and shrinks very little when cooked. It's incredibly easy to mix up a batch and make any breakfast special.
—*Jeannine Stallings*
East Helena, Montana

1/4 cup water
2 teaspoons salt
2 teaspoons rubbed sage
1 teaspoon pepper
1/2 teaspoon ground nutmeg
1/4 teaspoon crushed red pepper flakes
1/8 teaspoon ground ginger
2 pounds ground pork

In a bowl, combine water and seasonings. Add pork and mix well. Shape into eight 4-in. patties. In a skillet over medium heat, cook patties for 5-6 minutes on each side or until no longer pink in the center. **Yield:** 8 patties.

Italian Shepherd's Pie

(Pictured below)

For a stick-to-your-ribs main dish that's deliciously different, give this pie a try! The Italian sausage goes so well with mashed potatoes, and both get a new twist served in a crust and cut into wedges. My family is always glad to see me preparing this dish.
—Cindy Gage, Blair, Nebraska

      1 **unbaked pastry shell (9 inches)**
      1 **pound bulk Italian sausage**
      1 **cup cream-style cottage cheese**
      1 **egg**
1-1/2 **cups warm mashed potatoes (without added milk and butter)**
  1/4 **cup sour cream**
  1/2 **teaspoon dried oregano**
  1/2 **to 3/4 teaspoon salt**
  1/8 **teaspoon pepper**
      2 **teaspoons butter *or* margarine, melted**
      1 **cup (4 ounces) shredded cheddar cheese**
Cherry tomatoes, halved

Line unpricked pastry shell with a double thickness of heavy-duty foil. Bake at 450° for 7 minutes. Remove from oven and remove foil; set aside. Reduce heat to 350°. In a skillet, cook the sausage until no longer pink; drain well on paper towels. In a blender, process the cottage cheese and egg until smooth. Transfer to a large bowl; stir in potatoes, sour cream, oregano, salt and pepper. Place sausage in pastry shell; top with the potato mixture. Drizzle with butter. Bake for 50-60 minutes or until set. Sprinkle with cheese; let stand for a few minutes until cheese is melted. Garnish with tomatoes. **Yield:** 6-8 servings.

Peach Chutney

Golden chunks of sweet peaches are a wonderful part of this tangy chutney. We enjoy this and many other peach delicacies all year-round. —Julie Ann Morgan
Columbia, South Carolina

      2 **large onions, chopped**
      1 **tablespoon vegetable oil**
      3 **large peaches, peeled and cubed**
  1/2 **cup packed brown sugar**
  1/4 **cup sugar**
  1/4 **cup raisins**
      1 **tablespoon molasses**
      1 **teaspoon salt**
  1/2 **teaspoon pepper**
  1/4 **teaspoon ground allspice**
      8 **tablespoons vinegar, *divided***
      2 **tablespoons lemon juice**

In a large skillet, saute onions in oil until tender. Add peaches; cook and stir for 3 minutes. Add sugars, raisins, molasses, salt, pepper, allspice and 5 tablespoons vinegar; bring to a boil. Reduce heat; simmer, uncovered, for 45 minutes, stirring occasionally. Remove from the heat; stir in lemon juice and remaining vinegar. Serve at room temperature with ham, pork or chicken. Store in the refrigerator for up to 3 weeks. **Yield:** about 3 cups.

Spinach Burritos

I made up this recipe a couple years ago after trying a similar dish in a restaurant. Our oldest son tells me these burritos are "awesome"! Plus, they're easy and inexpensive to fix.
—Dolores Zornow
Poynette, Wisconsin

☑ Nutritional Analysis included

  1/2 **cup chopped onion**
      2 **garlic cloves, minced**
      2 **teaspoons butter *or* margarine**
      1 **package (10 ounces) frozen chopped spinach, thawed and drained**

1/8 teaspoon pepper
6 flour tortillas (10 inches)
3/4 cup picante sauce, divided
2 cups (8 ounces) shredded cheddar cheese, *divided*

In a skillet, saute onion and garlic in butter until tender. Add spinach and pepper; cook for 2-3 minutes or until heated through. Place about 3 tablespoonfuls on each tortilla; top with 1 tablespoon picante sauce and 2 tablespoons cheese. Place seam side down in a greased 13-in. x 9-in. x 2-in. baking dish. Top with remaining picante sauce and cheese. Bake, uncovered, at 350° for 20-25 minutes or until sauce is bubbly and cheese is melted. **Yield:** 6 servings. **Nutritional Analysis:** One serving (prepared with margarine, fat-free tortillas and reduced-fat cheese) equals 262 calories, 550 mg sodium, 25 mg cholesterol, 31 gm carbohydrate, 17 gm protein, 9 gm fat. **Diabetic Exchanges:** 1-1/2 meat, 1-1/2 starch, 1 vegetable.

Pork Chop Casserole

My family raves about this casserole with its tender chops and nicely seasoned potatoes. The best part is I can just pop it in the oven and spend time playing with my little grandson. —Linda Wynn Iowa Park, Texas

✓ Nutritional Analysis included

4 boneless pork loin chops (3/4 inch thick)
1/4 teaspoon Italian seasoning
1/4 teaspoon pepper
2 large potatoes, peeled and sliced 1/4 inch thick
1 medium onion, chopped
1 tablespoon all-purpose flour
3 tablespoons butter *or* margarine
1 tablespoon chopped green pepper

Sprinkle pork chops with Italian seasoning and pepper. Arrange in the center of a greased 13-in. x 9-in. x 2-in. baking dish. Combine potatoes, onion and flour; place around chops. Dot with butter; sprinkle with green pepper. Cover and bake at 325° for 55 minutes. Uncover and bake 10-15 minutes longer or until potatoes are tender and meat juices run clear. **Yield:** 4 servings. **Nutritional Analysis:** One serving (prepared with reduced-fat margarine) equals 278 calories, 137 mg sodium, 63 mg cholesterol, 14 gm carbohydrate, 27 gm protein, 13 gm fat. **Diabetic Exchanges:** 3 lean meat, 1 starch.

Sweet-and-Sour Elk
(Pictured above)

Baked elk steaks smothered with a simple, savory sauce is a special dinner we've enjoyed for years. My husband, Ralph, and I used to do quite a bit of hunting, so I accumulated lots of terrific recipes like this one. —Susan Bowdle, Ephrata, Washington

1 envelope onion soup mix
1/4 cup water
1 jar (12 ounces) apricot preserves
1/2 cup Russian *or* Catalina salad dressing
1/4 cup packed brown sugar
1 tablespoon cider vinegar
1-1/2 pounds elk steaks, cut into 1/2-inch strips
1 teaspoon salt
1/4 teaspoon pepper
Hot cooked rice

In a bowl, combine soup mix and water; let stand for 15 minutes. Add the preserves, salad dressing, brown sugar and vinegar; mix well. Place elk in a greased 13-in. x 9-in. x 2-in. baking dish. Sprinkle with salt and pepper. Pour apricot mixture over the elk. Cover and bake at 350° for 45 minutes. Uncover and bake 30-40 minutes longer or until meat is fork-tender. Serve over rice. **Yield:** 4-6 servings.

Pork Chops with Apricot Rice

(Pictured above)

I came up with this recipe to use some of my favorite ingredients in a quick-to-fix entree. I love the combination of apricots, golden raisins and celery with the crunch of almonds. I've gotten raves with this dish.
—Fayne Lutz, Taos, New Mexico

    1 can (15-1/4 ounces) apricot halves,
       undrained
    6 pork chops (1/2 inch thick)
    3 tablespoons butter *or* margarine
  1/4 cup chopped celery
2-1/2 cups uncooked instant rice
  3/4 cup hot water
  1/4 cup golden raisins
  1/2 teaspoon ground ginger
  1/2 teaspoon salt
  1/4 teaspoon white pepper
  1/4 cup slivered almonds

In a blender or food processor, puree the apricots until smooth; set aside. In a skillet over medium heat, brown pork chops in butter for 2-3 minutes on each side; remove and keep warm. In the same skillet, saute celery until tender. Add rice, water, raisins, ginger, salt, pepper and apricot puree; bring to a boil. Remove from the heat; stir in almonds. Pour into an ungreased 13-in. x 9-in. x 2-in. bak-

ing dish. Place the chops on top. Cover and bake at 350° for 15-20 minutes or until the pork is no longer pink and the rice is tender. **Yield:** 6 servings.

Scalloped Chicken Casserole

This is a great catchall meal-in-one dish. Any meat can be used, and vegetables may be substituted based on what you have available. —Marion White
La Center, Washington

    1 cup chopped green onions
    1 cup chopped celery
    1 small green *or* sweet red pepper, chopped
  1/2 cup shredded carrots
    2 garlic cloves, minced
    2 tablespoons vegetable oil
    2 cups cubed cooked chicken
    1 cup (4 ounces) shredded cheddar cheese
    1 cup (4 ounces) shredded mozzarella
       cheese
  1/2 cup mayonnaise
    1 tablespoon minced fresh parsley *or* 1
       teaspoon dried parsley flakes
   14 slices day-old whole wheat bread, cubed
    4 eggs
    2 cups milk
    1 can (10-3/4 ounces) condensed cream of
       chicken soup, undiluted
    1 tablespoon Worcestershire sauce
Paprika

In a skillet, saute the onions, celery, green pepper, carrots and garlic in oil until crisp-tender. Transfer to a large bowl; add chicken, cheeses, mayonnaise and parsley. Place half of the bread cubes in a greased 13-in. x 9-in. x 2-in. baking dish. Top with chicken mixture and remaining bread. In a bowl, beat eggs; add milk, soup and Worcestershire sauce. Pour over casserole. Sprinkle with paprika. Bake, uncovered, at 350° for 1 hour and 10 minutes or until a knife inserted near the center comes out clean. **Yield:** 12-16 servings.

Potato Omelet

Even folks who don't care for eggs will like this dish since the great taste of potatoes, bacon and garlic comes through. —Edie DeSpain, Logan, Utah

    2 medium potatoes, peeled and diced
  1/4 cup olive *or* vegetable oil
  1/2 cup sliced green onions
  1/4 cup minced fresh parsley

1 garlic clove, minced
6 eggs
1/4 cup water
1/2 teaspoon salt
1/8 teaspoon pepper
**Sour cream and crumbled cooked bacon,
  optional**

In a 12-in. skillet, cook potatoes in oil over medi-um-high heat for 10 minutes or until golden brown, stirring occasionally. Add onions, parsley and gar-lic; cook until tender. Reduce heat to medium. In a bowl, beat eggs, water, salt and pepper. Pour over potato mixture; cover and cook for 8-10 minutes or until completely set. Cut into wedges. Serve with sour cream and bacon if desired. **Yield:** 4-6 servings.

Sole with Cucumber Sauce

Cucumbers take on a mild pickle flavor as they cook with dill, herbs and sole fillets in this quick and deli-cious fish dish. —*Emily Chaney, Penobscot, Maine*

2 medium cucumbers, peeled and thinly
  sliced
1/2 cup chopped green onions
1/4 cup chopped celery
1 tablespoon minced fresh parsley
1 teaspoon dill weed
1 cup chicken broth
4 sole fillets (about 1-1/2 pounds)
2 teaspoons cornstarch
1/2 cup whipping cream
1 teaspoon prepared horseradish
Salt and pepper to taste

In a large skillet, layer cucumbers, onions, celery, parsley and dill; add broth. Top with fillets; bring to a boil. Cover and simmer for 8-10 minutes or un-til fish flakes easily with a fork. Transfer fish to a serving platter and keep warm; reserve cucumber mixture in skillet. Combine cornstarch and cream until smooth; add horseradish, salt and pepper. Stir into skillet. Simmer for 2 minutes or until thick-ened. Pour over fish; serve immediately. **Yield:** 4 servings.

Savory Meat Pie

(Pictured at right)

A friend gave me this recipe after I mentioned that my meat pies lacked "punch". This pie has a delicious, distinctive flavor thanks to lots of seasonings. Flecks of carrots peek out of each neat slice. My family espe-cially enjoys this dinner when the weather turns chilly.
—*Paula L'Hirondelle, Red Deer, Alberta*

2 medium potatoes, peeled and quartered
1 pound ground beef
3/4 cup sliced green onions
1 large carrot, finely chopped
1 garlic clove, minced
1/2 teaspoon dried thyme
1/2 teaspoon rubbed sage
1/2 teaspoon salt
1/2 teaspoon pepper
1/4 teaspoon celery salt
Pinch ground cinnamon
1/4 cup minced fresh parsley
1/4 cup chili sauce
Pastry for double-crust pie (9 inches)
1 tablespoon Dijon mustard
1 tablespoon milk

In a saucepan, cook potatoes in boiling water un-til tender; mash and set aside. Meanwhile, in a skil-let, brown beef; drain. Stir in the next nine ingre-dients. Simmer for 4-5 minutes. Stir in the pota-toes, parsley and chili sauce; remove from the heat. Place the bottom pastry in a 9-in. pie plate; brush with mustard. Add meat mixture. Top with re-maining pastry; seal and flute edges. Cut slits in the top crust. Brush with milk. Bake at 450° for 10 min-utes. Reduce heat to 350°; bake 25 minutes longer or until golden brown. **Yield:** 6 servings.

Sausage Florentine Bake

(Pictured below)

Prepare once and eat twice with this delicious lasagna-like casserole! Just bake one pan and freeze the second. —*Janice Mitchell, Aurora, Colorado*

1-1/2 pounds bulk Italian sausage
   2 cans (28 ounces *each*) crushed tomatoes
   1 bay leaf
   3 to 4 garlic cloves, minced
   2 teaspoons sugar
   1 teaspoon dried basil
  1/2 teaspoon dried oregano
  1/2 teaspoon salt
  1/4 teaspoon pepper
   4 eggs, beaten
  1/2 cup grated Parmesan cheese, *divided*
  1/8 teaspoon ground nutmeg
   2 packages (10 ounces *each*) frozen chopped spinach, thawed and well drained
   1 package (12 ounces) extra wide noodles, cooked and drained
   4 green onions, sliced
   4 cups (1 pound) shredded mozzarella cheese

In a Dutch oven or soup kettle, cook sausage until no longer pink; drain. Add tomatoes, bay leaf, garlic, sugar, basil, oregano, salt and pepper; bring to a boil. Reduce heat; simmer, uncovered, for 1 hour, stirring occasionally. Meanwhile, in a bowl, combine eggs, 1/4 cup Parmesan cheese and nutmeg; mix well. Stir in spinach, noodles and onions. Discard bay leaf from sausage mixture. In two greased 9-in. square baking pans, layer a fourth of the noodles, then a fourth of the sausage mixture. Top each with 1 cup mozzarella cheese. Repeat layers. Top with remaining Parmesan cheese. Bake, uncovered, at 350° for 30 minutes or until bubbly. Let stand for 10 minutes before serving. **Yield:** 2 casseroles (4 servings each). **Editor's Note:** Casseroles may be frozen before baking. Thaw in the refrigerator. Bake at 350° for 1 hour or until heated through.

Honey-Dijon Chicken

Honey, Dijon mustard and soy sauce blend perfectly to season these golden baked chicken breasts. A beekeeper shared the recipe with me. —*Julie Rowe Fort McMurray, Alberta*

✓ Nutritional Analysis included

   4 boneless skinless chicken breast halves (1 pound)
  1/4 cup honey
   2 tablespoons lemon juice
   2 tablespoons soy sauce
   1 teaspoon Dijon mustard

Place chicken in an ungreased 11-in. x 7-in. x 2-in. baking dish. Combine remaining ingredients; pour over chicken. Bake, uncovered, at 350° for 35-40 minutes or until juices run clear, turning and basting with pan juices every 15 minutes. **Yield:** 4 servings. **Nutritional Analysis:** One serving (prepared with light soy sauce) equals 197 calories, 340 mg sodium, 63 mg cholesterol, 19 gm carbohydrate, 24 gm protein, 3 gm fat. **Diabetic Exchanges:** 3 very lean meat, 1-1/2 fruit.

Turkey 'n' Stuffing Pie

Stuffing serves as the crust for this attractive cheese-latticed turkey pie. Try it the day after Thanksgiving to use up leftovers. —*Ruth Hastings Louisville, Illinois*

   1 egg, beaten
   1 cup chicken broth
  1/3 cup butter *or* margarine, melted
   5 cups herb-seasoned stuffing
FILLING:
   1 can (4 ounces) mushroom stems and pieces, drained
  1/2 cup chopped onion
   1 tablespoon butter *or* margarine
   1 tablespoon all-purpose flour

3 cups cubed cooked turkey
1 cup frozen peas
1 tablespoon minced fresh parsley
1 teaspoon Worcestershire sauce
1/2 teaspoon dried thyme
1 jar (12 ounces) turkey gravy
5 slices process American cheese, cut into strips

In a large bowl, combine egg, broth and butter. Add stuffing; mix well. Pat onto the bottom and up the sides of a greased 9-in. pie plate; set aside. In a skillet, saute mushrooms and onion in butter until tender. Sprinkle with flour; mix well. Add turkey, peas, parsley, Worcestershire sauce and thyme; mix well. Stir in gravy. Bring to a boil; boil and stir for 2 minutes. Spoon into the crust. Bake at 375° for 20 minutes. Arrange cheese strips in a lattice pattern over filling. Bake 5-10 minutes longer or until cheese is melted. **Yield:** 4-6 servings.

Gingered Beef Stir-Fry

You won't feel deprived in any way when you make this delicious main dish. The beef is tender and tasty, and the colorful vegetables keep a bit of their crunch.
—*Grace Nicholson, Willow Grove, Pennsylvania*

✓ Nutritional Analysis included

1 egg white
1 tablespoon cornstarch
1/2 teaspoon sugar
1/4 teaspoon ground ginger
1/4 teaspoon pepper
1 flank steak (1 pound), cut into thin strips
1 tablespoon vegetable oil
1/2 cup chopped green onions
2 tablespoons soy sauce
2 medium carrots, thinly sliced
1 medium zucchini, thinly sliced
1/4 pound fresh or frozen snow peas, thawed
Hot cooked rice

In a medium bowl, whisk egg white, cornstarch, sugar, ginger and pepper until smooth. Add beef and toss to coat; set aside. Heat oil in a 10-in. nonstick skillet; stir-fry onions for 1 minute. Add beef; stir-fry for 6-7 minutes or until browned and tender. Stir in soy sauce. Add carrots, zucchini and peas; stir-fry for 4-5 minutes or until crisp-tender. Serve over rice. **Yield:** 5 servings. **Nutritional Analysis:** One 1-cup serving (prepared with light soy sauce; calculated without rice) equals 240 calories, 246 mg sodium, 47 mg cholesterol, 14 gm carbohydrate, 23 gm protein, 10 gm fat. **Diabetic Exchanges:** 3 lean meat, 1 vegetable, 1/2 starch.

Beef Barley Stew

(Pictured above)

On cool days, I like to get out my slow cooker and make up a batch of this comforting stew. Trying to appeal to 10 picky eaters in our large household isn't easy, but with this recipe, everyone asks for seconds.
—*Barb Smith, Regina, Saskatchewan*

1-1/2 pounds beef stew meat, cut into 1-inch pieces
1 medium onion, chopped
2 tablespoons vegetable oil
1 quart water
1 can (15 ounces) tomato sauce
5 medium carrots, cut into 1/2-inch pieces
1 celery rib, thinly sliced
2 teaspoons salt
1/2 teaspoon dried oregano
1/2 teaspoon paprika
1/4 teaspoon pepper
2 cups fresh *or* frozen green beans
2 cups fresh *or* frozen corn
3/4 cup medium pearl barley

In a skillet, brown beef and onion in oil; drain. Transfer to a 5-qt. slow cooker. Add water, tomato sauce, carrots, celery, salt, oregano, paprika and pepper. Cover and cook on low for 4-5 hours. Add beans, corn and barley; cover and cook on low 2 hours longer or until barley, beef and vegetables are tender. **Yield:** 6-8 servings.

Saucy Bratwurst Supper

(Pictured above)

For a change-of-pace dinner menu, I pull out this sensational bratwurst recipe. The caraway and other seasonings give this meaty main dish wonderful old-world flair. My husband thinks it's terrific.
—*Robin Huber, Calgary, Alberta*

4 to 6 fresh bratwurst links
1 medium onion, chopped
3 garlic cloves, minced
1 tablespoon vegetable oil
2 cups sliced fresh mushrooms
2 medium tomatoes, chopped
2 tablespoons cider vinegar
1 bay leaf
1 teaspoon caraway seeds
1/2 teaspoon salt
1/2 teaspoon pepper
1 cup apple juice
2 tablespoons cornstarch
1/4 cup water

In a large skillet, brown bratwurst; drain. Remove and set aside. In the same skillet, saute onion and garlic in oil until tender. Add mushrooms, tomatoes, vinegar, bay leaf, caraway, salt and pepper. Cook and stir for 2-3 minutes. Return bratwurst to skillet. Add apple juice; bring to a boil. Reduce heat; cover and simmer for 18-22 minutes or until bratwurst is no longer pink. Discard bay leaf. Remove bratwurst; keep warm. Combine cornstarch and water until smooth. Gradually add to sauce mixture; bring to a boil. Boil and stir for 2 minutes. Serve with bratwurst. **Yield:** 4-6 servings.

Cucumber Relish

Folks often say this colorful, tangy relish reminds them of bread-and-butter pickles. It's a great topping for hot dogs or grilled chicken breasts.
—*Mildred Sherrer, Bay City, Texas*

4-1/2 cups chopped cucumbers
3-1/2 cups chopped celery
3 cups chopped onion
2 cups chopped sweet red pepper
2 cups chopped green pepper
1/4 cup canning salt
4 cups water
4 cups vinegar
3 cups sugar
2 teaspoons mustard seed
2 teaspoons celery seed

Combine cucumbers, celery, onion and peppers in a large bowl; add salt and water. Cover and refrigerate overnight. Drain; rinse and drain again. Combine remaining ingredients in a large kettle; bring to a boil. Add vegetables; simmer for 10 minutes. Ladle the hot mixture into hot jars, leaving 1/4-in. headspace. Adjust caps. Process for 10 minutes in a boiling-water bath. **Yield:** 10 half-pints.

Old-World Kielbasa

I've been making this recipe for most of my some 70 years. No one can resist this hearty old-fashioned fare.
—*Ethel Harrison, North Fort Myers, Florida*

☑ Nutritional Analysis included

1 medium onion, sliced
2 tablespoons butter *or* margarine
8 cups shredded cabbage
1 pound fully cooked kielbasa, cut into 1/4-inch slices
1 can (14-1/2 ounces) stewed tomatoes
1/2 cup water
4 teaspoons caraway seeds
1 teaspoon paprika

In a Dutch oven, saute onion in butter. Add remaining ingredients; bring to a boil. Reduce heat; cover and simmer for 30 minutes. Serve with a slotted spoon. **Yield:** 10 servings. **Nutritional Analysis:** One 1-cup serving (prepared with margarine, low-fat smoked turkey sausage and no-salt-added tomatoes) equals 115 calories, 454 mg sodium, 30 mg cholesterol, 8 gm carbohydrate, 8 gm protein, 6 gm fat. **Diabetic Exchanges:** 1-1/2 vegetable, 1 meat.

Savory Steak Rub

Keep the ingredients for this easy rub on hand to simply season steaks at a moment's notice.
—Donna Brockett, Kingfisher, Oklahoma

- 1 tablespoon dried marjoram
- 1 tablespoon dried basil
- 2 teaspoons garlic powder
- 2 teaspoons dried thyme
- 1 teaspoon dried rosemary, crushed
- 3/4 teaspoon dried oregano

Combine all ingredients; store in a covered container. Rub over steaks before grilling or broiling. Will season four to five steaks. **Yield:** 1/4 cup.

Lamb's-Quarter Quiche

Lamb's-quarter (also called "goosefoot") is one of my favorite salad greens. I add the leaves to stir-fries, soups and salads. Cook them alone or mix them with other greens. *—Dorothy Holderbaum*
Allegan, Michigan

- 1 medium onion, chopped
- 2 tablespoons vegetable oil
- 4 cups chopped lamb's-quarter (tender new leaves) *or* fresh spinach
- 3 eggs
- 1 can (12 ounces) evaporated milk *or* 1-2/3 cups milk
- 1/2 teaspoon salt
- 1/2 teaspoon pepper
- 2 cups (8 ounces) shredded cheddar cheese, *divided*
- 1 unbaked pie pastry (9 inches)

In a skillet, saute onion in oil until tender. Add lamb's-quarter; cook and stir until wilted. Cover and remove from the heat. In a mixing bowl, beat eggs and milk. Stir in salt, pepper, 1 cup cheese and lamb's-quarter mixture. Pour into pie shell. Sprinkle with remaining cheese. Bake at 400° for 10 minutes. Reduce heat to 350°; bake 30 minutes more or until a knife inserted near center comes out clean. Let stand 5-10 minutes before cutting. **Yield:** 6-8 servings.

'I Wish I Had That Recipe...'

A HIGHLIGHT of an Arkansas vacation was dinner at The 178 Club Restaurant in Bull Shoals, reports Linda Martin, Bartlett, Tennessee.

"My husband and I enjoyed spectacular Stuffed Pork Chops. They were so delicious that I'd like to enjoy their great taste at home."

Dee Fox, owner of The 178 Club with husband Robert, revealed, "I used to make these chops for our three children when they were growing up. Now they've become a popular special at our restaurant and are often requested for banquets.

"Everything on our menu, which features steaks, seafood, chicken, pasta and burgers, is made to order from scratch, using fresh ingredients."

Son Wade, who is head cook, and his wife, Vickie, have joined the Foxes in catering to hungry patrons.

Find The 178 Club on Highway 178 in Bull Shoals, Arkansas. Lunch is served 11 a.m. to 4 p.m.; dinner, 5 p.m. to 10 p.m.; Sunday breakfast-brunch, 9:30 a.m. to noon. The restaurant is closed Mondays. For reservations, call 1-870/445-4949.

Stuffed Pork Chops

- 4 pork chops (1 inch thick)
- 2 tablespoons vegetable oil
- 3 cups day-old French bread cubes (1/2 inch)
- 1/4 cup butter *or* margarine, melted
- 1/4 cup chicken broth
- 2 tablespoons chopped celery
- 2 tablespoons chopped onion
- 1/4 teaspoon poultry seasoning
- 1 can (10-3/4 ounces) condensed cream of mushroom soup, undiluted
- 1/3 cup water

In a skillet, brown pork chops in oil. Place chops in an ungreased shallow baking pan. Toss bread cubes, butter, broth, celery, onion and poultry seasoning. Mound about 1/2 cup stuffing on each pork chop. Combine soup and water; pour over chops. Cover and bake at 350° for 30 minutes. Uncover; bake 10-15 minutes longer or until juices run clear and a meat thermometer reads 160°-170°. **Yield:** 4 servings.

Simple Glazes Make Ham Holiday-Special

IS HAM on your holiday menu? Add festive Yuletide color and flavor to it with fruity glazes!

Glazes are so simple and economical that you may decide to serve several different ones along with your Christmas ham or on a party buffet.

Tangy cranberries are a "natural" with ham, says Hormel's chef, Horst Kruppa. His Elegant Holiday Ham Glaze mixes whole cranberries in a fruity medley with just a hint of mustard.

Another even simpler recipe, Fruity Ham Glaze features your homemade or purchased cranberry-orange sauce with peach or apricot preserves for a jewel-toned look and traditional taste your dinner crowd will savor.

Ruby Nelson of Mountain Home, Arkansas shares her recipe for another fruity favorite that's bound to please your family. Raspberry Ham Glaze stirs up in a wink and is sure to perk up the palate.

Holiday Ham Hints

Chef Kruppa also shares hints for cooking great holiday ham:

• Today's hams are lean, so remember to baste the ham frequently with your glaze or with moisture you've added to the pan.

• For ham glazes with fewer calories, substitute fresh fruit puree in your favorite recipes or use an artificial sweetener. (Don't add until the last moment, because artificial sweeteners tend to turn bitter when cooked.)

• You can cook many side dishes right in your glaze as you bake your ham. Some examples: apple halves, pears, dates, figs, chestnuts (without shell), small red potatoes, brussels sprouts or sweet potatoes.

• Try combining part of your glaze with ground nuts or fruit for basting toward the end of your baking time.

• Your glaze does not always have to be cooked with the ham. Mix a glaze you've made with slices of exotic fresh fruit like kiwi, passion fruit, mango or star fruit to serve as a pretty and delicious holiday ham accompaniment.

• Ham is best when served between 120° and 140°.

• If you microwave ham, use a covered microwave-safe dish and medium setting. To get a traditional oven-baked look, brush your ham with a "browning agent" such as egg yolk, honey or mustard and finish cooking on full power for a few minutes.

Microwave-cooked ham will be less salty than ham prepared in a conventional oven because less moisture evaporates. Make your glaze a little thicker to begin with because of extra moisture present.

Elegant Holiday Ham Glaze

Juice and grated peel of 1 orange
Juice and grated peel of 1 lemon
  1 cup cranberry juice *or* sweet red wine
1/2 cup light corn syrup
1/2 teaspoon ground mustard
  1 can (16 ounces) whole-berry cranberry sauce
Drippings from a baked ham, optional
  2 tablespoons cornstarch, optional
  2 tablespoons cold water, optional

In a saucepan, combine orange and lemon juices and peel, cranberry juice or wine, corn syrup and mustard. Simmer for 30 minutes. Add the cranberry sauce and ham drippings if desired; heat

Carving the Perfect Whole Ham

Place ham on its side on platter so fat side faces away from you. Cut a few slices off the bottom.

Turn ham so it rests on the cut side. Make even vertical slices starting at shank end down to the bone.

Run knife horizontally along bone to release slices.

TASTY TOPPINGS. Glazes like Raspberry Ham Glaze (recipe below right) beautifully top off baked ham and add a festive touch without a lot of fuss.

through. If a thicker glaze is desired, bring just to a boil. Combine cornstarch and water; add to glaze. Cook and stir until slightly thickened. Serve warm over sliced ham. **Yield:** 3-1/2 cups.

—— 🝰 🝰 🝰 ——

Fruity Ham Glaze

1/4 cup cranberry-orange sauce
1/4 cup apricot *or* peach preserves

Combine ingredients in a small bowl. About 30 minutes before ham is done, remove from the oven. Score surface; spoon glaze over entire ham. Return to the oven, basting occasionally during the last 30 minutes of baking. **Yield:** 1/2 cup.

Raspberry Ham Glaze

(Pictured above)

1/4 cup apple juice *or* dry white wine
2 tablespoons lemon juice
2 teaspoons cornstarch
1/3 cup seedless raspberry jam, *divided*
1 tablespoon butter *or* margarine

In a saucepan, combine the apple juice, lemon juice and cornstarch; stir until smooth. Stir in half of the jam. Cook and stir over medium heat until thickened and bubbly. Stir in butter and remaining jam. Cook and stir until the butter is melted. During the last 10 minutes of the ham's baking time, spoon glaze over the entire ham. **Yield:** about 2/3 cup.

Add enough water to juice to equal 1-1/2 cups; stir into vinegar mixture. Add sugar and soy sauce; cook and stir over medium heat until thickened. Add the meatballs, pineapple and green pepper; cook until heated through and the green pepper is tender. Serve over noodles. **Yield:** 3-4 servings.

Crab and Spinach Quiche

This savory quiche makes a great main dish, but I also serve it as an appetizer at my annual cookie exchange party. The recipe makes two pies, so it's convenient when you need to feed a crowd.
—*Arliene Hillinger, Rancho Palos Verdes, California*

>   5 eggs
> 1-1/2 cups milk
>   1/4 teaspoon salt
>   1/8 teaspoon pepper
>   1/8 teaspoon ground nutmeg
>   1 cup (4 ounces) shredded Swiss cheese
> 1-1/2 cups grated Parmesan cheese
>   3 tablespoons all-purpose flour
>   6 to 8 ounces canned *or* frozen crabmeat, thawed, drained and flaked
>   1 package (10 ounces) frozen chopped spinach, thawed and well-drained

Pastry for double-crust pie (9 inches)

In a large bowl, lightly beat eggs. Add milk, salt, pepper and nutmeg; set aside. Combine cheeses and flour; add to egg mixture with the crab and spinach. Mix well. Pour into two pastry-lined 9-in. pie plates or quiche pans. Bake at 350° for 50 minutes or until a knife inserted near center comes out clean. Cut into wedges. Serve warm. **Yield:** 12-16 servings.

Sauerkraut 'n' Sausage

I've fixed this satisfying stovetop supper for dozens of groups gatherings, and everyone seems to enjoy the wonderful blend of flavors. Sweet and tart ingredients balance nicely, complemented with bacon and spices.   —*Edna Hoffman, Hebron, Indiana*

>   1 small onion, chopped
>   1 tablespoon butter *or* margarine
>   1 jar (32 ounces) sauerkraut, rinsed and drained
>   1 pound fully cooked Polish sausage, cut into 1/2-inch chunks
> 3-1/2 cups diced cooked peeled potatoes
>   1 cup apple juice
>   1 medium unpeeled apple, diced

Moose Meatballs

(Pictured above)

Our family has found these meatballs in tangy sauce a great use for moose. I was glad to find a good recipe that incorporates ground moose meat, since we eat a lot of moose steaks and I like to use it differently for a change.   —*Janis Plourde*
Smooth Rock Falls, Ontario

>   1 pound ground moose meat *or* ground beef
>   1 egg, lightly beaten
>   4 tablespoons cornstarch, *divided*
>   1 teaspoon salt
>   1/4 teaspoon pepper
>   2 tablespoons chopped onion
>   1 tablespoon vegetable oil
>   3 tablespoons vinegar
>   1 can (8 ounces) pineapple chunks
>   1/2 cup sugar
>   1 tablespoon soy sauce
>   1 medium green pepper, cut into strips

Hot cooked wide egg noodles

In a bowl, combine meat, egg, 1 tablespoon cornstarch, salt, pepper and onion. Shape into 1-1/2-in. balls. In a large skillet, brown meatballs in oil. Cover and cook over low heat until the meatballs are done, about 10 minutes. In a saucepan, stir vinegar and remaining cornstarch until smooth. Drain pineapple, reserving juice. Set pineapple aside.

2 tablespoons brown sugar
2 tablespoons all-purpose flour
1 tablespoon caraway seeds
3 bacon strips, cooked and crumbled

In a large saucepan, saute onion in butter until tender. Add sauerkraut, sausage, potatoes, apple juice and apple. In a small bowl, combine the brown sugar, flour and caraway; stir into saucepan. Simmer for 35 minutes, stirring occasionally. Garnish with bacon. **Yield:** 10-12 servings.

Dan's Peppery London Broil

I was bored making the usual London Broil, so I got a little creative and sparked up the flavor with crushed red pepper, garlic and Worcestershire sauce.
—Dan Wright, San Jose, California

1 beef flank steak (about 3/4 pound)
1 garlic clove, minced
1/2 teaspoon seasoned salt
1/8 teaspoon crushed red pepper flakes
1/4 cup Worcestershire sauce

With a meat fork, poke holes in both sides of the meat. Make a paste with garlic, seasoned salt and red pepper; rub over both sides of meat. Place the steak in a gallon-size plastic bag. Add Worcestershire sauce and close bag. Refrigerate for at least 4 hours, turning once. Remove meat; discard marinade. Broil or grill over hot coals until meat reaches desired doneness, 4-5 minutes per side. To serve, slice thinly across the grain. **Yield:** 2 servings.

No-Salt Seasoning

When you first start on a low-salt diet, everything tastes bland until your taste buds have time to adjust. This seasoning will help overcome that blandness.
—Roma Lea Short, Baldwyn, Mississippi

5 teaspoons onion powder
1 tablespoon garlic powder
1 tablespoon paprika
1 tablespoon ground mustard
1 teaspoon dried thyme
1/2 teaspoon pepper
1/2 teaspoon celery seed

Combine all ingredients in a small jar with a shaker top. Use for seasoning broiled fish, poultry, cooked vegetables, soups and stews, or place it on the table to be used individually. **Yield:** about 1/3 cup.

Dilly Barbecued Turkey
(Pictured below)

This is my brother-in-law's recipe. The special marinade makes a tasty, tender turkey, and the tempting aroma prompts the family to gather around the grill.
—Sue Walker, Greentown, Indiana

✓ Nutritional Analysis included

1 turkey breast half with bone (2-1/2 to 3 pounds)
1 cup plain yogurt
1/4 cup lemon juice
3 tablespoons vegetable oil
1/4 cup minced fresh parsley
1/4 cup chopped green onions
2 garlic cloves, minced
2 tablespoons fresh minced dill *or* 2 teaspoons dill weed
1/2 teaspoon dried rosemary, crushed
1/2 teaspoon salt, optional
1/4 teaspoon pepper

Place turkey in a shallow glass container. Combine all remaining ingredients; spread over the turkey. Cover and refrigerate for 6-8 hours or overnight. Remove turkey and reserve marinade. Grill turkey, covered, over medium-hot heat, basting often with marinade, for 1 to 1-1/4 hours or until juices run clear and a meat thermometer reaches 170°. **Yield:** 6 servings. **Nutritional Analysis:** One serving (prepared with nonfat yogurt and without salt) equals 245 calories, 127 mg sodium, 40 mg cholesterol, 5 gm carbohydrate, 28 gm protein, 12 gm fat. **Diabetic Exchanges:** 3 lean meat, 1 vegetable, 1 fat.

Breads, Rolls & Muffins

An enticing assortment of homemade breads will satisfy morning, noon and night.

——— 🥄 🥄 🥄 ———

BREAD BASKET. Clockwise from upper left: Luscious Lemon Muffins (p. 118); Delicious Pumpkin Bread (p. 111); Apple Pull-Apart Bread (p. 113); French Toast Fingers, Hearty French Toast and Coconut French Toast (pp. 114 and 115).

brown. Remove from pan and cool on a wire rack for 10 minutes. Serve warm. **Yield:** 1 dozen. **Nutritional Analysis:** One roll equals 143 calories, 200 mg sodium, 4 mg cholesterol, 26 gm carbohydrate, 4 gm protein, 2 gm fat. **Diabetic Exchange:** 2 starch.

Basic Banana Muffins

As a snack or with a meal, these moist muffins go over great with the kids. The muffins fill them up and get them to eat nutritious bananas at the same time.
—Lorna Greene, Harrington, Maine

      1-1/2 cups all-purpose flour
          1 cup sugar
          1 teaspoon baking soda
        1/2 teaspoon salt
          3 medium ripe bananas
          1 egg
        1/3 cup vegetable oil
          1 teaspoon vanilla extract

In a large bowl, combine dry ingredients. In another bowl, mash the bananas; add egg, oil and vanilla. Mix well. Stir into the dry ingredients just until moistened. Fill greased or paper-lined muffin cups half full. Bake at 375° for 18-22 minutes or until muffins test done. Cool for 10 minutes; remove from pan to a wire rack to cool completely. **Yield:** 1 dozen.

Tasty White Bread

It's worth the time making this bread just to fill the house with its heavenly scent as it bakes. But eating a thick slice is even better!
—Angel Olvey
Kokomo, Indiana

✓ Nutritional Analysis included

          1 package (1/4 ounce) active dry yeast
          3 teaspoons sugar, *divided*
      2-1/4 cups warm water (110° to 115°), *divided*
          2 teaspoons salt
          6 to 6-1/2 cups all-purpose flour

In a mixing bowl, dissolve yeast and 1 teaspoon sugar in 1/4 cup water; let stand for 10 minutes. Combine salt and remaining sugar and water; add to yeast mixture. Add 3 cups of flour; beat until smooth. Add enough remaining flour to form a soft dough. Turn onto a floured surface; knead until smooth and elastic, about 6-8 minutes. Place in a greased bowl, turning once to grease top. Cover and let rise in a warm place until doubled, about 1 hour.

Cucumber Pan Rolls

(Pictured above)

When I have plenty of fresh cucumbers from my garden, I make these delicately flavored rolls often.
—Dorothy Showalter, Broadway, Virginia

✓ Nutritional Analysis included

          1 large cucumber, peeled and diced
        1/2 cup sour cream
        1/4 cup water
          1 tablespoon sugar
          1 teaspoon salt
      3-3/4 to 4-1/4 cups all-purpose flour
          1 package (1/4 ounce) active dry yeast
          2 tablespoons minced fresh *or* dried chives
          2 teaspoons minced fresh dill *or* 3/4
              teaspoon dill weed

Place cucumber in a blender or food processor; cover and process until smooth. Place 3/4 cup of puree in a saucepan (discard remaining puree or save for another use). Add sour cream, water, sugar and salt to saucepan; heat to 120°-130° (mixture will appear separated). In a mixing bowl, combine 1-1/4 cups flour, yeast, chives and dill; add the cucumber mixture. Beat on low speed just until moistened; beat on high for 3 minutes. Add enough remaining flour to form a stiff dough. Turn onto a floured surface; knead until smooth and elastic, about 6-8 minutes. Place in a greased bowl, turning once to grease top. Cover and let rise in a warm place until doubled, about 1 hour. Punch dough down; let rest 10 minutes. Shape into 12 balls; place in a greased 13-in. x 9-in. x 2-in. baking pan. Cover and let rise until doubled, about 45 minutes. Bake at 375° for 30-35 minutes or until golden

Punch dough down; divide in half. Shape into two loaves; place in 8-in. x 4-in. x 2-in. loaf pans that have been coated with nonstick cooking spray. Cover and let rise until doubled, about 1 hour. Bake at 350° for 35-40 minutes. Remove from pans to cool on wire racks. **Yield:** 2 loaves (32 slices). **Nutritional Analysis:** One slice equals 87 calories, 146 mg sodium, 0 cholesterol, 18 gm carbohydrate, 3 gm protein, trace fat. **Diabetic Exchange:** 1 starch.

☞ ☞ ☞

Multi-Grain English Muffin Bread

There's no need to knead the dough, which bakes into a hearty bread with the texture of English muffins. Good-for-you bread never tasted so delicious!
—Carol Forcum, Marion, Illinois

☑ Nutritional Analysis included

   1 package (1/4 ounce) active dry yeast
1-1/4 cups warm water (110° to 115°)
   1/3 cup whole wheat flour
   1/3 cup quick-cooking oats
   1/3 cup wheat germ
   1 tablespoon sugar
   3/4 teaspoon salt
   2 cups all-purpose flour
   1/4 cup cornmeal

In a mixing bowl, dissolve yeast in water. Add whole wheat flour, oats, wheat germ, sugar, salt and 1-1/4 cups of all-purpose flour; beat until smooth. Add enough remaining all-purpose flour to form a soft dough. Place in a greased bowl, turning once to grease top. Cover and let rise in a warm place until doubled, about 1 hour. Punch dough down (do not knead). Shape into a loaf. Coat a 9-in. x 5-in. x 3-in. loaf pan with nonstick cooking spray and sprinkle with half of the cornmeal. Place loaf in pan; sprinkle with remaining cornmeal. Cover and let rise until doubled, about 30 minutes. Bake at 400° for 30 minutes or until golden brown. Remove from pan and cool on a wire rack. **Yield:** 1 loaf (16 slices). **Nutritional Analysis:** One slice equals 93 calories, 110 mg sodium, 0 cholesterol, 19 gm carbohydrate, 3 gm protein, 1 gm fat. **Diabetic Exchange:** 1 starch.

Time-Saving Trick

To grease plastic wrap for covering yeast dough as it rises, simply press the wrap into the prepared loaf pan or empty greased bowl, then peel off and place greased side down over the dough.

Delicious Pumpkin Bread

(Pictured below)

An enticing aroma wafts through my house when this tender cake-like bread is in the oven. I bake extra loaves to give as holiday gifts. My friends wait eagerly for it every year.   *—Linda Burnett, Stanton, California*

   5 eggs
1-1/4 cups vegetable oil
   1 can (15 ounces) solid-pack pumpkin
   2 cups all-purpose flour
   2 cups sugar
   2 packages (3 ounces *each*) cook-and-serve vanilla pudding mix
   1 teaspoon baking soda
   1 teaspoon ground cinnamon
1/2 teaspoon salt

In a mixing bowl, beat the eggs. Add oil and pumpkin; beat until smooth. Combine remaining ingredients; gradually beat into pumpkin mixture. Pour batter into five greased 5-in. x 2-1/2-in. x 2-in. loaf pans. Bake at 325° for 50-55 minutes or until a toothpick inserted near the center comes out clean. Cool for 10 minutes; remove from pans to wire racks to cool completely. **Yield:** 5 miniature loaves. **Editor's Note:** Bread may also be baked in two greased 8-in. x 4-in. x 2-in. loaf pans for 75-80 minutes.

Handy Sausage Biscuits

(Pictured below)

These are similar to old-fashioned biscuits made from scratch, but even better thanks to the addition of tasty browned sausage. I like to serve these savory biscuits with an egg dish or with soup. —Nancy Parker
Seguin, Texas

    3/4 pound bulk pork sausage
2-2/3 cups all-purpose flour
    2 tablespoons sugar
1-1/2 teaspoons baking powder
    1/2 teaspoon baking soda
    1/2 teaspoon salt
    1/2 cup shortening
    1 package (1/4 ounce) active dry yeast
    1/4 cup warm water (110° to 115°)
    1 cup buttermilk
Melted butter *or* margarine

In a skillet, brown sausage; drain well and set aside. In a bowl, combine flour, sugar, baking powder, baking soda and salt; cut in the shortening until crumbly. Stir in sausage. In another bowl, dissolve yeast in water; let stand for 5 minutes. Add buttermilk. Stir into dry ingredients just until moistened. On a lightly floured surface, gently knead dough 6-8 times. Roll out to 1/2-in. thickness; cut with a 2-in. biscuit cutter. Place on lightly greased baking sheets. Brush tops with butter. Bake at 450° for 10-12 minutes or until golden brown. Serve warm. **Yield:** 2-3 dozen. **Editor's Note:** No rising time is necessary before baking these biscuits. The dough can be rerolled.

Refrigerator Rolls

I use this dough as a substitute in recipes that call for frozen bread dough. I like to make things from scratch, including rolls. —Nick Welty, Smithville, Ohio

    2 packages (1/4 ounce *each*) active dry yeast
1-3/4 cups warm water (110° to 115°)
    2 eggs
    1/2 cup sugar
    1/4 cup butter *or* margarine, softened
    1 teaspoon salt
    6 cups all-purpose flour

In a mixing bowl, dissolve yeast in water. Add eggs, sugar, butter, salt and 3 cups of flour; beat until smooth. Add enough remaining flour to form a soft dough. Turn onto a floured surface and knead until smooth and elastic, about 6-8 minutes. Place in a greased bowl, turning once to grease top. Cover and refrigerate for 2 hours or up to 2 days. Punch dough down and divide in half; shape each portion into 12 rolls. Place in two greased 9-in. round baking pans. Cover and let rise until nearly doubled, about 30 minutes. Bake at 350° for 20 minutes or until golden brown. **Yield:** 2 dozen.

Braided Date Coffee Cake

At Christmas, I decorate these braids with candies cherries and pecans. No one can eat just one slice of this festive bread. —Muriel Lerdal, Humboldt, Iowa

    2 packages (1/4 ounce *each*) active dry yeast
    1/2 cup warm water (110° to 115°)
    1/2 cup sugar
    1/2 cup warm milk (110° to 115°)
    1/4 cup vegetable oil
1-1/2 teaspoons salt
    2 eggs
    4 to 4-1/2 cups all-purpose flour
FILLING:
    1 cup chopped dates
    2/3 cup water
    1/2 cup chopped pecans
    1/4 cup sugar
    1 teaspoon lemon juice
    1/2 cup apricot preserves
ICING:
1-1/2 cups confectioners' sugar
    3 tablespoons butter *or* margarine, softened
    2 tablespoons boiling water
    1/2 teaspoon vanilla extract
Candied cherries, optional

In a mixing bowl, dissolve the yeast in water; let stand for 5 minutes. Add sugar, milk, oil, salt, eggs and 2 cups flour; beat on low for 3 minutes. Stir in enough remaining flour to form a soft dough. Turn onto a floured surface; knead until smooth and elastic, 6-8 minutes. Place in a greased bowl; turn once to grease top. Cover and let rise in a warm place until doubled, about 1 hour. Combine the first five filling ingredients in a saucepan. Cook and stir over medium heat until thickened, 7-8 minutes; remove from the heat. Stir in preserves; cool. Punch dough down; divide into thirds. On a floured surface, roll each portion into a 15-in. x 6-in. rectangle. Place on a greased baking sheet. Spread a third of filling down center third of each rectangle. On each long side, cut 1-1/2-in.-wide strips 1-3/4 in. into center or to the filling. Starting at one end, fold alternating strips at an angle across filling. Cover and let rise for 30 minutes or until doubled. Bake at 375° for 15-20 minutes or until browned. Cool on wire racks. Combine the first four icing ingredients; drizzle over braids. Decorate with cherries if desired. **Yield:** 3 loaves.

Apple Pull-Apart Bread

(Pictured at right)

For a fun sweet treat that's sure to satisfy, try this recipe. Drizzled with icing, each finger-licking "piece" has a yummy surprise filling of apples and pecans. It's well worth the bit of extra effort.
—*Carolyn Gregory, Hendersonville, Tennessee*

   1 **package (1/4 ounce) active dry yeast**
   1 **cup warm milk (110° to 115°)**
1/2 **cup butter *or* margarine, melted, *divided***
   1 **egg**
2/3 **cup plus 2 tablespoons sugar, *divided***
   1 **teaspoon salt**
   3 **to 3-1/2 cups all-purpose flour**
   1 **medium tart apple, peeled and chopped**
1/2 **cup finely chopped pecans**
1/2 **teaspoon ground cinnamon**
ICING:
   1 **cup confectioners' sugar**
   3 **to 4-1/2 teaspoons hot water**
1/2 **teaspoon vanilla extract**

In a mixing bowl, dissolve yeast in milk. Add 2 tablespoons butter, egg, 2 tablespoons sugar, salt and 3 cups of flour; beat until smooth. Add enough remaining flour to form a stiff dough. Turn onto a floured surface; knead until smooth and elastic, about 6-8 minutes. Place in a greased bowl, turning once to grease top. Cover and let rise in a warm place until doubled, about 1 hour. Meanwhile, combine apple, pecans, cinnamon and remaining sugar; set aside. Punch dough down and divide in half. Cut each half into 16 pieces. On a lightly floured surface, pat or roll out each piece into a 2-1/2-in. circle. Place 1 teaspoon apple mixture in center of circle; pinch edges together and seal, forming a ball. Dip in remaining butter. In a greased 10-in. tube pan, place 16 balls, seam side down; sprinkle with 1/4 cup apple mixture. Layer with remaining balls; sprinkle evenly with remaining apple mixture. Cover and let rise until nearly doubled, about 45 minutes. Bake at 350° for 35-40 minutes or until golden brown. Cool for 10 minutes; remove from pan to a wire rack. Combine icing ingredients; drizzle over bread. **Yield:** 1 loaf.

Quicker Quick Breads

If you like to prepare quick breads often, save time by premeasuring several batches of dry ingredients and storing in small containers. When you want to make a loaf, just grab a premeasured mix and add the remaining ingredients.

Feast on French Toast

VARIATIONS on this popular breakfast and brunch choice carry French toast to new heights! Here's how some creative cooks fix it:

Hearty French Toast
(Pictured below)

Since you make it ahead, this dish is wonderful for brunch. The slightly tart sauce pairs nicely with ham, turkey and cheese. —Page Alexander
Baldwin City, Kansas

24 slices day-old French bread (3/4 inch thick)
12 thin slices fully cooked ham
12 thin slices cooked turkey
 1 to 2 medium tart apples, peeled and thinly sliced
12 thin slices provolone *or* mozzarella cheese
 4 eggs
 1 cup milk
1/4 teaspoon ground nutmeg
APPLE CRANBERRY SAUCE:
1-1/2 cups cranberry juice

WAKE UP to the mmm-mouth-watering flavors of Coconut French Toast, French Toast Fingers and Hearty French Toast (shown above, clockwise from top left).

2 tablespoons cornstarch
1 tablespoon brown sugar
1 teaspoon grated orange peel
1/8 teaspoon ground cinnamon
1 medium tart apple, peeled and finely
   chopped

Place half of the bread in a greased 13-in. x 9-in. x 2-in. baking dish; top each with a slice of ham, turkey, two to three apple slices and a piece of cheese (cut or fold meat and cheese to fit). Top with remaining bread. In a bowl, beat eggs, milk and nutmeg; pour over bread. Cover and refrigerate 6 hours or overnight. Remove from the refrigerator 30 minutes before baking. Bake, uncovered, at 350° for 30 minutes or until a knife inserted near the center comes out clean. Let stand for 10 minutes. Meanwhile, in a saucepan, combine the first five sauce ingredients; cook and stir over medium heat until thickened. Cook and stir 2 minutes longer. Stir in apple. Serve warm over French toast. **Yield:** 12 servings.

Coconut French Toast

(Pictured at left)

Coated with coconut, these special slices are sure to please your family. —*Charlotte Baillargeon*
Hinsdale, Massachusetts

12 eggs
1-1/4 cups milk
  2 teaspoons sugar
  1 teaspoon ground cinnamon
14 slices day-old bread
  1 package (7 ounces) flaked coconut
Maple syrup

In a large bowl, beat eggs; add milk, sugar and cinnamon. Add bread, a few slices at a time; let soak for 1 minute on each side. Coat both sides with coconut. Place on greased baking sheets. Bake at 475° for 5 minutes on each side or until golden brown and cooked through. Serve with syrup. **Yield:** 7 servings.

French Toast Fingers

(Pictured at left)

Bite-size French toast "fingers" are great for a buffet...and kids of all ages love them. —*Mavis Diment*
Marcus, Iowa

 Nutritional Analysis included

2 eggs

1/4 cup milk
1/4 teaspoon salt
1/2 cup strawberry preserves
  8 slices day-old white bread
Confectioners' sugar, optional

In a small bowl, beat eggs, milk and salt; set aside. Spread preserves on four slices of bread; top with remaining bread. Trim crusts; cut each sandwich into three strips. Dip both sides in egg mixture. Cook on a lightly greased hot griddle for 2 minutes on each side or until golden brown. Dust with confectioners' sugar if desired. **Yield:** 4 servings. **Nutritional Analysis:** One serving of three strips (prepared with egg substitute, skim milk and sugar-free preserves and without confectioners' sugar) equals 235 calories, 500 mg sodium, 2 mg cholesterol, 42 gm carbohydrate, 10 gm protein, 4 gm fat. **Diabetic Exchanges:** 2 starch, 1 meat, 1/2 fruit.

Cherry Strata

Whenever I present this dressed-up French toast at a party I'm catering, it always gets rave reviews.
—*Carrie Sherrill, Forestville, Wisconsin*

12 cups day-old Italian bread cubes
    (1/2-inch cubes)
  1 package (8 ounces) cream cheese,
    softened
1/2 cup sugar, *divided*
1/2 teaspoon almond extract
1/2 cup dried cherries *or* cranberries
1/2 cup chopped pecans
  4 eggs
1-1/2 cups half-and-half cream
  1 teaspoon ground cinnamon
CHERRY SYRUP:
  1 can (14-1/2 ounces) sour cherries,
    chopped
  1 cup sugar
  1 cup corn syrup
1/2 teaspoon almond extract

Place 8 cups of the bread cubes in a greased 13-in. x 9-in. x 2-in. baking pan. In a mixing bowl, beat cream cheese, 1/4 cup of sugar and extract until smooth. Stir in cherries and pecans; spoon over bread. Top with remaining bread cubes. In a bowl, whisk eggs, cream, cinnamon and remaining sugar; pour over bread. Bake, uncovered, at 350° for 35-40 minutes or until browned. Let stand 5 minutes before serving. For syrup, combine cherries, sugar and corn syrup in a saucepan; bring to a boil. Reduce heat; simmer for 15 minutes. Remove from the heat; stir in extract. Serve warm over strata. **Yield:** 6-8 servings.

a floured surface; knead 4-6 minutes. Place in a greased bowl, turning once to grease top. Cover and let rise in a warm place until doubled, about 1 hour. Beat filling ingredients until smooth. Punch dough down. Roll into an 18-in. x 12-in. rectangle. Spread filling over dough to within 1 in. of edges. Starting at the long end, roll up tightly and seal edges. Place on a greased baking sheet, sealing ends to form a ring. Cover and let rise until doubled, about 30 minutes. Bake at 375° for 20-25 minutes or until golden. Remove to a wire rack. Combine milk and extract; whisk in sugar until smooth. Drizzle over coffee cake. Sprinkle with almonds if desired. **Yield:** 8-10 servings.

Clover Honey

This recipe comes from my mother-in-law, Myrtress Harrington, who enjoyed the pretty golden spread over pancakes, French toast and breakfast cereal when she was a girl.   —Heidi Harrington, Steuben, Maine

> 60 **fresh white clover blossoms**
> 40 **fresh red clover blossoms**
> 3 **tablespoons wild rose petals**
> 5 **pounds sugar**
> 3 **cups water**
> 1 **teaspoon powdered alum**

Wash clover and rose petals thoroughly in cool running water; drain well. Pat dry. Place in a large metal bowl; set aside. In a large heavy saucepan, bring sugar, water and alum to a boil, stirring constantly. Boil without stirring until a candy thermometer reads 220°; remove from the heat. Pour over clover and rose petals; let stand for 45 minutes. Pour through a double thickness of cheesecloth; discard clover and rose petals. Pour honey into jars; store in the refrigerator. **Yield:** 4-1/2 pints. **Editor's Note:** Make sure the clover and wild roses you use have not been chemically treated.

Yogurt Biscuits

Scoring the dough instead of cutting out individual pieces keeps these biscuits nice and moist. They have old-fashioned flavor that's very satisfying. They're most delicious served fresh from the oven.
—Rosemarie Kondrk, Old Bridge, New Jersey

☑ Nutritional Analysis included

> 1 **cup plus 2 tablespoons all-purpose flour**
> 1-1/2 **teaspoons baking powder**

Almond Ring Coffee Cake

(Pictured above)

*At our farm, we sometimes host tours of visitors to New England. I serve this special yeast bread to our guests first thing in the morning with coffee. It's also a regular on our family's Christmas menu.   —Vie Spence
Woburn, Massachusetts*

> 3-1/2 **to 3-3/4 cups all-purpose flour,** *divided*
> 1 **package (1/4 ounce) active dry yeast**
> 1 **cup milk**
> 1/3 **cup butter** *or* **margarine**
> 1/3 **cup sugar**
> 1/2 **teaspoon salt**
> 1 **egg**
> **FILLING:**
> 1/4 **cup butter** *or* **margarine, softened**
> 1/2 **cup sugar**
> 1/2 **teaspoon almond extract**
> **GLAZE:**
> 2 **to 3 tablespoons milk**
> 1 **teaspoon almond extract**
> 1-3/4 **cups confectioners' sugar**
> **Sliced almonds, toasted, optional**

In a mixing bowl, combine 2 cups flour and yeast. In a saucepan over low heat, bring milk, butter, sugar and salt to 120°-130°; stir into flour mixture. Add egg; beat for 3 minutes. Stir in enough remaining flour to form a soft dough. Turn onto

1/2 teaspoon salt
1/4 teaspoon baking soda
   2 tablespoons cold butter *or* margarine
1/2 cup plain yogurt
   1 teaspoon sugar
1/2 teaspoon milk

In a bowl, combine flour, baking powder, salt and baking soda; cut in butter until crumbly. Combine yogurt and sugar; stir into dry ingredients just until moistened. Turn onto a floured surface; knead 4-5 times. Place on a greased baking sheet; pat into a 6-in. x 4-in. rectangle. Cut into six square biscuits (do not separate biscuits). Brush tops with milk. Bake at 450° for 12-15 minutes or until golden. Serve warm. **Yield:** 6 biscuits. **Nutritional Analysis:** One biscuit (prepared with margarine, nonfat yogurt and skim milk) equals 134 calories, 429 mg sodium, trace cholesterol, 21 gm carbohydrate, 4 gm protein, 4 gm fat. **Diabetic Exchanges:** 1-1/2 starch, 1 fat.

Date Waffles

Instead of using traditional maple syrup, these moist waffles have a yummy cream cheese topping that appeals to all palates. —*Jean Gaines*
Bullhead City, Arizona

   2 cups all-purpose flour
1/4 cup packed brown sugar
1/4 cup finely chopped pecans
   1 tablespoon baking powder
   1 teaspoon salt
   1 cup finely chopped dates
1-3/4 cups milk
   2 eggs, *separated*
1/2 cup butter *or* margarine, melted
TOPPING:
   1 package (8 ounces) cream cheese, softened
1/4 cup half-and-half cream
   3 tablespoons sugar
   2 tablespoons orange juice
   1 tablespoon grated orange peel

In a mixing bowl, combine flour, brown sugar, pecans, baking powder and salt. Add dates. Combine milk, egg yolks and butter; stir into dry ingredients and mix well. In another mixing bowl, beat egg whites until stiff peaks form; fold into batter. Bake in a preheated waffle iron according to manufacturer's directions until golden brown. Combine topping ingredients in a mixing bowl; beat until smooth. Serve with waffles. **Yield:** 8-10 waffles (about 6-3/4 inches).

Cinnamon Rhubarb Muffins

(Pictured below)

When I was young, a good cook originally from Poland recommended this recipe to me. The tangy rhubarb center makes these fluffy muffins extra scrumptious and perfect for breakfast or snacking.
—*Barbara Perry, Saginaw, Michigan*

1-1/2 cups all-purpose flour
   1/2 cup plus 1 tablespoon sugar, *divided*
      2 teaspoons baking powder
1-1/4 teaspoons ground cinnamon, *divided*
   1/4 teaspoon salt
      1 egg, beaten
   2/3 cup buttermilk
   1/4 cup butter *or* margarine, melted
   1/2 cup chopped fresh *or* frozen rhubarb, thawed and drained
   1/4 cup peach preserves

In a bowl, combine flour, 1/2 cup sugar, baking powder, 1 teaspoon cinnamon and salt. Combine egg, buttermilk and butter; stir into dry ingredients just until moistened. Spoon 1 tablespoonful of batter into nine greased or paper-lined muffin cups. Combine rhubarb and preserves; place 1 tablespoonful in the center of each cup (do not spread). Top with remaining batter. Combine remaining sugar and cinnamon; sprinkle over batter. Bake at 400° for 20 minutes or until top of muffin springs back when lightly touched in the center. **Yield:** 9 muffins.

Luscious Lemon Muffins

(Pictured below)

I've had this recipe since my college days, when it was served in one of my foods classes. These tempting, light lemony muffins go well at a luncheon with chicken salad. Even our two middle-school-aged children love to munch on them.
—Mary-Lynne Mason
Janesville, Wisconsin

    1/2 cup butter *or* margarine, softened
    1/2 cup sugar
      2 eggs, *separated*
      1 cup all-purpose flour
      1 teaspoon baking powder
    1/4 teaspoon salt
      3 tablespoons lemon juice
      1 tablespoon grated lemon peel
Cinnamon-sugar

In a mixing bowl, cream the butter and sugar. Add egg yolks; mix well. Combine flour, baking powder and salt; add alternately with lemon juice to the creamed mixture. Beat egg whites until stiff peaks form; fold into batter with lemon peel. Fill greased or paper-lined muffin cups two-thirds full. Sprinkle with cinnamon-sugar. Bake at 350° for 20-25 minutes or until light golden brown and a toothpick inserted in the center comes out clean. **Yield:** 9 muffins.

No-Knead Tarragon Rolls

These golden brown rolls only look like a lot of trouble to make. But because no kneading is required, they're quite simple. Why not prepare them for your family soon and see for yourself?
—Polly Miller
Himrod, New York

☑ Nutritional Analysis included

2-3/4 cups all-purpose flour, *divided*
      1 package (1/4 ounce) active dry yeast
      2 tablespoons sugar
      1 tablespoon dried parsley flakes
      1 tablespoon minced fresh tarragon *or*
        1 teaspoon dried tarragon
    1/2 teaspoon celery seed
    1/2 teaspoon salt
      1 cup warm water (120° to 130°)
      1 egg
      2 tablespoons vegetable oil

In a mixing bowl, combine 1-1/2 cups of flour, yeast, sugar, parsley, tarragon, celery seed and salt. Add water, egg and oil; beat on low speed for 30 seconds, scraping the bowl occasionally. Beat on high for 1 minute. Stir in remaining flour. Do not knead. Cover and let rise in a warm place until doubled, about 30 minutes. Stir dough and spoon into greased muffin cups. Cover and let rise in a warm place until doubled, about 20-30 minutes. Bake at 375° for 15-18 minutes or until golden brown. Cool on wire racks. **Yield:** 1 dozen. **Nutritional Analysis:** One roll equals 141 calories, 104 mg sodium, 18 mg cholesterol, 24 gm carbohydrate, 4 gm protein, 3 gm fat. **Diabetic Exchanges:** 1-1/2 starch, 1/2 fat.

Stuffed French Toast with Berry Sauce

As the oldest of seven children growing up on a farm, if I wasn't milking the cows, I was making the meals. My love for cooking has continued throughout the years.
—Mary Kay Morris, Cokato, Minnesota

FILLING:
      1 package (8 ounces) cream cheese, softened
      1 tablespoon sugar
      1 teaspoon grated orange peel
    1/4 teaspoon ground cinnamon
FRENCH TOAST:
      2 eggs, lightly beaten
    1/4 cup milk
      1 teaspoon vanilla extract
      8 slices French bread (1 inch thick)

SYRUP:
  1/2 cup water
  1/4 cup maple syrup
    2 tablespoons sugar
    1 tablespoon cornstarch
1-1/2 cups frozen blueberries

In a mixing bowl, beat cream cheese, sugar, orange peel and cinnamon until smooth; set aside. In a shallow bowl, combine eggs, milk and vanilla. Cut a pocket in the crust of each slice of bread. Stuff each pocket with 1-2 tablespoons filling. Dip both sides of bread in egg mixture. Fry on a greased hot griddle for 3-4 minutes on each side or until golden brown. For syrup, combine water, maple syrup, sugar and cornstarch in a saucepan. Bring to a boil; boil for 2 minutes or until thickened. Reduce heat; add blueberries. Simmer for 5-7 minutes or until berries are tender. Serve over French toast. **Yield:** 4-6 servings (1-1/2 cups syrup).

Carrot Zucchini Bread

When my husband became diabetic, many of the treats he enjoyed were off-limits. This moist, flavorful bread satisfies his sweet tooth...and I like it, too.
—Edna Bright, Paris, Illinois

✓ Nutritional Analysis included

    1 cup unsweetened applesauce
  3/4 cup shredded carrots
  3/4 cup shredded peeled zucchini
  1/2 cup sugar
    2 eggs *or* 1/2 cup egg substitute
1-1/2 teaspoons pumpkin pie spice
    1 teaspoon ground cinnamon
  1/2 teaspoon ground nutmeg
    3 cups all-purpose flour
    1 tablespoon baking powder
  1/2 teaspoon baking soda
  1/2 teaspoon salt
  3/4 cup orange juice

In a bowl, combine the first eight ingredients. Combine flour, baking powder, baking soda and salt; add alternately with orange juice to carrot mixture. Pour into two greased and floured 8-in. x 4-in. x 2-in. loaf pans. Bake at 350° for 45 minutes or until bread tests done. Cool for 10 minutes; remove from pans to a wire rack to cool completely. **Yield:** 2 loaves (16 slices each). **Nutritional Analysis:** One slice (prepared with egg substitute) equals 68 calories, 110 mg sodium, trace cholesterol, 15 gm carbohydrate, 2 gm protein, trace fat. **Diabetic Exchange:** 1 starch.

'I Wish I Had That Recipe...'

ONE TASTE of the Mormon Muffins at The Greenery Restaurant near Ogden, Utah convinced Dolores O'Keefe of Lake Charles, Louisiana she'd like the recipe as a "souvenir" of her visit.

"While on a winter trip to Utah, I was treated to lunch at The Greenery by my daughter-in-law Brenda," Dolores recollects. "The muffins were so moist and tasty I ended up eating two!"

Russel King, a partner in the family-owned eatery, was delighted to share the recipe, re-created from memories of wonderful bran muffins his great-grandmother used to make. "They've been a specialty here since 1976," he reports. "We serve about 300 a day and also sell them to go."

Located at 1875 Valley Dr., The Greenery serves soups, sandwiches, salads and full meals 11 a.m. to 10 p.m. Monday through Thursday, 11 a.m. to 11 p.m. Friday and Saturday and 11 a.m. to 9 p.m. Sunday. 1-801/392-1777.

Mormon Muffins

    5 teaspoons baking soda
    2 cups boiling water
    1 cup shortening
    2 cups sugar
    4 eggs
    5 cups all-purpose flour
    1 teaspoon salt
    1 quart buttermilk
    4 cups All-Bran
    2 cups Bran Flakes
    1 cup chopped walnuts

In a bowl, stir baking soda in water until dissolved. Cool. In a mixing bowl, cream shortening and sugar. Add eggs, one at a time, beating well after each addition. Combine flour and salt; add to the creamed mixture alternately with buttermilk. Mix well. Beat in the baking soda mixture. Fold in cereals and nuts. Fill greased or paper-lined muffin cups three-fourths full. Bake at 350° for 25-30 minutes or until the muffins test done. **Yield:** about 5 dozen. **Editor's Note:** Muffin batter will keep in the refrigerator for 1 week.

Zucchini-Chocolate Chip Muffins

(Pictured above)

Whenever I make these muffins, I freeze several. As I'm leaving for work in the morning, I pull one out and enjoy it at the office with a cup of coffee.
—Janet Pierce, Westminster, Colorado

1-1/2 cups all-purpose flour
   3/4 cup sugar
      1 teaspoon baking soda
      1 teaspoon ground cinnamon
   1/2 teaspoon salt
      1 egg, lightly beaten
   1/2 cup vegetable oil
   1/4 cup milk
      1 tablespoon lemon juice
      1 teaspoon vanilla extract
      1 cup shredded zucchini
   1/4 cup semisweet miniature chocolate chips
   1/4 cup chopped walnuts

In a bowl, combine flour, sugar, baking soda, cinnamon and salt. Combine the egg, oil, milk, lemon juice and vanilla; mix well. Stir into dry ingredients just until moistened. Fold in zucchini, chocolate chips and walnuts. Fill greased or paper-lined muffin cups two-thirds full. Bake at 350° for 20-25 minutes or until the muffins test done. **Yield:** about 1 dozen.

Garden Herb Braid

This pretty golden round loaf is speckled with herbs. It's simply delicious and is so impressive to serve dinner guests!   —Deb Lipinski, Fremont, Nebraska

      4 to 4-1/2 cups all-purpose flour
      3 tablespoons sugar
      2 packages (1/4 ounce *each*) active dry yeast
1-1/2 teaspoons salt
1-1/2 teaspoons dried marjoram
   3/4 teaspoon dried thyme
   3/4 teaspoon dried rosemary, crushed
   3/4 cup milk
   1/2 cup water
   1/4 cup plus 1 tablespoon butter *or* margarine, *divided*
      1 egg, beaten
Additional dried marjoram, thyme and rosemary, optional

In a mixing bowl, combine 1-1/2 cups flour, sugar, yeast, salt, marjoram, thyme and rosemary. In a saucepan over low heat, heat milk, water and 1/4 cup butter to 120°-130°. Pour over the dry ingredients. Add egg and blend well. Beat on medium speed for 3 minutes. Add enough remaining flour to form a soft dough. Turn onto a floured surface and knead until smooth and elastic, about 6-8 minutes. Place in a greased bowl, turning once to grease top. Cover and let rise in a warm place until doubled, about 30 minutes. Punch dough down. Divide into three equal portions. Shape each into a 28-in. rope. Braid ropes; pinch ends to seal. Tie braid into a knot. Place on a greased baking sheet. Cover and let rise until doubled, about 30 minutes. Bake at 375° for 30-35 minutes or until golden brown; cover with foil during the last 15 minutes to prevent overbrowning. Melt remaining butter; brush over bread. Sprinkle with additional herbs if desired. Remove from pan and cool on a wire rack. **Yield:** 1 loaf.

Whole Wheat Herb Bread

When our kids were still at home, I'd make eight loaves of this bread at a time. Now that it's just my husband and me, I share with neighbors.
—Madeleine DeGruchy, Frankville, Nova Scotia

✓ Nutritional Analysis included

      1 package (1/4 ounce) active dry yeast
      2 cups warm water (110° to 115°)
      1 cup whole wheat flour
   1/4 cup sugar

4 teaspoons snipped fresh *or* dried chives
4 teaspoons snipped fresh dill *or* 1-1/2
    teaspoons dill weed
1-1/2 teaspoons shortening
1 teaspoon salt
4 to 4-1/2 cups all-purpose flour

In a mixing bowl, dissolve yeast in water. Add the whole wheat flour, sugar, chives, dill, shortening, salt and 1-1/2 cups all-purpose flour; beat until smooth. Add enough remaining all-purpose flour to form a soft dough. Turn onto a floured surface; knead until smooth and elastic, about 8-10 minutes. Place in a greased bowl, turning once to grease top. Cover and let rise in a warm place until doubled, about 1 hour. Punch dough down; divide in half. Shape into two loaves; place in 8-in. x 4-in. x 2-in. loaf pans that have been coated with nonstick cooking spray. Cover and let rise until doubled, about 40 minutes. Bake at 375° for 30-35 minutes or until golden brown. Remove from pans to cool on wire racks. **Yield:** 2 loaves (16 slices each). **Nutritional Analysis:** One slice equals 78 calories, 73 mg sodium, 0 cholesterol, 16 gm carbohydrate, 2 gm protein, trace fat. **Diabetic Exchange:** 1 starch.

Banana Crunch Muffins

I earned a blue ribbon when I submitted these good-for-you muffins in a competition at a local fair years ago. Even folks not on restricted diets enjoy them.
    —Chelsea Ferguson, Holdrege, Nebraska

✓ Nutritional Analysis included

3 cups all-purpose flour
1 cup packed brown sugar
1 tablespoon baking powder
1 teaspoon baking soda
1 teaspoon salt
1/4 teaspoon ground nutmeg
4 ripe bananas
3/4 cup egg substitute
1/3 cup vegetable oil
1 cup (8 ounces) low-fat strawberry yogurt
1-1/2 cups banana nut cereal, slightly crushed

In a large bowl, combine the flour, brown sugar, baking powder, baking soda, salt and nutmeg; set aside. In a small bowl, mash three bananas; stir in egg substitute, oil and yogurt. Coarsely chop the remaining banana; fold into yogurt mixture. Stir into dry ingredients just until moistened. Fill greased or paper-lined muffin cups one-third full. Spoon 1-1/2 teaspoons cereal on each. Top with remaining batter until the cups are three-fourths full. Sprin-

kle with remaining cereal. Bake at 375° for 15-18 minutes or until the muffins test done. **Yield:** 2 dozen. **Nutritional Analysis:** One muffin equals 161 calories, 244 mg sodium, 1 mg cholesterol, 27 gm carbohydrate, 3 gm protein, 4 gm fat.

Heart-Shaped Cheese Scones

(Pictured below)

When you set out a plate of these golden scones flecked with bits of cheddar cheese, everyone will know you've put your heart into your baking. They're a nice alternative to biscuits. —*Edna Hoffman, Hebron, Indiana*

2 cups all-purpose flour
2 tablespoons sugar
1 tablespoon baking powder
1 teaspoon salt
1/4 teaspoon baking soda
1-1/2 cups (6 ounces) shredded cheddar cheese
1 egg
1/2 cup sour cream
1/4 cup vegetable oil
3 tablespoons milk

In a large bowl, combine the flour, sugar, baking powder, salt and baking soda; stir in cheese. In another bowl, combine egg, sour cream, oil and milk; stir into dry ingredients just until moistened. Turn onto a floured surface and knead gently 10-12 times. Gently pat out to 1/3-in. thickness. Cut with a 3-in. heart-shaped cutter. Place on a greased baking sheet. Bake at 425° for 15-20 minutes or until golden brown. **Yield:** about 1 dozen.

Caraway Wheat Biscuits

My family can't eat just one of these fresh-from-the-oven biscuits. Onions make them moist and savory.
—*Nancy Messmore, Silver Lake Village, Ohio*

2-1/2 cups whole wheat flour
    2 tablespoons caraway seeds
    1 tablespoon baking powder
    1/8 teaspoon salt
1-1/3 cups grated onions (about 3 medium)
    2 eggs, beaten
    1/2 cup vegetable oil

In a large bowl, combine flour, caraway, baking powder and salt. Combine onions, eggs and oil; add to dry ingredients just until moistened. Turn onto a floured surface. Roll dough to 3/4-in. thickness; cut with a 2-in. biscuit cutter. Place on a greased baking sheet. Bake at 425° for 10-15 minutes or until golden brown. Serve hot. **Yield:** about 1 dozen.

———— 🧁 🧁 🧁 ————

Oatmeal Waffles

(Pictured below)

This recipe can be used to make pancakes as well as waffles. Both are delicious because of their hearty, whole-grain flavor. For a special treat, serve them topped with fruit. —*Mrs. Francis Stoops*
Stoneboro, Pennsylvania

    2 eggs
    2 cups buttermilk
    1 cup quick-cooking oats
    1 tablespoon molasses

    1 tablespoon vegetable oil
    1 cup whole wheat flour
    1/2 teaspoon salt
    1 teaspoon baking powder
    1 teaspoon baking soda
Milk, optional

In a large bowl, beat eggs and buttermilk. Add oats and mix well. Stir in molasses and oil. Combine flour, salt, baking powder and baking soda; stir into the egg mixture. If batter becomes too thick, thin with a little milk. Pour about 3/4 cup batter onto a greased preheated waffle maker. Bake according to manufacturer's directions. **To make pancakes:** Drop batter by 1/4 cupfuls onto a hot greased griddle. Turn when bubbles begin to form on top of pancake. **Yield:** 5 waffles (7 inches) or about 15 standard-size pancakes.

———— 🧁 🧁 🧁 ————

Holiday Ribbon Loaf

The trick to this gift bread is to wrap strips of aluminum foil around the dough before it's put into the oven. The foil creates a pattern in the bread during baking. Once the bread is cool, I remove the foil and replace it with holiday craft ribbon, then tie a bow—it's ready to go! —*Kay Ulmer, Roscoe, South Dakota*

    1 package (1/4 ounce) active dry yeast
    1/4 cup warm water (110° to 115°)
3-1/2 to 4 cups all-purpose flour, *divided*
    1/4 cup sugar
    1 teaspoon salt
    1/2 cup milk
    2 eggs, beaten
    3 tablespoons butter *or* margarine, *divided*
    1/2 cup raisins
    1 cup red *or* green candied cherries, halved, optional

Dissolve yeast in water; set aside. In a mixing bowl, combine 1 cup of flour, sugar and salt. Add milk, eggs, 2 tablespoons butter and yeast mixture. Beat on low speed until mixed; beat on medium for 3 minutes. Stir in the raisins, cherries if desired and enough of the remaining flour to form a soft dough. Turn onto a floured board; knead until smooth and elastic, about 6-8 minutes. Place in a greased

---

No-Fail Fluffy Pancakes

For very light and tender pancakes, separate the egg and beat the white until stiff. Stir the yolk and other liquid ingredients into the dry ingredients, then fold in the beaten egg white.

owl, turning once to grease top. Cover and let rise
a warm place until doubled, about 1-1/2 hours.
unch dough down; let rest 10 minutes. Shape in-
an 8-in. x 5-in. rectangle. Fold heavy-duty alum-
um foil into two strips, one 20 in. x 1-1/2 in.
d one 15 in. x 1-1/2 in. Grease strips; place on
greased baking sheet in the shape of a cross. Cen-
r dough over strips. Melt remaining butter and
rush over dough. Wrap foil strips loosely around
ough, overlapping edges 1 in. and securing with
paper clip. Cover and let rise until doubled, about
0 minutes. Bake at 350° for 35-40 minutes or
ntil golden brown. Cool on a wire rack. Remove
aper clips and foil strips. Replace foil with 1-1/2-
.-wide ribbon; tie ribbon into a bow. **Yield:** 1 loaf.

Violet Jam

*have several recipes that call for wild violet blossoms.
hildren especially like this jam on toast and bis-
uits.* —*Jeanne Conte, Columbus, Ohio*

-1/2 cups wild violet blossoms*
-1/2 cups water, *divided*
ice of 1 medium lime
-1/3 cups sugar
  1 package (1-3/4 ounces) powdered pectin

inse violet blossoms well and place in a blender.
dd 3/4 cup water and the lime juice; blend well.
radually add sugar, blending until a smooth paste
formed. In a saucepan, combine the pectin and
emaining water; bring to a boil and boil for 1
inute. Add to blender and blend for 1 minute.
Quickly pour into prepared jars or glasses and seal.
Editor's Note: Be sure to use the common wild
urple violet, not the African violet (often grown as
houseplant).

Chili Corn Muffins

(Pictured above right)

*ot corn bread was one of my childhood favorites.
his muffin version with a Southwest flavor that I de-
ised is now my and my husband's favorite.*
  —*Sarah Hovley, Santa Cruz, California*

-1/2 cups all-purpose flour
  1 cup yellow cornmeal
1/4 cup sugar
  5 teaspoons baking powder
-1/2 teaspoons salt
  1 teaspoon chili powder
  2 eggs
-1/2 cups milk

2/3 cup vegetable oil
1/2 cup finely chopped onion
  1 can (4 ounces) chopped green chilies,
    drained

In a large bowl, combine flour, cornmeal, sugar,
baking powder, salt and chili powder. In a small
bowl, beat eggs; add milk, oil, onion and chilies.
Stir into dry ingredients just until moistened. Fill
greased or paper-lined muffin cups two-thirds full.
Bake at 400° for 20-25 minutes or until muffins test
done. **Yield:** about 1-1/2 dozen.

Bunny Biscuits

*When my granddaughter comes to visit, I reach into my
file of fun recipes to try when she arrives. We look
forward to spending time together creating special
foods like this.* —*Flo Burtnett, Gage, Oklahoma*

  1 tube (8 ounces) refrigerated biscuits
10 raisins
  5 red-hot candies *or* red candied cherries
20 slivered almonds
  1 tube pink decorator icing

Separate biscuits; place five of them on a greased
baking sheet about 2 in. apart. Cut remaining biscuits in half. Shape biscuit halves to form ears and
firmly attach to whole biscuits. On each biscuit,
press on two raisin eyes, one candy or cherry nose
and four slivered almond whiskers. Bake at 375°
for 8-10 minutes or until biscuits are browned.
Cool slightly; frost ears with icing. **Yield:** 5 biscuits.

Cookies & Bars

You'll make your family's day when you offer a cookie jar brimming with mouth-watering morsels or a pretty platter stacked with tempting bars and brownies!

SWEET TREATS. Clockwise from upper left: Toffee Almond Sandies (p. 127), Very Chocolate Brownies (p. 126), Lo-Cal Molasses Cookies (p. 131) and Peanut Butter Swirl Brownies (p. 137).

Very Chocolate Brownies

(Pictured on page 124)

I've spent years trying brownie recipes in search of the perfect one. This scrumptious version might be it. The fluffy top layer is absolutely heavenly.
—Arlene Kay Butler, Ogden, Utah

    4 squares (1 ounce *each*) unsweetened
        chocolate
  3/4 cup butter (no substitutes)
    2 cups sugar
    3 eggs
    1 teaspoon vanilla extract
    1 cup all-purpose flour
    1 cup coarsely chopped walnuts
TOPPING:
    1 cup (6 ounces) semisweet chocolate chips
  1/4 cup water
    2 tablespoons butter (no substitutes)
    1 cup whipping cream, whipped

In a microwave or double boiler, melt chocolate and butter; cool for 10 minutes. Add sugar; mix well. Stir in eggs and vanilla. Add flour; mix well. Stir in walnuts. Line a 13-in. x 9-in. x 2-in. baking pan with foil and grease the foil. Pour batter into pan. Bake at 350° for 25-30 minutes or until a toothpick inserted near the center comes out with moist crumbs (do not overbake). Cool completely. For topping, melt chocolate chips, water and butter in a microwave or double boiler; stir until smooth. Cool to room temperature. Fold in whipped cream. Spread over brownies. Chill before cutting. Store leftovers in the refrigerator. **Yield:** 3 dozen.

Cherry-Filled Heart Cookies

These crisp, flaky cookies are a wonderful way to show you care. They take a little effort, but the smiles of satisfaction make it worthwhile. —Audrey Groe
Lake Mills, Iowa

  1/2 cup butter *or* margarine, softened
  1/2 cup shortening
    1 cup sugar
    1 egg
  1/2 cup milk
    1 teaspoon vanilla extract
3-1/2 cups all-purpose flour
    2 teaspoons baking powder
    1 teaspoon baking soda
  1/2 teaspoon salt
FILLING:
  1/2 cup sugar
4-1/2 teaspoons cornstarch

Chocolate Meringue Stars

(Pictured above)

These light, delicate chewy cookies sure make for merry munching. Their big chocolate flavor makes it difficult to keep the kids away from them long enough to get any on the cookie tray. —Edna Lee
Greeley, Colorado

    3 egg whites
  3/4 teaspoon vanilla extract
  3/4 cup sugar
  1/4 cup baking cocoa
GLAZE:
    3 squares (1 ounce *each*) semisweet
        chocolate
    1 tablespoon shortening

In a mixing bowl, beat egg whites and vanilla until soft peaks form. Gradually add sugar, about 2 tablespoons at a time, beating until stiff peaks form. Gently fold in cocoa. Place in a pastry bag with a large open star tip (#8b). Line baking sheets with foil and coat the foil with nonstick cooking spray. Pipe stars, about 1-1/4-in. diameter, onto foil, or drop by rounded teaspoonfuls. Bake at 300° for 30-35 minutes or until lightly browned. Remove from foil; cool on wire racks. In a microwave or double boiler, melt chocolate and shortening; stir until smooth. Dip the cookies halfway into glaze; place on waxed paper to harden. **Yield:** about 4 dozen.

1/2 cup orange juice
1/4 cup red maraschino cherry juice
12 red maraschino cherries, chopped
1 tablespoon butter *or* margarine
Additional sugar

In a mixing bowl, cream the butter and shortening; gradually add sugar. Add egg, milk and vanilla. Combine dry ingredients; gradually add to the creamed mixture. Mix well. Cover and refrigerate for at least 2 hours. Meanwhile, for filling, combine sugar and cornstarch in a small saucepan. Add the juices, cherries and butter. Bring to a boil; boil and stir for 1 minute. Chill. Roll out dough on a lightly floured surface to 1/8-in. thickness; cut with a 2-1/2-in. heart-shaped cookie cutter dipped in flour. Place half of the cookies on greased baking sheets; spoon 1/2 teaspoon filling in the center of each. Use a 1-1/2-in. heart-shaped cutter to cut small hearts out of the other half of the cookies. (Bake small heart cutouts separately.) Place the remaining hearts over filled cookies; press edges together gently. Fill centers with additional filling if needed. Sprinkle with sugar. Bake at 375° for 8-10 minutes or until lightly browned. Cool on wire racks. **Yield:** about 4-1/2 dozen filled cookies.

Chocolate Peanut Bars

This homemade version of the popular Baby Ruth candy bar is unbeatable and appeals to kids of all ages. A pan of these rich, chocolaty bars goes a long way.
—*Carol Johnson, West Covina, California*

1-1/2 cups light corn syrup
1 cup sugar
1 cup packed brown sugar
1 cup peanut butter
7 cups cornflakes
1 can (12 ounces) salted peanuts
TOPPING:
2 cups (12 ounces) semisweet chocolate chips
3 tablespoons peanut butter
2 tablespoons shortening

In a 3-qt. saucepan, combine corn syrup and sugars. Bring to a boil over medium heat; boil and stir for 1 minute. Remove from the heat; add peanut butter and mix well. Stir in the cornflakes and peanuts. Press into a greased 15-in. x 10-in. x 1-in. baking pan. In a microwave or double boiler, melt chocolate chips, peanut butter and shortening; pour over bars and quickly spread evenly. Refrigerate for 2-3 hours or until set before cutting. **Yield:** 3 dozen.

Toffee Almond Sandies

(Pictured below)

Crisp and loaded with goodies, these are my husband's favorite cookies. I used to bake them in large batches when our four sons still lived at home. Now I whip them up for our grandchildren. —*Alice Kahnk Kennard, Nebraska*

1 cup butter (no substitutes), softened
1 cup sugar
1 cup confectioners' sugar
1 cup vegetable oil
2 eggs
1 teaspoon almond extract
3-1/2 cups all-purpose flour
1 cup whole wheat flour
1 teaspoon baking soda
1 teaspoon cream of tartar
1 teaspoon salt
2 cups chopped almonds
1 package (6 ounces) English toffee bits
Additional sugar

In a mixing bowl, cream butter and sugars. Add oil, eggs and extract; mix well. Combine flours, baking soda, cream of tartar and salt; gradually add to the creamed mixture. Stir in almonds and toffee bits. Shape into 1-in. balls; roll in sugar. Place on ungreased baking sheets; flatten with a fork. Bake at 350° for 12-14 minutes or until lightly browned. **Yield:** about 12 dozen.

Chocolate Dipped Brownies

(Pictured below)

My family calls these delicious bars "the world's chocolatiest brownies" and is more than happy to gobble up a batch whenever I make them.
—Jackie Archer, Clinton, Iowa

3/4 cup sugar
1/3 cup butter *or* margarine
2 tablespoons water
4 cups (24 ounces) semisweet chocolate chips, *divided*
1 teaspoon vanilla extract
2 eggs
3/4 cup all-purpose flour
1/2 teaspoon salt
1/4 teaspoon baking soda
2 tablespoons shortening
1/2 cup chopped pecans, toasted

In a saucepan over medium heat, bring the sugar, butter and water to a boil; remove from the heat. Stir in 1 cup of chocolate chips and vanilla; stir until smooth. Cool for 5 minutes. Beat in eggs, one at a time, until well mixed. Combine flour, salt and baking soda; stir into the chocolate mixture. Stir in another cup of chips. Pour into a greased 9-in. square baking pan. Bake at 325° for 35 minutes. Cool completely. Place in the freezer for 30-40 minutes (do not freeze completely). Cut into bars. In a microwave or double boiler, melt remaining chips with shortening; stir until smooth. Using a small fork, dip brownies to completely coat; shake off excess. Place on waxed paper-lined baking sheets; immediately sprinkle with pecans. Allow to harden. Store in an airtight container in a cool dry place. **Yield:** 3 dozen.

Peanut Butter Brownies

I've prepared lots of pies, cookies, bars and cakes to share at family gatherings and church potlucks. These chewy brownies are one of my favorite treats.
—Nick Welty, Smithville, Ohio

3/4 cup shortening
3/4 cup peanut butter
2-1/4 cups sugar
5 eggs
1-1/2 teaspoons vanilla extract
1-1/2 cups all-purpose flour
1-1/2 teaspoons baking powder
3/4 teaspoon salt
1-1/2 cups semisweet chocolate chips
3/4 cup chopped peanuts

In a mixing bowl, cream the shortening, peanut butter and sugar. Add eggs and vanilla; mix well. Combine flour, baking powder and salt; stir into the creamed mixture. Stir in the chocolate chips and peanuts. Spread into a greased 15-in. x 10-in. x 1-in. baking pan. Bake at 350° for 30 minutes or until golden brown. **Yield:** about 3 dozen.

Soft Molasses Jumbles

These old-fashioned cookies are given a new twist with raisins and chocolate chips. —Meg Adamson
Gaithersburg, Maryland

2/3 cup butter *or* margarine, softened
1/2 cup sugar
1 egg
2-1/2 cups all-purpose flour
1 teaspoon baking soda
1/2 teaspoon ground cinnamon
1/4 teaspoon salt
1/8 teaspoon ground ginger
1/2 cup molasses
1/2 cup buttermilk
1/2 cup raisins
1/2 cup semisweet chocolate chips

In a mixing bowl, cream butter and sugar. Add egg; mix well. Combine dry ingredients. Combine molasses and buttermilk; add to creamed mixture alternately with dry ingredients. Stir in the raisins and chocolate chips. Drop by tablespoonfuls 2 in. apart onto greased baking sheets. Bake at 350° for 10-12 minutes or until set. Cool for 2 minutes before removing to a wire rack. **Yield:** 4 dozen.

Chewy Maple Cookies

My husband, Bob, and I have a small sugaring operation with Bob's father. I love to put some of our syrup to use in these golden cookies.
—*Reba Legrand, Jericho, Vermont*

- 1/2 **cup shortening**
- 1 **cup packed brown sugar**
- 1 **egg**
- 1/2 **cup pure maple syrup**
- 1/2 **teaspoon vanilla extract** *or* **maple flavoring**
- 1-1/2 **cups all-purpose flour**
- 2 **teaspoons baking powder**
- 1/2 **teaspoon salt**
- 1 **cup flaked coconut**

In a mixing bowl, cream shortening and brown sugar until fluffy. Beat in the egg, syrup and vanilla until well mixed. Combine flour, baking powder and salt; add to the creamed mixture. Stir in coconut. Drop by tablespoonfuls 2 in. apart onto greased baking sheets. Bake at 375° for 12-15 minutes or until lightly browned. **Yield:** 3 dozen.

Rhubarb Custard Bars

(Pictured above right)

Once I tried these rich gooey bars, I just had to have the recipe so I could make them for my family and friends. The shortbread-like crust and rhubarb and custard layers inspire folks to fix a batch for themselves. —*Shari Roach, South Milwaukee, Wisconsin*

- 2 **cups all-purpose flour**
- 1/4 **cup sugar**
- 1 **cup cold butter** *or* **margarine**

FILLING:
- 2 **cups sugar**
- 7 **tablespoons all-purpose flour**
- 1 **cup whipping cream**
- 3 **eggs, beaten**
- 5 **cups finely chopped fresh** *or* **frozen rhubarb, thawed and drained**

TOPPING:
- 2 **packages (3 ounces** *each***) cream cheese, softened**
- 1/2 **cup sugar**
- 1/2 **teaspoon vanilla extract**
- 1 **cup whipping cream, whipped**

In a bowl, combine flour and sugar; cut in butter until the mixture resembles coarse crumbs. Press into a greased 13-in. x 9-in. x 2-in. baking pan. Bake at 350° for 10 minutes. Meanwhile, for filling, combine sugar and flour in a bowl. Whisk in cream and eggs. Stir in the rhubarb. Pour over crust. Bake at 350° for 40-45 minutes or until custard is set. Cool. For topping, beat cream cheese, sugar and vanilla until smooth; fold in whipped cream. Spread over top. Cover and chill. Cut into bars. Store in the refrigerator. **Yield:** 3 dozen.

Peanut Butter 'n' Jelly Cookies

This classic combination makes a great sandwich cookie. —*Margaret Wilson, Moreno Valley, California*

- 1/2 **cup shortening**
- 1/2 **cup peanut butter**
- 1/2 **cup sugar**
- 1/2 **cup packed brown sugar**
- 1 **egg**
- 1-1/4 **cups all-purpose flour**
- 3/4 **teaspoon baking soda**
- 1/2 **teaspoon baking powder**
- 1/4 **teaspoon salt**
Jam *or* **jelly**

In a mixing bowl, cream shortening, peanut butter and sugars. Beat in egg. Combine dry ingredients; gradually add to creamed mixture. Cover and chill for 1 hour. Roll into 1-in. balls; place 2 in. apart on greased baking sheets. Flatten slightly. Bake at 375° for 10 minutes or until golden brown. Cool on wire racks. Spread jam on the bottom of half of the cookies; top with remaining cookies. **Yield:** about 4-1/2 dozen.

Volcano Brownie Cups

(Pictured above)

I cherish recipes like this. It produces a chocolaty and elegant dessert without fuss or extra time but looks like I've been cooking all day. I enjoy entertaining, and with two young children, ages 6 and 4, this is what I use. —Kellie Durazo, Merced, California

> 1 cup butter (no substitutes), softened
> 1/2 cup sugar
> 3 eggs
> 3 egg yolks
> 1 teaspoon vanilla extract
> 2 cups (12 ounces) semisweet chocolate chips, melted
> 1 cup all-purpose flour
> 1/4 teaspoon salt
> 1 cup ground toasted pecans
> 6 squares (1 ounce *each*) white baking chocolate

Confectioners' sugar, optional

In a mixing bowl, cream butter and sugar. Add eggs, yolks and vanilla; mix well. Add melted chocolate. Combine flour and salt; add to creamed mixture. Stir in pecans. Spoon into six greased 10-oz. custard cups; place on a baking sheet. Bake at 350° for 10 minutes. Push one square of chocolate into the center of each brownie. Bake 18-20 minutes longer or until a toothpick inserted in the brownie comes out clean. Remove from the oven and let stand for 5 minutes. Run a knife around edge of custard cups; invert onto serving plates. Dust with confectioners' sugar if desired. Serve warm. **Yield:** 6

servings. **Editor's Note:** To reheat, return brownie to custard cup and bake at 350° for 10 minutes.

Pistachio Thumbprints

These mild pistachio-flavored cookies disappear in a wink around our house. —Liz Probelski
Port Washington, Wisconsin

> 1 cup butter *or* margarine, softened
> 1/3 cup confectioners' sugar
> 1 egg
> 1 teaspoon vanilla extract
> 3/4 teaspoon almond extract
> 2 cups all-purpose flour
> 1 package (3.4 ounces) instant pistachio pudding mix
> 1/2 cup miniature chocolate chips
> 2 cups finely chopped pecans

FILLING:
> 2 tablespoons butter *or* margarine, softened
> 2 cups confectioners' sugar
> 1 teaspoon vanilla extract
> 2 to 3 tablespoons milk

GLAZE (optional):
> 1/2 cup semisweet chocolate chips
> 2 teaspoons shortening

In a mixing bowl, cream butter and sugar until smooth. Add egg and extracts; mix well. Combine flour and pudding mix; add to the creamed mixture. Stir in the chocolate chips. Shape into 1-in. balls; roll in pecans. Place 2 in. apart on greased baking sheets; make a thumbprint in the center of each cookie. Bake at 350° for 10-12 minutes. Remove to a wire rack to cool. For filling, cream butter, sugar, vanilla and milk. Spoon into center of cooled cookies. For glaze, if desired, melt chocolate chips and shortening; drizzle over cookies. Let stand until set. **Yield:** about 7 dozen.

Pumpkin Cookie Dip

This creamy, delicious dip is fun for a snack or quick dessert and so easy to make! —Gloria Kirchman
Eden Prairie, Minnesota

> 1 package (8 ounces) cream cheese, softened
> 2 jars (7 ounces *each*) marshmallow creme
> 1 can (15 ounces) solid-pack pumpkin
> 1 teaspoon ground cinnamon
> 1 teaspoon grated orange peel

Gingersnaps *or* vanilla wafers

In a mixing bowl, beat cream cheese and marshmallow creme until smooth. Stir in pumpkin, cinnamon and orange peel. Serve as a dip with cookies. Store in the refrigerator. **Yield:** 4 cups.

Fudgy Brownies

No one will ever guess that these soft, chocolaty brownies are made with light ingredients like yogurt and egg whites. —Denise Baumert, Dalhart, Texas

✓ Nutritional Analysis included

    1 cup sugar
1/2 cup baking cocoa
    6 tablespoons nonfat plain *or* vanilla yogurt
    2 egg whites
    1 teaspoon vanilla extract
1/2 cup all-purpose flour
1/4 cup chopped walnuts
Confectioners' sugar

In a bowl, combine sugar, cocoa and yogurt. Add egg whites and vanilla; mix well. Stir in flour and walnuts. Pour into an 8-in. square baking pan that has been coated with nonstick cooking spray. Bake at 350° for 25-28 minutes or until a toothpick inserted near the center comes out clean. Dust with confectioners' sugar. **Yield:** 16 servings. **Nutritional Analysis:** One serving equals 87 calories, 12 mg sodium, trace cholesterol, 18 gm carbohydrate, 2 gm protein, 2 gm fat. **Diabetic Exchanges:** 1 starch, 1/2 fat.

Sunflower Kernel Cookies

For a deliciously different treat, try these soft fruity cookies. They're packed with crisp sunflower kernels. —Bonnie Neuberger, Clark, South Dakota

1/2 cup chopped raisins
1/3 cup chopped dried apricots
    3 tablespoons apple juice
1/2 cup butter *or* margarine, softened
3/4 cup packed brown sugar
1/2 cup sugar
    1 egg
1-1/2 cups all-purpose flour
1-1/2 cups quick-cooking oats
1/2 teaspoon baking powder
1/2 cup roasted salted sunflower kernels, *divided*

In a bowl, combine raisins, apricots and apple juice; set aside. In a mixing bowl, cream butter and sugars. Add egg and mix well. Combine flour,

oats and baking powder; add to the creamed mixture. Stir in raisin mixture and 1/3 cup sunflower kernels. Chill. Shape dough into 1-in. balls. Place 2 in. apart on greased baking sheets; flatten slightly. Sprinkle with remaining sunflower kernels. Bake at 375° for 10 minutes or until lightly browned. Cool on wire racks. **Yield:** about 5 dozen.

Lo-Cal Molasses Cookies
(Pictured below)

For the holidays or anytime we want a super snack, I bake up a batch of these yummy molasses cookies. —Kim Marie Van Rheenen, Mendota, Illinois

✓ Nutritional Analysis included

1/2 cup vegetable oil
1/4 cup molasses
1/4 cup plus 2 tablespoons sugar, *divided*
    1 egg
    2 cups all-purpose flour
    2 teaspoons baking soda
    1 teaspoon ground cinnamon
1/2 teaspoon ground ginger
1/4 teaspoon ground cloves

In a mixing bowl, beat oil, molasses, 1/4 cup sugar and egg. Combine flour, baking soda, cinnamon, ginger and cloves; add to molasses mixture and mix well. Cover and refrigerate for at least 2 hours. Shape into 1-in. balls; roll in remaining sugar. Place on ungreased baking sheets. Bake at 375° for 10-12 minutes or until cookies are set and surface cracks. **Yield:** 5 dozen. **Nutritional Analysis:** One cookie equals 41 calories, 44 mg sodium, 4 mg cholesterol, 5 gm carbohydrate, 1 gm protein, 2 gm fat. **Diabetic Exchange:** 1/2 starch.

Cookies Capture Christmas Magic

BAKING Christmas cookies is a jolly job—what other holiday gift can you sample before giving? For sincere holiday cheer, whip up a batch of these merry morsels.

Raspberry Swirls

(Pictured below)

My mother-in-law shared the recipe for these old-fashioned cookies. Swirls of raspberry jam give them a yummy Yuletide twist. —Marcia Hostetter
Canton, New York

> 1 cup butter (no substitutes), softened
> 2 cups sugar
> 2 eggs
> 1 teaspoon vanilla extract
> 1/2 teaspoon lemon extract
> 3-3/4 cups all-purpose flour
> 2 teaspoons baking powder
> 1 teaspoon salt
> 1 jar (12 ounces) seedless raspberry jam
> 1 cup flaked coconut
> 1/2 cup chopped pecans

In a mixing bowl, cream butter and sugar. Add the eggs and extracts; mix well. Combine flour, baking powder and salt; add to creamed mixture and mix well. Cover and chill for at least 2 hours. Divide dough in half. On a lightly floured surface, roll each half into a 12-in. x 9-in. rectangle. Combine jam, coconut and pecans; spread over rectangles. Carefully roll up, starting with the long end, into a tight jelly roll. Wrap in plastic wrap. Refrigerate overnight or freeze for 2-3 hours. Cut into 1/4-in. slices; place on greased baking sheets. Bake at 375° for 10-12 minutes or until lightly browned. Cool on wire racks. **Yield:** 8 dozen.

A SNACK of milk or coffee band cookies has extra appeal around the holidays with treats like Raspberry Swirls, Dipped Vanillas and Almond Butter Cutouts (shown above, clockwise from top left).

Almond Butter Cutouts

(Pictured below left)

Ground almonds spread festive flavor throughout these cookies. My grandchildren love to dress them up with colored sugar or frosting. They're a nice twist on traditional butter cookies. —Edie DeSpain
Logan, Utah

    1 cup butter (no substitutes), softened
    1 cup sugar
    2 egg yolks
    1 teaspoon almond extract
    2 cups all-purpose flour
  1/2 teaspoon salt
  1/2 teaspoon baking powder
    1 cup ground almonds
Colored sugar and frosting, optional

In a mixing bowl, cream butter and sugar. Beat in egg yolks and extract. Combine flour, salt and baking powder; gradually add to creamed mixture. Stir in almonds. Cover and chill at least 2 hours. Roll out on a lightly floured surface to 3/8-in. thickness. Cut with cookie cutters; place on ungreased baking sheets. Sprinkle with sugar if desired. Bake at 375° for 10-13 minutes or until the edges begin to brown. Cool on wire racks. Frost if desired. **Yield:** 3-4 dozen.

Dipped Vanillas

(Pictured at left)

A touch of chocolate makes these classics stand out on the holiday cookie tray. They're a tradition at our home every Christmas. —Karen Bourne
Magrath, Alberta

  1/2 cup butter (no substitutes), softened
  1/2 cup ground almonds
  1/4 cup sugar
    1 teaspoon vanilla extract
    1 cup all-purpose flour
    2 tablespoons cornstarch
    2 squares (1 ounce *each*) semisweet
        chocolate
  1/2 teaspoon shortening

In a mixing bowl, cream butter, almonds, sugar and vanilla; add flour and cornstarch. Roll into 1-in. balls; shape into crescents and place on greased baking sheets. Bake at 375° for 8-10 minutes or until lightly browned. Cool completely on wire racks. Melt chocolate and shortening in a microwave or double boiler; stir until smooth. Dip one end of each crescent into chocolate; cool on waxed paper. Refrigerate for about 30 minutes to firm the chocolate. **Yield:** about 2-1/2 dozen.

Finnish Christmas Cookies

My friend bakes these cookies at Christmas. They're popular at cookie exchanges, but my friend's husband urges her not to trade any of them!
—Judith Outlaw, Portland, Oregon

    2 cups butter (no substitutes), softened
    1 cup sugar
    4 cups all-purpose flour
    1 egg, beaten
  2/3 cup finely chopped almonds
Colored sugar, optional

In a mixing bowl, cream butter and sugar until fluffy. Beat in flour. Cover and refrigerate for 1 hour. Roll out on a well-floured surface or pastry cloth to 1/4-in. thickness. Brush lightly with egg. Sprinkle with almonds and sugar if desired. Using a fluted pastry cutter or knife, cut into 2-in. x 1-in. strips. Place 1 in. apart on ungreased baking sheets. Bake at 350° for 10-12 minutes or until lightly browned. Cool on wire racks. **Yield:** about 6 dozen.

Crisp Gingerbread Cutouts

My grandsons Nathan and Caleb Wray started cooking by helping their grandpa mix up waffle and pancake batter. Now we make these cookies together.
—Shelia Hanauer, Reidsville, North Carolina

  1/2 cup shortening
  1/2 cup sugar
  1/2 cup molasses
    1 egg
2-1/4 cups all-purpose flour
1-1/2 teaspoons ground cinnamon
    1 teaspoon baking powder
    1 teaspoon ground ginger
    1 teaspoon ground cloves
  1/2 teaspoon ground nutmeg
  1/2 teaspoon baking soda
  1/2 teaspoon salt
Raisins, halved
Red-hot candies

In a mixing bowl, cream shortening and sugar. Add molasses and egg; mix well. Combine dry ingredients; add to the creamed mixture and mix well (dough will be soft). Cover and refrigerate for 1 hour. On a lightly floured surface, roll dough to 1/8-in. thickness. Cut with a floured 2-1/2-in. gingerbread cookie cutter and place on greased baking sheets. Add raisins for eyes and red-hots for buttons. Bake at 350° for 8-10 minutes or until the edges are lightly browned. Remove to wire racks to cool. **Yield:** about 4-1/2 dozen.

Chocolate Truffle Cookies

(Pictured below)

Here's a snack for serious chocolate lovers. These enticing cookies are crisp on the outside and soft on the inside, somewhat bittersweet and very chocolaty. I usually make them to share at get-togethers...otherwise, I'd eat them all myself!
—Delaine Fortenberry
McComb, Mississippi

     4 squares (1 ounce *each*) unsweetened chocolate
     2 cups (12 ounces) semisweet chocolate chips, *divided*
 1/3 cup butter *or* margarine
     1 cup sugar
     3 eggs
 1-1/2 teaspoons vanilla extract
 1/2 cup all-purpose flour
     2 tablespoons baking cocoa
 1/4 teaspoon baking powder
 1/4 teaspoon salt
Confectioners' sugar

In a microwave or double boiler, melt unsweetened chocolate, 1 cup of chocolate chips and butter; cool for 10 minutes. In a mixing bowl, beat sugar and eggs for 2 minutes. Beat in vanilla and the chocolate mixture. Combine flour, cocoa, baking powder and salt; beat into chocolate mixture. Stir in remaining chocolate chips. Cover and chill for at least 3 hours. Remove about 1 cup of dough. With lightly floured hands, roll into 1-in. balls. Place on ungreased baking sheets. Bake at 350° for 10-12 minutes or until lightly puffed and set. Cool for 3-4 minutes before removing from pan to a wire rack to cool completely. Repeat with remaining dough. Dust with confectioners' sugar. **Yield:** about 4 dozen.

Glazed Banana Nut Bars

I rely on this recipe when I need a sweet treat for a crowd. They're moist bars with the perfect balance of glaze, cake and nuts.
—Marion White
La Center, Washington

 1/2 cup butter *or* margarine, softened
 1-1/2 cups sugar
     2 eggs
     1 teaspoon vanilla extract
     2 cups all-purpose flour
     1 teaspoon baking powder
     1 teaspoon salt
 1/2 teaspoon baking soda
     1 teaspoon ground cinnamon
 1/8 teaspoon ground allspice
     1 cup mashed ripe bananas
 1/2 cup milk
     1 cup finely chopped walnuts
GLAZE:
 1/4 cup butter *or* margarine, softened
 1-1/2 cups confectioners' sugar
     1 teaspoon vanilla extract
     2 to 3 tablespoons boiling water
 1/2 cup chopped walnuts

In a mixing bowl, cream butter and sugar until light and fluffy. Add eggs, one at a time, beating well after each addition. Add vanilla. Combine flour, baking powder, salt, baking soda, cinnamon and allspice. Combine bananas and milk. Add the dry ingredients to creamed mixture alternately with banana mixture; mix well. Stir in nuts. Pour into a greased 15-in. x 10-in. x 1-in. baking pan. Bake at 350° for 20-25 minutes or until a toothpick inserted near the center comes out clean. Cool on a wire rack. For glaze, cream butter and sugar in a small mixing bowl. Stir in vanilla and enough water until glaze reaches desired consistency. Spread over bars. Sprinkle with walnuts. **Yield:** about 3 dozen.

Snowballs

I first tried this recipe because it's low in fat, but now I make these treats for their fruity taste. The folks in my pinochle clubs love them. —Madeline Scholfield
Winchester, Illinois

☑ Nutritional Analysis included

     4 cups All-Bran cereal
     1 cup dried pitted prunes
 1-2/3 cups raisins
 1-1/2 cups dried apricots
     2 cups chopped pecans
Confectioners' sugar

Place the cereal and prunes in a food processor or blender; cover and process until cereal is crumbled. Add raisins, apricots and pecans; process until finely chopped. Shape into 1-in. balls; roll in confectioners' sugar. Store in an airtight container in the refrigerator. Roll again in sugar before serving. **Yield:** about 5-1/2 dozen. **Nutritional Analysis:** One piece equals 64 calories, 59 mg sodium, 0 cholesterol, 11 gm carbohydrate, 1 gm protein, 3 gm fat. **Diabetic Exchanges:** 1/2 starch, 1/2 fat.

Oatmeal Breakfast Treats

These wholesome, economical treats are great for a meal on the go. They're not crumbly, plus they pack a lot of hearty ingredients in a small package.
—Angie Provence, Fayetteville, Georgia

   2 eggs
3/4 cup packed brown sugar
1/2 cup vegetable oil
1/4 cup evaporated milk
   1 teaspoon vanilla extract
2-1/2 cups old-fashioned oats
1/2 cup whole wheat flour
1/2 cup all-purpose flour
1/2 teaspoon salt
3/4 cup raisins
1/2 cup chopped walnuts

In a mixing bowl, combine the first five ingredients; mix well. Combine oats, flours and salt; add to brown sugar mixture and mix well. Stir in raisins and walnuts. Drop by rounded tablespoonfuls onto greased baking sheets. Bake at 350° for 12-14 minutes or until set. **Yield:** about 2-1/2 dozen.

Butter Fudge Fingers

(Pictured above right)

These scrumptious brownies get dressed up with a delicious browned butter frosting. The combination is delightfully different and assures that they vanish fast around the house or at a party.   *—Peggy Mangus Worland, Wyoming*

2/3 cup butter (no substitutes)
   4 squares (1 ounce *each*) unsweetened chocolate
   4 eggs
   1 teaspoon salt
   2 cups sugar
1-1/2 cups all-purpose flour
   1 teaspoon baking powder

   1 cup chopped pecans
BROWNED BUTTER FROSTING:
1/2 cup butter (no substitutes)
1/3 cup whipping cream
   2 teaspoons vanilla extract
   4 cups confectioners' sugar
GLAZE:
   1 square (1 ounce) unsweetened chocolate
   1 tablespoon butter (no substitutes)

In a microwave or double boiler, melt butter and chocolate; cool for 10 minutes. In a mixing bowl, beat eggs and salt until foamy. Gradually add sugar; mix well. Stir in chocolate mixture. Combine flour and baking powder; gradually add to chocolate mixture. Stir in pecans. Pour into a greased 15-in. x 10-in. x 1-in. baking pan. Bake at 350° for 20-25 minutes or until a toothpick inserted near the center comes out clean. Cool. For frosting, heat butter in a saucepan over medium heat until golden brown, about 7 minutes. Remove from the heat; add cream and vanilla. Beat in sugar until smooth and thick. Frost bars. For glaze, melt the chocolate and butter in a microwave or double boiler; cool slightly. Drizzle over bars. **Yield:** about 5 dozen.

Single Servings

To bake brownies in a hurry, pour the batter into muffin cups coated with nonstick cooking spray. You'll have individual servings in no time.

In a saucepan over low heat, melt butter and chocolate. Remove from the heat. Blend in sugar and vanilla. Beat in eggs. Combine flour, baking powder and salt; add to chocolate mixture. Stir in walnuts. Pour into a greased 13-in. x 9-in. x 2-in. baking pan. Bake at 350° for 25-30 minutes or until top springs back when lightly touched. For the topping, combine sugar, milk and butter in a heavy saucepan; bring to a boil over medium heat. Reduce heat; simmer for 5 minutes, stirring constantly. Remove from the heat. Stir in chocolate chips, marshmallow creme and vanilla; beat until smooth. Add nuts. Spread over warm brownies. Freeze for 3 hours or until firm. Cut into 1-in. squares. Store in the refrigerator. **Yield:** about 10 dozen.

Special Chocolate Treats

I usually bake and freeze a big batch of these lovely cookies. That way, I have a special treat on hand to serve when friends and family drop in.
—*Mrs. Walter Marx, Wabasha, Minnesota*

 3/4 cup butter *or* margarine, softened
 3/4 cup packed brown sugar
 1-1/2 teaspoons vanilla extract
 1/2 teaspoon salt
 1-3/4 cups all-purpose flour
FILLING/GLAZE:
 1 cup (6 ounces) semisweet chocolate chips
 1 tablespoon shortening
 2/3 cup finely chopped pecans
 1/2 cup sweetened condensed milk
 1 teaspoon vanilla extract
 1/8 teaspoon salt
 1 tablespoon light corn syrup
 1 teaspoon water

In a mixing bowl, cream butter and brown sugar until fluffy. Beat in vanilla and salt. Add flour; mix well. Cover and refrigerate. For filling, melt the chocolate chips and shortening in a microwave or double boiler until smooth. Remove from the heat; reserve 1/4 cup for glaze. To remaining chocolate, add pecans, milk, vanilla and salt; blend well. Cover and refrigerate until cool, about 15 minutes. Place a 16-in. x 12-in. piece of foil on a greased baking sheet; lightly sprinkle with flour. Divide dough in half; place one portion on foil. Roll into a 14-in. x 5-in. rectangle. Spread half of the filling lengthwise on half of the dough to within 1/2 in. of edges. Using foil, fold dough over filling; seal edges. Repeat with remaining dough and filling. Bake at 350° for 15-20 minutes or until golden brown. Cool on a wire rack for 10 minutes. For glaze, warm reserved chocolate; stir in corn syrup

Fudge-Topped Brownies

(Pictured above)

Why have just brownies or fudge when you can combine them? Mix up a pan of these exquisite brownies for any holiday or special gathering or just when you want to treat yourself to the ultimate chocolate dessert.
—*Judy Olson, Whitecourt, Alberta*

 1 cup butter (no substitutes)
 4 squares (1 ounce *each*) unsweetened chocolate
 2 cups sugar
 2 teaspoons vanilla extract
 4 eggs
 1-1/2 cups all-purpose flour
 1 teaspoon baking powder
 1/2 teaspoon salt
 1 cup chopped walnuts
TOPPING:
 4-1/2 cups sugar
 1 can (12 ounces) evaporated milk
 1/2 cup butter (no substitutes)
 1 package (12 ounces) semisweet chocolate chips
 1 package (11-1/2 ounces) milk chocolate chips
 1 jar (7 ounces) marshmallow creme
 2 teaspoons vanilla extract
 2 cups coarsely chopped walnuts

and water. Spread over cookies. Cool completely. Cut crosswise into 3/4-in. strips. **Yield:** about 3-1/2 dozen.

— 🥄 🥄 🥄 —

Ginger Cookies

Granddaughter Sarah first helped me stir up a batch when she was just 4. The best part for me is seeing the pride on her face when she serves these treats to her mom and dad and the rest of our family.
—Dixie Wicks, Central Point, Oregon

  3/4 **cup shortening**
    1 **cup sugar**
  1/4 **cup molasses**
    1 **egg**
    2 **tablespoons water**
    2 **cups all-purpose flour**
1-1/2 **teaspoons baking soda**
    1 **teaspoon ground cinnamon**
    1 **teaspoon ground ginger**
  1/4 **teaspoon salt**
Additional sugar, optional

In a mixing bowl, cream shortening and sugar. Add molasses; mix well. Combine egg and water; add to molasses mixture and mix well. Combine flour, baking soda, cinnamon, ginger and salt; add to molasses mixture and mix well. Cover and refrigerate for at least 20 minutes. Shape into 1-in. balls. Place on ungreased baking sheets; flatten with a fork. Sprinkle with additional sugar if desired. Bake at 350° for 9-11 minutes or until set. Cool for 5 minutes; remove to wire racks. **Yield:** 3 dozen.

— 🥄 🥄 🥄 —

Peanut Butter Swirl Brownies

(Pictured at right)

Peanut butter and chocolate are always a delicious duo, but they're extra special paired in this tempting treat. Even with a sizable collection of brownie recipes, I reach for this one quite often. The marbled look prompts curious tasters—the flavor brings them back for seconds.
—Linda Craig
Hay River, Northwest Territories

1/2 **cup butter *or* margarine, softened**
2/3 **cup sugar**
1/2 **cup packed brown sugar**
  2 **eggs**
  2 **tablespoons milk**
3/4 **cup all-purpose flour**
1/2 **teaspoon baking powder**
1/4 **teaspoon salt**
1/4 **cup creamy peanut butter**

Better Use Butter

Some brownie and cookie recipes call for butter only. For best results, don't substitute with a "light" butter or margarine product. (They can contain water, causing the recipe to "flop".)

1/3 **cup peanut butter chips**
1/3 **cup baking cocoa**
1/2 **cup semisweet chocolate chips**

In a mixing bowl, cream the butter and sugars. Add eggs and milk; mix well. Combine flour, baking powder and salt; add to creamed mixture and mix well. Divide the batter in half. To one portion, add peanut butter and peanut butter chips; mix well. To the other portion, add cocoa and chocolate chips; mix well. In a greased 9-in. square baking pan, spoon the chocolate batter in eight mounds in a checkerboard pattern. Spoon seven mounds of peanut butter batter between the chocolate batter. Cut through batters with a knife to swirl. Bake at 350° for 25-30 minutes or until a toothpick inserted in the center comes out clean. Cool on a wire rack. **Yield:** 3 dozen.

Moist Cake Brownies

(Pictured below)

In their original form, these brownies have been in my recipe collection since I was 9 years old. I've added to and altered the recipe over the years. My husband and son think they now have the perfect amount of everything, including semisweet and milk chocolate chips and pecans. —Louise Stacey, Dane, Wisconsin

>   2/3 cup butter *or* margarine
>   3/4 cup baking cocoa
>   1/4 cup vegetable oil
>   2 cups sugar
>   4 eggs
>   2 teaspoons vanilla extract
>   1-1/2 cups all-purpose flour
>   1 teaspoon baking powder
>   1 teaspoon salt
>   2/3 cup semisweet chocolate chips
>   1/2 cup milk chocolate chips
>   1 cup coarsely chopped pecans
>   Confectioners' sugar
>   Pecan halves, toasted, optional

Melt butter in a large saucepan. Whisk in cocoa and oil until smooth. Cook and stir over low heat until cocoa is blended. Remove from the heat; stir in sugar. Add eggs, one at a time, stirring well after each addition. Stir in vanilla. Combine flour, baking powder and salt; add to cocoa mixture. Stir in chocolate chips and pecans. Spread into a greased 13-in. x 9-in. x 2-in. baking pan. Bake at 350° for 25-30 minutes or until a toothpick inserted near the center comes out clean. Cool. Dust with confectioners' sugar. Garnish with pecan halves if desired. **Yield:** 2 dozen.

Butterfinger Cookies

These wonderful candy-like cookies don't last long around our house—when I want to serve company, I make a double batch! No one can resist their sweet chocolaty flavor. —Carol Kitchens
Ridgeland, Mississippi

>   1/2 cup butter *or* margarine, softened
>   3/4 cup sugar
>   2/3 cup packed brown sugar
>   2 egg whites
>   1-1/4 cups chunky peanut butter
>   1-1/2 teaspoons vanilla extract
>   1 cup all-purpose flour
>   1/2 teaspoon baking soda
>   1/4 teaspoon salt
>   5 Butterfinger candy bars (2.1 ounces *each*), coarsely chopped

In a mixing bowl, cream butter and sugars. Add egg whites; beat well. Blend in peanut butter and vanilla. Combine flour, baking soda and salt; add to creamed mixture and mix well. Stir in candy bars. Shape into 1-1/2-in. balls; place on greased baking sheets. Bake at 350° for 10-12 minutes or until golden brown. Cool on wire racks. **Yield:** 4 dozen.

Mocha Bars

I get a lot of requests for these moist bars when we make box lunches for church meetings. Chocolate chips and nuts make an easy tempting topping for these coffee-flavored treats. —Flossie Alers
Clinton, Maryland

>   2 eggs
>   1 cup vegetable oil
>   1 cup cold coffee
>   1 teaspoon vanilla extract
>   3 cups all-purpose flour
>   2-1/2 cups packed brown sugar
>   1 teaspoon salt
>   1 teaspoon baking soda
>   1 cup (6 ounces) semisweet chocolate chips
>   3/4 cup chopped walnuts

In a mixing bowl, beat eggs, oil, coffee and vanilla. Combine flour, brown sugar, salt and baking soda; add to coffee mixture. Beat until smooth. Pour into a greased 15-in. x 10-in. x 1-in. baking pan. Bake at 375° for 30-35 minutes or until top springs back when lightly touched. Sprinkle with chocolate chips and nuts. Cool before cutting. **Yield:** about 3 dozen.

Cookies 'n' Cream Brownies

You won't want to frost these brownies since the marbled top is too pretty to cover up. Besides, the cream cheese mixture makes them taste like they are already frosted. The crushed cookies add extra chocolate flavor and a fun crunch. —Darlene Markel
Sublimity, Oregon

CREAM CHEESE LAYER:
    1 package (8 ounces) cream cheese, softened
1/4 cup sugar
    1 egg
1/2 teaspoon vanilla extract
BROWNIE LAYER:
1/2 cup butter *or* margarine, melted
1/2 cup sugar
1/2 cup packed brown sugar
1/2 cup baking cocoa
    2 eggs
1/2 cup all-purpose flour
    1 teaspoon baking powder
    1 teaspoon vanilla extract
  12 cream-filled chocolate sandwich cookies, crushed

In a small mixing bowl, beat cream cheese, sugar, egg and vanilla until smooth; set aside. For brownie layer, combine butter, sugars and cocoa in a large mixing bowl; blend well. Add eggs, one at a time, beating well after each addition. Combine flour and baking powder; stir into cocoa mixture. Stir in the vanilla and cookie crumbs. Pour into a greased 11-in. x 7-in. x 2-in. baking pan. Spoon cream cheese mixture over batter; cut through batter with a knife to swirl. Bake at 350° for 25-30 minutes or until a toothpick inserted near the center comes out with moist crumbs. Cool completely. **Yield:** 2 dozen.

Brownie Kiss Cupcakes
(Pictured above right)

It's fun to prepare individual brownie "cupcakes" with a chocolaty "surprise" inside. My goddaughter, Cara, asks *me to make them for her birthday to share with her class at school. One year, she requested 32. I later found out she only needed 27. I wonder where the other five went!* —Pamela Lute
Mercersburg, Pennsylvania

1/3 cup butter *or* margarine, softened
    1 cup sugar
    2 eggs
    1 teaspoon vanilla extract
3/4 cup all-purpose flour
1/2 cup baking cocoa
1/4 teaspoon baking powder
1/4 teaspoon salt
    9 milk chocolate kisses

In a mixing bowl, cream butter and sugar. Add eggs and vanilla; mix well. Combine flour, cocoa, baking powder and salt; add to the creamed mixture and mix well. Fill paper- or foil-lined muffin cups two-thirds full. Place a chocolate kiss, tip end down, in the center of each. Bake at 350° for 20-25 minutes or until top springs back when lightly touched. **Yield:** 9 cupcakes.

In a small saucepan over medium heat, bring sugar, butter and water to a boil. Remove from the heat; stir in the chocolate chips until melted. In a mixing bowl, beat eggs and vanilla. Add chocolate mixture; mix well. Combine flour, baking soda and salt; add to chocolate mixture. Stir in walnuts. Pour into a greased 9-in. pie plate. Bake at 350° for 28-30 minutes or until a toothpick inserted near the center comes out clean. Cool on a wire rack. For fudge sauce, heat chocolate chips, milk, sugar and butter in a microwave or double boiler until chocolate and butter are melted; stir until smooth. Drizzle some over pie. Cut into wedges; serve with ice cream and additional fudge sauce. **Yield:** 6-8 servings.

Chewy Brownies

Corn syrup helps keep these brownies moist and fudgy. Instead of using frosting, I simply sprinkle them with confectioners' sugar. It's impossible to eat just one! —Shelia Wood, Macksville, Kansas

    2 cups sugar
1-1/2 cups all-purpose flour
   1/3 cup baking cocoa
1-1/2 teaspoons salt
    1 teaspoon baking powder
    1 cup vegetable oil
    4 eggs
    2 tablespoons light corn syrup
    1 teaspoon vanilla extract
    1 cup chopped nuts, optional
Confectioners' sugar, optional

In a mixing bowl, combine sugar, flour, cocoa, salt and baking powder. Combine oil, eggs, corn syrup and vanilla; add to dry ingredients. Fold in nuts if desired. Spread in a greased 13-in. x 9-in. x 2-in. baking pan. Bake at 350° for 25-27 minutes or until a toothpick inserted near the center comes out clean. If desired, dust with confectioners' sugar while warm. **Yield:** about 3 dozen.

Double Chip Cookies

These soft, yummy cookies were an instant hit the first time I made them. The combination of peanut butter and chocolate is classic. —Lori Daniels
Elkins, West Virginia

   3/4 cup creamy peanut butter
   1/2 cup butter-flavored shortening
1-1/4 cups packed brown sugar

Brownie Pie a la Mode

(Pictured above)

This is an easy brownie recipe when you need something good, fancy and chocolaty. My family loves these brownies. My 11-year-old daughter makes them all by herself and gets raves every time.
—Beverly Thornton, Cortlandt Manor, New York

   1/2 cup sugar
    2 tablespoons butter *or* margarine
    2 tablespoons water
1-1/2 cups semisweet chocolate chips
    2 eggs
    1 teaspoon vanilla extract
   2/3 cup all-purpose flour
   1/4 teaspoon baking soda
   1/4 teaspoon salt
   3/4 cup chopped walnuts
FUDGE SAUCE:
    1 cup (6 ounces) semisweet chocolate chips
   1/2 cup evaporated milk
   1/4 cup sugar
    1 tablespoon butter *or* margarine
Vanilla ice cream

1 egg
3 tablespoons milk
1 tablespoon vanilla extract
1-3/4 cups all-purpose flour
3/4 teaspoon baking soda
3/4 teaspoon salt
1/2 cup peanut butter chips
1/2 cup semisweet chocolate chips

In a mixing bowl, cream peanut butter, shortening and brown sugar. Add egg; mix well. Stir in milk and vanilla. Combine flour, baking soda and salt; gradually add to the creamed mixture. Stir in the chips. Drop by rounded teaspoonfuls onto ungreased baking sheets. Bake at 350° for 7-9 minutes or until golden brown. **Yield:** 10 dozen.

Apricot Coconut Cookies

These fancy, chewy cookies are made without eggs. Our son's allergy got me searching for treats he can enjoy...and we love them, too. —Sara Kennedy
Manassas, Virginia

1-1/4 cups all-purpose flour
1/4 cup sugar
1-1/2 teaspoons baking powder
1/2 cup butter *or* margarine
1 package (3 ounces) cream cheese
1/2 cup shredded coconut
1/2 cup apricot preserves
GLAZE:
1/2 cup confectioners' sugar
2 tablespoons apricot preserves
1-1/2 teaspoons butter *or* margarine, softened
1-1/2 teaspoons milk

In a large bowl, combine flour, sugar and baking powder. Cut in butter and cream cheese until the mixture resembles coarse crumbs. Add coconut and preserves; mix well. Drop by rounded teaspoonfuls 2 in. apart onto greased baking sheets. Bake at 350° for 10-12 minutes or until golden brown. Remove to wire racks to cool completely. Combine glaze ingredients in a small bowl; mix well. Spoon over cookies. **Yield:** about 3 dozen.

Snow Flurry Brownies

(Pictured at right)

This brownie recipe is the greatest dessert in my recipe box. I've even prepared them on the spur of the moment while company was over for dinner. They take just min-

utes to mix up, are out of my oven in less than a half hour and generate many compliments.
—*Sherry Olson, Boulder, Colorado*

1 cup sugar
1/2 cup butter *or* margarine, melted
2 eggs
1/2 teaspoon vanilla extract
2/3 cup all-purpose flour
1/2 cup baking cocoa
1/2 teaspoon baking powder
1/2 teaspoon salt
1/2 cup vanilla chips
1/2 cup chopped macadamia nuts

In a bowl, whisk together sugar, butter, eggs and vanilla. Combine the flour, cocoa, baking powder and salt; add to sugar mixture and mix well. Stir in vanilla chips and nuts. Spread in a greased 8-in. square baking pan. Bake at 350° for 25-30 minutes or until a toothpick inserted near the center comes out with moist crumbs (do not overbake). Cool on a wire rack. Cut into diamond shapes if desired. **Yield:** 16 brownies.

Chunky Blond Brownies

(Pictured below)

Every bite of these chewy blond brownies is packed with chunks of white and semisweet chocolate and macadamia nuts. We have lots of excellent cooks in this rural community, so it's a challenge coming up with a potluck offering that stands out. These usually do.
—Rosemary Dreiske, Keldron, South Dakota

  1/2 **cup butter *or* margarine, softened**
  3/4 **cup sugar**
  3/4 **cup packed brown sugar**
    2 **eggs**
    2 **teaspoons vanilla extract**
1-1/2 **cups all-purpose flour**
    1 **teaspoon baking powder**
  1/2 **teaspoon salt**
    1 **cup vanilla chips**
    1 **cup semisweet chocolate chunks**
    1 **jar (3-1/2 ounces) macadamia nuts *or* 3/4 cup blanched almonds, chopped, *divided***

In a mixing bowl, cream butter and sugars. Add eggs and vanilla; mix well. Combine flour, baking powder and salt; add to creamed mixture and mix well. Stir in vanilla chips, chocolate chunks and 1/2 cup nuts. Spoon into a greased 13-in. x 9-in. x 2-in. baking pan; spread to evenly cover bottom of pan. Sprinkle with the remaining nuts. Bake at 350° for 25-30 minutes or until golden brown. Cool on a wire rack. **Yield:** 2 dozen.

Carol's Springerle Cookies

I make these traditional cookies every Christmas using Springerle molds that my husband, Don, makes. They have a distinctive anise flavor. —Carol Dillon
Camp Hill, Pennsylvania

4 **eggs**
2 **cups sugar**
1 **teaspoon anise extract *or* 4 tablespoons aniseed***
4 **cups cake flour (no substitutes)**
1 **teaspoon baking powder**

In a mixing bowl, beat eggs at high speed until thick and light-colored. Gradually add sugar, beating until dissolved, about 10 minutes. Add anise. Sift flour and baking powder; fold into egg mixture. Cover and let rest for 15 minutes. Divide dough into thirds. On a well-floured board or pastry cloth, roll one piece of dough with a floured rolling pin to 1/4-in. thickness. Flour Springerle mold and quickly press design. Cut around design and place on a greased baking sheet. Repeat with remaining dough. Cover lightly with a towel. Allow cookies to dry for 12 hours or overnight. Dust off excess flour with a pastry brush. Bake at 300° for 15-18 minutes or until light brown on bottom only. Cookies will "spring" or rise during baking. Cool. Store in an airtight container. **Yield:** 15 cookies. ***Editor's Note:** Lemon or almond extract can be substituted for the anise extract or aniseed. After cookies have cooled, the design can be "painted" with food coloring. If cookies become too hard, place a cut apple in the storage container to soften.

Banana Spice Cookies

My grandchildren love these tasty soft cookies. With banana, walnuts and raisins, they're a nice wholesome snack. —Peggy Burdick, Burlington, Michigan

1/2 **cup shortening**
  1 **cup packed brown sugar**
  2 **eggs**
  1 **cup mashed ripe bananas (2 to 3 medium)**
  2 **cups all-purpose flour**
  2 **teaspoons baking powder**
1/2 **teaspoon ground cinnamon**
1/4 **teaspoon baking soda**
1/4 **teaspoon ground cloves**

1/4 teaspoon salt
1/2 cup chopped walnuts
1/2 cup raisins

In a mixing bowl, cream the shortening and brown sugar. Add eggs and bananas; mix well. Combine dry ingredients; add to creamed mixture and mix well. Stir in nuts and raisins. Chill (the dough will be very soft). Drop by rounded teaspoonfuls onto greased baking sheets. Bake at 350° for 8-10 minutes or until lightly browned. **Yield:** 3 dozen.

Pumpkin Chocolate Chip Cookies

I was one of the cooking project leaders for my daughter's 4-H club, and these soft delicious cookies were a big hit with the kids. —Marietta Slater
Augusta, Kansas

1 cup butter *or* margarine, softened
3/4 cup packed brown sugar
3/4 cup sugar
1 egg
1 teaspoon vanilla extract
2 cups all-purpose flour
1 cup quick-cooking oats
1 teaspoon baking soda
1 teaspoon ground cinnamon
1 cup cooked *or* canned pumpkin
1-1/2 cups semisweet chocolate chips

In a mixing bowl, cream butter and sugars. Beat in egg and vanilla. Combine the flour, oats, baking soda and cinnamon; stir into creamed mixture alternately with pumpkin. Fold in chocolate chips. Drop by tablespoonfuls onto greased baking sheets. Bake at 350° for 12-13 minutes or until lightly browned. **Yield:** 4 dozen.

Dark Chocolate Mocha Brownies

(Pictured above right)

Dark chocolate is a favorite at our house, so these frosted brownies are popular. I came up with this treat by reworking a recipe I've used for a long time. We have six children, so these brownies disappear quickly. —Linda McCoy, Oostburg, Wisconsin

2 cups packed brown sugar
1 cup butter *or* margarine, melted
3 eggs
1 tablespoon instant coffee granules
2 teaspoons vanilla extract
1 cup all-purpose flour

1 cup baking cocoa
1/2 teaspoon baking powder
1/2 teaspoon salt
6 ounces bittersweet chocolate, coarsely chopped
FROSTING:
1/4 cup butter *or* margarine, melted
3 tablespoons sour cream
2 teaspoons vanilla extract
2-3/4 to 3 cups confectioners' sugar
2 ounces grated bittersweet chocolate

In a mixing bowl, combine brown sugar and butter. Beat in eggs, one at a time. Add coffee and vanilla; mix well. Combine the flour, cocoa, baking powder and salt; add to sugar mixture and mix well. Stir in chocolate. Spread into a greased 13-in. x 9-in. x 2-in. baking pan. Bake at 350° for 25-30 minutes or until a toothpick inserted near the center comes out clean. Cool on a wire rack. For frosting, combine butter, sour cream and vanilla; mix well. Gradually stir in sugar until frosting is smooth and reaches desired consistency. Frost brownies. Sprinkle with grated chocolate. **Yield:** 5 dozen.

Cakes & Pies

Any way you slice it, cakes and pies add a flavorful finishing touch to everyday dinners and special-occasion meals.

SAVORY SLICES. Clockwise from upper left: Orange Pineapple Torte (p. 152), Potluck Apple Pie (p. 161), Chocolate Angel Cake (p. 146) and Peach Plum Pie (p. 147).

a fourth at a time. Spoon into an ungreased 10-in. tube pan. Carefully run a metal spatula or knife through batter to remove air pockets. Bake on lowest oven rack at 375° for 35-40 minutes or until the top springs back when lightly touched and cracks feel dry. Immediately invert pan; cool completely. Run a knife around edges and center tube to loosen; remove cake. In a mixing bowl, combine the first five frosting ingredients; cover and chill for 1 hour. Beat until stiff peaks form. Spread over top and sides of cake. Store in the refrigerator. Garnish with chocolate leaves if desired. **Yield:** 12-16 servings.

Chocolate Leaves

Wash and dry mint, lemon or rose leaves; set aside. In a microwave or double boiler, melt 1 cup of semisweet chocolate chips and 1 tablespoon of shortening. Brush evenly on the underside of leaves. Refrigerate until chocolate is set, about 10 minutes. Apply a second layer; refrigerate until set. Gently peel each leaf away from chocolate. Cover and refrigerate until ready to use.

Chocolate Angel Cake

(Pictured above)

When I married in 1944, I could barely boil water. My dear mother-in-law taught me her specialty—making the lightest of angel food cakes ever. This chocolate version is an easy, impressive treat.
—*Joyce Shiffler, Manitou Springs, Colorado*

1-1/2 cups confectioners' sugar
　1 cup cake flour
　1/4 cup baking cocoa
1-1/2 cups egg whites (about 10 eggs)
1-1/2 teaspoons cream of tartar
　1/2 teaspoon salt
　1 cup sugar
FROSTING:
1-1/2 cups whipping cream
　1/2 cup sugar
　1/4 cup baking cocoa
　1/2 teaspoon salt
　1/2 teaspoon vanilla extract
Chocolate leaves, optional (see tip box above right)

Sift together confectioners' sugar, flour and cocoa three times; set aside. In a mixing bowl, beat egg whites, cream of tartar and salt until soft peaks form. Add sugar, 2 tablespoons at a time, beating until stiff peaks form. Gradually fold in cocoa mixture, about

Zucchini Chocolate Cake

Using a food processor to shred zucchini, I bake up this lightly sweet cake often. There's just the right amount of chocolate in every bite. —*Leon Kingsley*
Marshfield, Massachusetts

　1/2 cup butter *or* margarine, softened
　1/2 cup vegetable oil
1-3/4 cups sugar
　2 eggs
　1 teaspoon vanilla extract
2-1/2 cups all-purpose flour
　1/4 cup baking cocoa
　1 teaspoon baking soda
　1/2 teaspoon baking powder
　1/2 teaspoon ground cinnamon
　1/4 to 1/2 teaspoon ground cloves
　1/2 cup sour milk*
　2 cups shredded peeled zucchini
　1/2 cup semisweet chocolate chips

In a mixing bowl, cream the butter, oil and sugar. Beat in the eggs and vanilla. Combine the flour, cocoa, baking soda, baking powder, cinnamon and cloves; add to the creamed mixture alternately with milk. Mix well. Stir in zucchini. Pour into a greased 13-in. x 9-in. x 2-in. baking pan. Sprinkle with the chocolate chips. Bake at 350° for 40-45 minutes or until a toothpick inserted near the center comes out clean. Cool on a wire rack. **Yield:** 12-

15 servings. ***Editor's Note:** To sour milk, place 1-1/2 teaspoons white vinegar in a measuring cup. Add milk to equal 1/2 cup.

Creamy Banana Pecan Pie

I always get compliments when I serve this layered banana beauty. Its old-fashioned flavor is terrific.
—*Isabel Fowler, Fairbanks, Alaska*

> 1 cup all-purpose flour
> 1/2 cup butter *or* margarine, softened
> 1 cup finely chopped pecans
> 1 package (8 ounces) cream cheese, softened
> 1 cup confectioners' sugar
> 1 carton (8 ounces) frozen whipped topping, thawed, *divided*
> 3 large firm bananas, sliced
> 1 package (3.4 ounces) instant vanilla pudding mix
> 1-1/3 cups cold milk
> Additional chopped pecans, optional

Combine flour, butter and pecans. Press onto the bottom and up the sides of a greased 9-in. pie plate. Bake at 350° for 25 minutes. Cool completely. In a mixing bowl, beat cream cheese and sugar. Fold in 1 cup of whipped topping. Spread over the crust. Arrange bananas on top. In a bowl, whisk pudding mix and milk. Immediately pour over bananas. Top with remaining whipped topping. Garnish with pecans if desired. Refrigerate until serving. **Yield:** 6-8 servings.

Pineapple Cherry Cake

When our granddaughter visits us on weekends, I try to find something fun for her to do. Since packaged ingredients are simply layered in a pan, this is an easy treat that even a young child can fix.
—*Geraldine Griffin, Prudenville, Michigan*

> 1 can (20 ounces) crushed pineapple, undrained
> 1 can (21 ounces) cherry *or* blueberry pie filling
> 1 package (18-1/4 ounces) yellow cake mix
> 1/2 cup butter *or* margarine

Evenly spread pineapple in a greased 13-in. x 9-in. x 2-in. baking pan. Carefully spread pie filling on top. Sprinkle with dry cake mix. Dot with butter. Bake at 350° for 50-60 minutes or until the top is browned. **Yield:** 12-16 servings.

Peach Plum Pie

(Pictured below)

When I want to impress guests, this is the pie I prepare. Peaches, plums and a bit of lemon peel are a refreshing trio that wakes up taste buds. —*Susan Osborne Hatfield Point, New Brunswick*

> 2 cups sliced peeled fresh *or* frozen peaches, thawed and drained
> 2 cups sliced peeled fresh purple plums
> 1 tablespoon lemon juice
> 1/4 teaspoon almond extract
> 1-1/2 cups sugar
> 1/4 cup quick-cooking tapioca
> 1/2 to 1 teaspoon grated lemon peel
> 1/4 teaspoon salt
> Pastry for double-crust pie (9 inches)
> 2 tablespoons butter *or* margarine

In a large bowl, combine the peaches, plums, lemon juice and extract. In another bowl, combine sugar, tapioca, lemon peel and salt. Add to fruit mixture and stir gently; let stand for 15 minutes. Line a 9-in. pie plate with bottom crust; add the filling. Dot with butter. Roll out remaining pastry to fit top of pie; cut slits in pastry. Place over filling. Trim, seal and flute edges. Cover the edges loosely with foil. Bake at 450° for 10 minutes. Reduce heat to 350°. Remove foil; bake 35 minutes longer or until crust is golden brown and filling is bubbly. **Yield:** 6-8 servings.

Apricot Torte

(Pictured below)

This yummy dessert is simple to prepare and oh-so-pretty. The chocolate buttercream nicely complements the apricot filling. I like to ornament my holiday table with this delectable dessert.—Dorothy Pritchett Wills Point, Texas

> 6 eggs, *separated*
> 1/2 cup plus 5 tablespoons sugar, *divided*
> 1 cup all-purpose flour

CHOCOLATE BUTTERCREAM:

> 1/4 cup sugar
> 3 eggs plus 2 egg yolks
> 1 teaspoon vanilla extract
> 1 teaspoon instant coffee granules
> 2 squares (1 ounce *each*) semisweet chocolate
> 1 cup butter (no substitutes), softened

APRICOT FILLING:

> 2 cans (17 ounces each) apricot halves, drained
> 1 cup apricot preserves

Chocolate curls, optional

In a large mixing bowl, beat egg yolks and 1/2 cup sugar until thickened. In a small mixing bowl, beat egg whites until foamy. Gradually add remaining sugar, beating until stiff peaks form. Fold into yolk mixture. Gradually fold in flour. Divide batter between three greased and floured 9-in. round cake pans. Bake at 350° for 15 minutes or until golden. Cool in pans for 5 minutes; remove to

wire racks to cool. For buttercream, whisk sugar, eggs, yolks, vanilla and coffee in a saucepan. Add chocolate; cook and stir over low heat until thickened (do not boil). Cool completely. In a mixing bowl, cream butter. Gradually add the chocolate mixture; set aside. Finely chop apricots; drain and place in a bowl. Stir in preserves; set aside. Split each cake into two horizontal layers; place one on a serving plate. Spread with 2/3 cup buttercream. Top with another cake layer and 2/3 cup apricot filling. Repeat layers twice. Cover and refrigerate 3 hours before serving. Garnish with chocolate curls if desired. **Yield:** 12 servings.

Blueberry Crunch Cake

At 94 years of age, I don't have the energy to do all the things I once did...but I can still get enthused about whipping up my favorite culinary concoctions! I tend to bake many desserts due to my sweet tooth.
—Leon Kingsley, Marshfield, Massachusetts

STREUSEL:

> 1/2 cup packed brown sugar
> 1/3 cup all-purpose flour
> 1/2 teaspoon ground cinnamon
> 1/3 cup finely chopped pecans
> 1/3 cup cold butter *or* margarine

CAKE:

> 1/2 cup butter *or* margarine, softened
> 3/4 cup sugar
> 2 eggs
> 2 teaspoons vanilla extract
> 2 cups all-purpose flour
> 2 teaspoons baking powder
> 1/2 teaspoon salt
> 3/4 cup milk

1-1/2 cups fresh *or* frozen blueberries
Confectioners' sugar

In a bowl, combine the first four ingredients; cut in butter until crumbly. Set aside. In a mixing bowl, cream butter and sugar. Beat in eggs, one at a time.

Buying and Storing Berries

When purchasing fresh blueberries, look for ones that are plump and taut. Avoid wrinkled berries—they're past their prime. Place unwashed berries in a covered container and refrigerate up to 10 days. (Or freeze in a single layer, then transfer to a freezer container.) Only wash berries when you're ready to use them.

Stir in vanilla. Combine flour, baking powder and salt; add to the creamed mixture alternately with milk. Mix well. Spoon two-thirds of the batter into a greased 9-in. springform pan. Sprinkle with two-thirds of the streusel. Spoon blueberries evenly over streusel. Top with remaining batter and streusel. Bake at 350° for 65-70 minutes or until a toothpick inserted near the center comes out clean. Cool for 10 minutes before removing sides of pan. Dust with confectioners' sugar. **Yield:** 8-10 servings.

Cheddar Pear Pie

I take this pie to lots of different gatherings, and I make sure to have copies of the recipe with me since people always ask for it. It's amusing to see some folks puzzling over what's in the filling—they expect apples but love the subtle sweetness of the pears.
—Cynthia LaBree, Elmer, New Jersey

> **4 large ripe pears, peeled and thinly sliced**
> **1/3 cup sugar**
> **1 tablespoon cornstarch**
> **1/8 teaspoon salt**
> **1 unbaked pastry shell (9 inches)**
> **TOPPING:**
> **1/2 cup shredded cheddar cheese**
> **1/2 cup all-purpose flour**
> **1/4 cup butter *or* margarine, melted**
> **1/4 cup sugar**
> **1/4 teaspoon salt**

In a bowl, combine pears, sugar, cornstarch and salt. Pour into pastry shell. Combine topping ingredients until crumbly; sprinkle over filling. Bake at 425° for 25-35 minutes or until crust is golden and cheese is melted. Cool on a wire rack for 15-20 minutes. Serve warm. Store in the refrigerator. **Yield:** 6-8 servings.

Lemon Supreme Pie

(Pictured above right)

A friend and I often visit a local restaurant for pie and coffee. When they stopped carrying our favorite, I got busy in the kitchen and created this version, which we think tastes even better! The combination of the cream cheese and tart lemon is wonderful.
—Jana Beckman, Wamego, Kansas

> **1 unbaked deep-dish pastry shell (9 inches)**
> **LEMON FILLING:**
> **1-1/2 cups sugar**
> **6 tablespoons cornstarch**

> **1/2 teaspoon salt**
> **1-1/4 cups water**
> **2 tablespoons butter *or* margarine**
> **2 teaspoons grated lemon peel**
> **4 to 5 drops yellow food coloring, optional**
> **2/3 cup lemon juice**
> **CREAM CHEESE FILLING:**
> **2 packages (one 8 ounces, one 3 ounces) cream cheese, softened**
> **3/4 cup confectioners' sugar**
> **1-1/2 cups whipped topping**
> **1 tablespoon lemon juice**

Line unpricked pastry shell with a double thickness of heavy-duty foil. Bake at 450° for 8 minutes. Remove foil; bake 5 minutes longer. Cool on a wire rack. In a saucepan, combine sugar, cornstarch and salt. Stir in water; bring to a boil over medium-high heat. Reduce heat; cook and stir for 2 minutes or until thickened and bubbly. Remove from the heat; stir in butter, lemon peel and food coloring if desired. Gently stir in lemon juice (do not overmix). Cool to room temperature, about 1 hour. In a mixing bowl, beat the cream cheese and sugar until smooth. Fold in whipped topping and lemon juice. Refrigerate 1/2 cup for garnish. Spread remaining cream cheese mixture into pastry shell; top with lemon filling. Chill overnight. Place reserved cream cheese mixture in a pastry bag with a #21 star tip; pipe stars onto pie. Store in the refrigerator. **Yield:** 6-8 servings.

1 tablespoon confectioners' sugar
1 teaspoon vanilla extract

Line unpricked pastry shell with a double thickness of heavy-duty foil. Bake at 450° for 5 minutes. Remove foil and set shell aside. Reduce heat to 375°. In a heavy saucepan, melt chocolate and butter. Remove from the heat; stir in milk and water. Add a small amount of hot chocolate mixture to eggs; return all to the pan. Stir in vanilla and salt. Pour into shell; sprinkle with nuts. Cover edges with foil. Bake for 35 minutes or until a knife inserted near the center comes out clean. Remove to a wire rack to cool completely. In a mixing bowl, beat the milk and pudding mix until smooth. Fold in whipped topping. Spread over nut layer; cover and refrigerate. In a mixing bowl, beat cream until soft peaks form. Add sugar and vanilla, beating until stiff peaks form. Spread over pudding layer. Refrigerate until set, about 4 hours. **Yield:** 6-8 servings.

Autumn Apple Cake

I think you'll agree this apple cake is simply irresistible. It's nicely crisp on top and moist and chewy inside. —Leon Kingsley, Marshfield, Massachusetts

   1/4 cup shortening
     1 cup sugar
     1 egg
     1 teaspoon vanilla extract
     1 cup all-purpose flour
   1/2 teaspoon baking soda
   1/2 teaspoon baking powder
   1/2 teaspoon salt
   1/2 teaspoon ground cinnamon
   1/2 teaspoon ground nutmeg
     3 cups diced peeled tart apples
   1/4 cup chopped pecans *or* walnuts, optional
Ice cream, optional

In a mixing bowl, cream shortening and sugar. Add egg and vanilla. Combine flour, baking soda, baking powder, salt, cinnamon and nutmeg; add to the creamed mixture. Stir in apples and nuts if desired. Spoon into a greased 8-in. square baking pan. Bake at 350° for 45-50 minutes or until a toothpick inserted near the center comes out clean. Serve warm with ice cream if desired. **Yield:** 9 servings.

Butternut Cake

This recipe has been in our family for years. It's always included on holiday menus. Preparing the cake is a

Fudgy Pecan Pie

(Pictured above)

This started out as just a plain chocolate pie that I "dressed up" for company. Now when I serve it, guests often tell me, "Your pie looks too good to eat—but I won't let that stop me!" —Ellen Arndt
Cologne, Minnesota

     1 unbaked pastry shell (9 inches)
     1 package (4 ounces) German sweet chocolate
   1/4 cup butter *or* margarine
     1 can (14 ounces) sweetened condensed milk
   1/2 cup water
     2 eggs, beaten
     1 teaspoon vanilla extract
   1/4 teaspoon salt
   1/2 cup chopped pecans
FILLING:
     1 cup cold milk
     1 package (3.9 ounces) instant chocolate pudding mix
     1 cup whipped topping
TOPPING:
     1 cup whipping cream

family project—the men crack the shells, and the children help pick out the nut meats.
—*Betty Zeltwanger, Canisteo, New York*

 1/2 **cup shortening**
   1 **cup sugar**
   2 **eggs**
   1 **teaspoon vanilla extract**
   2 **cups all-purpose flour**
   1 **teaspoon baking powder**
   1 **teaspoon baking soda**
 1/2 **teaspoon salt**
   1 **cup sour milk***
   1 **cup chopped butternuts *or* walnuts**
Frosting of your choice

In a mixing bowl, cream shortening and sugar until fluffy. Beat in eggs and vanilla. Combine flour, baking powder, baking soda and salt; add to the creamed mixture alternately with milk. Stir in nuts. Pour into a greased 13-in. x 9-in. x 2-in. baking pan. Bake at 350° for 30-35 minutes or until a toothpick inserted near the center comes out clean. Cool on a wire rack. Frost cooled cake. **Yield:** 15 servings. ***Editor's Note:** To sour milk, place 1 tablespoon white vinegar in a measuring cup. Add milk to equal 1 cup.

Frosted Orange Pie

(Pictured at right)

I discovered the recipe for this distinctive pie in an old church cookbook. With its fresh-tasting filling and fluffy frosting, it's truly an elegant final course. I'm happy to make it all year-round.
—*Delores Edgecomb, Atlanta, New York*

   1 **unbaked pastry shell (9 inches)**
 3/4 **cup sugar**
 1/2 **cup all-purpose flour**
 1/4 **teaspoon salt**
1-1/4 **cups water**
   2 **egg yolks, lightly beaten**
   2 **to 3 tablespoons grated orange peel**
 1/2 **teaspoon grated lemon peel**
 1/2 **cup orange juice**
   2 **tablespoons lemon juice**
FROSTING:
 1/2 **cup sugar**
   2 **egg whites**
   2 **tablespoons water**
 1/8 **teaspoon cream of tartar**
 1/8 **teaspoon salt**
 1/2 **cup flaked coconut, toasted, optional**

Line unpricked pastry shell with a double thickness of heavy-duty foil. Bake at 450° for 8 minutes. Re-

move foil; bake 5 minutes longer. Cool on a wire rack. In a saucepan, combine the sugar, flour and salt; gradually add water. Cook and stir over medium-high heat for 2-3 minutes or until thickened and bubbly. Remove from the heat. Gradually stir 1/2 cup of hot filling into egg yolks; return all to the pan. Bring to a gentle boil; cook and stir for 2 minutes. Remove from the heat; stir in orange and lemon peels. Gently stir in juices. Pour into baked shell. Cool on a wire rack for 1 hour. Refrigerate for at least 3 hours. In a heavy saucepan or double boiler, combine sugar, egg whites, water, cream of tartar and salt. With a portable mixer, beat on low speed for 1 minute. Continue beating on low over low heat until frosting reaches 160°, about 8-10 minutes. Pour into a large mixing bowl. Beat on high speed until frosting forms stiff peaks, about 7 minutes. Spread over chilled pie filling. Just before serving, sprinkle with coconut. Store in the refrigerator. **Yield:** 6-8 servings. **Editor's Note:** A stand mixer is recommended for beating the frosting after it reaches 160°.

Chocolate Marvel Cake

(Pictured below)

This attractive chocolaty cake with its fluffy mocha frosting is deliciously moist. It's a treat I'm proud to prepare for family and guests alike. —Pearl Watts
Cincinnati, Ohio

✓ Nutritional Analysis included

  1 cup strong brewed coffee
  1 cup milk
  2 jars (4 ounces *each*) pureed prune baby food
  4 egg whites
  2 teaspoons vanilla extract
  2 cups all-purpose flour
  2 cups sugar
3/4 cup baking cocoa
  2 teaspoons baking soda
  1 teaspoon baking powder
1/4 teaspoon salt
FROSTING:
  6 tablespoons butter *or* margarine, softened
2-2/3 cups confectioners' sugar
1/4 cup baking cocoa
  2 tablespoons milk
  2 tablespoons strong brewed coffee
  1 teaspoon vanilla extract

In a mixing bowl, combine coffee, milk, baby food, egg whites and vanilla; beat until well blended. Combine flour, sugar, cocoa, baking soda, baking powder and salt; add to coffee mixture. Beat for 2 minutes or until well blended (batter will be thin). Pour into two greased and floured 9-in. round cake pans. Bake at 350° for 30-35 minutes or until cake pulls away from sides of pan. Cool for 10 minutes; remove from pans to wire racks to cool completely. For frosting, in a mixing bowl, cream butter, sugar and cocoa. Gradually add the milk, coffee and vanilla, beating well. Frost between layers and top and sides of cake. **Yield:** 16 servings. **Nutritional Analysis:** One serving (prepared with skim milk and margarine) equals 306 calories, 614 mg sodium, trace cholesterol, 64 gm carbohydrate, 4 gm protein, 5 gm fat. **Diabetic Exchanges:** 3 starch, 1 fruit, 1 fat.

Orange Pineapple Torte

(Pictured on page 144)

Special family dinners wouldn't be complete without this beautiful, impressive cake. It's surprisingly rich-tasting and not too sweet. —Karen Mellinger Baker
Dover, Ohio

✓ Nutritional Analysis included

  1 package (18-1/4 ounces) yellow light cake mix
  2 packages (1 ounce *each*) instant sugar-free vanilla pudding mix, *divided*
  4 egg whites
  1 cup water
1/4 cup vegetable oil
1/4 teaspoon baking soda
  1 cup cold skim milk
  1 carton (8 ounces) frozen light whipped topping, thawed
  1 can (20 ounces) unsweetened crushed pineapple, well drained
  1 can (11 ounces) mandarin oranges, drained, *divided*
Fresh mint, optional

In a mixing bowl, combine cake mix, one package of pudding mix, egg whites, water, oil and baking soda. Beat on low speed for 1 minute; beat on medium for 4 minutes. Pour into two greased and floured 9-in. round cake pans. Bake at 350° for 25-30 minutes or until a toothpick inserted near the center comes out clean. Cool for 10 minutes; remove from pans to a wire rack to cool completely. For filling, combine milk and remaining pudding mix. Whisk for 2 minutes; let stand for 2 minutes.

Fold in whipped topping. In a medium bowl, combine 1-1/2 cups pudding mixture with pineapple and half of the oranges. Slice each cake layer in half horizontally. Spread pineapple mixture between the layers. Frost top and sides of cake with remaining pudding mixture. Garnish with remaining oranges and mint if desired. Store in the refrigerator. **Yield:** 12 servings. **Nutritional Analysis:** One serving equals 335 calories, 516 mg sodium, trace cholesterol, 58 gm carbohydrate, 4 gm protein, 9 gm fat. **Diabetic Exchanges:** 2 starch, 2 fruit, 2 fat.

— 🍷 🍷 🍷 —

Apple Cranberry Tart

I love the tangy sweetness of this elegant-looking dessert and the fact that it doesn't take long to make.
—Suzanne Strocsher, Bothell, Washington

Pastry for double-crust pie
   2 cups fresh *or* frozen cranberries, coarsely chopped
   2 medium tart apples, peeled and coarsely chopped
1-1/4 cups packed brown sugar
   2 tablespoons all-purpose flour
1/2 teaspoon ground cinnamon
   1 to 2 tablespoons butter *or* margarine

Roll half of the pastry into a 13-in. circle. Press onto the bottom and up the sides of an ungreased 11-in. fluted tart pan with removable bottom, or press into the bottom and 1 in. up the sides of a 10-in. springform pan. In a bowl, combine cranberries, apples, brown sugar, flour and cinnamon; pour into crust. Dot with butter. Cut remaining pastry with a 1-in. apple cookie cutter. Place over filling. Place tart pan on a warm baking sheet. Bake at 425° for 35-40 minutes or until filling is hot and bubbly and crust is golden. Serve warm. **Yield:** 12-16 servings.

— 🍷 🍷 🍷 —

Peanutty Ice Cream Pie

(Pictured above right)

A friend gave me this recipe almost 20 years ago. The unique crust makes these cool slices extra peanutty and perfect for a party. I keep the recipe handy since it's great for any occasion. —Donna Cline
Pensacola, Florida

1-1/3 cups finely chopped peanuts
   3 tablespoons butter *or* margarine, melted
   2 tablespoons sugar

FILLING:
   1/4 cup peanut butter
   1/4 cup light corn syrup
   1/4 cup flaked coconut
   3 tablespoons chopped peanuts
   1 quart vanilla ice cream, softened
Miniature M&M's *or* semisweet chocolate chips

Combine the peanuts, butter and sugar; press onto the bottom and up the sides of a greased 9-in. pie plate. Cover and refrigerate for 15 minutes. In a large bowl, combine peanut butter and corn syrup. Add coconut and peanuts. Stir in ice cream just until combined. Spoon into crust. Cover and freeze overnight or until firm. Just before serving, sprinkle with M&M's or chocolate chips. **Yield:** 6-8 servings.

Delicious Decoration

Looking for an economical and fun way to dress up plain frosted cakes? Just crush some sweetened breakfast cereal (cocoa or multicolored) and scatter across the top.

heat for 2-3 minutes or until thickened and bubbly. Remove from the heat. Gradually stir 1/4 cup into egg yolk; return all to pan. Cook for 2 minutes. Remove from the heat; add vanilla. Cool to room temperature. Pour over apples. Chill until set, about 2 hours. In a mixing bowl, beat cream until soft peaks form. Add cinnamon. Gradually add sugar, beating until stiff peaks form. Serve with pie. Store in the refrigerator. **Yield:** 6-8 servings.

Banana Split Snack Cake

This rich and delicious treat is fun to serve. It was a blue-ribbon winner for me at the county fair several years ago. —Renee Schwebach, Dumont, Minnesota

> 1/3 cup butter *or* margarine, softened
> 1 cup sugar
> 1 egg
> 1 medium ripe banana, mashed
> 1/2 teaspoon vanilla extract
> 1-1/4 cups all-purpose flour
> 1 teaspoon baking powder
> 1/4 teaspoon salt
> 1/3 cup chopped walnuts
> 2 cups miniature marshmallows
> 1 cup (6 ounces) semisweet chocolate chips
> 1/3 cup maraschino cherries, quartered

In a mixing bowl, cream butter and sugar. Beat in the egg, banana and vanilla. Combine flour, baking powder and salt; stir into creamed mixture. Add walnuts. Spread evenly into a greased 13-in. x 9-in. x 2-in. baking pan. Bake at 350° for 20 minutes. Sprinkle with the marshmallows, chocolate chips and cherries. Bake 10 minutes longer or until lightly browned. Cool on a wire rack. Cut into squares. **Yield:** 24-30 servings.

Sour Cream Chocolate Cake

(Pictured on front cover)

This melt-in-your-mouth cake is a good old-fashioned "Sunday supper" dessert. —Marsha Lawson Pflugerville, Texas

> 1 cup baking cocoa
> 1 cup boiling water
> 1 cup butter *or* margarine, softened
> 2-1/2 cups sugar
> 4 eggs
> 2 teaspoons vanilla extract
> 3 cups cake flour
> 2 teaspoons baking soda
> 1/2 teaspoon baking powder

Maple Apple Cream Pie

(Pictured above)

Who can resist this pie's tender apples smothered in a silky maple-flavored cream? —Christi Paulton Phelps, Wisconsin

> 1 unbaked pastry shell (9 inches)
> 2 tablespoons butter *or* margarine
> 6 medium Golden Delicious apples (about 2 pounds), peeled and cut into eighths
> 1/2 cup packed brown sugar
> 1/3 cup maple syrup
> 2 tablespoons cornstarch
> 1 can (12 ounces) evaporated milk
> 1 egg yolk
> 1 teaspoon vanilla extract
> 1/2 cup whipping cream
> 1/4 teaspoon ground cinnamon
> 1 tablespoon sugar

Line unpricked pastry shell with a double thickness of heavy-duty foil. Bake at 450° for 8 minutes. Remove foil; bake 5 minutes longer. Cool on a wire rack. In a skillet, melt butter. Add apples and brown sugar; cook and stir until apples are tender and coated, 15-20 minutes. Cool to room temperature. Spread evenly into pie shell. In a saucepan, combine syrup and cornstarch until smooth. Gradually add milk. Cook and stir over medium-high

1/2 teaspoon salt
   1 cup (8 ounces) sour cream
FROSTING:
   2 cups (12 ounces) semisweet chocolate
     chips
1/2 cup butter *or* margarine
   1 cup (8 ounces) sour cream
   1 teaspoon vanilla extract
4-1/2 to 5 cups confectioners' sugar

Dissolve the cocoa in water; set aside. In a mixing bowl, cream butter and sugar. Add eggs, one at a time, beating well after each. Add vanilla. Combine the flour, baking soda, baking powder and salt; add to the creamed mixture alternately with cocoa mixture and sour cream. Pour into three greased and floured 9-in. round cake pans. Bake at 350° for 30-35 minutes or until a toothpick inserted near the center comes out clean. Cool for 10 minutes; remove from pans to wire racks to cool completely. In a heavy saucepan, melt chocolate chips and butter over low heat. Remove from the heat; cool for 5 minutes. Transfer to a mixing bowl; add sour cream and vanilla. Mix well. Add confectioners' sugar; beat until light and fluffy. Spread between layers and over top and sides of cake. Refrigerate any leftovers. **Yield:** 16 servings.

— 🥄 🥄 🥄 —

Refreshing Lime Pie

Everyone can enjoy a fluffy slice of this tart, refreshing pie. This dessert is a real gem for diabetics.
—*Mildred Baker, Youngstown, Ohio*

☑ Nutritional Analysis included

   1 envelope unflavored gelatin
1/2 cup cold water
   1 package (3 ounces) lime gelatin
1/2 cup boiling water
   3 cartons (8 ounces *each*) key lime pie
     yogurt *or* lemon yogurt
1-1/2 cups whipped topping
   1 shortbread crust (8 inches)

In a small bowl, sprinkle gelatin over cold water; let stand for 1 minute. In another bowl, dissolve lime gelatin in boiling water; stir in unflavored gelatin until dissolved. Refrigerate for 10 minutes. Stir in yogurt. Chill until partially set. Fold in the whipped topping. Pour into crust. Chill until firm. **Yield:** 8 servings. **Nutritional Analysis:** One serving (prepared with sugar-free gelatin, sugar-free fat free yogurt and light whipped topping) equals 172 calories, 183 mg sodium, 1 mg cholesterol, 24 gm carbohydrate, 6 gm protein, 6 gm fat. **Diabetic Exchanges:** 1 starch, 1 fat, 1/2 skim milk.

— 🥄 🥄 🥄 —

'I Wish I Had That Recipe...'

"TURTLE PIE at the House of Plenty restaurant in Highland, Illinois is the most wonderful dessert!" reports Joan Gocking of Carlinville.

"I'd thought twice about ordering dessert after enjoying a big delicious sandwich at this charming restaurant in an old house. But I'm glad I didn't miss trying this wonderfully rich pie."

Delighted with Joan's compliment, owner Judy Ernst happily shares the recipe. "Manager Debbie Poehling and I like to put our heads together to create delicious desserts," Joan explains.

"We combined some favorite ingredients for this pie and soon put it on the daily dessert menu."

The Highland House of Plenty is also known for homemade soups, a variety of sandwich breads and home-style dinners. Located at 802 Ninth St., the restaurant serves from 11 a.m. to 3 p.m. Sunday through Wednesday and 7 a.m. to 9 p.m. Thursday through Saturday. 1-618/654-4868.

House of Plenty's Turtle Pie

   1 cup (6 ounces) semisweet chocolate
     chips, *divided*
1/4 cup chopped pecans
   1 pastry shell (9 inches), baked
1/4 cup caramel topping
   2 packages (8 ounces *each*) cream
     cheese, softened
3/4 cup confectioners' sugar
   2 tablespoons whipping cream
Whipped cream and additional chocolate
   chips, pecans and caramel topping for
   garnish, optional

Sprinkle 1/4 cup of chocolate chips and the pecans into pastry shell. Pour caramel topping over chips and pecans. In a mixing bowl, beat cream cheese and sugar until smooth. In a saucepan over low heat, cook and stir cream and remaining chips until smooth. Gradually add to the cream cheese mixture; mix well. Carefully spread into pastry shell. Garnish as desired. **Yield:** 8 servings.

— 🥄 🥄 🥄 —

You'll Flip Over These Cakes

PINEAPPLE upside-down cakes were first developed in the 1920's to promote canned pineapple and were traditionally baked in cast-iron skillets.

Grandma's been making this topsy-turvy dessert ever since, but it hasn't gone out of style! Your idea of a delightful dessert will be turned upside down when you taste one of these variations on the traditional pineapple upside-down cake.

These recipes feature an interesting mix of ingredients in the bottom of the pan that make this luscious lineup "tops" when the cakes are turned out to serve.

Spiced Apple Upside-Down Cake
(Pictured below)

I like unusual desserts like this one. Judging from the condition of my recipe card, it must be very good—a messy, well-worn card shows I've made this countless times. —Mavis Diment, Marcus, Iowa

- 1 jar (14 ounces) spiced apple rings
- 6 tablespoons butter *or* margarine, softened, *divided*
- 1/2 cup packed brown sugar

TAKE THE CAKE with special desserts like Spiced Apple Upside-Down Cake and Peach Upside-Down Cake (shown above, top to bottom). Compliments are bound to turn up when you try these treats!

1/4 **cup sliced almonds, toasted**
   1 **egg**
1/2 **cup milk**
   1 **teaspoon vanilla extract**
   1 **cup all-purpose flour**
1/2 **cup sugar**
1-1/2 **teaspoons baking powder**
Whipped cream, optional

Drain the apple rings, reserving 1 tablespoon syrup; set apple rings aside. Melt 2 tablespoons butter; add brown sugar and reserved syrup. Spread evenly in a greased 8-in. round baking pan; sprinkle with almonds. Top with apple rings; set aside. In a mixing bowl, beat egg, milk, vanilla and remaining butter. Combine flour, sugar and baking powder; add to egg mixture and mix well. Spoon over apple rings. Bake at 350° for 35-40 minutes or until a toothpick inserted near the center comes out clean. Let stand for 5 minutes. Run a knife around the edge of pan; invert cake onto a serving plate. Cool. Serve with whipped cream if desired. **Yield:** 6-8 servings.

Peach Upside-Down Cake

(Pictured at left)

Sweet peaches and coconut give this variation of pineapple upside-down cake a refreshing flavor that's especially nice for spring and summer.
— *Terri Holmgren, Swanville, Minnesota*

1/3 **cup butter *or* margarine, melted**
1/2 **cup packed brown sugar**
   1 **can (29 ounces) peach halves**
1/4 **cup shredded coconut**
   2 **eggs**
2/3 **cup sugar**
1/2 **teaspoon almond extract**
   1 **cup all-purpose flour**
   1 **teaspoon baking powder**
1/4 **teaspoon salt**

Pour butter into a 9-in. round baking pan; sprinkle with brown sugar. Drain peaches, reserving 6 tablespoons of syrup. Arrange peach halves, cut side down, in a single layer over the sugar. Sprinkle coconut around peaches; set aside. In a mixing bowl, beat the eggs until thick and lemon-colored; gradually beat in sugar. Add extract and reserved syrup. Combine flour, baking powder and salt; add to egg mixture and mix well. Pour over peaches. Bake at 350° for 50-60 minutes or until a toothpick inserted near the center comes out clean. Cool for 10 minutes; invert cake onto a serving plate. Serve warm. **Yield:** 6-8 servings.

Banana Upside-Down Cake

For a fun and distinctive way to use bananas, try this version. Every time I serve this treat, someone requests the recipe.
— *Ruth Andrewson*
Leavenworth, Washington

1/2 **cup packed brown sugar**
   2 **tablespoons lemon juice, *divided***
   1 **tablespoon butter *or* margarine**
1/2 **cup pecan halves**
   2 **medium firm bananas, sliced**
CAKE:
1-1/2 **cups all-purpose flour**
1/2 **cup sugar**
   1 **teaspoon baking soda**
   1 **teaspoon baking powder**
1/4 **teaspoon salt**
1/4 **cup cold butter *or* margarine**
   1 **cup plain yogurt**
   2 **eggs, beaten**
   2 **teaspoons grated lemon peel**
   1 **teaspoon vanilla extract**
Whipped cream, optional

In a small saucepan, combine brown sugar, 1 tablespoon of lemon juice and butter; bring to a boil. Reduce heat to medium; cook without stirring until the sugar is dissolved. Pour into a greased 9-in. springform pan. Arrange pecans on top with flat side up. Pour remaining lemon juice into a small bowl; add the bananas and stir carefully. Drain. Arrange the bananas in a circular pattern over the pecans; set aside. In a large bowl, combine flour, sugar, baking soda, baking powder and salt. Cut in butter until mixture resembles coarse crumbs. Combine yogurt, eggs, lemon peel and vanilla; stir into the dry ingredients just until moistened. Spoon over bananas. Bake at 375° for 35-40 minutes or until a toothpick inserted near the center comes out clean. Cool for 10 minutes. Run a knife around edge of pan; invert cake onto a serving plate. Serve with whipped cream if desired. **Yield:** 6-8 servings.

Upside-Down Advice

So that you don't disturb the fruit in the bottom of the pan, be sure to *carefully* spoon the cake batter on top.

If some of the fruit topping sticks to the bottom of the pan after inverting the baked cake onto a serving plate, gently scrape it off of the pan and replace it on top of the warm cake.

Upside-down cakes are best served warm on the same day they're made.

Triple Fruit Pie

(Pictured below)

My goal is to create pies as good as my mother's. I came up with this recipe to use up fruit in my freezer. The first time I made it, my family begged for seconds. If I continue making pies this good, maybe someday our two daughters will be striving to imitate mine!
—Jeanne Freybler, Grand Rapids, Michigan

1-1/4 cups *each* fresh blueberries, raspberries
    and chopped rhubarb*
1/2 teaspoon almond extract
1-1/4 cups sugar
1/4 cup quick-cooking tapioca
1/4 teaspoon ground nutmeg
1/4 teaspoon salt
1 tablespoon lemon juice
Pastry for double-crust pie (9 inches)

In a large bowl, combine fruits and extract; toss to coat. In another bowl, combine sugar, tapioca, nutmeg and salt. Add to fruit; stir gently. Let stand for 15 minutes. Line a 9-in. pie plate with bottom crust; trim pastry even with edge. Stir lemon juice into fruit mixture; spoon into the crust. Roll out the remaining pastry and make a lattice crust. Seal and flute edges. Bake at 400° for 20 minutes. Reduce heat to 350°; bake 30 minutes longer or until the crust is golden brown and the filling is bubbly. **Yield:** 6-8 servings. ***Editor's Note:** Frozen berries and rhubarb may be substituted for fresh; thaw and drain before using.

Pumpkin Cake Roll

This special cake is delicious—especially if you love cream cheese and pumpkin. It tastes so good in fall.
—Elizabeth Montgomery, Taylorville, Illinois

3 eggs
1 cup sugar
2/3 cup cooked *or* canned pumpkin
1 teaspoon lemon juice
3/4 cup all-purpose flour
2 teaspoons ground cinnamon
1 teaspoon baking powder
1/2 teaspoon salt
1/4 teaspoon ground nutmeg
1 cup finely chopped walnuts
CREAM CHEESE FILLING:
2 packages (3 ounces *each*) cream cheese, softened
1 cup confectioners' sugar
1/4 cup butter *or* margarine, softened
1/2 teaspoon vanilla extract
Additional confectioners' sugar, optional

In a mixing bowl, beat eggs on high for 5 minutes. Gradually beat in sugar until thick and lemon-colored. Add pumpkin and lemon juice. Combine flour, cinnamon, baking powder, salt and nutmeg; fold into pumpkin mixture. Grease a 15-in. x 10-in. x 1-in. baking pan and line with waxed paper. Grease and flour the paper. Spread batter into pan; sprinkle with walnuts. Bake at 375° for 15 minutes or until cake springs back when lightly touched. Immediately turn out onto a linen towel dusted with confectioners' sugar. Peel off paper and roll cake up in towel, starting with a short end. Cool. Meanwhile, in a mixing bowl, beat cream cheese, sugar, butter and vanilla until fluffy. Carefully unroll cake. Spread filling over cake to within 1 in. of edges. Roll up again. Cover and chill until serving. Dust with confectioners' sugar if desired. **Yield:** 8-10 servings.

Marble Chiffon Cake

(Pictured on back cover)

This beautiful high cake won me a blue ribbon for "best chiffon cake" at our county fair years ago.
—Sharon Evans, Rockwell, Iowa

1/3 cup baking cocoa
1/4 cup boiling water
1-1/2 cups plus 3 tablespoons sugar, *divided*
1/2 cup plus 2 tablespoons vegetable oil, *divided*
2-1/4 cups all-purpose flour
1 tablespoon baking powder
1 teaspoon salt
7 eggs, *separated*
3/4 cup water
1/2 teaspoon cream of tartar
2 teaspoons grated orange peel

ORANGE GLAZE:
2 cups confectioners' sugar
1/3 cup butter *or* margarine, melted
3 to 4 tablespoons orange juice
1/2 teaspoon grated orange peel

In a small bowl, combine cocoa, boiling water, 3 tablespoons sugar and 2 tablespoons oil; whisk until smooth. Cool. In a mixing bowl, combine flour, baking powder, salt and remaining sugar. In another bowl, whisk egg yolks, water and remaining oil; add to dry ingredients. Beat until well blended. In another mixing bowl, beat egg whites and cream of tartar until soft peaks form; fold into batter. Remove 2 cups batter; stir into cocoa mixture. To remaining batter, add orange peel. Alternately spoon orange and chocolate batters into an ungreased 10-in. tube pan. Swirl with a knife. Bake at 325° for 70-75 minutes or until top springs back when lightly touched. Immediately invert the cake pan on a wire rack; cool completely. For glaze, combine sugar, butter and enough orange juice to reach desired consistency. Add orange peel; spoon over cake. **Yield:** 12-14 servings.

🍴 🍴 🍴

Chocolate Raspberry Pie

(Pictured above right)

After tasting this pie at my sister-in-law's house, I had to have the recipe. I love the chocolate and raspberry layers separated by a dreamy cream layer.
—Ruth Bartel, Morris, Manitoba

1 unbaked pastry shell (9 inches)
3 tablespoons sugar
1 tablespoon cornstarch
2 cups fresh *or* frozen unsweetened raspberries, thawed

FILLING:
1 package (8 ounces) cream cheese, softened
1/3 cup sugar
1/2 teaspoon vanilla extract
1/2 cup whipping cream, whipped

TOPPING:
2 squares (1 ounce *each*) semisweet chocolate
3 tablespoons butter *or* margarine

Line unpricked pastry shell with a double thickness of heavy-duty foil. Bake at 450° for 8 minutes. Remove foil; bake 5 minutes longer. Cool on a wire rack. In a saucepan, combine sugar and cornstarch. Stir in the raspberries; bring to a boil over medium heat. Boil and stir for 2 minutes. Remove from the heat; cool for 15 minutes. Spread into shell; refrigerate. In a mixing bowl, beat cream cheese, sugar and vanilla until fluffy. Fold in the whipped cream. Carefully spread over the raspberry layer. Cover and refrigerate for at least 1 hour. For topping, melt chocolate and butter; cool for 4-5 minutes. Pour over filling. Cover and chill at least 2 hours. Store in the refrigerator. **Yield:** 6-8 servings.

No-Mess Meringue

When cutting meringue-topped pies, oil the knife first so the meringue won't tear or pull.

For frosting, melt chocolate in a heavy saucepan over medium heat. Gradually stir in cream and sugar if desired until well blended. Heat to a gentle boil; boil and stir for 1 minute. Remove from the heat and transfer to a mixing bowl. Refrigerate for 2-3 hours or until mixture reaches pudding-like consistency, stirring a few times. Beat until soft peaks form. Immediately spread between layers and over top and sides of cake. Sprinkle with grated chocolate. Store in the refrigerator. **Yield:** 16-20 servings.

Applesauce Spice Cupcakes

I began making these moist cupcakes in elementary school and still bake them frequently.
—Edna Hoffman, Hebron, Indiana

   1/3 cup butter *or* margarine, softened
   3/4 cup sugar
     2 eggs
     1 teaspoon vanilla extract
1-1/3 cups all-purpose flour
     1 teaspoon baking powder
   1/2 teaspoon baking soda
   1/2 teaspoon salt
     1 teaspoon ground cinnamon
   1/2 teaspoon ground nutmeg
   1/8 teaspoon ground cloves
   3/4 cup applesauce
Cream cheese frosting

In a mixing bowl, cream butter and sugar. Add eggs and vanilla; mix well. Combine the dry ingredients; add to creamed mixture alternately with applesauce. Fill greased or paper-lined muffin cups two-thirds full. Bake at 350° for 25 minutes or until cupcakes test done. Cool for 10 minutes before removing to a wire rack. Frost cooled cupcakes. **Yield:** 1 dozen.

Fluffy Caramel Pie

I bake a variety of pies, but this is the one my husband likes best. The gingersnap crumb crust is a tangy contrast to the sweet, lighter-than-air caramel filling.
—Ginger Hendricksen, Wisconsin Rapids, Wisconsin

1-1/2 cups crushed gingersnaps (about 30 cookies)
   1/4 cup butter *or* margarine, melted
FILLING:
   1/4 cup cold water
     1 envelope unflavored gelatin
    28 caramels
     1 cup milk
Dash salt

Triple Layer Brownie Cake

(Pictured above)

A little of this tall rich brownie cake goes a long way, so you'll have plenty to share with grateful family members and friends. It's a sure way to satisfy chocolate lovers. —*Barbara Dean, Littleton, Colorado*

1-1/2 cups butter (no substitutes)
     6 squares (1 ounce *each*) unsweetened chocolate
     3 cups sugar
     5 eggs
1-1/2 teaspoons vanilla extract
1-1/2 cups all-purpose flour
   3/4 teaspoon salt
FROSTING:
     2 packages (8 ounces *each*) semisweet baking chocolate
     3 cups whipping cream
   1/2 cup sugar, optional
     2 milk chocolate candy bars (1.55 ounces *each*), grated

In a microwave or double boiler, melt butter and chocolate. Stir in sugar. Add eggs, one at a time, beating well after each addition. Stir in vanilla, flour and salt; mix well. Pour into three greased and floured 9-in. round cake pans. Bake at 350° for 23-25 minutes or until a toothpick inserted near the center comes out clean. Cool for 10 minutes; remove from pan to a wire rack to cool completely.

1/2 cup chopped pecans
1 teaspoon vanilla extract
1 cup whipping cream, whipped
Caramel ice cream topping and additional pecans, optional

Combine the cookie crumbs and butter; press onto the bottom and up the sides of a greased 9-in. pie plate. Cover and chill. Meanwhile, place cold water in a heavy saucepan; sprinkle with gelatin. Let stand for 1 minute. Add caramels, milk and salt; cook and stir over low heat until gelatin is dissolved and caramels are melted. Refrigerate for 1-2 hours or until mixture mounds when stirred with a spoon. Stir in pecans and vanilla. Fold in whipped cream. Pour into crust. Refrigerate for 6 hours or overnight. Garnish with ice cream topping and pecans if desired. Store in the refrigerator. **Yield:** 6-8 servings.

Colonial Caraway Cake

A dusting of confectioners' sugar is all that's needed to top this beautiful cake. The combination of caraway and lemon is unique and flavorful. —Eleanor Davis *Pittsburgh, Pennsylvania*

5 eggs, *separated*
1/4 teaspoon salt
1-1/2 cups sugar, *divided*
1 cup butter *or* margarine, softened
1-2/3 cups cake flour
2 teaspoons caraway seeds
1 teaspoon lemon extract
Confectioners' sugar

In a mixing bowl, beat egg whites and salt until foamy. Gradually beat in 1/2 cup sugar until stiff peaks form; set aside. In another mixing bowl, cream butter and remaining sugar until light and fluffy. Add egg yolks, one at a time, beating well after each addition. Add flour, caraway and lemon extract; mix well. Fold in egg white mixture. Spoon into a greased and floured 10-in. fluted tube pan. Bake at 300° for 65-70 minutes or until a toothpick inserted near the center comes out clean. Cool for 10 minutes; remove from pan to a wire rack to cool completely. Dust with confectioners' sugar before serving. **Yield:** 12-16 servings.

Potluck Apple Pie

(Pictured at right)

In charge of dessert for a fund-raising dinner at our church, I experimented and came up with this scrumptious pie made in a jelly roll pan. It fed a group and got rave reviews. With flavorful apples and maple syrup, it gives a true taste of the Northeast.
—Alma Lynne Gravel, Trappe, Pennsylvania

2-1/4 cups all-purpose flour, *divided*
1/4 cup water
Pinch salt
1 cup shortening
FILLING:
1/2 cup maple syrup, *divided*
3 pounds tart apples (8 to 9 medium), peeled and thinly sliced
1-1/4 cups sugar
1/4 cup lemon juice
2 teaspoons ground cinnamon
1 teaspoon vanilla extract
TOPPING:
1 cup all-purpose flour
1/2 cup packed brown sugar
1/2 cup cold butter *or* margarine
1 cup chopped pecans

In a small bowl, combine 1/4 cup flour and water until smooth; set aside. In a large bowl, combine salt and remaining flour; cut in shortening until mixture resembles coarse crumbs. Add reserved flour mixture; knead gently until dough forms a ball. Press dough onto the bottom and up the sides of an ungreased 15-in. x 10-in. x 1-in. baking pan. Spread 1/4 cup syrup over crust. Arrange apples over syrup. Combine sugar, lemon juice, cinnamon, vanilla and remaining syrup; drizzle over apples. For topping, combine flour and sugar in a bowl; cut in butter until the mixture resembles coarse crumbs. Stir in pecans. Sprinkle over filling. Bake at 350° for 1 hour or until apples are tender. **Yield:** 18-24 servings. **Editor's Note:** Pastry can be easily pressed into pan by placing a large sheet of plastic wrap on top of the dough.

Cherry Pineapple Pie

My husband never cared for cherry pie. Then one day I added pineapple and he raved about it!
—Carolyn Bartley, Curtice, Ohio

- 1 cup sugar
- 1/3 cup all-purpose flour
- 1/8 teaspoon salt
- 2 cans (16 ounces *each*) pitted tart red cherries, well drained
- 2 cans (8 ounces *each*) crushed pineapple, well drained
- 3 drops almond extract
- Pastry for double-crust pie (9 inches)
- 2 tablespoons butter *or* margarine
- 1 tablespoon milk
- Additional sugar

In a bowl, combine sugar, flour and salt. Stir in cherries, pineapple and extract. Line a 9-in. pie pan with the bottom crust. Add filling; dot with butter. Top with a lattice crust. Brush with milk and sprinkle with sugar. Bake at 375° for 50-60 minutes or until bubbly and golden brown. **Yield:** 6-8 servings.

Peachy Rhubarb Pie

(Pictured below)

My husband especially loves the combination of peaches and homegrown rhubarb in this pie.
—Phyllis Galloway, Roswell, Georgia

- 1 can (8-1/2 ounces) sliced peaches
- 2 cups chopped fresh *or* frozen rhubarb, thawed and drained
- 1 cup sugar
- 1/4 cup flaked coconut

- 3 tablespoons quick-cooking tapioca
- 1 teaspoon vanilla extract
- Pastry for double-crust pie (9 inches)
- 1 tablespoon butter *or* margarine

Drain peaches, reserving syrup; chop the peaches. Place peaches and syrup in a bowl; add rhubarb, sugar, coconut, tapioca and vanilla. Line a 9-in. pie plate with the bottom pastry. Add filling; dot with butter. Top with remaining pastry or a lattice crust; flute edges. If using a full top crust, cut slits in it. Bake at 350° for 1 hour or until crust is golden brown and filling is bubbly. **Yield:** 6-8 servings.

Pear Apple Pie

When it's apple season, I reach for this recipe from The Apple Fare restaurant in Grass Valley. Owner Joyce Rollings says homemade pies are paramount at this family eatery. —Gloria Curtis, Marysville, California

- 1 cup plus 1 tablespoon all-purpose flour, *divided*
- 1/2 teaspoon salt
- 1/3 cup shortening
- 2 to 3 tablespoons cold water
- 1/3 cup sugar
- 1/2 teaspoon ground cinnamon
- 3-1/2 cups sliced peeled tart apples
- 1-1/2 cups sliced peeled pears
- **TOPPING:**
- 1/2 cup all-purpose flour
- 1/2 cup packed brown sugar
- 1/4 cup cold butter *or* margarine
- 3 tablespoons chopped walnuts
- Whipped cream, optional

In a bowl, combine 1 cup flour and salt; cut in shortening until mixture resemble coarse crumbs. Gradually add water, 1 tablespoon at a time, tossing lightly with a fork until dough forms a ball. On a floured surface, roll out dough to fit a 9-in. pie plate. Flute edges. In a large bowl, combine sugar, cinnamon and remaining flour. Add apples and pears; toss. Pour into crust. For topping, combine flour and brown sugar; cut in butter until crumbly. Stir in walnuts. Sprinkle over filling. Bake at 375° for 50-60 minutes or until fruit is tender. Serve with whipped cream if desired. **Yield:** 8 servings.

Fresh Apricot Pie

This is a nice change of pace from the more traditional fruit and berry pies. Apricots are very nutritious and delicious! —Ruth Peterson, Jenison, Michigan

4 cups sliced fresh apricots
1 cup sugar
1/3 cup all-purpose flour
Pinch ground nutmeg
1 tablespoon lemon juice
Pastry for double-crust pie (9 inches)
Milk
Additional sugar

In a bowl, toss apricots, sugar, flour and nutmeg. Sprinkle with lemon juice; mix well. Line a 9-in. pie plate with bottom crust; add filling. Roll out remaining pastry to make a lattice crust. Place over filling; seal and flute edges. Brush with milk and sprinkle with sugar. Cover edges of pastry loosely with foil. Bake at 375° for 45-55 minutes or until golden brown. **Yield:** 6-8 servings.

— ▛ ▛ ▛ —

White Chocolate Pound Cake

I'm always asked to make this moist bundt cake, drizzled with two types of chocolate glaze, for special occasions. —Kimberly Thompson, Fayetteville, Georgia

8 squares (1 ounce _each_) white baking chocolate
1 cup butter (no substitutes), softened
2 cups plus 2 tablespoons sugar, _divided_
5 eggs
2 teaspoons vanilla extract
1/2 teaspoon almond extract
3 cups all-purpose flour
1 teaspoon baking powder
1/2 teaspoon salt
1/4 teaspoon baking soda
1 cup (8 ounces) sour cream
GLAZE:
4 squares (1 ounce _each_) semisweet baking chocolate, melted
4 squares (1 ounce _each_) white baking chocolate, melted
Whole fresh strawberries, optional

Chop four squares of white chocolate and melt the other four; set both aside. In a mixing bowl, cream butter and 2 cups sugar until light and fluffy, about 5 minutes. Add eggs, one at a time, beating well after each addition. Stir in extracts and melted chocolate. Combine flour, baking powder, salt and baking soda; add to the creamed mixture alternately with sour cream. Beat just until combined. Grease a 10-in. fluted tube pan. Sprinkle with remaining sugar. Pour a third of the batter into the pan. Sprinkle with half of the chopped chocolate. Repeat. Pour remaining batter on top. Bake 350° for 55-60 minutes or until a toothpick

inserted near the center comes out clean. Cool for 10 minutes; remove from pan to a wire rack to cool completely. Drizzle semisweet and white chocolate over cake. Garnish with strawberries if desired. **Yield:** 16 servings.

Ricotta Nut Pie

(Pictured above)

Similar to a traditional Italian ricotta pie but with a few fun twists, this is a satisfying dessert that's not overly sweet. —Renee Bennett, Manlius, New York

1-1/2 cups crushed vanilla wafers (about 45 cookies)
1/4 cup butter _or_ margarine, softened
1/3 cup apricot preserves
1 carton (15 ounces) ricotta cheese
1/2 cup sugar
1 teaspoon vanilla extract
3 squares (1 ounce _each_) semisweet baking chocolate, chopped
1/2 cup finely chopped toasted almonds
1/4 cup chopped dried apricots
1 cup whipping cream, whipped
1/4 cup slivered almonds, toasted

Combine the wafer crumbs and butter; press onto the bottom and up the sides of an ungreased 9-in. pie plate. Bake at 375° for 6-8 minutes or until the crust is lightly browned; cool. Spread preserves over crust. In a mixing bowl, beat ricotta, sugar and vanilla until smooth. Stir in chocolate, chopped almonds and apricots. Fold in whipped cream. Spoon into the crust. Sprinkle with slivered almonds. Cover and refrigerate overnight. **Yield:** 6-8 servings.

Just Desserts

Put a flavorful finishing touch on every meal with a mouth-watering medley of candies, cobblers, cheesecakes, cream puffs, puddings, sweet sauces and more.

HAPPY ENDINGS. Clockwise from upper left: Black and Blue Cobbler (p. 180), Orange Chocolate Meltaways (p. 170), White Chocolate Mousse (p. 175), Rich Truffle Wedges (p. 168) and Neapolitan Cheesecake (p. 167).

Mocha Fondue

(Pictured above)

People have such fun dipping pieces of cake and fruit into this heavenly melted chocolate mixture. It's an exquisite treat to serve at special gatherings.
—*Gloria Jarrett, Loveland, Ohio*

  3 cups (18 ounces) milk chocolate chips
1/2 cup whipping cream
  1 tablespoon instant coffee granules
  2 tablespoons hot water
  1 teaspoon vanilla extract
1/8 teaspoon ground cinnamon
  1 pound cake (16 ounces), cut into 1-inch cubes
Strawberries, kiwi *or* other fresh fruit

In a heavy saucepan, melt chocolate chips with cream over low heat, stirring constantly. Dissolve coffee in water; add to chocolate mixture with vanilla and cinnamon. Mix well. Serve warm, using cake pieces and fruit for dipping. **Yield:** 2 cups.

Cherry Rice Dessert

I cook with rice at least four times a week. This special rice pudding is a terrific example of a sweet rice treat. —*Naomi Jackson, McCrory, Arkansas*

  3 cups cooked long grain rice
1/2 cup chopped pecans

  1 package (8 ounces) cream cheese, softened, *divided*
  1 can (21 ounces) cherry *or* strawberry pie filling
  1 cup confectioners' sugar
  1 carton (12 ounces) frozen whipped topping, thawed, *divided*
  1 package (3.4 ounces) instant coconut cream pudding mix
1-1/2 cups cold milk
  1 cup flaked coconut, toasted

In a bowl, combine rice, pecans and a third of the cream cheese; mix well. Spread into a greased 13-in. x 9-in. x 2-in. baking dish. Refrigerate for 30 minutes; spread with pie filling. Refrigerate for 15 minutes. In a bowl, combine sugar and the remaining cream cheese. Fold in half of the whipped topping; spread over pie filling. Refrigerate for 30 minutes. In a mixing bowl, beat pudding mix and milk for 2 minutes or until thickened. Pour over top; refrigerate for 30 minutes. Spread with the remaining whipped topping; sprinkle with coconut. **Yield:** 16-20 servings.

Date Nut Cracker Dessert

This chewy treat has a refreshing lemon topping. It's always a hit. —*Billie Moss, El Sobrante, California*

  3 eggs
3/4 cup sugar, *divided*
  1 teaspoon baking powder
  2 cups vanilla wafer crumbs
  1 cup chopped dates
  1 cup chopped pecans *or* walnuts
  2 tablespoons grated orange peel
  1 teaspoon vanilla extract
TOPPING:
1/4 cup sour cream
1/4 cup whipping cream
  1 tablespoon lemon juice
  1 tablespoon sugar

In a mixing bowl, beat eggs and 1/2 cup sugar until thickened, about 4-5 minutes. Combine baking powder and remaining sugar; beat into egg mixture. Add wafer crumbs, dates, nuts, orange peel and vanilla; stir well. Pour into a well-greased 10-in. pie plate or 11-in. x 7-in. x 2-in. baking pan. Bake at 350° for 30-40 minutes or until a toothpick inserted near the center comes out clean. Meanwhile, combine topping ingredients; let stand at room temperature until the pie has cooled for 30 minutes (topping will thicken). Spread over pie. Cool completely before serving. Store in the refrigerator. **Yield:** 6-8 servings.

Almond Coconut Candies

These special candies have the irresistible combination of coconut, almonds and deep dark chocolate. They make great gifts—if you can get yourself to part with any! —*Janet Loomis, Terry, Montana*

4-1/2 cups confectioners' sugar
   3 cups flaked coconut
   1 cup sweetened condensed milk
 1/2 cup butter *or* margarine, melted
   1 teaspoon vanilla extract
  60 whole unblanched almonds
FROSTING:
1-1/2 cups confectioners' sugar
 1/2 cup baking cocoa
 1/2 cup butter *or* margarine, melted
   3 tablespoons hot coffee

In a large bowl, combine the first five ingredients; stir until well mixed. Shape into 1-in. balls; place on lightly greased baking sheets. Press an almond on top of each ball. Chill for 1 hour. Combine frosting ingredients until smooth; immediately frost tops of candies. Chill until frosting is firm. Store in the refrigerator. **Yield:** 5 dozen.

Raspberry Crisp

My raspberry patch keeps my family well supplied with luscious treats in summer. We enjoy these beautiful sweet berries in many desserts, including this one. —*Patricia Staudt, Marble Rock, Iowa*

   4 cups fresh *or* frozen raspberries
 1/3 cup sugar
 1/3 cup plus 3 tablespoons all-purpose flour, *divided*
 3/4 cup quick-cooking oats
 1/3 cup packed brown sugar
 1/4 cup cold butter *or* margarine

In a bowl, gently toss raspberries with sugar and 3 tablespoons flour. Transfer to a greased 9-in. square baking dish. In a bowl, combine the oats, brown sugar and remaining flour; cut in butter until mixture resembles coarse crumbs. Sprinkle over berries. Bake at 350° for 30 minutes or until golden brown. **Yield:** 6 servings.

Neapolitan Cheesecake

(Pictured at right)

This rich, creamy cheesecake won first-place ribbons at many fairs and is my family's favorite dessert. —*Sherri Regalbuto, Carp, Ontario*

   1 cup chocolate wafer crumbs
   5 tablespoons butter *or* margarine, melted, *divided*
   3 packages (8 ounces *each*) cream cheese, softened
 3/4 cup sugar
   3 eggs
   1 teaspoon vanilla extract
   5 squares (1 ounce *each*) semisweet chocolate, divided
2-1/2 squares (2-1/2 ounces) white baking chocolate, *divided*
 1/3 cup mashed sweetened strawberries
   2 teaspoons shortening, *divided*

Combine crumbs and 3 tablespoons of butter; press onto the bottom of an ungreased 9-in. springform pan. Bake at 350° for 8 minutes; cool. In a mixing bowl, beat cream cheese and sugar until smooth. Beat in eggs, one at a time. Add vanilla. Divide into three portions, about 1-2/3 cups each. Melt 2 squares semisweet chocolate; stir into one portion of batter. Melt 2 squares of white chocolate; stir into second portion. Stir strawberries into remaining batter. Spread semisweet mixture evenly over crust. Carefully spread with white chocolate mixture, then strawberry mixture. Bake at 425° for 10 minutes; reduce heat to 300°. Bake for 50-55 minutes or until center is nearly set. Remove from oven; immediately run a knife around edge. Cool; remove from pan. Melt remaining semisweet chocolate, remaining butter and 1 teaspoon of shortening; cool for 2 minutes. Pour over cake. Melt remaining white chocolate and shortening; drizzle over glaze. Refrigerate leftovers. **Yield:** 12-14 servings.

Rich Truffle Wedges

(Pictured below)

This decadent dessert has a fudgy consistency and big chocolate taste. The tart raspberry sauce complements the flavor. —Patricia Vatta, Norwood, Ontario

- 1/2 cup butter *or* margarine
- 6 squares (1 ounce *each*) semisweet chocolate, chopped
- 3 eggs
- 2/3 cup sugar
- 1 teaspoon vanilla extract
- 1/4 teaspoon salt
- 2/3 cup all-purpose flour

GLAZE:
- 1/4 cup butter *or* margarine
- 2 squares (1 ounce *each*) semisweet chocolate
- 2 squares (1 ounce *each*) unsweetened chocolate
- 2 teaspoons honey

SAUCE:
- 2 cups fresh *or* frozen unsweetened raspberries
- 2 tablespoons sugar

Whipped cream, fresh raspberries and mint, optional

In a microwave or double boiler, melt butter and chocolate; stir until smooth. Cool for 10 minutes. In a mixing bowl, beat the eggs, sugar, vanilla and salt until thick, about 4 minutes. Blend in chocolate mixture. Stir in flour; mix well. Pour into a greased and floured 9-in. springform pan. Bake at 350° for 25-30 minutes or until a toothpick inserted near the center comes out clean. Cool completely on a wire rack. Combine glaze ingredients in a small saucepan; cook and stir over low heat until melted and smooth. Cool slightly. Run a knife around the edge of springform pan to loosen; remove cake to serving plate. Spread glaze over the top and sides; set aside. For sauce, puree raspberries in a blender or food processor. Press through a sieve if desired; discard seeds. Stir in sugar; chill until serving. Spoon sauce over individual servings. Garnish with whipped cream, raspberries and mint if desired. **Yield:** 12 servings.

Cashew Crickle

Instead of traditional brickle that calls for peanuts, this recipe uses cashews. Everyone agrees this holiday candy is excellent. —Kathy Kittell, Lenexa, Kansas

- 2 cups sugar
- 1 cup corn syrup
- 1/2 cup water
- 3 tablespoons butter *or* margarine
- 1 teaspoon vanilla extract
- 1/2 teaspoon baking soda
- 2 cups salted cashews

In a large saucepan, combine sugar, corn syrup and water; bring to a boil, stirring constantly, until sugar is dissolved. Cook, without stirring, over medium heat until a candy thermometer reads 300° (hard-crack stage). Remove from the heat; stir in butter, vanilla and baking soda. Add cashews. Pour into a greased 15-in. x 10-in. x 1-in. baking pan. Cool before breaking into pieces. **Yield:** about 2 pounds.

Low-Fat Cheesecake

No one would ever guess this smooth, rich-tasting dessert is low in fat. Drizzled with cherry pie filling, it's a delicious lovely treat. —Vera Reid Laramie, Wyoming

☑ Nutritional Analysis included

- 2 packages (8 ounces *each*) fat-free cream cheese, softened
- 2/3 cup plus 3 tablespoons sugar, *divided*
- 1-1/2 teaspoons vanilla extract, *divided*

Egg substitute equivalent to 3 eggs
- 1 cup (8 ounces) nonfat sour cream
- 1 cup reduced-sugar cherry pie filling

In a mixing bowl, beat cream cheese, 2/3 cup of sugar and 1/2 teaspoon vanilla until fluffy. Gradually add egg substitute; beat until smooth. Pour

to a 9-in. pie plate that has been coated with non-stick cooking spray. Bake at 350° for 30-35 minutes or until puffy and light brown around the edges. Cool on a wire rack for 10 minutes. Meanwhile, combine sour cream and remaining sugar and vanilla. Spread over cheesecake. Bake 15 minutes longer. Cool completely on a wire rack. Refrigerate. Before serving, top each serving with 2 tablespoons cherry pie filling. **Yield:** 8 servings. **Nutritional Analysis:** One serving equals 214 calories, 342 mg sodium, 5 mg cholesterol, 37 gm carbohydrate, 14 gm protein, 1 gm fat. **Diabetic Exchanges:** 2 starch, 1 very lean meat, 1/2 fruit.

South Carolina Cobbler

With peach orchards just a couple miles from home, I'm happy to treat family to this traditional dessert.
—Mattie Carter, Rock Hill, South Carolina

   4 cups sliced peeled fresh *or* frozen peaches, thawed
   1 cup sugar, *divided*
   1/2 teaspoon almond extract
   1/3 cup butter *or* margarine, melted
   3/4 cup all-purpose flour
   2 teaspoons baking powder
Pinch salt
   3/4 cup milk

Gently toss peaches, 1/2 cup sugar and extract; set aside. Pour butter into a 2-qt. baking dish. In a bowl, combine flour, baking powder, salt and remaining sugar; stir in milk. Mix well. Pour evenly over butter (do not stir). Top with peach mixture. Bake at 350° for 50-55 minutes. **Yield:** 8 servings.

Strawberry Rhubarb Sauce

(Pictured above right)

This versatile sauce brings a sunny new taste to pound cake, ice cream and bread pudding. I wouldn't be without it! —Mary Pittman, Shawnee, Kansas

2-1/2 cups chopped fresh *or* frozen rhubarb (1-inch pieces)
   1 cup water
   1/2 cup sugar
   2 tablespoons grated lemon peel
   1/4 teaspoon salt
   1 cup sliced fresh *or* frozen unsweetened strawberries
   2 tablespoons lemon juice
   1/4 teaspoon ground cinnamon

   3 to 4 drops red food coloring, optional
Pound *or* angel food cake

In a saucepan, combine the rhubarb, water, sugar, lemon peel and salt; bring to a boil. Reduce heat. Cook, uncovered, over medium heat until rhubarb is soft, about 10-15 minutes. Remove from the heat and let stand for 5 minutes. Stir in strawberries, lemon juice and cinnamon. Add food coloring if desired. Cool. Serve over cake. **Yield:** 3 cups.

Fluffy Rice Dessert

Working in food-related jobs over the years, I've collected lots of wonderful recipes like this one.
—Janice Todd, La Crosse, Wisconsin

✓ Nutritional Analysis included

   1 package (.3 ounce) sugar-free cherry gelatin
   1 cup boiling water
   1 can (20 ounces) unsweetened crushed pineapple
1-1/2 cups hot cooked rice
   1 cup light whipped topping

In a bowl, dissolve gelatin in boiling water. Drain pineapple, reserving juice; set pineapple aside. Add juice to gelatin; stir in rice. Chill until mixture begins to thicken. Fold in whipped topping and pineapple. Chill for 1 hour. **Yield:** 10 servings. **Nutritional Analysis:** One 1/2-cup serving equals 79 calories, 19 mg sodium, 0 cholesterol, 16 gm carbohydrate, 1 gm protein, 1 gm fat. **Diabetic Exchanges:** 1/2 starch, 1/2 fruit.

Orange Chocolate Meltaways

(Pictured above)

The terrific combination of chocolate and orange makes these some of the best truffles I've ever had. As holiday gifts, they're showstoppers. I have little time to cook, but when I do, I like to "get fancy". In this case, "fancy" doesn't have to be difficult. —Lori Kostecki
Wausau, Wisconsin

        1 package (11-1/2 ounces) milk chocolate
          chips
        1 cup (6 ounces) semisweet chocolate chips
      3/4 cup whipping cream
        1 teaspoon grated orange peel
    2-1/2 teaspoons orange extract
    1-1/2 cups finely chopped toasted pecans
    COATING:
        1 cup (6 ounces) milk chocolate chips
        2 tablespoons shortening

Place chocolate chips in a mixing bowl; set aside. In a saucepan, bring cream and orange peel to a gentle boil; immediately pour over chips. Let stand for 1 minute; whisk until smooth. Add the extract. Cover and chill for 35 minutes or until mixture begins to thicken. Beat for 10-15 seconds or just until mixture lightens in color (do not overbeat). Spoon rounded teaspoonfuls onto waxed paper-lined baking sheets. Cover and chill for 5 minutes. Gently shape into balls; roll half in pecans. In a microwave or double boiler, melt chocolate and shortening; stir until smooth. Dip remaining balls in chocolate. Place on waxed paper to harden. Store in the refrigerator. **Yield:** 6 dozen.

Strawberry Chocolate Shortcake

I like to make this luscious layered dessert for Valentine's Day. It's simple to prepare, but so elegant and impressive. —Suzanne McKinley, Lyons, Georgia

    3-1/2 cups biscuit/baking mix
      2/3 cup plus 2 teaspoons sugar, *divided*
      1/2 cup baking cocoa
        1 cup milk
      1/3 cup butter *or* margarine, melted
        1 egg white
    2-1/2 pints fresh strawberries
        2 cups whipping cream
        3 tablespoons confectioners' sugar
        1 cup chocolate syrup

In a bowl, combine biscuit mix, 2/3 cup of sugar and cocoa. Stir in milk and butter; mix well. Drop by 1/3 cupfuls at least 2 in. apart onto a greased baking sheet. Beat egg white until foamy; brush over shortcakes. Sprinkle with remaining sugar. Bake at 400° for 15-18 minutes. Cool on wire racks. Set aside 10 whole strawberries; slice remaining strawberries. In a mixing bowl, beat cream and confectioners' sugar until soft peaks form. Just before serving, split shortcakes horizontally. Spoon half of the whipped cream and all of the sliced berries between cake layers. Spoon the remaining whipped cream on top. Drizzle with chocolate syrup; top with a whole berry. **Yield:** 10 servings.

Maple Praline Supreme

This is such an easy dessert to fix well in advance and tuck in the freezer for a special treat anytime. Maple syrup has the right flavor to make it dynamite.
—Pat Bixby, Lake Elmore, Vermont

    1-1/2 cups chopped pecans *or* hazelnuts
      1/2 cup packed brown sugar
        3 tablespoons butter *or* margarine, melted
        1 jar (7 ounces) marshmallow creme
      1/2 cup pure maple syrup
        2 cups whipping cream, whipped

Combine nuts, brown sugar and butter until well mixed. Spread onto a greased baking sheet. Bake at 350° for 12 minutes or until browned. Cool; crumble and set aside. In a bowl, combine marshmallow creme and syrup until smooth; fold in whipped cream. Place half of the nut mixture in a greased 9-in. x 5-in. x 3-in. loaf pan. Top with marshmallow mixture and remaining nut mixture. Cover and freeze overnight or until firm. Invert onto a serving plate and slice. **Yield:** 8-10 servings.

Creamy Lime Sherbet

(Pictured on back cover)

The lime flavor in this cool treat is perfect, and the pastel color is pretty. —May Dell Spiess, Industry, Texas

  1 package (3 ounces) lime gelatin
  1 cup boiling water
1-1/4 cups sugar
  1 can (6 ounces) frozen limeade
     concentrate, thawed
Dash salt
  1 quart milk
  1 pint half-and-half cream
  8 drops green food coloring, optional

In a large bowl, dissolve gelatin in water. Add the sugar, limeade and salt; mix until sugar is dissolved. Add remaining ingredients; blend well. Pour into the cylinder of an ice cream freezer and freeze according to manufacturer's directions. **Yield:** about 2 quarts. **Editor's Note:** Orange gelatin and orange juice concentrate may be substituted for the lime gelatin and limeade.

Sweet Potato Crunch

Mississippi farmers grow wonderful sweet potatoes, and we put them to good use in recipes like this.
     —Ruth Carter, Van Vleet, Mississippi

1-1/2 cups all-purpose flour
  3/4 cup finely chopped pecans
  3/4 cup butter *or* margarine, melted
FILLING:
  3 medium sweet potatoes, peeled and cubed
  1/3 cup sugar
  3 tablespoons butter *or* margarine
  1 teaspoon vanilla extract
  1/4 teaspoon almond extract
TOPPING:
  1 package (8 ounces) cream cheese, softened
  4 cups confectioners' sugar
  1 carton (8 ounces) frozen whipped
     topping, thawed
Additional chopped pecans, optional

In a bowl, combine flour and pecans. Stir in butter. Press into a greased 13-in. x 9-in. x 2-in. baking pan. Bake at 350° for 12-14 minutes. Cool on a wire rack. Place sweet potatoes in a large saucepan and cover with water; bring to a boil. Cover and boil for 15 minutes or just until tender; drain and mash. Add the sugar, butter and extracts; stir until smooth. Spread over crust. For topping, beat cream cheese and sugar in a mixing bowl until smooth. Fold in whipped topping. Spread over filling. Sprin-

kle with pecans if desired. Refrigerate for 4-6 hours. **Yield:** 12-16 servings.

Caramel Rhubarb Cobbler

(Pictured below)

My son especially likes rhubarb, and this old-fashioned dessert lets those special stalks star.
     —Beverly Shebs, Pinehurst, North Carolina

  7 tablespoons butter *or* margarine, *divided*
  3/4 cup packed brown sugar
  1/2 cup sugar, *divided*
  3 tablespoons cornstarch
1-1/4 cups water
  6 cups chopped fresh *or* frozen rhubarb,
     thawed
  3 to 4 drops red food coloring, optional
1-1/4 cups all-purpose flour
1-1/2 teaspoons baking powder
  1/4 teaspoon salt
  1/3 cup milk
Cinnamon-sugar
Whipped cream *or* ice cream, optional

In a saucepan over medium heat, melt 3 tablespoons of butter. Add brown sugar, 1/4 cup of sugar and cornstarch. Gradually stir in water and rhubarb; cook and stir until thickened, about 5-8 minutes. Add food coloring if desired. Pour into a greased 2-qt. baking dish and set aside. In another bowl, combine flour, baking powder, salt and remaining sugar. Melt remaining butter; add to dry ingredients with milk. Mix well. Drop by tablespoonfuls onto rhubarb mixture. Bake at 350° for 35-40 minutes or until the fruit is bubbly and the top is golden brown. Sprinkle with cinnamon-sugar. Serve warm with whipped cream or ice cream if desired. **Yield:** 6 servings.

Chocolate Caramel Candy

(Pictured below)

This prize-winning treat tastes like a Snickers bar but has homemade flavor beyond compare. —Jane Meek
Pahrump, Nevada

    1 cup (6 ounces) milk chocolate chips
  1/4 cup butterscotch chips
  1/4 cup creamy peanut butter
FILLING:
  1/4 cup butter *or* margarine
    1 cup sugar
  1/4 cup evaporated milk
1-1/2 cups marshmallow creme
  1/4 cup creamy peanut butter
    1 teaspoon vanilla extract
1-1/2 cups chopped salted peanuts
CARAMEL LAYER:
    1 package (14 ounces) caramels
  1/4 cup whipping cream
ICING:
    1 cup (6 ounces) milk chocolate chips
  1/4 cup butterscotch chips
  1/4 cup creamy peanut butter

Line a 13-in. x 9-in. x 2-in. pan with foil; butter the foil and set aside. Combine the first three ingredients in a small saucepan; stir over low heat until melted and smooth. Spread into prepared pan. Chill until set. For filling, melt the butter in a heavy saucepan over medium heat. Add sugar and milk; bring to a gentle boil. Reduce heat to medium-low; boil and stir for 5 minutes. Remove from the heat; stir in marshmallow creme, peanut butter and vanilla. Add peanuts. Spread over first layer. Chill until set. Combine caramels and cream in a saucepan; stir over low heat until melted and smooth. Cook and stir 4 minutes longer. Spread over filling. Chill until set. In another saucepan, combine chips and peanut butter; stir over low heat until melted and smooth. Pour over the caramel layer. Chill for at least 4 hours. Remove from the refrigerator 20 minutes before cutting. Remove from the pan; cut into 1-in. squares. **Yield:** about 8 dozen.

Puffy Dessert Omelet

This unique fruity omelet is definitely worth the bit of extra time it takes to fix. —Carol Mead
Los Alamos, New Mexico

    6 eggs, *separated*
  1/2 teaspoon salt
  1/4 cup sugar
    2 tablespoons all-purpose flour
    2 teaspoons grated lemon peel
    1 teaspoon vanilla extract
    2 tablespoons butter *or* margarine
    1 pint fresh strawberries, sliced and
      sweetened
Whipped cream

In a mixing bowl, beat egg whites with salt until stiff peaks form; set aside. In another bowl, beat egg yolks, sugar, flour, lemon peel and vanilla until smooth. Fold in egg whites. In a 10-in. ovenproof skillet, melt butter over medium-low heat. Add egg mixture. Cook without stirring for 6-7 minutes or until bottom is golden brown. Remove from the heat. Broil 4 in. from the heat for 1 minute or just until top is golden (watch carefully). Fold omelet in half; transfer to a serving platter. Top with strawberries and whipped cream. **Yield:** 4 servings.

Peanut Butter Chocolate Pudding

Being a diabetic with several dietary restrictions, I was so pleased to find the recipe for this cool, satisfying pudding. I can even serve it to company.
—Shirlye Price, Hartford, Kentucky

✓ Nutritional Analysis included

    2 cups cold milk, *divided*
    2 tablespoons chunky peanut butter
    1 cup whipped topping, *divided*
    1 package (3.9 ounces) instant chocolate
      pudding mix

In a small bowl, mix 2 tablespoons milk and peanut butter until smooth. Fold in 3/4 cup whipped topping; set aside. In a mixing bowl, beat pudding mix and remaining milk until blended, about 2 minutes. Let stand for 5 minutes. Spoon half of the pudding into six parfait glasses or bowls; top with peanut butter mixture and remaining pudding. Garnish with remaining whipped topping. **Yield:** 6 servings.
Nutritional Analysis: One serving (prepared with skim milk, reduced-fat peanut butter, light whipped topping and sugar-free pudding) equals 102 calories, 144 mg sodium, 1 mg cholesterol, 13 gm carbohydrate, 5 gm protein, 3 gm fat. **Diabetic Exchanges:** 1 starch, 1/2 fat.

Pistachio Pudding Tarts

For St. Patrick's Day or anytime you want a treat that's colorful, refreshing and delightful, try these tempting tarts. —Bettye Linster, Atlanta, Georgia

1 cup butter *or* margarine, softened
1 package (8 ounces) cream cheese, softened
2 cups all-purpose flour
1 package (3.4 ounces) instant pistachio pudding mix
1-3/4 cups cold milk

In a mixing bowl, combine butter, cream cheese and flour; mix well. Shape into 48 balls (1 in. each); press onto the bottom and up the sides of ungreased miniature muffin cups. Bake at 400° for 12-15 minutes or until lightly browned. Cool for 5 minutes; carefully remove from pans to a wire rack to cool completely. For the filling, combine pudding and milk in a mixing bowl; beat on low speed for 2 minutes. Cover and refrigerate for 5 minutes. Spoon into tart shells; serve immediately. **Yield:** 4 dozen.

— 🍷 🍷 🍷 —

Espresso Chocolate Sauce

Our 30 acres of coffee plants produce tons of beans each year for smooth distinctive Kona coffee, which we use in this recipe. —Roz Roy, Honaunau, Hawaii

1/3 cup strong coffee
2 squares (1 ounce *each*) unsweetened chocolate
1/2 cup sugar
3 tablespoons butter *or* margarine
1/4 teaspoon vanilla extract
Ice cream

In a saucepan over low heat, cook and stir coffee and chocolate until chocolate is melted. Add sugar and butter; cook and stir until the sugar is dissolved and the butter is melted. Remove from the heat; stir in vanilla. Serve over ice cream. **Yield:** 1 cup.

— 🍷 🍷 🍷 —

Rhubarb Fritters

(Pictured above right)

I got this recipe from my niece's son. This treat is nice when rhubarb is plentiful. —Helen Budinock
Wolcott, New York

1 cup all-purpose flour
1 cup plus 1 tablespoon sugar, *divided*
1/2 teaspoon salt
2 eggs, *separated*
1/2 cup milk
1 tablespoon butter *or* margarine, melted

2 cups finely chopped fresh *or* frozen rhubarb, thawed and drained
Oil for deep-fat frying
Confectioners' sugar

In a medium bowl, combine flour, 1 cup sugar and salt. In another bowl, whisk egg yolks, milk and butter. Gradually add to the dry ingredients, stirring until smooth. Toss rhubarb with the remaining sugar; gently stir into batter. In a mixing bowl, beat egg whites until stiff. Fold into batter. In an electric skillet or deep-fat fryer, heat oil to 375°. Drop batter by tablespoonfuls into oil. Fry, a few at a time, turning with a slotted spoon until golden brown. Drain on paper towels. Dust with confectioners' sugar. Serve warm. **Yield:** about 3 dozen.

— 🍷 🍷 🍷 —

Berry Dessert Sauce

People are amazed to learn that this frothy, fruity sauce is actually whipped skim milk and frozen berries. —Patricia Brownlow, Gaithersburg, Maryland

✓ Nutritional Analysis included

1/2 cup skim milk
1 cup frozen unsweetened strawberries, partially thawed
Artificial sweetener equivalent to 4 teaspoons sugar
1/8 teaspoon vanilla extract
Angel food cake

Place the milk, berries, sweetener and vanilla in a blender; cover and process until whipped. Serve over cake. **Yield:** 1-1/4 cups. **Nutritional Analysis:** One 1/4-cup serving of sauce equals 21 calories, 13 mg sodium, trace cholesterol, 4 gm carbohydrate, 1 gm protein, trace fat. **Diabetic Exchange:** 1/2 fruit.

Rhubarb Mandarin Crisp

(Pictured above)

An attractive and unique dessert, this crisp is also a popular breakfast dish at our house, served with a glass of milk rather than topped with ice cream.
—Rachael VandenDool, Barry's Bay, Ontario

 6 cups chopped fresh **or** frozen rhubarb
1-1/2 cups sugar
 5 tablespoons quick-cooking tapioca
 1 can (11 ounces) mandarin oranges, drained
 1 cup packed brown sugar
 1 cup quick-cooking oats
 1/2 cup all-purpose flour
 1/2 teaspoon salt
 1/2 cup cold butter **or** margarine
Ice cream, optional

In a bowl, toss rhubarb, sugar and tapioca; let stand for 15 minutes, stirring occasionally. Pour into a greased 13-in. x 9-in. x 2-in. baking pan. Top with oranges. In a bowl, combine brown sugar, oats, flour and salt. Cut in butter until the mixture resembles coarse crumbs; sprinkle evenly over oranges. Bake at 350° for 40 minutes or until top is golden brown. Serve with ice cream if desired. **Yield:** 12 servings.

Pastel Torte

I've made this old-fashioned homemade dessert for many baby and bridal showers. —*Gloria Denton Courtenay, British Columbia*

 1/2 cup butter **or** margarine, softened
 1/2 cup packed brown sugar

 2 egg yolks
1-1/2 cups all-purpose flour
 1 teaspoon baking powder
TOPPING:
 3/4 cup sugar
 2 envelopes unflavored gelatin
Pinch salt
 1 cup cold water
 1 cup confectioners' sugar
 1 teaspoon baking powder
 1/2 teaspoon almond extract
 2 drops green food coloring
 2 drops red food coloring
 1/4 cup shredded coconut, toasted

In a mixing bowl, cream butter and brown sugar. Beat in egg yolks, one at a time. Combine flour and baking powder; add to creamed mixture. Press into a greased 9-in. square baking pan. Bake at 325° for 15-20 minutes or until light brown. Cool. In a saucepan, combine sugar, gelatin and salt; stir in water. Let stand for 1 minute. Cook and stir over medium heat until mixture comes to a boil. Reduce heat; simmer for 10 minutes, stirring occasionally. Remove from the heat; transfer to a mixing bowl. Add confectioners' sugar; beat on high until thick and creamy white, about 12 minutes. Add baking powder and extract. Divide into three equal portions. Add green food coloring to one portion and red food coloring to another; mix well. Leave the third portion white. Pour green mixture over crust; chill for 3 minutes. Top with white mixture; chill for 3 minutes. Top with pink mixture. Sprinkle with coconut. Cover and refrigerate for 1 hour or until set. **Yield:** 9 servings. **Editor's Note:** Varying room temperatures and humidity may cause the white and pink mixtures to become too firm to spread. To soften, microwave on high in 5-second segments until mixture is spreadable. The torte may be frozen.

Lemon-Lime Mousse

For a light and refreshing dessert after any meal, try this tangy citrus treat. —*Kathryn Anderson Wallkill, New York*

 1/2 cup sugar
 2 tablespoons cornstarch
Pinch salt
 3 egg yolks
 2/3 cup milk
 1/4 cup lemon juice
 1 tablespoon lime juice
1-1/2 teaspoons grated lemon peel
 1/2 teaspoon grated lime peel

1 cup whipping cream, whipped
Lime slices and additional lemon peel, optional

In a saucepan, combine sugar, cornstarch and salt. In a bowl, whisk egg yolks and milk; stir into sugar mixture. Add juices; whisk until smooth. Cook and stir over medium heat until mixture comes to a boil. Cook and stir 2 minutes longer. Add peels. Cover surface with plastic wrap; refrigerate until completely cooled. Fold in whipped cream. Spoon into dishes. Garnish with lime slices and lemon peel if desired. **Yield:** 6 servings.

— ⲙ ⲙ ⲙ —

Apple Cider Sundaes

I adapted one of my mother's recipes and came up with this terrific fall snack. Thanks to the tangy apple cider, these sundaes are a hit whenever I serve them!
—Jeanne Lee, Terrace Park, Ohio

 Nutritional Analysis included

1-1/2 cups apple cider
1/3 cup sugar
2 tablespoons cornstarch
1/2 teaspoon lemon juice
1/2 teaspoon ground cinnamon
1-1/2 cups finely chopped peeled tart apples
Vanilla ice cream

In a saucepan, combine cider, sugar, cornstarch, lemon juice and cinnamon; stir until smooth. Add apples. Bring to a boil; boil and stir for 2 minutes. Remove from the heat; cool slightly. Serve over ice cream. **Yield:** about 2 cups topping. **Nutritional Analysis:** One 2-tablespoon serving of topping equals 37 calories, 1 mg sodium, 0 cholesterol, 9 gm carbohydrate, trace protein, trace fat. **Diabetic Exchange:** 1/2 fruit.

— ⲙ ⲙ ⲙ —

Frozen Peach Dessert

I use peaches in most every way you can think of. In this recipe, some simple and delicious ingredients like fresh peaches, sugar and cream combine in a delightful way. *—Sharon Bickett, Chester, South Carolina*

2 cups sliced peeled fresh *or* frozen peaches
2/3 cup sugar
2 cups whipping cream
3 to 4 drops almond extract
Fresh mint and additional peaches, optional

In a blender or food processor, process peaches until smooth. Transfer to a bowl; add sugar. Let stand for 1 hour. In a mixing bowl, beat cream and extract until soft peaks form. Fold into peach mixture. Pour into a 6-cup mold or freezer-safe bowl. Cover and freeze overnight. Unmold onto a serving plate about 1 hour before serving. Return to freezer. Before serving, garnish with mint and peaches if desired. Cut into wedges. **Yield:** 10 servings.

— ⲙ ⲙ ⲙ —

White Chocolate Mousse

(Pictured below)

Since almost any fresh fruit may be used, this elegant dessert can grace special meals throughout the year.
—Susan Herbert, Aurora, Illinois

1 cup whipping cream
2 tablespoons sugar
1 package (3 ounces) cream cheese, softened
3 squares (1 ounce *each*) white baking chocolate, melted
2 cups blueberries, raspberries *or* strawberries
Additional berries, optional

In a mixing bowl, beat cream until soft peaks form. Gradually add the sugar, beating until stiff peaks form; set aside. In another mixing bowl, beat cream cheese until fluffy. Add chocolate and beat until smooth. Fold in whipped cream. Alternate layers of mousse and berries in parfait glasses, ending with mousse. Garnish with additional berries if desired. Serve immediately or refrigerate for up to 3 hours. **Yield:** 4-6 servings.

PERFECT PASTRIES like Chocolate-Filled Cream Puffs, Danish Puff and Graham Cream Puffs (shown above, clockwise from top) will quickly disappear from your dessert table.

Chocolate-Filled Cream Puffs

(Pictured above)

Chocolate lovers will enjoy these puffs, stuffed with a slightly sweet chocolate cream and drizzled with a chocolate glaze. —*Kathy Kittell, Lenexa, Kansas*

    1 cup water
    6 tablespoons butter (no substitutes)
    1 cup all-purpose flour
    1/4 teaspoon salt
    4 eggs
FILLING:
    1 cup whipping cream
    1/2 cup confectioners' sugar
    2 tablespoons baking cocoa
GLAZE:
    1 square (1 ounce) unsweetened chocolate
    1 tablespoon butter
    1/2 cup confectioners' sugar
    2 tablespoons water

In a saucepan over medium heat, bring water and butter to a boil. Add flour and salt all at once; stir until a smooth ball forms. Remove from the heat; let stand 5 minutes. Add eggs, one at a time, beating well after each. Beat until smooth. Cover a baking sheet with foil; grease foil. Drop batter into six mounds onto foil. Bake at 400° for 15 minutes. Reduce heat to 350°; bake 30 minutes longer. Remove puffs to a wire rack. Immediately cut a slit in each for steam to escape. In a mixing bowl, beat cream until soft peaks form. Gradually add sugar and cocoa, beating until almost stiff. Split puffs and remove soft dough. Add filling; replace tops. Melt chocolate and butter; stir in sugar and water. Drizzle over puffs. Chill. **Yield:** 6 servings.

Graham Cream Puffs

(Pictured above)

These "berry" special graham cracker puffs are filled with raspberries and cream and topped with a tangy raspberry sauce. —*Iola Egle, McCook, Nebraska*

    1 cup water
    1/2 cup butter (no substitutes)

1/2 cup all-purpose flour
1/2 cup graham cracker crumbs
1/4 teaspoon salt
4 eggs
GLAZE:
1/2 cup raspberries
2 tablespoons sugar
1 teaspoon cornstarch
1/2 cup orange juice
FILLING:
1 cup whipping cream
1 to 3 tablespoons sugar
1 teaspoon vanilla extract
2 cups raspberries, drained

In a saucepan over medium heat, bring water and butter to a boil. Add flour, crumbs and salt all at once; stir until a smooth ball forms. Remove from the heat; let stand for 5 minutes. Add eggs, one at a time, beating well after each. Beat until smooth. Cover baking sheets with foil; grease foil. Drop batter by 1/4 cupfuls 3 in. apart onto foil. Bake at 400° for 30-35 minutes or until golden brown. Meanwhile, for glaze, puree berries in a blender; strain and discard seeds. Set the puree aside. Remove puffs to wire racks; immediately cut a slit in each for steam to escape. In a saucepan, combine sugar and cornstarch; stir in orange juice and the reserved puree. Bring to a boil over medium heat, stirring constantly; boil for 1 minute. Remove from the heat; set aside. In a mixing bowl, beat cream until soft peaks form. Beat in sugar and vanilla. Fold in raspberries. Just before serving, split puffs and remove soft dough. Add filling; replace tops. Drizzle with glaze. **Yield:** 10 servings.

Danish Puff

(Pictured above left)

I remember Mom making this cream puff variation for special occasions. Now I make it as a treat for friends and family. —Susan Garoutte, Georgetown, Texas

1/2 cup butter (no substitutes)
1 cup all-purpose flour
1 to 2 tablespoons cold water
FILLING:
1 cup water
1/2 cup butter (no substitutes)
1 cup all-purpose flour
1/4 teaspoon salt
3 eggs
1/2 teaspoon almond extract
TOPPING:
1-1/2 cups confectioners' sugar
2 tablespoons butter, softened

1 to 2 tablespoons water
1-1/2 teaspoons vanilla extract
1/2 cup sliced almonds, toasted

In a bowl, cut butter into the flour until crumbly. Sprinkle with water; toss with a fork until moist enough to shape into a ball. Divide in half. On a floured surface, roll each portion into a 12-in. x 3-in. rectangle. Place on greased baking sheets. In a saucepan, bring water and butter to a boil. Add flour and salt all at once; stir until a smooth ball forms. Remove from the heat; let stand 5 minutes. Add eggs, one at a time, beating well after each. Add extract; beat until smooth. Spread over dough. Bake at 350° for 1 hour or until puffed and golden brown. Cool on pans for 10 minutes. Combine sugar, butter, water and vanilla until smooth; spread over warm puffs. Sprinkle with almonds. Refrigerate leftovers. **Yield:** 16 servings.

Sweet Potato Turnovers

My family refused to eat nutritious sweet potatoes as a side dish, so I decided to serve them for dessert.
—Doreen Kelly, Roslyn, Pennsylvania

FILLING:
2 cups mashed sweet potatoes (without added milk and butter)
1 can (20 ounces) crushed pineapple, drained
1-1/4 cups sugar
1 teaspoon grated lemon peel
1 teaspoon grated orange peel
1/4 teaspoon *each* ground allspice, cinnamon and ginger
PASTRY:
2-1/2 cups all-purpose flour
1 teaspoon baking powder
1/2 teaspoon salt
3/4 cup butter-flavored shortening
5 to 6 tablespoons cold water
Milk and additional sugar

In a saucepan, combine filling ingredients. Cook over medium-low heat for 12 minutes or until thickened, stirring occasionally. Cool. For pastry, combine flour, baking powder and salt in a bowl. Cut in shortening until crumbly. Gradually add water; toss with a fork until dough forms a ball. Divide into 12 portions. On a floured surface, roll each portion into a 6-in. circle. Spoon 1/4 to 1/3 cup filling on half of each circle. Moisten edges with water; fold dough over filling. Press edges with a fork to seal. Place on greased baking sheets. Brush with milk and sprinkle with sugar. Cut slits in top. Bake at 425° for 15-20 minutes. **Yield:** 12 servings.

Nutty Apple Streusel Dessert

(Pictured above)

Many people don't think of using a slow cooker to make dessert. But I like to start this scrumptious apple treat in the morning and not think about it all day.
—Jacki Every, Rotterdam, New York

```
     6 cups sliced peeled tart apples
1-1/4 teaspoons ground cinnamon
   1/4 teaspoon ground allspice
   1/4 teaspoon ground nutmeg
   3/4 cup milk
     2 tablespoons butter or margarine, softened
   3/4 cup sugar
     2 eggs
     1 teaspoon vanilla extract
   1/2 cup biscuit/baking mix
```
TOPPING:
```
     1 cup biscuit/baking mix
   1/3 cup packed brown sugar
     3 tablespoons cold butter or margarine
   1/2 cup sliced almonds
```
Ice cream *or* whipped cream, optional

In a large bowl, toss apples with cinnamon, allspice and nutmeg. Place in a greased slow cooker. In a mixing bowl, combine milk, butter, sugar, eggs, vanilla and baking mix; mix well. Spoon over apples. For topping, combine biscuit mix and brown sugar in a bowl; cut in butter until crumbly. Add almonds; sprinkle over apples. Cover and cook on low for 6-7 hours or until the apples are tender. Serve with ice cream or whipped cream if desired. **Yield:** 6-8 servings.

White Chocolate Fruit Tart

(Pictured on back cover)

It takes a little time to make, but this tart is absolutely marvelous, especially in summer! —Claire Darby
New Castle, Delaware

CRUST:
```
   3/4 cup butter or margarine, softened
   1/2 cup confectioners' sugar
1-1/2 cups all-purpose flour
```
FILLING:
```
     1 package (10 ounces) vanilla baking chips,
       melted
   1/4 cup whipping cream
     1 package (8 ounces) cream cheese,
       softened
     1 can (20 ounces) pineapple chunks
     1 pint fresh strawberries, sliced
     1 can (11 ounces) mandarin oranges,
       drained
     2 kiwifruit, peeled and sliced
```
GLAZE:
```
     3 tablespoons sugar
     2 teaspoons cornstarch
   1/2 teaspoon lemon juice
```

In a mixing bowl, cream butter and confectioners' sugar. Gradually add flour; mix well. Press into an ungreased 11-in. tart pan or 12-in. pizza pan with sides. Bake at 300° for 25-30 minutes or until lightly browned. Cool. In a mixing bowl, beat chips and cream. Add cream cheese; beat until smooth. Spread over crust. Chill for 30 minutes. Drain the pineapple, reserving 1/2 cup juice; set juice aside. Arrange strawberries, pineapple, oranges and kiwi over filling. For glaze, combine sugar, cornstarch, lemon juice and reserved pineapple juice in a saucepan; bring to a boil over medium heat. Boil for 2 minutes or until thickened, stirring constantly. Cool; brush over fruit. Chill for 1 hour before serving. Store in the refrigerator. **Yield:** 12-16 servings.

Rhubarb Crumble

When I met my English husband and served him just the crumble, he said it was fantastic but really needed a custard sauce over it. We found a terrific sauce recipe from England, and now the pair is perfect together.
—Amy Freeman, Cave Creek, Arizona

```
     8 cups chopped fresh or frozen rhubarb
1-1/4 cups sugar, divided
2-1/2 cups all-purpose flour
   1/4 cup packed brown sugar
   1/4 cup quick-cooking oats
     1 cup cold butter or margarine
```

CUSTARD SAUCE:
    6 egg yolks
    1/2 cup sugar
    2 cups whipping cream
  1-1/4 teaspoons vanilla extract

In a saucepan, combine rhubarb and 3/4 cup of sugar. Cover and cook over medium heat, stirring occasionally, until the rhubarb is tender, about 10 minutes. Pour into a greased 13-in. x 9-in. x 2-in. baking dish. In a bowl, combine flour, brown sugar, oats and remaining sugar. Cut in the butter until crumbly; sprinkle over rhubarb. Bake at 400° for 30 minutes. Meanwhile, in a saucepan, whisk the egg yolks and sugar; stir in cream. Cook and stir over low heat until a thermometer reads 160° and mixture thickens, about 15-20 minutes. Remove from the heat; stir in vanilla. Serve warm over rhubarb crumble. **Yield:** 12 servings (2-1/2 cups sauce).

Gelatin Torte

You can make this lovely summer torte ahead. It has a fluffy cake layer topped with a fruity gelatin mixture.
—Sophie Hilicki, Racine, Wisconsin

    3 eggs, *separated*
    1 cup sugar, *divided*
    1 can (8 ounces) crushed pineapple,
      drained
    1 cup graham cracker crumbs (about 16
      squares)
  1/2 teaspoon baking powder
  1/4 cup chopped pecans
    1 package (6 ounces) cherry gelatin
    2 cups boiling water
1-1/2 cups cold water
    3 medium firm bananas, sliced
    1 cup whipping cream
    3 tablespoons confectioners' sugar
Maraschino cherries, optional

In a mixing bowl, beat egg yolks and 1/2 cup sugar until thick and lemon-colored. Stir in pineapple. Combine cracker crumbs and baking powder; stir into pineapple mixture. Add pecans; set aside. In a mixing bowl, beat egg whites until foamy. Gradually beat in the remaining sugar until soft peaks form. Fold into pineapple mixture. Pour into an ungreased 9-in. springform pan. Bake at 350° for 30 minutes or until top springs back when lightly touched. Cool on a wire rack. (Do not remove sides of pan.) Dissolve gelatin in boiling water. Stir in cold water; refrigerate until mixture begins to thicken, about 40 minutes. Stir in bananas; pour over cooled cake layer. Refrigerate until firm, about 2 hours. In a mixing bowl, beat cream and sugar until soft peaks form; pipe or spoon over gelatin layer. Just before serving, run a knife around the edge of pan to loosen; remove sides of pan. Garnish with cherries if desired. **Yield:** 8 servings.

Caramel Pear Pudding

(Pictured below)

Don't expect this old-fashioned dessert to last long. The delicate pears and irresistible caramel topping make it a winner whenever I serve it.
—Sharon Mensing, Greenfield, Iowa

    1 cup all-purpose flour
  2/3 cup sugar
1-1/2 teaspoons baking powder
  1/2 teaspoon ground cinnamon
  1/4 teaspoon salt
Pinch ground cloves
  1/2 cup milk
    4 medium pears, peeled and cut into
      1/2-inch cubes
  1/2 cup chopped pecans
  3/4 cup packed brown sugar
  1/4 cup butter *or* margarine
  3/4 cup boiling water
Vanilla ice cream *or* whipped cream, optional

In a mixing bowl, combine the first six ingredients; beat in milk until smooth. Stir in pears and pecans. Spoon into an ungreased 2-qt. baking dish. In another bowl, combine brown sugar, butter and water; pour over batter. Bake, uncovered, at 375° for 45-50 minutes. Serve warm with ice cream or whipped cream if desired. **Yield:** 8 servings.

Bread Pudding for Two

My sister and I love the old-fashioned flavor of this bread pudding. We share it with each other often.
—Mildred Patterson, Guthrie, Oklahoma

  1 slice bread, cubed
  2 tablespoons raisins
  1 egg
1/2 cup evaporated milk
  3 tablespoons water
  2 tablespoons sugar
1/4 teaspoon ground cinnamon
1/4 teaspoon ground nutmeg

Divide bread and raisins between two greased 8-oz. baking dishes; set aside. In a bowl, beat egg, milk and water; pour over bread. Combine sugar, cinnamon and nutmeg; sprinkle over the top. Bake, uncovered, at 350° for 30-35 minutes or until a knife inserted near the center comes out clean. Cool slightly. Serve warm. **Yield:** 2 servings.

Black and Blue Cobbler

(Pictured below)

It never occurred to me that I could bake a cobbler in my slow cooker until I saw some recipes and decided to try it. —Martha Creveling, Orlando, Florida

    1 cup all-purpose flour
1-1/2 cups sugar, *divided*
    1 teaspoon baking powder
  1/4 teaspoon salt
  1/4 teaspoon ground cinnamon

1/4 teaspoon ground nutmeg
  2 eggs, beaten
  2 tablespoons milk
  2 tablespoons vegetable oil
  2 cups fresh *or* frozen blackberries
  2 cups fresh *or* frozen blueberries
3/4 cup water
  1 teaspoon grated orange peel

In a bowl, combine flour, 3/4 cup sugar, baking powder, salt, cinnamon and nutmeg. Combine eggs, milk and oil; stir into dry ingredients just until moistened. Spread batter evenly onto the bottom of a greased 5-qt. slow cooker. In a saucepan, combine berries, water, orange peel and remaining sugar; bring to a boil. Remove from the heat; immediately pour over batter. Cover and cook on high for 2 to 2-1/2 hours or until a toothpick inserted into the batter comes out clean. Turn cooker off. Uncover and let stand for 30 minutes before serving. **Yield:** 6 servings.

Peanut Butter Pudding

For a creamy, comforting dessert, this smooth pudding can't be beat. I hope you try it soon. —Edna Hoffman, Hebron, Indiana

  1/3 cup sugar
4-1/2 teaspoons cornstarch
  1/4 teaspoon salt
1-1/2 cups milk
  1/2 cup half-and-half cream
  1/2 cup creamy peanut butter
    1 teaspoon vanilla extract
Whipped cream, optional

In a saucepan, combine sugar, cornstarch and salt. Gradually stir in milk and cream; bring to a boil over medium heat. Cook and stir for 2 minutes. Remove from the heat; stir in peanut butter and vanilla until smooth. Pour into serving dishes; refrigerate. Garnish with whipped cream if desired. **Yield:** 4 servings.

Apricot Tarts

These tiny tarts are an extra-special treat for any holiday or occasion. We love the fruity, nutty flavor.
—Phyllis Hickey, Bedford, New Hampshire

1/2 cup butter *or* margarine, softened
  1 package (3 ounces) cream cheese, softened
  1 cup all-purpose flour
3/4 cup finely chopped dried apricots

3/4 cup water
1/3 cup chopped pecans
1/4 cup sugar
    2 tablespoons orange marmalade
1/2 teaspoon ground cinnamon
1/8 teaspoon ground cloves
TOPPING:
    2 tablespoons cream cheese, softened
    1 tablespoon butter *or* margarine
1/2 teaspoon vanilla extract
1/2 cup confectioners' sugar

In a mixing bowl, blend butter, cream cheese and flour. Chill for 1 hour. Meanwhile, in a saucepan, bring apricots and water to a boil. Reduce heat; simmer for 5 minutes. Drain. Add pecans, sugar, marmalade, cinnamon and cloves; set aside. Shape dough into 24 balls. Press onto the bottom and up the sides of greased miniature muffin cups. Spoon apricot mixture into cups. Bake at 350° for 25-30 minutes or until browned. Cool for 10 minutes; remove from pans to a wire rack to cool completely. For topping, combine cream cheese and butter in a small mixing bowl. Stir in vanilla until smooth. Beat in confectioners' sugar. Spoon a dollop onto each tart. **Yield:** 2 dozen.

Pumpkin Pudding

For a light and fluffy dessert with the great fall taste of pumpkin, give this simple recipe a try. —Sally Helfer Houston, Texas

☑ Nutritional Analysis included

    1 carton (8 ounces) vanilla yogurt
    1 cup cooked *or* canned pumpkin
1/4 teaspoon ground nutmeg
1/4 teaspoon ground cinnamon

Combine all of the ingredients in a bowl; stir until smooth. Refrigerate until serving. **Yield:** 4 servings. **Nutritional Analysis:** One serving (prepared with light yogurt) equals 75 calories, 38 mg sodium, 2 mg cholesterol, 15 gm carbohydrate, 4 gm protein, trace fat. **Diabetic Exchange:** 1 starch.

Rhubarb Cheesecake Dessert

(Pictured above right)

After moving to our current home, we were thrilled to discover a huge rhubarb patch. Each spring, my family looks forward to these sensational squares.
—Joyce Krumwiede, Mankato, Minnesota

    1 cup all-purpose flour
1/2 cup packed brown sugar
1/4 teaspoon salt
1/4 cup cold butter *or* margarine
1/2 cup chopped walnuts
    1 teaspoon vanilla extract
FILLING:
    2 packages (8 ounces *each*) cream cheese, softened
3/4 cup sugar
    3 eggs
    1 teaspoon vanilla extract
TOPPING:
    3 cups chopped fresh *or* frozen rhubarb, thawed and drained
    1 cup sugar
1/4 cup water
    1 tablespoon cornstarch
1/4 teaspoon ground cinnamon

In a bowl, combine flour, brown sugar and salt; cut in butter until mixture resembles coarse crumbs. Stir in walnuts and vanilla. Press into a greased 13-in. x 9-in. x 2-in. baking dish. Bake at 375° for 10 minutes. Cool slightly. In a mixing bowl, beat cream cheese and sugar until light and fluffy. Add eggs and vanilla; mix well. Pour over crust. Bake for 20-25 minutes or until center is set and edges are light brown. Cool. In a saucepan, combine rhubarb, sugar, water, cornstarch and cinnamon; bring to a boil over medium heat. Cook and stir until thickened, about 5 minutes. Cool. Pour over filling. Chill at least 1 hour. **Yield:** 12-15 servings.

Potluck Pleasers

Experienced cooks share a host of crowd-pleasing recipes that you can rely on when planning menus for 10, 100 or any number in between!

—— 🍶 🍶 🍶 ——

SUREFIRE SUCCESSES. Clockwise from upper left: Holiday Ham with Pineapple (p. 184), Cherry Punch (p. 193), Two-Cheese Tossed Salad (p. 190), Butterscotch Pecan Dessert (p. 190) and Golden Crescents (p. 191).

Holiday Ham with Pineapple

(Pictured above)

My husband and I have lots of family living in our area, so any gathering is bound to be big. This ham satisfies everyone and is often requested. One of my brothers-in-law will eat six slices before helping himself to anything else. —Sue Jackson-Tucker, Sunset, Utah

    1 whole bone-in fully cooked ham (12 to 14
        pounds), spiral-cut* or thinly sliced
    2 cans (6 ounces *each*) pineapple juice
    1 can (20 ounces) crushed pineapple,
        undrained
    2 cups packed brown sugar
   20 to 30 whole cloves
  1/4 cup golden raisins

Place ham in a roasting pan. Slowly pour pineapple juice over ham so it runs between slices. Spoon pineapple over ham. Sprinkle with brown sugar and cloves. Add raisins to pan juices. Cover and refrigerate overnight. Discard cloves. Cover and bake ham at 325° for 1-1/2 to 2 hours or until a meat thermometer reads 140°, basting every 20 minutes. **Yield:** 24-28 servings. ***Editor's Note:** If spiral-cut ham is not available, ask your butcher to cut a fully cooked ham into 1/8-inch-thick slices and tie it securely.

Beef Tips on Rice

Don't just rely on simple sandwiches when feeding a crowd. This is an easy, elegant main dish with tender pieces of beef. —Kathy Berndt, El Campo, Texas

   20 pounds beef stew meat, cut into 1-inch
        cubes
    2 tablespoons salt
    5 teaspoons pepper
    5 teaspoons dried thyme
   15 cans (10-3/4 ounces *each*) condensed
        cream of mushroom soup, undiluted
    4 cups water
    4 cups chopped onion
  2/3 cup chopped fresh parsley
2-1/2 teaspoons browning sauce, optional
6-1/2 to 7 pounds long grain rice, cooked

Combine beef, salt, pepper and thyme; mix well. Place in five greased 13-in. x 9-in. x 2-in. baking pans. Bake, uncovered, at 400° for 15 minutes; stir. Bake 15 minutes longer; drain. Combine the soup, water, onion, parsley and browning sauce if desired. Pour over beef; mix well. Cover and bake at 350° for 1-1/2 to 2 hours or until the beef is tender. Serve over rice. **Yield:** 75 servings (3/4 cup rice and 3/4 cup beef with sauce).

Make-Ahead Potatoes

There's no need to slave away making mashed potatoes at the last minute, not when this creamy, comforting potato side dish is so handy to prepare well in advance. Plus, it's an easy dish for people to serve themselves and it looks so appealing on a buffet.
—Margaret Twitched, Danbury, Iowa

   10 large potatoes, peeled and quartered
    1 cup (8 ounces) sour cream
    1 package (8 ounces) cream cheese, softened
    6 tablespoons butter *or* margarine, *divided*
    2 tablespoons dried minced onion
  1/2 to 1 teaspoon salt
Paprika

Place potatoes in a Dutch oven or large kettle; cover with water and bring to a boil. Reduce heat; cover and cook for 20-25 minutes or until the potatoes are tender. Drain and place in a bowl; mash. Add sour cream, cream cheese, 4 tablespoons butter, onion and salt; stir until smooth and the cream cheese and butter are melted. Spread in a greased 13-in. x 9-in. x 2-in. baking dish. Melt remaining butter; drizzle over potatoes. Sprinkle with paprika. Refrigerate or bake immediately, covered, at 350° for 40 minutes; uncover and bake 20 minutes longer. If potatoes are made ahead and refrigerated, let stand at room temperature for 30 minutes before baking. **Yield:** 12 servings.

Golden Punch

For a super addition to any celebration, you can't go wrong with this beverage. Pineapple and orange juices lend a terrific tropical taste! —Nancy Johnson
Laverne, Oklahoma

> 6 **cups water**
> 4 **cups sugar**
> 1 **can (46 ounces) pineapple juice**
> 1 **can (12 ounces) frozen orange juice concentrate**
> 1 **can (6 ounces) frozen lemonade concentrate**
> 1/2 **teaspoon almond _or_ vanilla extract**
> 1 **bottle (2 liters) lemon-lime soda**

In a large saucepan, bring the water and sugar to a boil; cook and stir for 2 minutes. Pour into a large container; add pineapple juice, concentrates and extract. Cover and freeze. Remove from freezer 1-2 hours before serving. Just before serving, mash the mixture with a potato masher and stir in soda. **Yield:** 48 (1/2-cup) servings.

Fluffy Mint Dessert

The cool, minty flavor of this fluffy dessert is perfect for Christmas or the hot summer months. Since it has to be made ahead of time, it's a great time-saver on potluck day. I received the recipe from a neighbor a couple years ago. —Carol Mixter
Lincoln Park, Michigan

> 1 **package (1 pound) cream-filled chocolate sandwich cookies (40 cookies), crushed**
> 1/2 **cup butter _or_ margarine, melted**
> 2 **cartons (12 ounces _each_) frozen whipped topping, thawed**
> 2 **cups pastel miniature marshmallows**
> 1-1/3 **cups small pastel mints (5-1/2 ounces)**

Reserve 1/4 cup of crushed cookies for garnish. Combine the remaining cookies with butter; press into an ungreased 13-in. x 9-in. x 2-in. baking dish. Fold together whipped topping, marshmallows and mints; pour over crust. Garnish with reserved cookies. Cover and refrigerate for 1-2 days before serving. **Yield:** 18-20 servings.

Onion Mustard Buns

(Pictured below)

This recipe makes delectable rolls that are a hit wherever I take them. The onion and mustard flavors go so well with ham or hamburgers and are special enough to serve alongside an elaborate main dish.
—Melodie Shumaker, Elizabethtown, Pennsylvania

✓ Nutritional Analysis included

> 1 **package (1/4 ounce) active dry yeast**
> 1/4 **cup warm water (110° to 115°)**
> 2 **cups warm milk (110° to 115°)**
> 3 **tablespoons dried minced onion**
> 3 **tablespoons prepared mustard**
> 2 **tablespoons vegetable oil**
> 2 **tablespoons sugar**
> 1-1/2 **teaspoons salt**
> 6 **to 6-1/2 cups all-purpose flour**

In a mixing bowl, dissolve yeast in water. Add milk, onion, mustard, oil, sugar, salt and 4 cups flour; beat until smooth. Add enough remaining flour to form a soft dough. Turn onto a floured surface; knead until smooth and elastic, about 6-8 minutes. Place in a greased bowl, turning once to grease top. Cover and let rise in a warm place until doubled, about 1 hour. Punch dough down; divide into 24 pieces. Flatten each piece into a 3-in. circle. Place 1 in. apart on greased baking sheets. Cover and let rise until doubled, about 45 minutes. Bake at 350° for 20-25 minutes or until golden brown. Cool on wire racks. **Yield:** 2 dozen. **Nutritional Analysis:** One bun (prepared with skim milk) equals 138 calories, 181 mg sodium, trace cholesterol, 26 gm carbohydrate, 4 gm protein, 2 gm fat. **Diabetic Exchanges:** 1-1/2 starch, 1/2 fat.

Fluffy Raspberry Salad

I've modified this recipe slightly since I first served it for Thanksgiving dinner many years ago. It's always a hit. —Teresa Shattuck, Oak Park, Illinois

    3 packages (3 ounces *each*) raspberry
        gelatin
    2 packages (3 ounces *each*) orange gelatin
    5 cups boiling water
    4 packages (10 ounces *each*) frozen
        sweetened raspberries
    1 jar (20 ounces) chunky applesauce
    3 cups miniature marshmallows
    2 cups whipping cream, whipped

Dissolve gelatin in boiling water. Add raspberries; stir until thawed. Stir in applesauce. Refrigerate until partially set. Fold in the marshmallows and whipped cream. Pour into two 13-in. x 9-in. x 2-in. dishes. Refrigerate until firm. **Yield:** 32-40 servings.

Potluck Chicken Casserole

(Pictured below)

I never bring home leftovers whenever I take this creamy, stick-to-your-ribs casserole to a potluck. Its mild flavor has broad appeal. I especially like the way that the crumb topping adds a bit of crunch to each meaty serving. —Faye Hintz, Springfield, Missouri

    8 cups cubed cooked chicken
    2 cans (10-3/4 ounces *each*) condensed
        cream of chicken soup, undiluted

    1 cup (8 ounces) sour cream
    1 cup butter-flavored cracker crumbs
        (about 25 crackers)
    2 tablespoons butter *or* margarine, melted
    1 teaspoon celery seed
Fresh parsley and sweet red pepper rings,
    optional

Combine chicken, soup and sour cream; spread into a greased 13-in. x 9-in. x 2-in. baking dish. Combine crumbs, butter and celery seed; sprinkle over the chicken mixture. Bake, uncovered, at 350° for 30-35 minutes or until bubbly. Garnish with parsley and red pepper if desired. **Yield:** 10-12 servings.

Peach-Cranberry Gelatin Salad

Harvest colors and flavors give this refreshing salad a delightful twist that's just right for Thanksgiving or any special meal. For Christmas, I use lime gelatin instead of peach for a green and red salad.
—Patty Kile, Greentown, Pennsylvania

    1 package (6 ounces) peach gelatin
    4 cups boiling water, *divided*
    1 cup orange juice
    2 cans (15 ounces *each*) sliced peaches,
        drained
    1 package (6 ounces) cranberry *or*
        raspberry gelatin
    1 cup cranberry juice
    2 large oranges, peeled
    2 cups fresh *or* frozen cranberries
    1 cup sugar

In a bowl, dissolve peach gelatin in 2 cups boiling water. Add orange juice; mix well. Chill until partially set. Fold in peaches. Pour into a 3-qt. serving bowl. Chill until firm. In a bowl, dissolve the cranberry gelatin in remaining boiling water. Add cranberry juice and mix well. In a blender or food processor, combine oranges, cranberries and sugar; process until fruit is coarsely chopped. Add to cranberry gelatin. Carefully spoon over peach gelatin. Chill until set. **Yield:** 14-18 servings.

Rice Dressing

To make this a meal in itself, I sometimes add finely chopped cooked chicken and a little more broth before baking. —Linda Emery, Tuckerman, Arkansas

    4 cups chicken broth, *divided*
1-1/2 cups uncooked long grain rice
    2 cups chopped onion

2 cups chopped celery
1/2 cup butter *or* margarine
2 cans (4 ounces *each*) mushroom stems
  and pieces, drained
3 tablespoons minced fresh parsley
1-1/2 to 2 teaspoons poultry seasoning
3/4 teaspoon salt
1/2 teaspoon pepper
Fresh sage and thyme, optional

In a saucepan, bring 3-1/2 cups of broth and rice to a boil. Reduce heat; cover and simmer for 20 minutes or until tender. Meanwhile, in a skillet, saute onion and celery in butter until tender. Stir in rice, mushrooms, parsley, poultry seasoning, salt, pepper and the remaining broth. Pour into a greased 13-in. x 9-in. x 2-in. baking dish. Bake, uncovered, at 350° for 30 minutes. Garnish with sage and thyme if desired. **Yield:** 10-12 servings.

Punch Bowl Trifle

This impressive-looking trifle is an easy way to serve a big group a little different dessert. It's cool, creamy and loaded with fruit. —Margaret Wagner Allen
Abingdon, Virginia

2 cans (20 ounces *each*) crushed pineapple
1 package (18-1/4 ounces) yellow cake mix
1 package (5.1 ounces) instant vanilla
  pudding mix
2 cans (21 ounces *each*) cherry pie filling
4 medium ripe bananas, sliced
2 cans (15-1/4 ounces *each*) fruit cocktail,
  drained
2 cans (11 ounces *each*) mandarin oranges,
  drained
1 carton (16 ounces) frozen whipped
  topping, thawed
1 package (7 ounces) flaked coconut,
  toasted

Drain pineapple, reserving juice; set the pineapple aside. Prepare cake batter according to package directions, substituting pineapple juice for the water (add water if necessary for the required measurement). Bake as directed in a greased 13-in. x 9-in. x 2-in. pan. Cool. Meanwhile, prepare pudding according to package directions. Cut the cake into 1-in. cubes; place half in a 6-qt. punch bowl. Top with half of the pudding, pie filling, pineapple, bananas, fruit cocktail, oranges, whipped topping and coconut. Repeat layers. Cover and refrigerate for 6 hours or overnight. **Yield:** 55 (1/2-cup) servings.

Fudgy Coconut Squares

(Pictured above)

Whenever I taste these rich, delicious layered bars, I think of my childhood. My parents were missionaries in Thailand, and Mother was able to get these common ingredients there—the squares reminded us of the candy bars back home. —Pam Tesh
Lexington, North Carolina

1 cup butter *or* margarine, softened
1-1/2 cups sugar
3 eggs
1 teaspoon vanilla extract
1 cup all-purpose flour
1/4 cup baking cocoa
1/2 cup chopped walnuts
1 can (14 ounces) sweetened condensed
  milk
1 cup shredded coconut
ICING:
2 cups confectioners' sugar
1/4 cup baking cocoa
5 tablespoons evaporated milk
2 tablespoons butter *or* margarine, melted
1/2 teaspoon vanilla extract

In a mixing bowl, cream butter and sugar. Add eggs and vanilla; mix well. Combine flour, cocoa and walnuts; add to the creamed mixture. Spread into a greased 13-in. x 9-in. x 2-in. baking pan. Bake at 350° for 30 minutes or until a toothpick inserted near the center comes out clean. Combine condensed milk and coconut; carefully spread over the hot chocolate layer. Bake at 350° for 20 minutes or until coconut is lightly browned. Combine icing ingredients until smooth; spread over warm bars. Refrigerate at least 1 hour before cutting. **Yield:** about 4 dozen.

Sunny Vegetable Salad

(Pictured above)

A terrific mixture of crisp, chewy, fresh and sweet ingredients makes this salad taste as good as it looks. A nutritious vegetable like broccoli is a lot more palatable "dressed up" this way. —Char Holm
Goodhue, Minnesota

    5 cups broccoli florets
    5 cups cauliflowerets
    2 cups (8 ounces) shredded cheddar cheese
 2/3 cup chopped onion
 1/2 cup raisins
    1 cup mayonnaise
 1/2 cup sugar
    2 tablespoons cider *or* red wine vinegar
    6 bacon strips, cooked and crumbled
 1/4 cup sunflower kernels

In a large salad bowl, toss broccoli, cauliflower, cheese, onion and raisins. In a small bowl, combine mayonnaise, sugar and vinegar. Pour over salad; toss to coat. Cover and refrigerate for 1 hour. Sprinkle with the bacon and sunflower kernels. **Yield:** 12-16 servings.

—— 🥤 🥤 🥤 ——

Heavenly Dinner Rolls

Several years ago, I entered this recipe in a contest sponsored by a local newspaper and was awarded a
first prize! Your family and friends will give these fluffy rolls high honors, too.* —Joan Priefert
Overland Park, Kansas

    2 packages (1/4 ounce *each*) active dry yeast
 1/4 cup warm water (110° to 115°)
    4 cups warm milk (110° to 115°)
    1 cup sugar
    1 cup shortening
    7 to 7-1/2 cups all-purpose flour, *divided*
    2 teaspoons baking powder
    1 teaspoon baking soda
    1 teaspoon salt
Melted butter *or* margarine, optional

In a mixing bowl, dissolve yeast in water. Add milk, sugar, shortening and 4 cups of flour; beat until smooth. Cover and let rise in a warm place for 2 hours. Add baking powder, baking soda, salt and enough remaining flour to form a soft, slightly sticky dough. Cover and refrigerate until ready to use. Turn onto a heavily floured surface; pat to 1/2-in. thickness. Cut with a biscuit cutter or drop by 1/4 cupfuls onto greased baking sheets. Cover and let rise until nearly doubled, about 30 minutes. Bake at 350° for 10-15 minutes or until lightly browned. Brush tops with butter if desired. Dough may be refrigerated up to 3 days. Punch down each day. **Yield:** about 5 dozen.

—— 🥤 🥤 🥤 ——

Stew for a Crowd

Need a no-fuss feast to feed a crowd? With lots of meat and vegetables, this big-batch stew is sure to satisfy. —Mike Morratzo, Florence, Alabama

   25 pounds beef stew meat
    5 pounds onions, diced (about 16 cups)
    2 celery stalks, cut into 1-inch pieces (about 14 cups)
About 5 quarts water
 1/2 cup browning sauce, optional
 1/4 cup salt
    3 tablespoons garlic powder
    3 tablespoons dried thyme
    3 tablespoons seasoned salt
    2 tablespoons pepper
   12 bay leaves
   15 pounds red potatoes, cut into 1-inch cubes (about 16 cups)
   10 pounds carrots, cut into 1-inch pieces (about 24 cups)
   10 cups frozen peas
   10 cups frozen corn
    4 cups all-purpose flour
    3 to 4 cups milk

Divide the stew meat, onions and celery between several large stockpots. Add water to fill pots half full. Add browning sauce if desired and seasonings. Cover and simmer for about 1-1/2 hours or until the meat is tender. Add potatoes and carrots; simmer for 40 minutes or until vegetables are tender. Add the peas and corn; simmer 1 hour longer. Combine flour and enough milk to make a smooth (not runny) paste; add to stew, stirring constantly, until thickened. Remove the bay leaves before serving. **Yield:** 120 (1-cup) servings.

Chicken Rolls

These rolls take some time to prepare, but it's worth it! Everyone enjoys the savory filling wrapped inside a soft, delicious dough. —*Susan Carter*
American Fork, Utah

- 2 cups chopped celery
- 1 large onion, chopped
- 2 cups butter *or* margarine
- 10 cups chopped cooked chicken
- 1 pound fresh mushrooms, sliced
- 4 packages (8 ounces *each*) cream cheese, softened

Salt and pepper to taste
DOUGH:
- 4 packages (1/4 ounce *each*) active dry yeast
- 2 cups warm milk (110° to 115°)
- 6 eggs
- 3/4 cup sugar
- 1 tablespoon salt
- 9 to 9-1/2 cups all-purpose flour

Melted butter *or* margarine
Dry bread crumbs

Saute celery and onion in butter until tender. Add the chicken, mushrooms, cream cheese, salt and pepper; mix well. Refrigerate. In a mixing bowl, dissolve yeast in milk. Add eggs, sugar, salt and 1 cup flour; beat until smooth. Add enough remaining flour to form a firm dough. Roll out on a floured surface to 1/4-in. thickness; cut into 4-in. circles. Reroll scraps and cut more circles. Roll circles to a 6-1/2-in. diameter. Place on greased baking sheets and let rise in a warm place for 15 minutes. Place about 1/3 cup chicken mixture in the center of each circle. Fold up edges to center; pinch tightly to seal in filling. Dip in butter; roll in crumbs. Place on greased baking sheets (do not cover); let rise for 20 minutes. Bake at 375° for 20 minutes. Serve immediately. **Yield:** about 3 dozen. **Editor's Note:** Rolls can be made ahead and frozen. Dip in butter and crumbs when ready to bake.

Italian Casserole
(Pictured below)

I come from a huge family, and it seems there is always a potluck occasion. Graduation parties are the perfect place for me to bring this hearty, crowd-pleasing Italian main dish. It's easy to make and serve.
—*Rita Goshaw, South Milwaukee, Wisconsin*

- 1-1/2 pounds bulk Italian sausage
- 1-1/2 pounds ground beef
- 1 cup chopped onion
- 1 cup chopped green pepper
- 2 cans (15 ounces *each*) tomato sauce
- 2 cans (6 ounces *each*) tomato paste
- 1/2 cup water
- 1 teaspoon dried basil
- 1 teaspoon dried oregano
- 1 teaspoon salt
- 1 teaspoon pepper
- 1/8 teaspoon garlic powder
- 2 cans (8-3/4 ounces *each*) whole kernel corn, drained
- 2 cans (2-1/4 ounces *each*) sliced ripe olives, drained
- 1 package (16 ounces) wide noodles, cooked and drained
- 8 ounces cheddar cheese, cut into strips

In a Dutch oven over medium heat, cook sausage, beef, onion and green pepper until meat is browned and vegetables are tender; drain. Add tomato sauce and paste, water and seasonings; bring to a boil. Reduce heat; cover and simmer for 15 minutes. Add corn and olives; cover and simmer for 5 minutes. Stir in noodles. Pour into two greased 13-in. x 9-in. x 2-in. baking dishes. Top with cheese. Cover and bake at 350° for 25-30 minutes or until heated through. **Yield:** 16-20 servings.

Apple Cabbage Coleslaw

This cool, crunchy salad is perfect for hot summer days when family reunions, picnics and weddings are in full bloom! —Emma Magielda, Amsterdam, New York

     3 cartons (16 ounces *each*) sour cream
     1 cup sugar
     2 tablespoons salt
     1 tablespoon pepper
     5 teaspoons ground mustard
     4 to 5 pounds unpeeled tart apples, julienned
  1/2 cup lemon juice
     3 large heads cabbage (3 to 4 pounds *each*), shredded

In a large bowl, combine the first five ingredients; mix well. Cover and chill for at least 1 hour. Toss apples with lemon juice. Combine apples and cabbage; mix well. Just before serving, add dressing and toss to coat. **Yield:** 90-95 (1/2-cup) servings.

Butterscotch Pecan Dessert

(Pictured below)

The fluffy cream cheese layer topped with cool butterscotch pudding is a lip-smacking combination.
—Becky Harrison, Albion, Illinois

  1/2 cup cold butter *or* margarine
     1 cup all-purpose flour
  3/4 cup chopped pecans, *divided*
     1 package (8 ounces) cream cheese, softened
     1 cup confectioners' sugar
     1 carton (8 ounces) frozen whipped topping, thawed, *divided*
3-1/2 cups milk
     2 packages (3.4 or 3.5 ounces *each*) instant butterscotch *or* vanilla pudding mix

In a bowl, cut butter into flour until crumbly; stir in 1/2 cup pecans. Press into an ungreased 13-in. x 9-in. x 2-in. baking pan. Bake at 350° for 20 minutes or until lightly browned. Cool. In a mixing bowl, beat cream cheese and sugar until fluffy. Fold in 1 cup whipped topping; spread over crust. Combine milk and pudding mix until smooth; pour over cream cheese layer. Refrigerate for 15-20 minutes or until set. Top with remaining whipped topping and pecans. Refrigerate for 1-2 hours. **Yield:** 16-20 servings.

Cookies for a Crowd

I'm a cook at a 4-H camp. Our campers go wild over these crisp cookies with an excellent peanutty flavor.
—Mary Green, Mishicot, Wisconsin

     4 cups shortening
     4 cups packed brown sugar
     4 cups sugar
     8 eggs
     4 cups peanut butter
     4 teaspoons vanilla extract
    10 cups all-purpose flour
     4 teaspoons baking soda
     4 teaspoons salt
     1 cup chopped salted peanuts, optional

Cream shortening and sugars. Add eggs, peanut butter and vanilla; mix well. Add the flour, baking soda and salt; mix well. Stir in peanuts if desired. Drop by rounded teaspoonfuls 2 in. apart onto ungreased baking sheets. Flatten with a fork if desired. Bake at 350° for 10-12 minutes or until set. **Yield:** about 20 dozen.

Two-Cheese Tossed Salad

(Pictured on page 182)

Colorful, hearty ingredients and a delectable dressing make second helpings of this salad hard to resist. Cottage cheese is an unusual but tasty addition.
—Barbara Birk, American Fork, Utah

  1/2 cup vegetable oil
  1/2 cup chopped red onion
  1/4 cup sugar
  1/4 cup vinegar
     1 teaspoon poppy seeds
  1/2 teaspoon dried minced onion
  1/4 to 1/2 teaspoon prepared mustard
  1/8 to 1/4 teaspoon salt
     5 cups torn fresh spinach
     5 cups torn iceberg lettuce

1/2 **pound fresh mushrooms, sliced**
1 **carton (8 ounces) cottage cheese**
1 **cup (4 ounces) shredded Swiss cheese**
2 **bacon strips, cooked and crumbled**

In a jar with tight-fitting lid, combine the first eight ingredients. Refrigerate overnight. Just before serving, toss spinach, lettuce, mushrooms and cheeses in a large salad bowl. Shake dressing and pour over salad. Sprinkle with bacon. **Yield:** 12-14 servings.

Carrot Coin Casserole

When I first started making this recipe 25 years ago, I think it was just a creamed vegetable dish. Over time, I've enhanced it by trying different combinations of vegetables and adding nutmeg. —Linda Phillippi
Ronan, Montana

12 **medium carrots, sliced**
1 **large onion, cut into 1/4-inch slices**
2 **cups frozen peas**
1-1/2 **cups (6 ounces) shredded cheddar cheese**
4 **tablespoons butter *or* margarine, *divided***
2 **tablespoons all-purpose flour**
1 **teaspoon salt**
1/4 **teaspoon pepper**
1/4 **teaspoon ground nutmeg**
2-1/2 **cups milk**
1 **cup crushed butter-flavored crackers (about 25 crackers)**

Place the carrots and a small amount of water in a saucepan; cover and cook over medium heat until crisp-tender, about 6 minutes. Add onion; bring to a boil. Reduce heat; cover and simmer for 4-6 minutes or until crisp-tender. Drain. Add peas and toss. Place 4 cups in a greased shallow 3-qt. baking dish; sprinkle with cheese. Top with remaining vegetables. In a saucepan over medium heat, melt 1 tablespoon butter. Stir in flour, salt, pepper and nutmeg until smooth. Gradually add milk, stirring constantly. Bring to a boil; boil and stir for 2 minutes. Pour over vegetables. In a small saucepan or skillet, combine cracker crumbs and remaining butter; cook and stir over medium heat until toasted. Sprinkle over the casserole. Bake, uncovered, at 350° for 30-40 minutes or until bubbly. **Yield:** 12 servings.

Golden Crescents

(Pictured above right)

My family loves these rolls so much they request them for every Sunday dinner. Pulling these slightly sweet,

tender rolls from out of the basket, my grandchildren say to me, "Grandma, you're the world's best cook."
—Bertha Johnson, Indianapolis, Indiana

2 **packages (1/4 ounce *each*) active dry yeast**
3/4 **cup warm water (110° to 115°)**
1/2 **cup sugar**
1/4 **cup plus 2 tablespoons butter *or* margarine, softened, *divided***
2 **tablespoons shortening**
2 **eggs**
1 **teaspoon salt**
4 **to 4-1/2 cups all-purpose flour**
Additional butter *or* margarine, melted, optional

In a mixing bowl, dissolve yeast in water. Add sugar, 1/4 cup of butter, shortening, eggs, salt and 2 cups flour; beat until smooth. Add enough of the remaining flour to form a soft dough. Turn onto a floured surface; knead until smooth and elastic, about 6-8 minutes. Place in a greased bowl; turn once to grease top. Cover and let rise in a warm place until doubled, about 1-1/2 hours. Punch the dough down; divide in half. Roll each portion into a 12-in. circle. Melt remaining butter; brush over dough. Cut each circle into 12 wedges. Roll up wedges from the wide end and curve to form crescents. Place with point down 2 in. apart on greased baking sheets. Cover and let rise until doubled, about 45 minutes. Bake at 375° for 8-10 minutes or until golden brown. Brush with butter if desired. **Yield:** 2 dozen.

Carrot Sheet Cake

We sold pieces of this cake at an art show and, before long, sold out of the 10 cakes we had made!
—Dottie Cosgrove, South El Monte, California

> 4 eggs
> 1 cup vegetable oil
> 2 cups sugar
> 2 cups all-purpose flour
> 2 teaspoons baking soda
> 1/4 teaspoon baking powder
> 2 teaspoons ground cinnamon
> 1/2 teaspoon salt
> 3 cups shredded carrots
> 2/3 cup chopped walnuts
> FROSTING:
> 1 package (8 ounces) cream cheese, softened
> 1/2 cup butter *or* margarine, softened
> 1 teaspoon vanilla extract
> 4 cups confectioners' sugar
> 2/3 cup chopped walnuts

In a mixing bowl, beat eggs, oil and sugar until smooth. Combine flour, baking soda, baking powder, cinnamon and salt; add to egg mixture and beat well. Stir in carrots and walnuts. Pour into a greased 15-in. x 10-in. x 1-in. baking pan. Bake at 350° for 35 minutes or until a toothpick inserted near the center comes out clean. Cool on a wire rack. For frosting, beat cream cheese, butter and vanilla in a mixing bowl until smooth; beat in sugar. Spread over cake. Sprinkle with nuts. **Yield:** 24-30 servings. **Editor's Note:** Frosted cake may be frozen.

Party Potato Salad

This salad has been a staple for the family for years. A friend and I prepared enough to serve 200 at my oldest son's wedding reception.
—Dona Sundsmo
Tacoma, Washington

> 10 pounds potatoes, peeled and cubed
> 3 cups mayonnaise
> 3 cups sweet pickle relish
> 2 cups chopped onion
> 1/2 cup prepared mustard
> 1 tablespoon salt
> 1 teaspoon pepper
> 15 hard-cooked eggs, chopped

Cook potatoes in boiling water until tender; drain. Combine mayonnaise, relish, onion, mustard, salt and pepper; mix well. Add eggs and warm potatoes; toss gently. Cover and refrigerate. **Yield:** 60 (1/2-cup) servings.

Sandwich for a Crowd

(Pictured above)

My husband and I live on a 21-acre horse ranch and are pleased to invite friends to enjoy it with us. When entertaining, I rely on no-fuss make-ahead entrees like this satisfying sandwich.
—Helen Hougland
Spring Hill, Kansas

> 2 unsliced loaves (1 pound *each*) Italian bread
> 1 package (8 ounces) cream cheese, softened
> 1 cup (4 ounces) shredded cheddar cheese
> 3/4 cup sliced green onions
> 1/4 cup mayonnaise
> 1 tablespoon Worcestershire sauce
> 1 pound thinly sliced fully cooked ham
> 1 pound thinly sliced roast beef
> 12 to 14 thin slices dill pickle

Cut the bread in half lengthwise. Hollow out top and bottom of loaves, leaving a 1/2-in. shell (discard removed bread or save for another use). Combine cheeses, onions, mayonnaise and Worcestershire sauce; spread over cut sides of bread. Layer ham and roast beef on bottom and top halves; place pickles on bottom halves. Gently press halves together. Wrap in plastic wrap and refrigerate for at least 2 hours. Cut into 1-1/2-in. slices. **Yield:** 12-14 servings.

Celery Seed Slaw

A simple cooked dressing gives this crisp cabbage mixture a delightful sweet-and-sour flavor.
—Ronnie Stone, Arapahoe, North Carolina

    3 pounds cabbage, coarsely shredded
1/2 cup finely shredded carrot
1/2 cup chopped green pepper
    1 cup sugar
    1 cup vinegar
    1 tablespoon salt
    1 teaspoon celery seed

In a large bowl, combine cabbage, carrot and green pepper. In a saucepan, combine sugar, vinegar, salt and celery seed; bring to a boil. Pour over cabbage mixture and toss. Cover and refrigerate for 4 hours or overnight. **Yield:** 12-16 servings.

Melon and Grape Salad

This fruit salad—with an easy-to-prepare refreshing citrus dressing—is a nice complement to any buffet.
—Mary Etta Buran, Olmsted Township, Ohio

       1 medium-large watermelon, cut into cubes *or* balls
       3 honeydew melons, cut into cubes *or* balls
       3 cantaloupe melons, cut into cubes *or* balls
1-1/2 pounds seedless green grapes
1-1/2 pounds seedless red grapes
       3 cups sugar
    1/3 cup lemon juice
    1/3 cup lime juice
    1/3 cup orange juice

Combine melons and grapes. Combine sugar and juices; pour over fruit and toss to coat. Cover and chill for 1 hour. Serve with a slotted spoon. **Yield:** 50-54 servings (about 1 cup each).

Au Gratin Potatoes and Ham

With hearty chunks of ham and red potato in a creamy cheese sauce, this dish appeals to all at any gathering.
—Evie Pond, Ipswich, South Dakota

   20 pounds red potatoes
    8 pounds fully cooked ham, cubed
    4 cans (10-3/4 ounces *each*) condensed cream of celery soup, undiluted
    2 quarts milk
 1/2 cup all-purpose flour
    6 pounds process American cheese, cubed
    2 teaspoons pepper
    2 teaspoons paprika

Cook potatoes until tender; cool. Peel if desired and cut into cubes. Place about 6 cups of potatoes each in eight greased 13-in. x 9-in. x 2-in. baking pans. Add about 3-1/2 cups of cubed ham to each pan. In a Dutch oven over medium heat, combine soup, milk and flour until smooth; bring to a boil. Cook and stir for 2 minutes or until thickened. Add cheese, pepper and paprika. Reduce heat; cook until the cheese is melted. Pour about 2-1/4 cups of sauce into each pan. Cover and bake at 350° for 40 minutes. Uncover and bake 5-10 minutes longer or until bubbly. **Yield:** 140 (1-cup) servings.

Cherry Punch

(Pictured below)

In 1952, a co-worker gave me the recipe for this versatile punch. It's not too sweet, so it really refreshes.
—Davlyn Jones, San Jose, California

    1 can (6 ounces) frozen lemonade concentrate, thawed
    1 can (6 ounces) frozen limeade concentrate, thawed
    1 can (20 ounces) pineapple chunks, undrained
    2 cups water
    2 liters cherry soda, chilled
    2 liters ginger ale, chilled
Lemon and lime slices, optional

In a blender, combine concentrates and pineapple; cover and blend until smooth. Pour into a gallon-size container; stir in water. Store in the refrigerator. To serve, pour the mixture into a punch bowl; add cherry soda and ginger ale. Garnish with lemon and lime slices if desired. **Yield:** about 6 quarts.

Layered Chicken Salad

(Pictured below)

This cool main-dish salad really hits the spot during the warm summer months. Plus, its colorful layers look so appealing. Served with a roll or muffin, it's a complete meal. —Kay Bridgeman, Lexington, Ohio

    3 cups cubed cooked chicken, *divided*
    2 cups torn lettuce
    1 cup cooked long grain rice
    1 package (10 ounces) frozen peas, thawed
  1/4 cup minced fresh parsley
    2 large tomatoes, seeded and chopped
    1 cup thinly sliced cucumber
    1 small sweet red pepper, chopped
    1 small green pepper, chopped
DRESSING:
    1 cup mayonnaise
  1/2 cup sour cream
  1/2 cup raisins
  1/2 cup finely chopped onion
  1/4 cup sweet pickle relish
    2 tablespoons milk
  1/2 teaspoon celery seed
  1/2 teaspoon dill seed
  1/2 teaspoon ground mustard
  1/2 teaspoon garlic salt
Sweet red pepper rings and fresh parsley sprigs, optional

In a 3-qt. glass bowl, layer 1-1/2 cups of chicken and the lettuce. Combine rice, peas and parsley; spoon over lettuce. Layer with tomatoes, cucumber, peppers and remaining chicken. Combine the first 10 dressing ingredients; spoon over salad. Garnish with red pepper and parsley if desired. Cover and refrigerate for 8 hours or overnight. Toss before serving. **Yield:** 10-12 servings.

Shortcake for 50

Folks are always impressed to see these individual shortcakes on the buffet table. They're surprisingly easy to make. —Clara Honeyager
Mukwonago, Wisconsin

10-1/2 cups all-purpose flour
 4-1/4 cups sugar, *divided*
   1/2 cup plus 1 tablespoon baking powder
     4 teaspoons salt
     1 cup cold butter *or* margarine
     3 cups whipping cream
 1-1/2 cups water
     8 quarts fresh strawberries, sliced
Whipped cream *or* ice cream

In a bowl, combine flour, 2-1/4 cups sugar, baking powder and salt; cut in butter until crumbly. Stir in the cream and water just until moistened. Drop by 1/4 cupfuls 2 in. apart onto ungreased baking sheets. Bake at 450° for 15 minutes or until golden brown. Cool on wire racks. Combine the berries and remaining sugar. To serve, split shortcakes lengthwise; spoon about 1/3 cup of berries and whipped cream on bottom halves. Replace tops; top with another 1/3 cup of berries and additional cream. **Yield:** 50 servings.

Tangy Meatballs

These tasty meatballs floating in a thick tangy sauce are a hearty main dish you can make ahead. They are sure to please. —Inez Orsburn, Demotte, Indiana

    2 cups cubed rye bread
    2 cups milk
    3 eggs
    1 envelope onion soup mix
    2 teaspoons salt
 1-1/2 teaspoons dried thyme
   1/2 teaspoon pepper
   1/4 teaspoon ground nutmeg
     5 pounds ground beef
     2 pounds bulk pork sausage
     1 bottle (40 ounces) ketchup
     2 cups crab apple *or* apple jelly, melted
     4 teaspoons browning sauce, optional

Combine bread cubes and milk; let stand for 5 minutes. Add the next six ingredients; mix well. Crumble meat into bread mixture; stir just until blended. Form into 1-1/2-in. balls. Place in four ungreased 13-in. x 9-in. x 2-in. baking pans. Bake, uncovered, at 350° for 45 minutes; drain. Combine ketchup, jelly and browning sauce if desired; spoon over meatballs. Reduce heat to 300°; cover and bake for 1 hour. **Yield:** 7 to 7-1/2 dozen.

Three-Bean Baked Beans

With ground beef and bacon mixed in, these satisfying beans are a big hit at backyard barbecues and church picnics. —Julie Currington, Gahanna, Ohio

- 1/2 **pound ground beef**
- 5 **bacon strips, diced**
- 1/2 **cup chopped onion**
- 2 **cans (16 ounces *each*) pork and beans, undrained**
- 1 **can (16 ounces) butter beans, rinsed and drained**
- 1 **can (16 ounces) kidney beans, rinsed and drained**
- 1/3 **cup packed brown sugar**
- 1/4 **cup sugar**
- 1/4 **cup ketchup**
- 1/4 **cup barbecue sauce**
- 2 **tablespoons molasses**
- 2 **tablespoons prepared mustard**
- 1/2 **teaspoon chili powder**
- 1/2 **teaspoon salt**

In a large skillet or saucepan over medium heat, brown beef, bacon and onion; drain. Add beans. Combine remaining ingredients; stir into bean mixture. Pour into a greased 2-1/2-qt. baking dish. Bake, uncovered, at 350° for 1 hour or until beans reach desired thickness. **Yield:** 12 servings.

— 🥄 🥄 🥄 —

Caramel Peanut Bars

(Pictured above right)

With chocolate, peanuts and caramel between golden oat and crumb layers, these bars are very popular. They taste like candy bars but with homemade goodness.
—Ardyce Piehl, Wisconsin Dells, Wisconsin

- 1-1/2 **cups quick-cooking oats**
- 1-1/2 **cups all-purpose flour**
- 1-1/4 **cups packed brown sugar**
- 3/4 **teaspoon baking soda**
- 1/4 **teaspoon salt**
- 3/4 **cup butter *or* margarine, melted**
- 1 **package (14 ounces) caramels**
- 1/2 **cup whipping cream**
- 1-1/2 **cups (9 ounces) semisweet chocolate chips**
- 3/4 **cup chopped peanuts**

In a bowl, combine the first five ingredients; stir in butter. Set aside 1 cup for topping. Press the remaining mixture into a greased 13-in. x 9-in. x 2-in. baking pan. Bake at 350° for 10 minutes or until lightly browned. Meanwhile, combine caramels and cream in a heavy saucepan or microwave-safe bowl. Cook over low heat or microwave until melt-

ed, stirring often. Sprinkle chocolate chips and peanuts over the crust; top with the caramel mixture. Sprinkle with reserved oat mixture. Bake for 15-20 minutes or until topping is golden brown. Cool completely before cutting. **Yield:** 3 dozen.

— 🥄 🥄 🥄 —

Corn Dog Casserole

Reminiscent of traditional corn dogs, this fun main dish really hits the spot on fall days. It's perfect for the football parties my husband and I often host.
—Marcy Suzanne Olipane, Belleville, Illinois

- 2 **cups thinly sliced celery**
- 2 **tablespoons butter *or* margarine**
- 1-1/2 **cups sliced green onions**
- 1-1/2 **pounds hot dogs**
- 2 **eggs**
- 1-1/2 **cups milk**
- 2 **teaspoons rubbed sage**
- 1/4 **teaspoon pepper**
- 2 **packages (8-1/2 ounces *each*) corn bread/muffin mix**
- 2 **cups (8 ounces) shredded sharp cheddar cheese, *divided***

In a skillet, saute celery in butter for 5 minutes. Add onions; saute for 5 minutes. Place in a large bowl; set aside. Cut hot dogs lengthwise into quarters, then cut into thirds. In the same skillet, saute hot dogs for 5 minutes or until lightly browned; add to vegetables. Set aside 1 cup. In a large bowl, combine eggs, milk, sage and pepper. Add remaining hot dog mixture. Stir in corn bread mixes. Add 1-1/2 cups cheese. Spread into a shallow 3-qt. baking dish. Top with reserved hot dog mixture and remaining cheese. Bake, uncovered, at 400° for 30 minutes or until golden brown. **Yield:** 12 servings.

Crunchy Peanut Butter Bars

(Pictured above)

These delicious bars are great holiday treats, but the kids like them all year long. I used this recipe over and over when our five children were at home. Now I'm thrilled to bake a batch for my grandchildren.
—Geraldine Grisdale, Mt. Pleasant, Michigan

2-3/4 cups all-purpose flour
1-1/4 cups packed brown sugar
   1 egg
1/2 cup butter *or* margarine, softened
1/2 cup shortening
1/3 cup chunky peanut butter
   1 teaspoon vanilla extract
1/2 teaspoon salt
TOPPING:
   1 cup (6 ounces) semisweet chocolate
     chips, melted
1/2 cup chunky peanut butter
1-1/2 cups crushed cornflakes

In a mixing bowl, combine the first eight ingredients and mix well (batter will be thick). Press into an ungreased 15-in. x 10-in. x 1-in. baking pan. Bake at 350° for 15-20 minutes or until set. Cool for 5 minutes. Meanwhile, combine the chocolate chips and peanut butter in a bowl; stir in cornflakes. Carefully spread on top. Cut into bars. **Yield:** 4 dozen.

Chocolate Peanut Torte

A crust of vanilla wafer crumbs and crushed peanuts gives this cool, creamy dessert an extra tasty base peo- *ple enjoy. It's almost guaranteed that I'll bring home an empty pan when I take it to a potluck.*
—Ardyce Piehl, Wisconsin Dells, Wisconsin

   2 cups vanilla wafer crumbs
1/3 cup butter *or* margarine, melted
   1 cup peanuts, finely chopped, *divided*
   1 package (8 ounces) cream cheese,
     softened
   1 cup confectioners' sugar
1/2 cup peanut butter
   4 cups whipped topping, *divided*
   3 cups cold milk
   2 packages (3.9 ounces *each*) instant
     chocolate pudding mix
   1 milk chocolate candy bar (1.55 ounces),
     grated

Combine the wafer crumbs, butter and 2/3 cup of peanuts. Press onto the bottom of an ungreased 13-in. x 9-in. x 2-in. baking dish. Bake at 350° for 8-10 minutes or until lightly browned. Cool. In a mixing bowl, beat cream cheese, sugar and peanut butter until smooth. Fold in 2 cups whipped topping. Spread over crust. In a mixing bowl, beat milk and pudding mixes on low for 2 minutes. Carefully spread over cream cheese layer. Cover and refrigerate for 4-6 hours. Just before serving, carefully spread remaining topping over pudding layer. Sprinkle with grated chocolate and remaining peanuts. **Yield:** 16-20 servings.

Turkey Salad for 60

The mild seasonings in this salad certainly have mass appeal. It's a substantial main dish with a delightful crunch.
—Terry Smith, Campbell Hall, New York

   1 turkey (20 to 22 pounds)
   4 packages (7 ounces *each*) ring macaroni,
     cooked and drained
   3 bunches celery, thinly sliced
   3 cans (8 ounces *each*) sliced water
     chestnuts, drained
   2 packages (16 ounces *each*) frozen tiny
     sweet peas, thawed
   1 large onion, diced
   2 quarts mayonnaise
   2 tablespoons seasoned salt
   4 cups slivered almonds, toasted

Roast the turkey. Cool; debone and cut into chunks. Combine turkey, macaroni, celery, water chestnuts, peas and onion. Combine mayonnaise and seasoned salt; stir into salad. Cover and refrigerate for several hours. Add almonds just before serving. **Yield:** 60 servings.

Glazed Apple Pan Pie

Potluck gatherings keep us busy around the year, so I appreciate foods that feed a crowd. With a sweet apple filling and delicious crust, this pan pie is always a hit. —Barbara Keith, Faucett, Missouri

    5 cups all-purpose flour
    4 teaspoons sugar
  1/2 teaspoon salt
  1/2 teaspoon baking powder
1-1/2 cups shortening
    2 egg yolks
  2/3 cup cold water
FILLING:
  14 cups thinly sliced peeled tart apples
    4 teaspoons lemon juice
    1 teaspoon vanilla extract
  3/4 cup sugar
  3/4 cup packed brown sugar
    2 teaspoons ground cinnamon
  1/4 teaspoon salt
    3 tablespoons butter _or_ margarine
    2 tablespoons milk
GLAZE:
  1/2 cup confectioners' sugar
    1 tablespoon water
  1/8 teaspoon vanilla extract

In a bowl, combine flour, sugar, salt and baking powder. Cut in shortening until crumbly. Beat egg yolks and water; add to flour mixture, tossing with a fork until dough forms a ball. Divide dough in half. Roll out one half to fit the bottom and up the sides of an ungreased 15-in. x 10-in. x 1-in. baking pan. Toss apples with lemon juice and vanilla; set aside. Combine sugars, cinnamon and salt. Place half of the apples over crust; sprinkle with half of the sugar mixture. Repeat; dot with butter. Roll out remaining pastry to fit top of pie; place over filling. Seal and flute edges. Brush with milk. Bake at 375° for 50-55 minutes or until golden brown. Cool for 10 minutes. Combine glaze ingredients; drizzle over pie. **Yield:** 24 servings.

— 🍲 🍲 🍲 —

Savory Pork Turnovers

(Pictured at right)

Apples, potatoes, ground pork and seasonings tucked inside flaky golden pastry crust never fail to win praise from my family at home and friends at church functions. The assembly requires a bit of effort, but these impressive little turnovers are worth it.
—Ruby Carves, Litchfield, Maine

    6 cups all-purpose flour
    2 teaspoons sugar
1-1/2 teaspoons salt
    1 cup shortening
    1 cup cold butter _or_ margarine
  12 to 18 tablespoons cold water
FILLING:
    2 pounds ground pork
    3 tablespoons butter _or_ margarine
  1/2 cup chopped onion
    2 cups cooked cubed peeled potatoes
    2 cups diced peeled tart apples
    3 tablespoons all-purpose flour
    1 tablespoon brown sugar
1-1/2 teaspoons rubbed sage
    1 teaspoon pepper
  1/2 teaspoon salt
    2 egg yolks
    2 tablespoons water

In a bowl, combine flour, sugar and salt; cut in shortening and butter until crumbly. Add water, 1 tablespoon at a time, tossing lightly with a fork until dough forms a ball. Cover and chill for at least 1 hour. In a Dutch oven over medium heat, brown pork until no longer pink; drain. Add butter and onion; saute until onion is tender. Add potatoes, apples, flour, sugar, sage, pepper and salt; cook and stir for 2 minutes. Cool. Meanwhile, on a heavily floured surface, roll pastry to 1/8-in. thickness; cut into 3-1/2-in. circles. Place 1-2 tablespoons filling on each circle. Moisten edges with water; fold dough in half. Seal edges with fingers or a fork. Place on ungreased baking sheets. Beat egg yolks and water; brush over turnovers. Bake at 375° for 20-25 minutes or until golden brown. Serve warm. **Yield:** about 4 dozen.

Cooking for One or Two

*These perfectly portioned recipes—
featuring savory entrees,
side dishes, desserts and more—
deliciously prove good things
really do come in small packages!*

IDEAL QUANTITIES. Clockwise from upper left:
Beef Tenderloin in Mushroom Sauce, Vegetable
Ramekins and Little Dixie Pound Cake (pages
206 and 207); Cornish Hens with Rice Stuffing
and Sweet Potato Souffles (page 210); Scallop
and Potato Saute and Greens with Mustard
Vinaigrette (page 200); Mini Meat Loaf, Wilted
Coleslaw and Mac 'n' Cheese for One (page 204).

Singling Out Good Food

RECIPES that serve only one can have as much appeal as those that feed a bunch. The delightful duo pictured at right makes a mighty good meal for one.

Mildred Sherrer of Bay City, Texas shares her recipe for Scallop and Potato Saute. "I make this special seafood dish for the holidays to treat myself," informs Mildred.

Greens with Mustard Vinaigrette comes from Mississippi cook Shirley Glaab of Hattiesburg. "It tastes extra-fresh every time since you make the dressing when you need it," Shirley remarks.

Becky Bolte of Jewell, Kansas loves Chinese food, but her family doesn't. "So I make Teriyaki Chicken Breast just for me," says Becky.

"Baked Pear is a nice side dish to go with pork or chicken," offers Valerie Lee of Snellville, Georgia. "It also makes a delicious light dessert."

Scallop and Potato Saute

2 small red potatoes, sliced 1/4 inch thick
2 tablespoons olive *or* vegetable oil, *divided*
1/4 pound bay scallops
1 garlic clove, minced
1 tablespoon lemon juice
1 tablespoon chopped fresh parsley
1/8 teaspoon salt
Dash pepper
Lemon slice *or* wedge, optional

In a small skillet over medium heat, cook potatoes in 1 tablespoon oil until golden brown and tender, about 12 minutes. Remove and keep warm. In the same skillet, heat remaining oil. Cook and stir the scallops for 2 minutes. Add garlic and lemon juice; cook and stir 1-2 minutes longer or until scallops are firm and opaque. Add parsley, salt and pepper. Return potatoes to pan; heat through. Serve with lemon if desired. **Yield:** 1 serving.

Greens with Mustard Vinaigrette

1 tablespoon olive *or* vegetable oil
2 teaspoons apple juice
1 teaspoon cider *or* red wine vinegar
1/2 to 1 teaspoon lemon juice
1/2 teaspoon Dijon mustard

1 cup torn mixed greens
Tomato wedges

In a small bowl, combine oil, apple juice, vinegar, lemon juice and mustard; mix well. Serve over greens and tomatoes. **Yield:** 1 serving.

Teriyaki Chicken Breast

(Not pictured)

2 tablespoons chicken broth
1 tablespoon soy sauce
2 teaspoons sugar
1 teaspoon vegetable oil

1 garlic clove, minced
Pinch ground ginger
1 boneless skinless chicken breast half
Additional chicken broth
1/2 cup uncooked instant rice
2 tablespoons frozen peas

In a resealable bag or shallow glass container, combine the first six ingredients. Add chicken; cover and refrigerate for 1 hour. Remove chicken and set marinade aside. Broil the chicken for 12 minutes or until juices run clear, turning once. Add broth to marinade to measure 2/3 cup. Pour into a small saucepan; bring to a boil. Boil for 5 minutes. Add rice and peas; cover and let stand for 5 minutes. Serve with chicken. **Yield:** 1 serving.

Baked Pear

(Not pictured)

1 pear, cored and thinly sliced
1 tablespoon butter *or* margarine
1 teaspoon sugar
Dash ground nutmeg

Place pear slices in an ungreased 2-cup baking dish. Dot with butter; sprinkle with sugar and nutmeg. Cover and bake at 350° for 40-50 minutes or until tender. **Yield:** 1 serving. **Editor's Note:** This recipe may be prepared in a microwave oven. Use a microwave-safe dish; cover and cook on high for 3-4 minutes (using a 700-watt microwave) or until the pear is tender.

ARE YOU looking for ways to wake up tired taste buds? You're sure to enjoy satisfying helpings of the single-serving recipes featured here.

Margery Bryan of Royal City, Washington shares the recipe for a tasty and colorful main dish—Stir-Fry for One. "Whenever I ask my husband what he'd like for dinner, this is what he requests," says Margery. "Then I double the recipe so that I can enjoy it with him. He thinks this rivals the stir-fries served in many restaurants."

For a light fluffy dessert with big banana flavor, try Banana Whip, shared by Marie Crumpacker of Creswell, Oregon. "For chocolate lovers, substitute chocolate cookie crumbs for the graham cracker crumbs and sprinkle with mini chocolate chips instead of chopped walnuts," she suggests.

Another no-fuss way to combine meat and vegetables in one dish is by preparing Chicken Veggie Packet. "The chicken and vegetables bake together in foil, so there's no pan to wash," explains Mildred Stubbs of Hamlet, North Carolina.

_____ 🍽 🍽 🍽 _____

Stir-Fry for One

 Nutritional Analysis included

- **1 tablespoon soy sauce**
- **2 teaspoons cider *or* red wine vinegar**
- **1 garlic clove, minced**
- **1/2 teaspoon sugar**
- **1/4 pound sirloin steak, cut into 1/4-inch strips**
- **1/4 cup broccoli florets**
- **1/4 cup cauliflowerets**
- **1/2 teaspoon vegetable oil**
- **1/4 cup diced green *or* sweet red pepper**
- **1/4 cup diced cabbage**
- **1/4 cup sliced water chestnuts**
- **2 green onions, sliced**
- **3 tablespoons beef broth**
- **1 teaspoon cornstarch**

Hot cooked rice

In a large resealable plastic bag or shallow glass container, combine the first four ingredients; add beef and turn to coat. Seal or cover and refrigerate for at least 10 minutes. In a skillet or wok, stir-fry broccoli and cauliflower in oil until vegetables begin to soften. Add beef and marinade; cook on medium-high for 3 minutes. Add green pepper, cabbage and water chestnuts; stir-fry for 2-3 minutes or until the vegetables are crisp-tender. Add onions. Combine broth and cornstarch until smooth; add to skillet. Bring to a boil; cook and stir for 2 minutes or until thickened. Serve over rice. **Yield:** 1 serving. **Nutritional Analysis:** One serving (prepared with light soy sauce and low-sodium broth; calculated without rice) equals 291 calories, 600 mg sodium, 77 mg cholesterol, 20 gm carbohydrate, 31 gm protein, 10 gm fat. **Diabetic Exchanges:** 3-1/2 lean meat, 1 starch, 1 vegetable.

_____ 🍽 🍽 🍽 _____

Banana Whip

- **1 cup miniature marshmallows**
- **1/4 cup milk**
- **1/4 cup whipping cream, whipped**
- **1/4 cup diced ripe banana**
- **1/8 teaspoon vanilla extract**
- **1/3 cup graham cracker crumbs**
- **1 tablespoon finely chopped walnuts**

In a small saucepan, combine marshmallows and milk. Cook and stir over low heat until marshmallows are melted. Remove from the heat and let cool. Fold in whipped cream. Add banana and vanilla. Spread crumbs in the bottom of a 2-cup serving dish. Top with the banana mixture. Sprinkle with nuts. Chill for at least 30 minutes. **Yield:** 1 serving.

Chicken Veggie Packet
(Not pictured)

1 bone-in chicken breast, skin removed
1 cup diced zucchini

1/2 cup diced green pepper
1/2 cup frozen mixed vegetables
  2 tablespoons diced onion
1/8 teaspoon dried basil
1/8 teaspoon dried parsley flakes
1/8 teaspoon paprika
1/8 teaspoon salt
1/8 teaspoon pepper

Place chicken and vegetables in the center of a large piece of heavy-duty aluminum foil, about 18 in. x 13 in. Sprinkle with seasonings. Fold foil around mixture and seal tightly. Place on a baking sheet. Bake at 350° for 40 minutes or until meat juices run clear. Open the foil carefully to allow steam to escape. **Yield:** 1 serving.

JUST BECAUSE you're cooking for one doesn't mean you have to forgo the down-home flavor of home-style meals. Treat yourself to the single-serving foods featured here and warm your body, soul and kitchen!

Lethea Weber of Newport, Arkansas suggests a tempting main dish of Mini Meat Loaf. "This recipe is a nice way to add vegetables to your diet...they add color, flavor and nutrition," Lethea remarks. "Chili sauce makes a pretty and tasty topping for the single-serving loaf."

Belleville, Illinois cook Denise Albers is happy to share the recipe for Wilted Coleslaw. "I fix this snappy salad for myself whenever I have a taste for it," Denise says. "The crisp ingredients and sweet-and-sour dressing are irresistible."

Mac 'n' Cheese for One is a creamy, comforting casserole you can enjoy without days of leftovers. "It's easy to make and goes well with any meat," assures Lucy Holland of Derby Line, Vermont. Pop this casserole in the oven during the last 15 minutes of the meat loaf's baking time.

Microwave Fruit Crisp is recommended by Luella Bogner of Attica, Ohio. "This simple dessert has lots of fruit and a golden oat topping," Luella explains. She typically uses apples, but pears also work nicely.

Mini Meat Loaf

  1/2 **slice bread, crumbled**
    2 **tablespoons finely shredded carrot**
    1 **tablespoon** *each* **chopped onion, celery and green pepper**
  1/4 **teaspoon salt**
Dash pepper
    2 **tablespoons chili sauce** *or* **ketchup,** *divided*
  1/4 **pound ground beef**

In a bowl, combine bread, carrot, onion, celery, green pepper, salt, pepper and 1 tablespoon chili sauce. Add beef and mix well. Shape into a 3-in. x 2-1/2-in. loaf; place in an ungreased shallow baking dish. Top with remaining chili sauce. Bake, uncovered, at 350° for 35-40 minutes. **Yield:** 1 serving.

Wilted Coleslaw

    1 **cup shredded cabbage**
    1 **green onion, sliced**
  1/8 **teaspoon celery seed**
  1/8 **teaspoon salt**
    2 **bacon strips**

    2 **tablespoons sugar**
4-1/2 **teaspoons vinegar**
Dash paprika

In a small bowl, combine cabbage, onion, celery seed and salt; set aside. In a skillet, cook bacon until crisp. Drain, reserving 1 tablespoon drippings. Crumble bacon over cabbage mixture. To the drippings, add sugar, vinegar and paprika; heat until sugar is dissolved. Pour over cabbage mixture and toss to coat. Serve immediately. **Yield:** 1 serving.

Mac 'n' Cheese for One

    2 **tablespoons butter** *or* **margarine,** *divided*
    1 **tablespoon all-purpose flour**
  1/4 **teaspoon salt**

Pinch pepper
1/2 cup milk
1/3 cup diced cheddar cheese
1/4 teaspoon prepared mustard
1/4 teaspoon Worcestershire sauce
1/2 teaspoon chopped onion
3 tablespoons elbow macaroni, cooked and drained
2 saltines, crushed

In a saucepan, melt 1 tablespoon of butter; stir in flour, salt and pepper. Whisk in milk until smooth. Cook and stir for 2 minutes. Reduce heat to low. Add cheese, mustard, Worcestershire sauce and onion; stir until cheese is melted. Add macaroni. Transfer to a greased 1-cup baking dish. Sprinkle with saltines; dot with remaining butter. Bake, uncovered, at 350° for 15 minutes or until heated through. **Yield:** 1 serving.

Microwave Fruit Crisp

(Not pictured)

1 medium apple *or* pear, peeled and thinly sliced
2 tablespoons brown sugar
2 tablespoons quick-cooking oats
1 tablespoon all-purpose flour
1/8 teaspoon ground cinnamon
1 tablespoon cold butter *or* margarine

Place fruit in a small microwave-safe dish. In another bowl, combine the dry ingredients; cut in butter until crumbly. Sprinkle over fruit. Microwave, uncovered, on high for 2-1/2 minutes or until fruit is tender. **Yield:** 1 serving. **Editor's Note:** This recipe was tested in a 700-watt microwave. It can also be baked in a small baking dish, uncovered, at 375° for 25-30 minutes.

Cooking for 'Just the Two of Us'

IT'S SAID that "good things come in twos"…but finding good recipes that serve just two can be tricky. So, here and on the pages that follow, we offer perfectly portioned meals.

"It doesn't take much fuss to fix a special meal for two," assures Denise McNab of Warrington, Pennsylvania. "When our kids are visiting Grandma, I make Beef Tenderloin in Mushroom Sauce for just my husband, Derek, and me. It's a recipe my mother-in-law has been using for more than 30 years. I especially look forward to preparing it as part of a special Valentine's Day menu."

Says Dona Alsover of Upland, California, "Our children and grandchildren live far away, so my husband, Jim, and I frequently plan a quiet dinner by candlelight. We have Vegetable Ramekins often since we can pull fresh things from our garden all year. It's a colorful and delicious side dish. You can easily mix and match your favorite vegetables."

Little Dixie Pound Cake is a moist quick-to-fix cake with a mild orange flavor. "When my great-grandson and I eat dinner together, we're always happy to share this delightful dessert," informs Ruby Williams of Bogalusa, Louisiana.

Beef Tenderloin in Mushroom Sauce

- 1 teaspoon vegetable oil
- 4 tablespoons butter *or* margarine, ***divided***
- 2 beef tenderloin steaks *or* fillets (1 inch thick)
- 1/2 cup chopped fresh mushrooms
- 1 tablespoon chopped green onions
- 1 tablespoon all-purpose flour
- 1/8 teaspoon salt
Dash pepper
- 2/3 cup chicken *or* beef broth
- 1/8 teaspoon browning sauce, optional

In a skillet, heat oil and 2 tablespoons of butter over medium-high heat. Cook steaks for 6-7 minutes on each side or until meat is done as desired (for rare, a meat thermometer should read 140°; medium, 160°; well-done, 170°). Remove to a serving platter and keep warm. To pan juices, add mushrooms, onions and remaining butter; saute until tender. Add flour, salt and pepper; gradually stir in broth until smooth. Add browning sauce if desired. Bring to a boil; boil and stir for 2 minutes. Spoon over the steaks. Serve immediately. **Yield:** 2 servings.

Vegetable Ramekins

- 1 small zucchini *or* yellow summer squash, halved and cut into 1/2-inch slices
- 1/4 cup chopped green pepper
- 1/3 cup broccoli florets
- 1 medium carrot, julienned
- 1 medium potato, peeled, cooked and cubed
- 2 tablespoons butter *or* margarine

2 tablespoons all-purpose flour
3/4 cup milk
1/4 teaspoon garlic salt
1/8 teaspoon coarse black pepper
1/4 cup shredded cheddar cheese
1 tablespoon minced fresh parsley
1 tablespoon chopped walnuts

In a saucepan over medium heat, cook squash, green pepper, broccoli and carrot in boiling water until crisp-tender; drain. Stir in the potato. Spoon into two greased ovenproof 10-oz. custard cups or casseroles. In a saucepan, melt the butter; stir in flour, milk, garlic salt and pepper until smooth. Cook for 2-3 minutes, gradually adding the cheese in small amounts; cook and stir until cheese is melted. Pour over vegetables. Sprinkle with parsley and walnuts. Bake, uncovered, at 350° for 20-25 minutes or until sauce is bubbly. **Yield:** 2 servings.

Little Dixie Pound Cake

3 tablespoons butter (no substitutes), softened
6 tablespoons sugar
1 egg
6 tablespoons all-purpose flour
Pinch baking soda
7 teaspoons buttermilk
1/4 teaspoon vanilla extract
1/8 teaspoon orange extract

In a small mixing bowl, cream the butter and sugar. Beat in egg. Combine flour and baking soda; add alternately with buttermilk to creamed mixture. Blend in extracts. Pour into a greased 5-3/4-in. x 3-in. x 2-in. loaf pan. Bake at 350° for 30-35 minutes or until cake tests done. Cool for 10 minutes; remove from the pan to cool on a wire rack. **Yield:** 1 mini loaf.

RECIPES that serve only two can have as much flavor as those that feed a bunch. Here's proof!

Quick Ginger Pork is the pick of Esther Johnson Danielson of Lawton, Pennsylvania. "My husband and I are empty nesters," she explains. "It was a challenge learning to cook for just two again, but recipes like this give us delicious scaled-down dinners."

Esther continues, "Ginger adds a spark to the sauce, which beautifully glazes tender strips of pork. Plus, the aroma while it's cooking is wonderful."

From Annandale, Virginia, Marge Killmon recommends Special Green Beans. "Simple seasonings give the popular vegetable a distinctive, tasty twist. They go well with many meals," she relates.

Says Emma Magielda of Amsterdam, New York, "When husband Frank and I yearn for something a little different at mealtime, I fix Honey-Lime Fruit Salad. It's really light and refreshing."

Quick Ginger Pork

☑ Nutritional Analysis included

    1 tablespoon vegetable oil
1/2 pound pork tenderloin, cut into thin strips
    1 garlic clove, minced
    2 tablespoons soy sauce
1/4 teaspoon sugar
1/8 to 1/4 teaspoon ground ginger
1/2 cup water
1-1/2 teaspoons cornstarch
Hot cooked rice

Heat oil in a large skillet over medium-high heat. Stir-fry the pork and garlic for 3 minutes. Combine soy sauce, sugar and ginger; add to skillet. Reduce heat to medium; stir-fry for 3-4 minutes or until pork is no longer pink. Combine water and cornstarch until smooth; add to skillet. Bring to a boil; boil and stir for 2 minutes. Serve over rice. **Yield:** 2 servings. **Nutritional Analysis:** One serving (prepared with light soy sauce; calculated without rice) equals 227 calories, 554 mg sodium, 67 mg cholesterol, 5 gm carbohydrate, 25 gm protein, 11 gm fat. **Diabetic Exchanges:** 3 lean meat, 1/2 starch, 1/2 fat.

Special Green Beans

☑ Nutritional Analysis included

1-1/4 cups cut fresh green beans (2-inch pieces)
    2 teaspoons vegetable oil
    1/3 cup water

    1 teaspoon soy sauce
Dash ground ginger

In a saucepan, saute beans in oil over medium heat for 4 minutes. Add water. Reduce heat; cover and simmer for 15 minutes or until the beans are crisp-tender. Drain; toss with soy sauce and ginger. **Yield:** 2 servings. **Nutritional Analysis:** One serving (prepared with light soy sauce) equals 64 calories, 88 mg sodium, 0 cholesterol, 5 gm carbohydrate,

2 gm protein, 5 gm fat. **Diabetic Exchanges:** 1 vegetable, 1 fat.

Honey-Lime Fruit Salad

1-1/2 cups torn salad greens
1 can (11 ounces) mandarin oranges, drained
1 small red apple, sliced
3 tablespoons limeade *or* lemonade concentrate
3 tablespoons honey
3 tablespoons vegetable oil
1/2 teaspoon poppy seeds

On salad plates, arrange the greens, oranges and apple. Combine remaining ingredients in a bowl; whisk until smooth. Pour over salads. **Yield:** 2 servings.

MUCH TO the delight of folks who cook for "just the two of us" even during the hectic holidays, the spectacular spread pictured at right showcases how a festive meal doesn't have to be produced in great quantities to be special.

Assures Kathy Meyer of Kenosha, Wisconsin, "I came across the recipe for Cornish Hens with Rice Stuffing a few years ago around Thanksgiving. The golden, juicy hens and festive rice stuffing make a memorable feast for two. Best of all, we're not eating leftovers for days on end."

For a super side dish that suits any season, try Sweet Potato Souffles from Mary Kay Dixson of Decatur, Alabama. "This is a delightfully new way to enjoy sweet potatoes. I know you'll agree these souffles are light, smooth and delicious," she says.

—— ☕ ☕ ☕ ——

Cornish Hens with Rice Stuffing

- 1 **package (6 ounces) long grain and wild rice mix**
- 2 **tablespoons butter** *or* **margarine,** *divided*
- 1/2 **cup chopped pecans**
- 1-1/3 **cups orange juice**
- 1 **cup water**
- 1/4 **cup raisins**
- 2 **Cornish game hens (1 to 1-1/2 pounds** *each***)**
- 1/2 **teaspoon salt**
- 1/4 **teaspoon pepper**

Set the seasoning packet from rice mix aside. In a saucepan, melt 1 tablespoon butter. Add rice and pecans; saute over low heat for 10 minutes or until rice is golden brown, stirring often. Stir in orange juice, water, raisins and contents of the seasoning packet; bring to a boil over medium heat. Reduce heat; cover and simmer for 25 minutes or until liquid is absorbed. Spoon about 1/2 cup rice mixture into each hen; set the remaining rice mixture aside. Tie the legs of each hen together; turn wing tips under backs. Place on a greased rack in a roasting pan. Melt remaining butter; brush over hens. Sprinkle with salt and pepper. Bake at 350° for 1 to 1-1/4 hours or until juices run clear and a thermometer inserted into the stuffing reads 165°. Baste occasionally with pan drippings. Heat the reserved rice mixture; serve with hens. **Yield:** 2 servings.

—— ☕ ☕ ☕ ——

Sweet Potato Souffles

- 4 **teaspoons sugar,** *divided*
- 1 **large sweet potato (about 12 ounces), peeled and cubed**
- 1 **teaspoon lemon juice**
- 1/2 **to 3/4 teaspoon salt**
- 1/8 **teaspoon ground nutmeg**
- 1 **tablespoon butter** *or* **margarine**
- 4 **teaspoons all-purpose flour**
- 1/2 **cup milk**
- 2 **eggs,** *separated*
- 1/4 **cup miniature marshmallows**

Grease two 2-cup souffle dishes or custard cups; sprinkle each with 1/2 teaspoon of sugar. Set aside. Place sweet potato in saucepan; cover with water. Cover and cook until tender, 10-15 minutes; drain well. Add lemon juice, salt and nutmeg. Mash potato mixture (should have about 1 cup); set aside to cool. In another saucepan, melt butter; stir in flour and remaining sugar until smooth. Gradually add milk; cook and stir until thickened and bubbly. Remove from heat. In small bowl, beat egg yolks; stir in mashed potato. Add milk mixture. In a mixing bowl, beat egg whites until stiff peaks form; gently fold into potato mixture. Spoon into prepared dishes. Top with marshmallows. Bake, uncovered, at 350° for 35 minutes or until knife inserted in center comes out clean. Serve immediately. **Yield:** 2 servings.

'My Mom's Best Meal'

Six cooks recall special times when they prepare the same meals for which their moms are fondly remembered.

MEMORABLE MEALS include, clockwise from upper left: Grade A Recipes (p. 230), Country-Style Cooking (p. 222), Homey Ham Dinner (p. 218) and Comforting Family Supper (p. 234).

***Timeless recipes
have a bit of
old-fashioned flair
that appeal to all
generations.***

By Gloria Grant, Sterling, Illinois

EVEN IN HER 80's, my mother (Berneda Grant, above, of Pekin, Illinois) works wonders in the kitchen! When we kids were growing up, she always made delicious, hearty meals with many special touches.

For example, Mom freezes sweet corn in the summer so we can enjoy that fresh taste at the holidays. She also makes pickles to round out many of her menus.

My two sisters, brother and I unanimously agree that our mom's Chuck Roast with Homemade Noodles is still our all-time favorite. Even her five grandchildren request this main dish to celebrate their birthdays. Simmered in beef broth, the noodles taste wonderfully old-fashioned. Sometimes she has to triple or quadruple the noodles to satisfy all of us.

My mom loves to cook and share recipes. She picked up the one for Carrot Casserole from a dear friend. It's a comforting and colorful side dish.

And Molded Strawberry Salad is a tasty recipe Mom makes year-round with berries she picks and freezes. For years, Mom has included this salad in meals she prepares for our family.

We typically like ice cream for dessert, but Mom often adds Surprise Meringues. She knows these sweet light cookies are a fitting finale to a big meal.

Some of us kids live close to Mom and Dad, and some are far away. So, going home for one of Mom's meals means a lot and sustains us when we're apart. We're pleased to honor Mom by sharing this meal.

PICTURED AT LEFT: Chuck Roast with Homemade Noodles, Mom's Carrot Casserole and Molded Strawberry Salad (recipes are on the next page).

or until tender. Drain; season with pepper. Serve with the roast. **Yield:** 8 servings. **Editor's Note:** Uncooked noodles may be stored in the refrigerator for 2-3 days or frozen for up to 1 month.

Mom's Carrot Casserole

Rich and cheesy, this casserole is the very best way to eat carrots. Pretty orange slices peek out from under a topping of buttery cracker crumbs.

> 2 pounds carrots, sliced
> 1/2 cup butter *or* margarine, ***divided***
> 6 ounces process American cheese, cubed
> 1/4 teaspoon dill weed
> 1/2 cup crushed saltines (about 15 crackers)

Place carrots in a saucepan and cover with water; bring to a boil. Reduce heat; cover and simmer until tender, about 10 minutes. Drain and place in a greased 1-1/2-qt. baking dish. In a small saucepan, melt 1/4 cup butter and cheese, stirring often. Stir in dill. Pour over the carrots. Melt remaining butter; toss with saltines. Sprinkle over carrots. Bake, uncovered, at 350° for 25-30 minutes or until lightly browned and bubbly. **Yield:** 8 servings.

Chuck Roast with Homemade Noodles

The whole family loves Mom's tender beef and hearty noodles. Mom has to make a huge batch since even the grandchildren gobble them up.

> 1 boneless chuck roast (3 to 4 pounds)
> 1/2 cup chopped onion
> 2 tablespoons vegetable oil
> 2-1/2 cups water, ***divided***
> 1 cup all-purpose flour
> 1/2 teaspoon salt
> 1 egg
> 2 tablespoons milk
> 1 can (14 ounces) beef broth

Pepper to taste

In a Dutch oven, brown roast and onion in oil. Add 1/2 cup of water. Cover and bake at 325° for 2-1/2 to 3 hours or until the meat is tender. Meanwhile, for noodles, combine flour and salt in a bowl; make a well in the center. Beat egg and milk; pour into well. Stir to form a stiff dough. Turn onto a well-floured surface; roll into a 15-in. x 12-in. rectangle. Cut into 1/8-in. strips. Cover and refrigerate until ready to cook. Remove roast and keep warm; add broth and remaining water to pan. Bring to a boil; add noodles. Cook for 8-10 minutes

3 egg whites
1/8 teaspoon cream of tartar
3/4 cup sugar
1/8 teaspoon salt
1 teaspoon vanilla extract
1 cup (6 ounces) miniature semisweet chocolate chips
1/4 cup chopped pecans *or* walnuts

In a mixing bowl, beat egg whites and cream of tartar until soft peaks form. Gradually add sugar, salt and vanilla, beating until stiff peaks form and sugar is dissolved, about 5-8 minutes. Fold in the chocolate chips and nuts. Drop by rounded teaspoonfuls onto greased baking sheets. Bake at 300° for 30 minutes or until lightly browned. Cool on baking sheets. Store in an airtight container. **Yield:** 4 dozen.

Molded Strawberry Salad

This refreshing salad has two layers—a pretty pink bottom that includes sour cream, and a ruby red top with strawberries and pineapple.

1 package (6 ounces) strawberry gelatin
1-1/2 cups boiling water
1 package (10 ounces) frozen sweetened strawberries, thawed
1 can (8-1/4 ounces) crushed pineapple, undrained
1 cup (8 ounces) sour cream
Leaf lettuce and fresh strawberries, optional

In a bowl, dissolve gelatin in water. Add strawberries and pineapple. Strain, reserving liquid and fruit. Set aside 1 cup of the liquid at room temperature. Pour fruit and remaining liquid into a 5-cup mold or 9-in. square pan that has been coated with non-stick cooking spray. Cover and refrigerate until set, about 1 hour. Whisk sour cream and reserved liquid; pour over top. Cover and refrigerate until set. Cut into squares and place on individual plates or unmold onto a serving platter. Garnish with lettuce and strawberries if desired. **Yield:** 8 servings.

Surprise Meringues

These crisp, delicate cookies are light as a feather. Mini chocolate chips and chopped nuts are a delightful and yummy surprise in every bite.

Shortcuts Worth Sharing

If you get some egg yolk in egg whites, just touch the yolk with a piece of bread. The yolk will adhere to the bread.

Let whites stand at room temperature for 30 minutes before beating to obtain maximum volume.

Her mother's gorgeous ham dinner made a lasting impression that she still cherishes today.

By Helen Vail, Glenside, Pennsylvania

WHEN I WAS growing up, my family's farm was complete with livestock, a garden, a fruit orchard, raspberry bushes and a strawberry patch.

In winter, Mother (Dorothy Wanamaker, above) would fire up the old stove and fix a hearty meal—no small task with 10 people in our family. This meal is one of my favorites.

It was always an occasion when my mother made this gorgeous golden Apple-Mustard Glazed Ham. I was thrilled to help her by inserting the cloves. It looked beautiful as it came out of the oven and tasted so good.

The perfect side dish was her Peppery Scalloped Potatoes. Once the first of us eight kids picked up this dish, it didn't hit the table again until we all helped ourselves to big servings.

We also couldn't wait to dig into the special Candied Carrots. They often looked too good to eat—but that didn't stop us!

Mother's Walnut Cake smelled wonderful while baking, and each tall slice was a joy to eat. She often made it with black walnuts since we also had three black walnut trees on the farm.

I can still picture how my dear mother stood in front of the hot stove, humming to herself as she cooked. Maybe that was her way of staying on track with us rambunctious children running in and out of the kitchen.

And maybe that's why I have such a love of cooking—Mother always made it look like such fun!

PICTURED AT LEFT: Apple-Mustard Glazed Ham, Peppery Scalloped Potatoes, Candied Carrots and Mother's Walnut Cake (recipes are on the next page).

Apple-Mustard Glazed Ham

The sweet and tangy glaze is so simple to mix up, but it turns an ordinary baked ham into a special feast.

- 1 cup apple jelly
- 1 tablespoon prepared mustard
- 1 tablespoon lemon juice
- 1/4 teaspoon ground nutmeg
- 1 fully cooked bone-in ham (5 to 7 pounds)
- Whole cloves
- Spiced apple rings, optional

In a small saucepan, combine jelly, mustard, lemon juice and nutmeg; bring to a boil, stirring constantly. Remove from the heat; set aside. Score the surface of the ham, making diamond shapes 1/2 in. deep; insert a clove in each diamond. Place ham on a rack in a shallow roasting pan. Bake, uncovered, at 325° for 20 minutes per pound or until a meat thermometer reads 140°. During the last 30 minutes of baking, brush with glaze twice. Garnish with apple rings if desired. **Yield:** 8-10 servings.

Peppery Scalloped Potatoes

Mother knew these rich, hearty potatoes are good on a cold day since the cayenne pepper warms you up.

- 1 can (10-3/4 ounces) condensed cream of mushroom soup, undiluted
- 1-1/2 cups milk
- 1/2 to 1 teaspoon salt
- 1/8 teaspoon cayenne pepper
- 5 cups thinly sliced peeled potatoes
- 1/4 cup butter *or* margarine, melted
- 1/4 cup all-purpose flour

In a small bowl, combine the soup, milk, salt and cayenne; set aside. Place a third of the potatoes in a greased 13-in. x 9-in. x 2-in. baking dish; layer with a third of the butter, flour and soup mixture. Repeat layers twice. Bake, uncovered, at 350° for 1 hour and 20 minutes or until the potatoes are tender. **Yield:** 6-8 servings.

Candied Carrots

When I was a girl, Mother made carrots taste more like candy than a vegetable with this recipe. She'd serve them, garnished with parsley, in a pretty bowl.

✓ Nutritional Analysis included

- **1-1/2 cups water**
- 2 pounds carrots, sliced 1/2 inch thick

2 **cinnamon sticks (3 inches)**
1 **teaspoon ground cumin**
1 **teaspoon ground ginger**
6 **tablespoons honey**
4 **teaspoons lemon juice**

Bring water to a boil in a large skillet; add carrots, cinnamon sticks, cumin and ginger. Reduce heat; cover and simmer for 10 minutes. Add honey and lemon juice. Bring to a boil. Boil, uncovered, for 4 minutes or until the liquid evaporates and the carrots are tender. **Yield:** 6-8 servings. **Nutritional Analysis:** One 1/2-cup serving equals 78 calories, 56 mg sodium, 0 cholesterol, 20 gm carbohydrate, 1 gm protein, trace fat. **Diabetic Exchange:** 1 starch.

Mother's Walnut Cake

Even though Mother baked this tall, beautiful cake often when I was growing up, it was a real treat every time. I like the walnuts in the cake and the frosting.

1/2 **cup butter *or* margarine, softened**
1/2 **cup shortening**
2 **cups sugar**
4 **eggs**
3-1/2 **cups all-purpose flour**
2 **teaspoons baking soda**
1/2 **teaspoon salt**
1-1/2 **cups buttermilk**
2 **teaspoons vanilla extract**
1-1/2 **cups ground walnuts**
FROSTING:
2 **packages (one 8 ounces, one 3 ounces) cream cheese, softened**
3/4 **cup butter *or* margarine, softened**
5 **to 5-1/2 cups confectioners' sugar**
1-1/2 **teaspoons vanilla extract**
1/3 **cup finely chopped walnuts**

In a large mixing bowl, cream butter, shortening and sugar. Add eggs, one at a time, beating well after each addition. Combine the flour, baking soda and salt; add to the creamed mixture alternately with buttermilk and vanilla. Beat on low speed just until combined. Stir in walnuts. Pour into three greased and floured 9-in. x 1-1/2-in. round cake pans. Bake at 350° for 20-25 minutes or until a toothpick inserted near the center comes out clean. Cool for 5 minutes; remove from pans to a wire rack to cool completely. For frosting, beat cream cheese and butter in a mixing bowl. Add sugar; mix well. Add vanilla; beat until smooth. Spread between layers and over top and sides of cake. Sprinkle with walnuts. Store in the refrigerator. **Yield:** 12-16 servings.

You, too, can "come home" to a mouth-watering spread that highlights fond food memories.

By Maria Costello, Monroe, North Carolina

MY MOTHER'S cooking was always a treat, but now that I live far away, going home to a meal Mom has prepared is extra-special.

Mom (Delores Briggs, above, of Houlton, Maine) is sure to have my favorite meal waiting when we walk in the door. Herbed Cornish Hens come out of the oven golden and flavorful. The seasonings in this recipe also work great on a whole roasted chicken. Either way, the result is a mouth-watering feast.

Mom's Macaroni and Cheese is old-fashioned comfort food, yet it's so simple to prepare. I can make a whole meal out of it, but it's also a good side dish with any meat. It has tender noodles and a crowd-pleasing golden crumb topping.

Her Homemade Brown Bread recipe produces beautiful crusty loaves. The moist slices are great even without butter.

And I know I'll never outgrow a fun dessert like Old-Fashioned Whoopie Pies. With all the delicious food Mom prepares, it's not easy to save room, but we always do. They're a treat that never lasted very long with me and my two brothers around.

Helping Mom in the kitchen and savoring her culinary creations continue to give me lots of wonderful memories. She still sends my husband, Robbie, and me "care packages" of goodies throughout the year. Nothing compares to her cookies and pies.

I've picked up Mom's love of cooking, and I hope our young son, Caleb, will see in me the same joy that comes from preparing foods for others.

PICTURED AT LEFT: Herbed Cornish Hens, Mom's Macaroni and Cheese, Homemade Brown Bread and Old-Fashioned Whoopie Pies (recipes are on the next page).

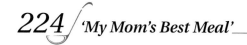

Mom's Macaroni and Cheese

The wonderful homemade goodness of this creamy macaroni and cheese makes it a staple side dish in my mother's kitchen and in mine as well.

1-1/2 **cups uncooked elbow macaroni**
   5 **tablespoons butter *or* margarine, *divided***
   3 **tablespoons all-purpose flour**
1-1/2 **cups milk**
   1 **cup (4 ounces) shredded cheddar cheese**
   2 **ounces process American cheese, cubed**
1/2 **teaspoon salt**
1/4 **teaspoon pepper**
   2 **tablespoons dry bread crumbs**

Cook macaroni according to package directions; drain. Place in a greased 1-1/2-qt. baking dish; set aside. In a saucepan, melt 4 tablespoons of butter over medium heat. Stir in flour until smooth. Gradually add milk; bring to a boil. Cook and stir for 2 minutes; reduce heat. Stir in cheeses, salt and pepper until the cheese is melted. Pour over macaroni; mix well. Melt the remaining butter; add the bread crumbs. Sprinkle over casserole. Bake, uncovered, at 375° for 30 minutes. **Yield:** 6 servings.

Herbed Cornish Hens

The refreshing basting sauce that Mom makes with thyme, lemon juice and butter gives these hens savory flavor throughout.

   6 **Cornish game hens (about 20 ounces *each*)**
   1 **cup lemon juice**
3/4 **cup butter *or* margarine, melted**
1/2 **teaspoon paprika**
1-1/2 **teaspoons dried thyme, *divided***
1-1/4 **teaspoons seasoned salt, *divided***
1-1/8 **teaspoons garlic powder, *divided***
1/4 **teaspoon salt**
1/8 **teaspoon pepper**

Place the hens on a wire rack in a large roasting pan. In a small bowl, combine the lemon juice, butter, paprika and 1 teaspoon each of thyme, seasoned salt and garlic powder. Pour half over the hens; set the remaining mixture aside for basting. Combine the salt, pepper and remaining thyme, seasoned salt and garlic powder; sprinkle evenly over the hens. Bake, uncovered, at 375° for 30 minutes. Baste with the reserved lemon juice mixture. Bake 30 minutes longer, basting occasionally, or until the meat is tender and juices run clear. **Yield:** 6 servings.

Homemade Brown Bread

This yummy bread has a light texture and includes richly flavored ingredients like molasses, brown sugar and oats. One slice absolutely calls for another!

1-1/2 cups boiling water
   1 cup old-fashioned oats
   2 tablespoons shortening
   2 teaspoons salt
   1 package (1/4 ounce) active dry yeast
  3/4 cup warm water (110° to 115°)
  1/2 teaspoon sugar
  1/4 cup packed brown sugar
  1/4 cup molasses
4-3/4 to 5-1/4 cups all-purpose flour
Melted butter *or* margarine

In a bowl, combine boiling water, oats, shortening and salt. Cool to 110°- 115°. In a mixing bowl, dissolve yeast in warm water. Sprinkle with sugar. Add oat mixture, brown sugar, molasses and 3 cups of flour; mix well. Add enough remaining flour to form a soft dough. Turn onto a floured surface and knead until smooth and elastic, about 6-8 minutes. Place in a greased bowl, turning once to grease top. Cover and let rise in a warm place until doubled, about 1 hour. Punch dough down. Divide in half and shape into two loaves. Place in greased 9-in. x 5-in. x 3-in. loaf pans. Cover and let rise until doubled, about 30-45 minutes. Bake at 375° for 30-35 minutes or until golden brown. Remove from pans to cool on wire racks. Brush with melted butter. **Yield:** 2 loaves.

Old-Fashioned Whoopie Pies

Who can resist soft chocolate sandwich cookies filled with a layer of fluffy white frosting? Mom has made these for years.

  1/2 cup baking cocoa
  1/2 cup hot water
  1/2 cup shortening
1-1/2 cups sugar
   2 eggs
   1 teaspoon vanilla extract
2-2/3 cups all-purpose flour
   1 teaspoon baking powder
   1 teaspoon baking soda
  1/4 teaspoon salt
  1/2 cup buttermilk
FILLING:
   3 tablespoons all-purpose flour
Dash salt
   1 cup milk
  3/4 cup shortening
1-1/2 cups confectioners' sugar
   2 teaspoons vanilla extract

In a small bowl, combine cocoa and water; mix well. Cool for 5 minutes. In a mixing bowl, cream shortening and sugar. Add cocoa mixture, eggs and vanilla; mix well. Combine dry ingredients. Add to creamed mixture alternately with buttermilk; mix well. Drop by rounded tablespoonfuls 2 in. apart onto greased baking sheets. Flatten slightly with a spoon. Bake at 350° for 10-12 minutes or until firm to the touch. Remove to wire racks to cool. In a saucepan, combine flour and salt. Gradually whisk in milk until smooth; cook and stir over medium-high heat until thick, about 5-7 minutes. Remove from the heat. Cover and refrigerate until completely cool. In a mixing bowl, cream shortening, sugar and vanilla. Add chilled milk mixture; beat for 7 minutes or until fluffy. Spread filling on half of the cookies; top with remaining cookies. Store in the refrigerator. **Yield:** 2 dozen.

Her summer weekends weren't complete without Mom dishing out flavorful foods and Dad firing up the grill.

By Sue Gronholz, Columbus, Wisconsin

WHEN my sister and I were growing up, we eagerly awaited summer weekends. That's when Mom (Lila Koch, above, of Beaver Dam, Wisconsin) would fix one of her special suppers with the help of Dad at the grill.

My mouth waters just thinking about her delicious Tangy Ham Steak. Dad still grills it to perfection while basting it with a glaze of mustard, honey and orange peel, keeping the meat really tender. He's even made this ham for Christmas dinner, much to everyone's delight!

Everyone raves over Mom's fluffy Whipped Potatoes. She got the recipe from her sister, and it's a standard dish at all of our family get-togethers. Mom appreciates the fact that she can make them ahead and bake them just before serving.

Mom has always loved to serve fresh foods she's grown herself (a passion I inherited). Mom's Vegetable Medley uses lots of colorful tasty garden veggies, simply seasoned with convenient onion soup mix.

For dessert, my sister and I would regularly request Chocolate Cherry Torte. The chocolate-covered graham cracker crust and fluffy white filling are extra-special. Mom could never make that rich creamy treat too often as far as we were concerned.

Our family has grown a bit since those summer weekends of my childhood. Since my husband and I and our two kids don't live far from my parents, Mom and Dad treat us to their wonderful weekend meals now and then.

PICTURED AT LEFT: Tangy Ham Steak, Whipped Potatoes, Mom's Vegetable Medley and Chocolate Cherry Torte (recipes are on the next page).

Tangy Ham Steak

This glazed ham steak is a yummy quick-and-easy main dish. It tastes especially good heated on the grill but works well in the oven broiler, too. On summer weekends back home, Dad does the grilling while Mom prepares the rest of the meal.

1/3 cup spicy brown mustard
1/4 cup honey
1/2 teaspoon grated orange peel
1 fully cooked ham steak (about 2 pounds)

In a small bowl, combine mustard, honey and orange peel. Brush over one side of ham. Broil or grill, uncovered, over medium-hot heat for 7 minutes. Turn; brush with mustard mixture. Cook until well glazed and heated through, about 7 minutes. **Yield:** 6-8 servings.

Whipped Potatoes

"More, please," is what you'll hear when you serve these light and creamy potatoes. Seasoned with just a hint of garlic, they go great with any meat.

2-1/2 pounds potatoes, peeled, quartered and cooked
1 package (3 ounces) cream cheese, softened
1/2 to 3/4 cup sour cream
1/4 cup butter *or* margarine, softened
1/2 teaspoon garlic salt
Salt and pepper to taste
Paprika, optional

In a large bowl, mash the potatoes. Add the cream cheese, sour cream, butter, garlic salt, salt and pepper; mix until smooth. Transfer to a greased 1-1/2-qt. baking dish. Sprinkle with paprika if desired. Bake, uncovered, at 350° for 30 minutes or until heated through. **Yield:** 6-8 servings.

Mom's Vegetable Medley

A colorful mix of zucchini, onion, celery, green pepper and tomato is at its tasty best in this simple side dish. Mom came up with this recipe as a way to use up her garden vegetables. It has the taste of summer.

✓ Nutritional Analysis included

2 celery ribs, chopped
1 medium green pepper, chopped
2 tablespoons chopped onion
2 tablespoons butter *or* margarine
3 small zucchini, quartered lengthwise and sliced
1 medium tomato, chopped
1 tablespoon onion soup mix

In a skillet, saute celery, green pepper and onion in butter for 6-8 minutes. Add zucchini; cook and stir over medium heat until tender. Add tomato and soup mix; cook and stir until the tomato is tender. **Yield:** 8 servings. **Nutritional Analysis:** One 1/2-cup serving equals 42 calories, 127 mg sodium, 0 cholesterol, 4 gm carbohydrate, 1 gm protein, 3 gm fat. **Diabetic Exchanges:** 1 vegetable, 1/2 fat.

1 package (8 ounces) cream cheese, softened
2 cans (21 ounces *each*) cherry pie filling

Set aside 1/4 cup of crushed cookies for topping. Combine the remaining cookies with butter; spread into a 13-in. x 9-in. x 2-in. dish. Set aside. In a mixing bowl, combine whipped topping mixes, milk and vanilla; beat on low speed until blended. Beat on high for 4 minutes or until thickened and stiff peaks form. Add cream cheese and beat until smooth. Spread over the crust; top with pie filling. Sprinkle with reserved cookies. Refrigerate for 12-24 hours before serving. **Yield:** 12-16 servings.

Chocolate Cherry Torte

Mom has made this sweet treat for years. Since she knows how much my sister and I like it, she's still happy to serve this torte when we're home for a meal.

56 chocolate-covered graham crackers
    (about 1 pound), crushed
1 cup butter *or* margarine, melted
2 envelopes whipped topping mix
1 cup cold milk
1 teaspoon vanilla extract

Buying and Cooking Potatoes

Look for firm potatoes that are free from cuts, decay, blemishes and green discoloration.

To cook potatoes for use in the Whipped Potatoes recipe, scrub them with a vegetable brush; remove all eyes and sprouts. Peel and quarter. Place in a saucepan; cover with water. Cover and cook for 15-30 minutes or until tender; drain well.

Hardworking mom taught this cook and her sister how to make the grade in the kitchen.

By Brenda DuFresne, Midland, Michigan

MOM WAS a hardworking grade-school teacher when I lived at home, but she still took time to make wonderful meals for our family. She also made a point of sharing her kitchen skills with me and my sister.

Every summer, Mom (Susan Stancroff, above, of Ludington, Michigan) and I would put up lots of jams and jellies. One year we had so much peach jam that we needed to find creative new ways to use it.

Mom decided to experiment with pork chops. Her Peachy Pork Chops turned out delicious. Sweet peaches dot the stuffing, and peach preserves makes an appealing golden glaze. I've found that even the pickiest eaters love these tempting stuffed chops.

One of our favorite accompaniments to that main dish (or any others) were Cloverleaf Rolls. My sister and I ate more than our share of these versatile golden rolls.

In her Green Beans Amandine, a few simple ingredients sure give new life to plain beans. I always felt the crunchy almonds were a super addition.

There's no better way to top off a meal than with Mom's incredible Dutch Apple Pie. The delightful crust cuts beautifully to reveal a filling with tiny pieces of diced apple. I still like mine a la mode. At harvesttime or anytime, you can't beat this delectable variety of apple pie.

Now I use many of Mom's recipes for my own family. She'll retire from teaching soon and will have more time to cook and spend with her grandchildren.

PICTURED AT LEFT: Peachy Pork Chops, Cloverleaf Rolls, Green Beans Amandine and Dutch Apple Pie (recipes are on the next page).

Peachy Pork Chops

Pork and peaches are a palate-pleasing combination in this hearty main dish.

1-1/2 **cups finely chopped onion**
1-1/2 **cups finely chopped celery**
  1/3 **cup butter *or* margarine**
    6 **cups dry bread cubes**
  1/2 **teaspoon poultry seasoning**
  1/2 **teaspoon rubbed sage**
  1/8 **teaspoon pepper**
    1 **can (8 ounces) peaches, drained and diced**
    2 **eggs**
    1 **cup water**
    2 **tablespoons minced fresh parsley**
    6 **boneless pork chops (1-1/4 inches thick)**
    3 **tablespoons olive *or* vegetable oil**
Garlic salt and additional pepper to taste
  1/4 **cup peach preserves**

In a skillet, saute onion and celery in butter until tender; transfer to a large bowl. Add bread cubes, poultry seasoning, sage and pepper. Fold in peaches. Combine eggs, water and parsley; add to bread mixture. Toss gently until well mixed. Cut a large pocket in the side of each pork chop; spoon stuffing loosely into pockets. Tie with string to secure stuffing if necessary. Brush chops with oil. Sprinkle with garlic salt and pepper. In a large skillet, brown chops on both sides. Place remaining stuffing in a greased 13-in. x 9-in. x 2-in. baking dish. Top with chops. Spread preserves over chops. Cover and bake at 350° for 45 minutes. Uncover and bake 15 minutes longer or until juices run clear. If string was used, remove before serving. **Yield:** 6 servings.

Cloverleaf Rolls

When I was a girl, it was a rare occasion when Mom made a gourmet meal. Most often, she relied on traditional recipes like this one.

    1 **package (1/4 ounce) active dry yeast**
    3 **tablespoons sugar**
1-1/4 **cups warm milk (110° to 115°)**
  1/4 **cup butter *or* margarine, softened**
    1 **egg**
    1 **teaspoon salt**
    4 **to 4-1/2 cups all-purpose flour**
Additional butter *or* margarine, melted

In a mixing bowl, combine yeast, sugar and milk; beat until smooth. Add butter, egg and salt; mix well. Add 3 cups flour; beat until smooth. Add enough remaining flour to form a soft dough. Turn onto a floured surface; knead until smooth and elastic, about 6-8 minutes. Place in a greased bowl,

turning once to grease top. Cover and let rise in a warm place until doubled, about 1 hour. Punch dough down and divide in half. Divide each half into 36 pieces and shape into balls. Place three balls each in greased muffin cups. Cover and let rise until doubled, about 30 minutes. Brush with butter. Bake at 375° for 15-18 minutes or until lightly browned. Remove to wire racks. Serve warm. **Yield:** 2 dozen.

Green Beans Amandine

It's hard to improve on the taste Mother Nature gives to fresh green beans, but Mom has for years using this recipe.

☑ Nutritional Analysis included

  1 pound fresh *or* frozen green beans, cut into 2-inch pieces
1/2 cup water
1/4 cup slivered almonds
  2 tablespoons butter *or* margarine
  1 teaspoon lemon juice
1/4 teaspoon seasoned salt, optional

In a saucepan, bring beans and water to a boil; reduce heat to medium. Cover and cook for 10-15 minutes or until beans are crisp-tender; drain and set aside. In a large skillet, cook almonds in butter over low heat. Stir in lemon juice and seasoned salt if desired. Add beans and heat through. **Yield:** 6

servings. **Nutritional Analysis:** One 1/2-cup serving (prepared with margarine and without seasoned salt) equals 92 calories, 50 mg sodium, 0 cholesterol, 7 gm carbohydrate, 3 gm protein, 7 gm fat. **Diabetic Exchanges:** 1-1/2 fat, 1 vegetable.

Dutch Apple Pie

Everything about this dessert makes it the top request for family gatherings.

  2 cups all-purpose flour
  1 cup packed brown sugar
3/4 cup butter *or* margarine, melted
1/2 cup quick-cooking oats
FILLING:
2/3 cup sugar
  3 tablespoons cornstarch
1-1/4 cups water
  3 cups diced peeled tart apples
  1 teaspoon vanilla extract

Combine the first four ingredients; set aside 1 cup for topping. Press remaining crumb mixture into an ungreased 9-in. pie plate; set aside. For filling, combine sugar, cornstarch and water in a saucepan until smooth; bring to a boil. Cook and stir for 1 minute or until thickened. Remove from the heat; stir in apples and vanilla. Pour into crust; top with reserved crumb mixture. Bake at 350° for 40-45 minutes or until crust is golden brown. **Yield:** 6-8 servings.

Mom used simple ingredients to create comforting foods for friends and family.

By Barbara Hyatt, Folsom, California

I HAVE warm, happy memories of growing up in Lorain, Ohio. Many of them include the hearty, comforting meals Mom (Ruth Toth, above) prepared for Dad, Grandfather and me.

Mom's best meal started with City Chicken—a flavorful main dish actually made with cubes of pork on skewers, seasoned simply and served over mashed potatoes. I'm especially fond of the savory gravy.

In her Chunky Cinnamon Applesauce, red-hot candies give freshly cooked apples a rosy color and irresistible flavor. I'd always take a big helping. As a young girl, I was amazed when my mother transformed fresh apples into this delightful mixture.

Mom knew that a homemade salad topper like her Oil and Vinegar Dressing made even plain lettuce a super side dish.

In those days, Mom was an avid baker. It was nothing for her to bake 30 pies in 2 days for Dad's men's club dinner. Mom's Custard Pie was often requested for those gatherings and was a favorite dessert for our family meals as well.

Just as Mom did for many years, I love cooking for others. I've collected lots of recipes, but the best ones are those Mom passed on to me—now I'm sharing them with my daughter-in-law and granddaughter.

Mom, widowed in 1997 after 55 years of marriage, now lives nearby. She joins my husband, Bill, and me, our son, Scott, his wife, Lorna, and their two children for delicious meals like this one.

PICTURED AT LEFT: City Chicken, Chunky Cinnamon Applesauce, Oil and Vinegar Dressing and Mom's Custard Pie (recipes are on the next page).

City Chicken

This old-fashioned mock chicken dish, which is actually made with tender perfectly seasoned pork, is one my mother relied on for many years. The great gravy tastes so good over mashed potatoes.

    2 pounds boneless pork, cut into cubes
1/2 cup all-purpose flour
1/2 teaspoon garlic salt
1/4 teaspoon pepper
1/4 cup butter *or* margarine
    3 tablespoons vegetable oil
    1 envelope onion soup mix
    1 can (14-1/2 ounces) chicken broth
    1 cup water
Hot mashed potatoes

Thread pork on small wooden skewers. Combine flour, garlic salt and pepper on a plate; roll kabobs in flour mixture until coated. In a large skillet, heat butter and oil over medium heat. Brown the kabobs, turning frequently; drain. Sprinkle with soup mix. Add broth and water. Reduce heat; cover and simmer for 1 hour. Remove kabobs and keep warm. If desired, thicken pan juices and serve over mashed potatoes with the kabobs. **Yield:** 4-6 servings.

Chunky Cinnamon Applesauce

I'm not sure if I liked this so much because there were candies in it or because it tasted wonderful. Either way, Mom was delighted to see us gobble it up!

    8 medium tart apples, peeled and quartered
    1 cup water
    1 cup sugar
1/4 cup red-hot candies

Place apples and water in a 5-qt. saucepan. Cover and cook over medium-low heat for 20 minutes or until tender. Mash the apples. Add sugar and candies. Cook, uncovered, until sugar and candies are dissolved. Remove from the heat; cool. Refrigerate until serving. **Yield:** 6 cups.

Oil and Vinegar Dressing

The goodness of crisp salad ingredients comes through when topped with this simple homemade dressing. It tastes so fresh. My mother made it for us when I was growing up, and now I serve it to my family.

    1 cup sugar
    1 tablespoon ground mustard
    1 teaspoon salt
1/2 teaspoon pepper

1/2 teaspoon paprika
1/2 cup hot water
1/4 cup vinegar
  2 garlic cloves, halved
1/4 cup vegetable oil
Mixed salad greens and shredded red cabbage

In a 1-qt. jar with a tight-fitting lid, combine the first five ingredients. Add water, vinegar and garlic; shake until sugar is dissolved. Add oil; shake well. Store in the refrigerator. Just before serving, remove garlic from the dressing. Drizzle over greens and cabbage. **Yield:** 2 cups.

Mom's Custard Pie

Just a single bite of this old-fashioned treat takes me back to the days when my mom would fix this pie for my dad, my grandfather and me. Mom also regularly prepared this pie for one type of large gathering or another.

  1 **pastry shell (9 inches)**
  4 **eggs**
1/2 **cup sugar**
1/4 **teaspoon salt**
  1 **teaspoon vanilla extract**
2-1/2 **cups milk**
1/4 **teaspoon ground nutmeg**

Line unpricked pastry shell with a double thickness of heavy-duty foil. Bake at 450° for 8 minutes. Re-

move foil; bake 5 minutes longer. Remove from the oven and set aside. Separate one egg and set the white aside. In a mixing bowl, beat the yolk and remaining eggs just until combined. Blend in sugar, salt and vanilla. Stir in milk. Beat reserved egg white until stiff peaks form; fold into egg mixture. Carefully pour into crust. Cover edges of pie with foil. Bake at 350° for 25 minutes. Remove foil; bake 15-20 minutes longer or until a knife inserted near the center comes out clean. Cool on a wire rack. Sprinkle with nutmeg. Store in the refrigerator. **Yield:** 6-8 servings.

Cool It with Custard

It's important not to overbake custard pies. Check for doneness a few minutes before the minimum baking time by inserting a knife near the center. If the knife comes out clean, the pie is done. The center will remain soft but will continue to cook while cooling. After cooling a custard pie to room temperature, store it in the refrigerator.

Editors' Meals

Taste of Home magazine is edited by 1,000 cooks across North America. On the following pages, six of those cooks share a favorite meal that you and yours are sure to enjoy!

TRIED-AND-TRUE TASTES. Clockwise from upper left: A Harvest of Flavors (p. 260), Savory Down-Home Dinner (p. 244), Sunny Summertime Supper (p. 252) and Delightful Midday Meal (p. 248).

This cook's Christmas dinner is a feast for the eyes as well as the palate—and it's surprisingly easy to prepare!

By Betty Claycomb, Alverton, Pennsylvania

WE LIKE to spread Christmas all through the big old house where my husband, Harold (everyone calls him "Jake"), and I have lived for 33 of our 50 years together.

There's no place that better captures the flavor of our celebration than my busy kitchen. I love to cook and bake, especially for the holidays. One joyful job is planning and preparing our family Christmas Day dinner.

Like many of you, I used to serve ham or turkey as our Christmas dinner entree. But one year I decided on something different—Stuffed Crown Roast of Pork. It was a big hit!

Now our traditional feast, the roast looks spectacular garnished with a string of cranberries looped in and out of the bone tips. Impressive as it looks, this roast is easy enough for a new cook to prepare.

Christmas Cauliflower has a wonderful Swiss cheese sauce, while green pepper and pimientos add a dash of color. Any leftovers reheat well in the microwave.

Cranberry Gelatin Salad is a refreshing and very satisfying accompaniment for a roast or poultry. While the salad can be made in a 9 x 13 pan and cut into squares, I put it in a pretty cut-glass bowl for special occasions.

I took the best from two recipes and worked out this wonderfully moist Coconut Cake Supreme. Most folks can't believe it starts with a cake mix.

I place holly from our own trees around my punch bowl filled with Mock Champagne Punch. Even the children can enjoy this nonalcoholic beverage.

Each year adds treasured memories as we welcome loved ones and friends to our home—and our table—to celebrate the sacred and joyous Christmas season.

PICTURED AT LEFT: Stuffed Crown Roast of Pork, Christmas Cauliflower, Cranberry Gelatin Salad, Mock Champagne Punch and Coconut Cake Supreme (recipes are on the next page).

Stuffed Crown Roast of Pork

It looks so elegant that everyone thinks I really fussed when I serve this roast. But it's actually so easy! The biggest challenge is to remember to order the crown roast from the meat department ahead of time. My family loves the succulent pork and savory bread stuffing.

  1 pork loin crown roast (5 to 6 pounds, about 10 ribs)
1/2 teaspoon seasoned salt
MUSHROOM STUFFING:
  1 cup sliced fresh mushrooms
1/2 cup diced celery
1/4 cup butter *or* margarine
  3 cups day-old bread cubes
1/4 teaspoon salt
1/4 teaspoon pepper
1/3 cup apricot preserves
  1 cup whole fresh cranberries, optional

Place roast, rib ends up, in a shallow roasting pan; sprinkle with seasoned salt. Cover rib ends with foil. Bake, uncovered, at 325° for 1-1/2 hours. Meanwhile, saute mushrooms and celery in butter until tender. Stir in bread cubes, salt and pepper. Spoon into the center of the roast. Brush sides of roast with preserves. Bake 1 hour longer or until a meat thermometer inserted into meat between ribs reads 160°; remove foil. If desired, thread cranberries on a 20-in. piece of thin string or thread. Transfer roast to a serving platter. Loop the cranberry string in and out of the rib ends. **Yield:** 8 servings.

Christmas Cauliflower

A Swiss cheese sauce gives this vegetable casserole an extra-special taste. My family says Christmas dinner just wouldn't be as delicious without it.

  1 large head cauliflower, broken into florets
1/4 cup diced green pepper
  1 jar (7.3 ounces) sliced mushrooms, drained
1/4 cup butter *or* margarine
1/3 cup all-purpose flour
  2 cups milk
  1 cup (4 ounces) shredded Swiss cheese
  2 tablespoons diced pimientos
  1 teaspoon salt
Paprika, optional

In a large saucepan, cook cauliflower in a small amount of water for 6-7 minutes or until crisp-tender; drain well. In a medium saucepan, saute green pepper and mushrooms in butter for 2 minutes. Add flour; gradually stir in milk. Bring to a boil; boil for 2 minutes, stirring constantly. Remove from the heat; stir in cheese until melted. Add pimientos and salt. Place half of the cauliflower in a greased 2-qt. baking dish; top with half of the sauce. Repeat layers. Bake, uncovered, at 325° for 25 minutes or until bubbly. Sprinkle with paprika if desired. **Yield:** 8-10 servings.

Cranberry Gelatin Salad

Since this tangy salad keeps well, I make it a day ahead for my Christmas menu. It's also a great choice to take to a holiday potluck—even people who aren't fond of cranberries think it's yummy. I got the recipe from a friend at church who likes to cook and bake as much as I do.

☑ Nutritional Analysis included

> 1 package (6 ounces) cherry gelatin
> 1-1/2 cups boiling water
> 1 can (20 ounces) crushed pineapple, undrained
> 1 can (16 ounces) whole-berry cranberry sauce
> 1-1/2 cups seedless red grapes, halved
> 1/4 cup chopped pecans

In a large bowl, dissolve gelatin in water. Stir in pineapple and cranberry sauce. Refrigerate for 30 minutes. Stir in grapes and pecans. Pour into a 2-qt. serving bowl. Refrigerate until firm. **Yield:** 8-10 servings. **Nutritional Analysis:** One 1/2-cup serving (prepared with sugar-free gelatin and unsweetened pineapple) equals 146 calories, 62 mg sodium, 0 cholesterol, 32 gm carbohydrate, 1 gm protein, 2 gm fat. **Diabetic Exchanges:** 2 fruit, 1/2 fat.

Mock Champagne Punch

(Pictured on page 240)

Of all the punch recipes I've tried, I keep coming back to this one. It's so easy to keep the ingredients in the refrigerator and mix as much as needed.

> 1 quart white grape juice, chilled
> 1 quart ginger ale, chilled
> **Strawberries *or* raspberries**

Combine grape juice and ginger ale; pour into a punch bowl or glasses. Garnish with berries. **Yield:** 16 (1/2-cup) servings.

Coconut Cake Supreme

I make most cakes from scratch, but during the holidays, this recipe buys me some time. Eager eaters don't suspect the shortcut when you dress it up.

> 1 package (18-1/4 ounces) yellow cake mix
> 2 cups (16 ounces) sour cream
> 2 cups sugar
> 1-1/2 cups flaked coconut
> 1 carton (8 ounces) frozen whipped topping, thawed
> **Fresh mint and red gumdrops, optional**

Prepare and bake cake according to package directions in two 9-in. round cake pans. Cool in pans for 10 minutes before removing to a wire rack to cool completely. For filling, combine sour cream and sugar; mix well. Stir in coconut (filling will be soft). Set aside 1 cup of filling for frosting. To assemble, split each cake into two horizontal layers. Place one layer on a serving platter; cover with a third of the filling. Repeat layers. Fold reserved filling into whipped topping; frost cake. Refrigerate for at least 4 hours. Garnish with mint and gumdrops if desired. **Yield:** 10-12 servings.

Recipes that stand the test of time make up her down-home menu— it's a savory family feast that's satisfied for decades!

By Shirley Leister, West Chester, Pennsylvania

TALK ABOUT an "old standby"—my favorite meal is one I've used often for more than 40 years after first seeing the recipes on a TV cooking program.

The savory Stuffed Meat Loaf is hearty and moist. Plenty of mushrooms in the bread stuffing layer make it a little more special than other meat loaves. Even so, it's an economical main dish.

Crumb-Coated Potato Halves get their beautiful golden color from an easy seasoned bread-crumb coating. This side dish is simple to prepare but good enough for company.

Husband John and I grow a variety of vegetables, including tomatoes, peppers, onions, peas, beans and carrots. I can and freeze as much as we can use to prepare in recipes like Baked String Beans.

I keep the ingredients on hand to make the Creamy Fruit Mold whenever we have a taste for it. Refreshing and pretty, it's a gelatin mold that holds its shape well. Fruit cocktail and nuts add color and texture.

Apricot Cobbler makes a great dessert for my meal. Served warm and topped with a scoop of vanilla ice cream or whipped cream, this yummy, old-fashioned cobbler is so fruity, juicy and sweet...just thinking about it makes my mouth water.

Many friends and relatives have joined us for this meal over the years, and all have given it their stamp of approval. I especially like the fact that the meat, potatoes and beans all go into the oven at the same time and bake for an hour.

Sharing my favorite meal has been a pleasure and brought back many fond memories of happy times with family and friends. I hope you enjoy this meal as much as we have.

PICTURED AT LEFT: Stuffed Meat Loaf, Crumb-Coated Potato Halves, Creamy Fruit Mold, Baked String Beans and Apricot Cobbler (recipes are on the next page).

Stuffed Meat Loaf

I first tried this savory meat loaf recipe more than 40 years ago after seeing it demonstrated on a local TV cooking program. Since then, I've served it time and again to family and guests. The flavorful stuffing sets it apart from the ordinary.

    2 eggs
    2 tablespoons milk
  1/4 cup ketchup
1-1/2 teaspoons salt
  1/8 teaspoon pepper
1-1/2 pounds lean ground beef
STUFFING:
  1/2 pound fresh mushrooms, sliced
    1 medium onion, chopped
    2 tablespoons butter *or* margarine
    2 cups soft bread crumbs
    2 tablespoons chopped fresh parsley
  1/2 teaspoon dried thyme
  1/2 teaspoon salt
  1/8 teaspoon pepper

In a large bowl, beat eggs, milk, ketchup, salt and pepper. Add beef and mix well. Pat half of the meat mixture into a greased 9-in. x 5-in. x 3-in. loaf pan; set aside. For stuffing, saute the mushrooms and onion in butter until tender, about 3 minutes. Add bread crumbs, parsley, thyme, salt and pepper; saute until crumbs are lightly browned. Spoon over meat layer; cover with remaining meat mixture and press down gently. Bake at 350° for 1 hour or until no pink remains, draining fat when necessary. **Yield:** 6 servings.

Crumb-Coated Potato Halves

Dressing up potatoes is a snap with this easy method. What I like best about the recipe is that I can pop the baking dish of coated potatoes into the oven at the same time as my meat loaf. It's a great side dish with roasts, poultry and pork chops as well.

1/2 cup Italian-seasoned bread crumbs
  1 teaspoon paprika
  1 teaspoon salt
1/8 teaspoon pepper
  4 large potatoes, peeled and halved
  2 tablespoons butter *or* margarine, melted

In a shallow bowl, combine the bread crumbs, paprika, salt and pepper. Brush potatoes with butter; roll in crumb mixture until coated. Place in a greased 13-in. x 9-in. x 2-in. baking pan. Cover and bake at 350° for 1 hour or until tender. **Yield:** 6 servings.

Creamy Fruit Mold

Because it can be made ahead, a gelatin salad like this one, brimming with fruit and nuts, is so convenient. This salad (another old standby from the cooking show I watched years ago) comes out of the mold easily and looks very attractive when served.

  1 package (3 ounces) cream cheese, softened
  1 package (3 ounces) lime gelatin
  1 cup boiling water
1/4 cup mayonnaise
  1 can (15-1/4 ounces) fruit cocktail, drained
1/2 cup chopped pecans

In a mixing bowl, beat cream cheese and gelatin. Add water; stir until gelatin is dissolved. Refrigerate until thickened, about 1 hour, stirring frequently. Add mayonnaise; whisk until smooth. Stir in fruit cocktail and pecans. Pour into a 1-qt. mold that has been coated with nonstick cooking spray. Refrigerate until firm. Unmold onto a serving platter. **Yield:** 6 servings.

Baked String Beans

(Pictured on page 244)

Frozen string beans from our garden (or the grocery store) taste great in this side dish. Bouillon, garlic salt and crisp bacon give them a nice fresh flavor.

    1 package (16 ounces) frozen French-style
      green beans, thawed
    2 bacon strips
    1 beef bouillon cube
    1 cup hot water
1/4 to 1/2 teaspoon garlic salt
Pinch pepper

Place the beans in an ungreased 1-1/2-qt. baking dish; set aside. Cook bacon until crisp; remove with a slotted spoon. Crumble and set aside. Stir 1 tablespoon of drippings into beans. Dissolve bouillon in water; add garlic salt and pepper. Pour over beans. Cover and bake at 350° for 1 hour. Top with bacon. **Yield:** 6 servings.

Apricot Cobbler

Old-fashioned, comforting and mouth-watering perfectly describe this down-home dessert. It bakes up golden brown and bubbly, with a crunchy crumb topping. The recipe comes from the owner of a popular restaurant in our state's famous Lancaster County.

  3/4 cup sugar
    1 tablespoon cornstarch
  1/4 teaspoon ground cinnamon
  1/8 teaspoon ground nutmeg
    1 cup water
    3 cans (15-1/4 ounces *each*) apricot halves,
      drained
    1 tablespoon butter *or* margarine
TOPPING:
    1 cup all-purpose flour
    1 tablespoon sugar
1-1/2 teaspoons baking powder
  1/2 teaspoon salt
    3 tablespoons cold butter *or* margarine
  1/2 cup milk

In a saucepan, combine the sugar, cornstarch, cinnamon and nutmeg. Stir in water; bring to a boil over medium heat. Boil and stir for 1 minute; reduce heat. Add apricots and butter; heat through. Pour into a greased 2-qt. baking dish. For topping, combine flour, sugar, baking powder and salt in a bowl; cut in butter until crumbly. Stir in milk just until moistened. Spoon over hot apricot mixture. Bake at 400° for 30-35 minutes or until golden brown and a toothpick inserted into the topping comes out clean. **Yield:** 6 servings.

Her can't-miss combination of brunch recipes, relished by family and guests, makes a delightful midday meal perfect for a spring gathering.

By Patricia Throlson, Hawick, Minnesota

BRUNCH is a great meal to mark special occasions. At our house, we've celebrated birthdays, confirmations and graduations with this mid-morning menu. I also served it the morning of our son's wedding day.

Most of the recipes for my favorite brunch come from church and community cookbooks in my collection of more than 200 recipe-packed volumes.

Sunday Brunch Casserole moved from one of these into my personal file almost 20 years ago. Featuring eggs, bacon, hash browns, cheddar cheese and bits of green pepper, it's a hearty and wonderful meal-in-one that looks very attractive when you serve it.

If you prefer, you can substitute sausage or ham for the bacon or increase the amount of bacon called for. To speed thawing of the hash browns, I run cold water over them in a colander.

When our two boys were still at home, I often prepared this dish for supper, too.

I found Pineapple Ham Bake in a church cookbook from my grandfather's hometown.

Overnight Coffee Cake, another church cookbook "find", is convenient to make ahead when guests are coming. I frequently turn to this recipe when it's time to bring morning coffee treats to work.

Combining ingredients from two recipes, I came up with my own Blueberry Muffins. These bake up fluffy, light and pretty, with an appealing golden-brown top.

Frozen Fruit Cups are colorful and bursting with tart fruity taste. I freeze the mixture in clear plastic cups. This recipe was shared by a co-worker.

When strawberries and melons are abundant, I may substitute a fresh fruit cup in my brunch menu.

Maybe there's an upcoming special event on your calendar when you could test my dishes on your family.

PICTURED AT LEFT: Sunday Brunch Casserole, Pat's Blueberry Muffins, Overnight Coffee Cake and Frozen Fruit Cups (recipes are on the next page).

Pat's Blueberry Muffins

Yummy and golden, these muffins are packed with plenty of berries and are a great addition to a brunch menu. But at our house, muffins aren't relegated to mornings—we also enjoy them for supper or a snack.

    2 cups all-purpose flour
  1/3 cup plus 2 tablespoons sugar
    1 tablespoon baking powder
    1 teaspoon salt
    1 cup fresh or frozen blueberries, thawed
    1 egg
    1 cup milk
  1/4 cup butter or margarine, melted

In a large bowl, combine the flour, sugar, baking powder and salt. Add blueberries. In another bowl, beat egg and milk; stir in butter. Stir into dry ingredients just until moistened. Fill greased or paper-lined muffin cups two-thirds full. Bake at 400° for 20-25 minutes or until muffins test done. **Yield:** 1 dozen.

Sunday Brunch Casserole

"Isn't it about time for you to make your 'egg pie'?" my husband and sons inquire, using the nickname they've given this hearty casserole. It's nice enough for a special brunch and versatile enough for a satisfying family supper.

  1/2 pound sliced bacon
  1/2 cup chopped onion
  1/2 cup chopped green pepper
   12 eggs
    1 cup milk
    1 package (16 ounces) frozen hash brown potatoes, thawed
    1 cup (4 ounces) shredded cheddar cheese
    1 teaspoon salt
  1/2 teaspoon pepper
  1/4 teaspoon dill weed

In a skillet, cook bacon until crisp. Remove with a slotted spoon; crumble and set aside. In the drippings, saute onion and green pepper until tender; remove with a slotted spoon. Beat eggs and milk in a large bowl. Stir in hash browns, cheese, salt, pepper, dill, onion, green pepper and bacon. Transfer to a greased 13-in. x 9-in. x 2-in. baking dish. Bake, uncovered, at 350° for 35-45 minutes or until a knife inserted near the center comes out clean. **Yield:** 6-8 servings.

Overnight Coffee Cake

It's so convenient to mix up this old-fashioned breakfast treat the night before and bake it fresh the morning you serve it. We like the cake's light texture and nutty topping spiced with cinnamon and nutmeg.

  1/3 cup butter or margarine, softened
  1/2 cup sugar
  1/4 cup packed brown sugar
    1 egg, beaten
    1 cup all-purpose flour
  1/2 teaspoon baking powder

1/4 teaspoon baking soda
1/2 teaspoon ground cinnamon
1/2 cup buttermilk
TOPPING:
1/4 cup packed brown sugar
1/4 cup finely chopped pecans
1/4 teaspoon ground cinnamon
1/8 teaspoon ground nutmeg, optional

In a mixing bowl, cream butter and sugars. Add egg; mix well. Combine flour, baking powder, baking soda and cinnamon; add to creamed mixture alternately with buttermilk. Beat well. Spread into a greased 8-in. square baking pan. Combine topping ingredients; sprinkle over batter. Cover and refrigerate overnight. Bake, uncovered, at 350° for 40-45 minutes or until the cake tests done. **Yield:** 6-8 servings.

Pineapple Ham Bake

(Not pictured)

This side dish is simple to fix, and the tangy pineapple flavor goes well with the casserole.

2 cans (8 ounces *each*) crushed pineapple, undrained
2/3 cup packed brown sugar
1 tablespoon vinegar
2 teaspoons ground mustard
1 pound fully cooked ham, cut into bite-size pieces

Combine the first four ingredients in an ungreased 2-qt. baking dish; mix well. Stir in ham. Bake, uncovered, at 350° for 30-40 minutes or until heated through. Serve with a slotted spoon. **Yield:** 8 servings.

Frozen Fruit Cups

Individual servings of this rosy-orange fruit blend are a refreshing and attractive part of brunch. Freeze the salad in disposable clear plastic glasses or use cupcake liners to set in sauce dishes or sherbet glasses.

☑ Nutritional Analysis included

2 cans (20 ounces *each*) crushed pineapple, undrained
2 packages (10 ounces *each*) frozen sweetened strawberries, thawed
1 can (20 ounces) fruit cocktail, undrained
1 can (12 ounces) frozen orange juice concentrate, thawed
1 can (6 ounces) frozen lemonade concentrate, thawed
6 medium firm bananas, cubed

In a large bowl, combine all ingredients. Pour into foil-lined muffin cups or individual plastic beverage glasses. Freeze until solid. When ready to serve, thaw for 30-45 minutes before serving. **Yield:** 10 servings. **Nutritional Analysis:** One 3/4-cup serving (prepared with unsweetened pineapple and fruit cocktail in light syrup) equals 259 calories, 7 mg sodium, 0 cholesterol, 64 gm carbohydrate, 3 gm protein, 1 gm fat. **Diabetic Exchange:** 4 fruit.

Being an "early bird" in the kitchen pays off when her mouth-watering chicken dinner is ready to relish on a summer evening.

By Dorothy Bateman, Carver, Massachusetts

WHEN a hot summer day is forecast, I like to prepare our supper in the cool of the morning. Later, I can relax and enjoy eating with my husband, Wally, without spending a lot of time in a hot kitchen.

Crispy Potato Chicken is versatile since it can be served hot or cold. It bakes to a lovely golden brown, and the nicely seasoned coating stays on.

Zippy Skillet Rice (my version of Spanish rice) is a flavorful accompaniment to the chicken. It can also be made ahead and reheated in the microwave.

For a simple colorful salad, I turn to Tomatoes and Cukes. I cover my prettiest pottery plate with leaf lettuce, then arrange tomato and cucumber slices on top and drizzle them with a vinaigrette.

My favorite foods to prepare are desserts of all kinds. Strawberry Cheese Pie is one that Wally requests often. A beautiful variation on a cheesecake, this scrumptious pie requires chilling to set up. When we have a taste for it, I make it first thing in the morning or even the night before.

Guests rave over this elegant treat, too. We enjoy having people over for dessert and coffee, as that gives me a chance to make something really special. (If I could start over in life, I'd study to be a pastry chef!)

Using local fresh ingredients always makes any meal delicious. Carver is known as the "Cranberry Center of the Northeast", and there are bogs all around us. Years ago, I sent my best cranberry muffin recipe to *Country* magazine, *Taste of Home's* "brother" publication. It won first prize for the East region.

My sunny summertime supper is a staple at our house. I hope you'll give it a try.

PICTURED AT LEFT: Crispy Potato Chicken, Zippy Skillet Rice, Tomatoes and Cukes and Strawberry Cheese Pie (recipes are on the next page).

Crispy Potato Chicken

We think this savory chicken tastes just as good cold as it does hot. It's perfect for a family dinner at home or to take along on a picnic.

- 1 tablespoon grated Parmesan cheese
- 1 teaspoon paprika
- 1 teaspoon garlic salt
- 1 teaspoon salt
- 1 teaspoon pepper
- 1 broiler/fryer chicken (3-1/2 to 4 pounds), cut up and skin removed
- 2 eggs
- 2 tablespoons water
- 1-1/2 cups mashed potato flakes
- 1/2 cup butter *or* margarine, melted

In a large resealable plastic bag, combine the first five ingredients. Add chicken in two batches; shake to coat. In a shallow bowl, beat eggs and water. Dip chicken in the egg mixture, then coat with potato flakes. Pour butter into a 13-in. x 9-in. x 2-in. baking dish; add chicken. Bake, uncovered, at 375° for 30 minutes. Turn the chicken; bake 30 minutes longer or until juices run clear. **Yield:** 4 servings.

Zippy Skillet Rice

Tomatoes, pimientos and green pepper add festive color to this zippy rice side dish. To turn the recipe into a main dish for a light supper, just add 3/4 pound of browned ground beef.

- 1 cup uncooked long grain rice
- 2 tablespoons butter *or* margarine
- 1/2 cup chopped green pepper
- 1/2 cup chopped onion
- 2 garlic cloves, minced
- 2 cans (14-1/2 ounces *each*) diced tomatoes, undrained
- 1/2 cup diced pimientos
- 1 teaspoon chili powder
- 1 teaspoon salt
- 1/2 teaspoon pepper
- 1/2 teaspoon ground turmeric
- 1/2 cup shredded cheddar cheese

In a large skillet, saute rice in butter for 5 minutes or until golden brown, stirring constantly. Add green pepper, onion and garlic. Cook and stir for 2-3 minutes or until vegetables are tender. Add tomatoes, pimientos, chili powder, salt, pepper and turmeric; mix well. Cover and simmer for 20-25 minutes or until rice is tender. Sprinkle with cheese. Serve immediately. **Yield:** 4-6 servings.

Cranberry Muffins

(Not pictured)

Winning the Country magazine competition inspired me to enter the recipe contest held in conjunction with Carver's annual Cranberry Festival. I've won five awards so far.

- 1 cup fresh cranberries, quartered
- 8 tablespoons sugar, *divided*
- 1-3/4 cups all-purpose flour
- 2-1/2 teaspoons baking powder
- 1/4 teaspoon salt
- 1 egg
- 3/4 cup milk
- 1/3 cup vegetable oil
- 1 teaspoon grated lemon peel, optional

Cinnamon-sugar

Sprinkle the cranberries with 2 tablespoons of sugar; set aside. In a large bowl, combine flour, baking powder, salt and remaining sugar. In a small bowl, beat egg, milk and oil; stir into dry ingredients just until moistened. Fold in cranberries and lemon peel if desired. Fill greased muffin cups two-thirds full. Sprinkle with cinnamon-sugar. Bake at 400° for 18-22 minutes or until muffins test done. Cool for 10 minutes; remove from pan to a wire rack. **Yield:** 1 dozen. **Editor's Note:** This recipe was originally published in the Feb/Mar 1991 issue of *Country* magazine.

— ♥ ♥ ♥ —

Tomatoes and Cukes

Sometimes, simple is best. That's how I feel about this quick and refreshing summertime salad—a delightful dressing lets the garden-fresh vegetables star.

- 2 **tablespoons olive** *or* **vegetable oil**
- 1 **tablespoon vinegar**
- 1 **tablespoon minced fresh parsley**
- 1/4 **teaspoon salt**
- 1/4 **teaspoon pepper**
- 3 **medium tomatoes, sliced**
- 1/2 **large cucumber, sliced**

Leaf lettuce, optional

In a small bowl, whisk oil, vinegar, parsley, salt and pepper. On a serving plate, arrange tomato and cucumber slices over lettuce if desired. Drizzle with the vinaigrette. **Yield:** 4 servings.

Strawberry Cheese Pie

Impressive as it looks, this dessert is really easy to prepare. I make it often when strawberries are at their peak. My husband thinks it's terrific, and I receive compliments when I serve the pie to guests.

- 1 **unbaked pastry shell (9 inches)**
- 2 **packages (one 8 ounces, one 3 ounces) cream cheese, softened**
- 1/2 **cup plus 2 tablespoons sugar,** *divided*
- 1/2 **teaspoon vanilla extract**
- 2 **eggs**
- 1 **cup (8 ounces) sour cream**
- 2 **pints fresh strawberries, hulled**

Confectioners' sugar, optional

Line unpricked pastry shell with a double thickness of heavy-duty foil. Bake at 450° for 8 minutes. Remove foil and set shell aside. In a mixing bowl, combine cream cheese, 1/2 cup sugar and vanilla; beat until smooth. Add eggs; mix until combined. Pour into shell. Bake at 350° for 20-25 minutes or until center is almost set. Remove from the oven and let stand for 5 minutes. Meanwhile, combine sour cream and remaining sugar in a mixing bowl; mix well. Spread over filling. Turn oven off. Return pie to the oven for 15 minutes. Remove; cool on a wire rack. Refrigerate for 6 hours or overnight. Before serving, top with strawberries. Dust with confectioners' sugar if desired. **Yield:** 6-8 servings.

_**Fresh air's a main
ingredient in this
hospitable cook's
lip-smacking spread
of barbecued chicken,
sweet corn, salad,
bread and cake.**_

By Priscilla Weaver, Hagerstown, Maryland

DURING the summer months and into early autumn, I'm always eager to cook out. In fact, I'm on my fifth grill now—the first four wore out from frequent use!

Husband Leon (everyone calls him "Sonnie") and I often invite friends over for a casual outdoor dinner, either in our backyard or at our log cabin retreat. Everyone agrees that some foods just seem to taste better outside.

I've been told my Barbecued Picnic Chicken is "better than the best". The homemade barbecue sauce takes on a slightly sweet taste from brown sugar and gets its zip from garlic and hot pepper sauce. I add celery seed for interest and crunch.

Potato Tossed Salad is a hybrid I came up with when trying to decide whether to take potato salad or a tossed green salad to a carry-in dinner at church. On a whim, I combined the two for a dish with a different twist.

It's hard to top the taste of crisp sweet corn spread with butter...however, once you've tried my Herbed Corn on the Cob, you might not settle for plain buttered corn again!

Seasoned butter also dresses up plain French bread in my Grilled Garlic Bread recipe.

If I had to claim one dessert as my specialty, it would be Easy Red Velvet Cake. Conveniently, I start with a marble cake mix, which turns a lighter shade of red than chocolate cake mix when food coloring is added. Buttermilk or sour milk makes the high layers extra moist and tender.

Gather together some of your favorite folks and try my cookout menu. See if you agree that these recipes are ideal for a casual get-together in the great outdoors.

PICTURED AT LEFT: Barbecued Picnic Chicken, Potato Tossed Salad, Grilled Garlic Bread, Herbed Corn on the Cob and Easy Red Velvet Cake (recipes are on the next page).

that's met with many compliments. Slices of new potatoes take on added flavor as they marinate.

- **1/2 cup olive *or* vegetable oil**
- **2 tablespoons lemon juice**
- **2 teaspoons dried oregano**
- **1 garlic clove, minced**
- **1/4 teaspoon salt**
- **1/2 pound small red potatoes, cooked, peeled and sliced**
- **6 cups torn mixed salad greens**
- **2 small tomatoes, cut into wedges**
- **1 small cucumber, thinly sliced**
- **1 small red onion, thinly sliced into rings**
- **1/2 cup crumbled feta *or* blue cheese**

In a small bowl, whisk together the first five ingredients. Add potatoes; toss gently. Cover and refrigerate for 1 hour. Drain, reserving dressing. Place salad greens in a large bowl. Arrange tomatoes, cucumber, onion, cheese and potatoes on top. Drizzle with reserved dressing. **Yield:** 8 servings.

Barbecued Picnic Chicken

When we entertain friends for a picnic at our cabin, I like to serve this savory chicken. Cooked on a covered grill, the poultry stays so tender and juicy. Everyone loves the zesty, slightly sweet homemade basting sauce—and it's so easy to prepare!

- **2 garlic cloves, minced**
- **2 teaspoons butter *or* margarine**
- **1 cup ketchup**
- **1/4 cup packed brown sugar**
- **1/4 cup chili sauce**
- **2 tablespoons Worcestershire sauce**
- **1 tablespoon celery seed**
- **1 tablespoon prepared mustard**
- **1/2 teaspoon salt**
- **2 dashes hot pepper sauce**
- **2 broiler/fryer chickens (3-1/2 to 4 pounds *each*), quartered**

In a saucepan, saute garlic in butter until tender. Add the next eight ingredients. Bring to a boil, stirring constantly. Remove from the heat and set aside. Grill chicken, covered, over medium heat for 30 minutes, turning occasionally. Baste with sauce. Grill 15 minutes longer or until juices run clear, basting and turning several times. **Yield:** 8 servings.

------- 🍶 🍶 🍶 -------

Potato Tossed Salad

Instead of serving potato salad plus a tossed salad, I combine the two in a unique and colorful recipe

Grilled Garlic Bread

(Pictured on page 256)

Until several years ago, I'd never thought of making garlic bread outdoors, but with this recipe, it turns out nice and crispy.

- **1 loaf (16 ounces) French bread**
- **1/4 cup butter *or* margarine, softened**
- **1 teaspoon garlic powder**

Cut the bread into eight slices. In a small bowl, combine the butter and garlic powder. Spread on one side of each slice of bread. Place bread, buttered side up, on grill over medium heat for 2 minutes or until browned. Turn and grill 2 minutes longer or until both sides are browned. **Yield:** 8 servings.

Herbed Corn on the Cob

"What's in the butter?" people always ask me after tasting this herb-speckled blend on fresh sweet corn. I'm more than happy to share the secret. Once you've tried this recipe, you won't want to eat corn plain again!

  1/2 cup butter *or* margarine, softened
    2 tablespoons minced fresh chives
    2 tablespoons minced fresh parsley
  1/2 teaspoon Salad Supreme Seasoning*
    8 hot cooked ears sweet corn

Combine butter and seasonings; spread over corn. **Yield:** 8 servings. ***Editor's Note:** Salad Supreme Seasoning can be found in the spice section of most grocery stores.

Easy Red Velvet Cake

I've been making Red Velvet Cake for many years, trying slight changes in the recipe until coming up with

one I consider "tried and proven". Conveniently, it starts with a cake mix and turns out beautifully every time.

    1 package (18-1/4 ounces) fudge marble cake mix
    1 teaspoon baking soda
    2 eggs
1-1/2 cups buttermilk
    1 bottle (1 ounce) red food coloring
    1 teaspoon vanilla extract
FROSTING:
    5 tablespoons all-purpose flour
    1 cup milk
    1 cup butter *or* margarine, softened
    1 cup sugar
    2 teaspoons vanilla extract

In a mixing bowl, combine contents of cake mix and baking soda. Add eggs, buttermilk, food coloring and vanilla; blend on low until moistened. Beat on high for 2 minutes. Pour into two greased and floured 9-in. round cake pans. Bake at 350° for 30-35 minutes or until a toothpick inserted near the center comes out clean. Cool for 10 minutes; remove from pans to a wire rack to cool completely. For frosting, whisk flour and milk in a saucepan until smooth. Bring to a boil; cook and stir for 2 minutes or until thickened. Cover and cool to room temperature. In a mixing bowl, cream butter and sugar. Add milk mixture; beat for 10 minutes or until fluffy. Stir in vanilla. Frost between layers and top and sides of cake. **Yield:** 12 servings.

Celebrating harvesttime flavors, she roasts a succulent turkey and adds savory side dishes for a memorable holiday menu.

By Gloria Warczak, Cedarburg, Wisconsin

AUTUMN is my favorite time of year. To me, the sunny, crisp days and blazing foliage don't signify a "winding down" or ending, but rather a new beginning of good things yet to come. These festive recipes, which are perfect for Thanksgiving or any fall get-together, reflect this feeling.

My succulent Special Roast Turkey has crisp brown skin and tender moist meat. Rich turkey juices, orange juice, seasonings and chopped roasted giblets combine to produce the perfect gravy to accompany Old-Fashioned Riced Potatoes.

My husband, Pat, has been a fan of these home-style potatoes since I first made them early in our marriage. They seem lighter than mashed potatoes, so I always say, "Go ahead, have an extra helping!"

Flavorful Rice Dressing can be stuffed in the turkey or baked separately. The mixture is laden with wild rice and vegetables, including spinach and mushrooms. While it may seem unusual, the ingredients are drawn from different types of stuffing I've tried, and the combination is appealing.

In my recipe for Microwave Brussels Sprouts, the creamy, subtle cheese sauce offsets and "tames" the cabbage flavor.

I don't need to remind family members to save room for Traditional Pumpkin Pie. Calling for six eggs, the filling is rich and custard-like. The pastry recipe is one I've used for as long as I can remember. From the leftover pastry, I cut turkey, maple leaf and acorn shapes to bake for decorating the pies.

Family gatherings, especially around the holidays, are woven together by a common thread—good food.

PICTURED AT LEFT: Special Roast Turkey, Flavorful Rice Dressing, Microwave Brussels Sprouts and Traditional Pumpkin Pie (recipes are on the next page).

Special Roast Turkey

Before putting my turkey in the oven, I pour a savory sauce over it. It adds a pleasant citrus-soy flavor.

- 1 turkey (12 to 14 pounds)
- 2 cups water
- 2-1/2 cups chicken broth, *divided*
- 1-1/2 cups orange juice, *divided*
- 4 tablespoons soy sauce, *divided*
- 1 tablespoon chicken bouillon granules
- 1 teaspoon dried minced onion
- 1/2 teaspoon garlic powder

ORANGE GIBLET GRAVY:
- 3/4 cup chicken broth
- 1/4 cup orange juice
- 2 teaspoons Worcestershire sauce
- 1/2 teaspoon dried thyme
- 1/2 teaspoon sugar
- 1/4 teaspoon pepper
- 3 tablespoons cornstarch
- 1/2 cup water

Place turkey on a greased rack in a roasting pan. Add water, giblets and neck to pan. Combine 1-1/4 cups broth, 3/4 cup orange juice and 2 table-spoons soy sauce; pour over turkey. Combine bouillon, onion and garlic powder; sprinkle over turkey. Bake, uncovered, at 325° for 3-1/2 hours, basting every 30 minutes. When turkey begins to brown, cover lightly with foil. Remove giblets and neck when tender; set aside for gravy. Combine remaining broth, orange juice and soy sauce. Remove foil from turkey; pour broth mixture over turkey. Bake 30 minutes longer or until a meat thermometer reads 180°. For gravy, remove meat from neck;

discard bones. Chop giblets and neck meat; set aside. In a saucepan, combine 2 cups pan juices, broth, orange juice and Worcestershire sauce; mix well. Stir in thyme, sugar and pepper. Combine cornstarch and water until smooth. Whisk into broth mixture; bring to a boil. Cook and stir for 2 minutes. Stir in reserved giblets and neck meat. Carve turkey; serve with gravy. **Yield:** 8 servings.

Flavorful Rice Dressing

My original dressing recipe includes both bread and rice, plus spinach and a hint of orange for unexpected surprises.

- 7 slices day-old bread, torn
- 1 cup torn corn bread
- 2/3 cup hot water
- 1/2 cup thinly sliced celery
- 1/2 cup chopped onion
- 1/2 cup sliced fresh mushrooms
- 1 tablespoon vegetable oil
- 1 cup firmly packed sliced fresh spinach
- 1 cup cooked long grain rice
- 1/2 cup cooked wild rice
- 1/2 cup orange juice
- 1 egg, beaten
- 2 teaspoons rubbed sage
- 1/2 teaspoon dried thyme
- 1/2 teaspoon salt
- 1/4 teaspoon sugar
- 1/4 teaspoon pepper

In a large bowl, lightly toss bread and water. In a skillet, saute celery, onion and mushrooms in oil until tender, stirring constantly. Stir into bread mixture. Add remaining ingredients; mix well. Place in a 2-qt. baking dish. Cover and bake at 350° for 30 minutes. **Yield:** 8 servings.

Old-Fashioned Riced Potatoes

This traditional side dish is a nice change from mashed potatoes. My husband is a big fan of them.

> 8 **medium potatoes, peeled and quartered**
> 5 **whole peppercorns**
> 1 **large bay leaf**
> 1/4 **teaspoon celery salt**
> 1/4 **teaspoon sugar**
> **Minced fresh parsley, optional**

Place potatoes in a large kettle or Dutch oven; cover with water. Tie peppercorns and bay leaf in a double thickness of cheesecloth; add to pan. Add celery salt and sugar; bring to a boil. Reduce heat to medium; cover and cook for 20 minutes or until potatoes are tender. Drain. Discard spice bag. Using a potato ricer or grater, press or grate potatoes into a serving bowl. Sprinkle with parsley if desired. **Yield:** 8-10 servings.

Microwave Brussels Sprouts

(Pictured on page 260)

Preparing these in the microwave is a help when the oven is crowded with other foods.

> 1-1/2 **pounds brussels sprouts**
> 1/4 **cup water**
> 1/4 **teaspoon celery salt**
> **Pinch pepper**
> 1/2 **cup shredded cheddar cheese**
> 1/3 **cup finely crushed cornflakes**
> 1 **tablespoon butter *or* margarine, melted**

Place brussels sprouts in a 1-1/2-qt. microwave-safe dish; add water. Sprinkle with celery salt and pepper. Cover and microwave on high for 8-10 minutes or until tender, stirring and rotating a quarter turn every 3 minutes. Drain. Sprinkle with cheese; microwave on high for 1-2 minutes or until cheese begins to melt. Combine cornflakes and butter; sprinkle over sprouts. **Yield:** 8 servings. **Editor's Note:** This recipe was tested in a 700-watt microwave.

Traditional Pumpkin Pie

Usually I prepare two different desserts for our holiday dinner, but one must be this pumpkin pie!

> 2 **cups all-purpose flour**
> 3/4 **teaspoon salt**
> 2/3 **cup shortening**
> 4 to 6 **tablespoons cold water**
> **FILLING:**
> 6 **eggs**
> 1 **can (29 ounces) solid-pack pumpkin**
> 2 **cups packed brown sugar**
> 2 **teaspoons ground cinnamon**
> 1 **teaspoon salt**
> 1/2 **teaspoon *each* ground cloves, nutmeg and ginger**
> 2 **cups evaporated milk**

In a bowl, combine flour and salt; cut in shortening until crumbly. Sprinkle with water, 1 tablespoon at a time, tossing with a fork until dough forms a ball. Divide dough in half. On a floured surface, roll out each portion to fit a 9-in. pie plate. Place pastry in plates; trim pastry (set the scraps aside if leaf cutouts are desired) and flute edges. Set shells aside. For filling, beat eggs in a mixing bowl. Add pumpkin, brown sugar, cinnamon, salt, cloves, nutmeg and ginger; beat just until smooth. Gradually stir in milk. Pour into pastry shells. Bake at 450° for 10 minutes. Reduce heat to 350°; bake 40-45 minutes longer or until a knife inserted near the center comes out clean. Cool on wire racks. If desired, cut pastry scraps with a 1-in. leaf-shaped cookie cutter; place on an ungreased baking sheet. Bake at 350° for 10-15 minutes or until lightly browned. Place on baked pies. **Yield:** 2 pies (6-8 servings each).

Meals in Minutes

Mix and match these recipes to create countless meals that go from stovetop to tabletop in 30 minutes or less.

TIMELESS TREATS. Clockwise from upper left: Spring Supper Bursting with Flavor (p. 270), Bring a Taste of Italy to Your Table (p. 266), Reel in Raves on Warm Sunny Days (p. 272) and Rise and Shine with Bright Breakfast (p. 276).

Bring a Taste of Italy To Your Table

NOTHING warms your spirit on a cold winter evening like a hot and hearty meal. Plus, it's a nice gift to give you and your family after a hurried day during the holiday season!

The menu here is made up of favorite recipes shared by three great cooks and combined in our test kitchen.

Easy Italian Chicken, from Joan Rose of Langley, British Columbia, is a lovely fresh-tasting main course you can serve with pride and without fuss.

"When we want a hearty Italian dish but I don't want to spend hours cooking, this is the recipe I choose," Joan conveys. "Boneless skinless chicken breasts are convenient to have in the freezer because they thaw and cook quickly. Plus, I always have the other ingredients in my pantry."

Flaky Garlic Rolls are a fun and tasty way to dress up handy refrigerator biscuits. "Hot from the oven, these rolls are great alongside any meat and are also super with soup or as an evening snack," assures Peggy Burdick from Burlington, Michigan. "Garlic bread tastes especially nice with this saucy chicken and spaghetti."

Peppermint Mousse is a refreshing, mildly minty dessert suggested by Julie Moyer, from Union Grove, Wisconsin. "Although I've been known to prepare this delicious dessert throughout the year, it's a wonderful way to end a holiday meal," Julie remarks.

Easy Italian Chicken

✓ Nutritional Analysis included

- **4 boneless skinless chicken breast halves**
- **1 can (14-1/2 ounces) Italian stewed tomatoes**
- **1 can (4 ounces) mushroom stems and pieces, drained**
- **1/2 teaspoon dried basil**
- **1/4 teaspoon garlic powder**
- **1 tablespoon cornstarch**
- **1/3 cup cold water**
- **Hot cooked spaghetti**

In a large skillet coated with nonstick cooking spray, cook chicken for 5-6 minutes on each side or until the juices run clear. Meanwhile, in a saucepan over medium heat, bring tomatoes, mushrooms, basil and garlic powder to a boil.

Combine cornstarch and water; add to tomato mixture. Return to a boil; cook and stir for 2 minutes. Serve chicken over spaghetti; top with the tomato sauce. **Yield:** 4 servings. **Nutritional Analysis:** One serving (prepared with no-salt-added stewed tomatoes and calculated without spaghetti) equals 177 calories, 178 mg sodium, 73 mg cholesterol, 7 gm carbohydrate, 28 gm protein, 3 gm fat. **Diabetic Exchanges:** 3 very lean meat, 2 vegetable.

Flaky Garlic Rolls

- **1 tube (6 ounces) refrigerated flaky biscuits**
- **1 to 2 tablespoons butter *or* margarine, melted**
- **1/4 to 1/2 teaspoon garlic salt**

Separate each biscuit into three pieces; place on a greased baking sheet. Brush with butter; sprinkle with garlic salt. Bake at 400° for 8-10 minutes or until golden brown. Serve warm. **Yield:** 15 rolls.

Peppermint Mousse

- **1 envelope unflavored gelatin**
- **2 tablespoons cold water**
- **1 cup milk**
- **4 ounces chocolate-covered peppermint patties**
- **1/2 teaspoon vanilla extract**
- **1/4 teaspoon salt**
- **1 cup whipping cream, whipped**
- **Fresh mint and additional peppermint patties, optional**

In a saucepan, sprinkle gelatin over water; let stand for 1 minute. Add milk and peppermint patties; stir over low heat for 5 minutes or until candies and gelatin are dissolved. Add vanilla and salt. Pour into a mixing bowl; place in freezer for 15-20 minutes, stirring frequently until the mixture is cooled and thickened. Beat for 1 minute or until fluffy. Fold in whipped cream. Spoon into serving dishes. Garnish with mint and peppermint patties if desired. **Yield:** 4-6 servings.

Busy Cooks Depend on Classic Combination

WHEN time's short and hunger's high, you can always rely on soup and a sandwich. Whether you serve it as a hearty lunch or light supper, the comforting, tasty flavor just can't be beat.

The menu here is made up of family favorites from three country cooks. You can have everything ready to serve in just 30 minutes.

For a flavorful and filling part of a fast-to-fix meal, try Sausage Bean Soup from Marlene Muckenhirn, Delano, Minnesota. The recipe calls for canned beans and quick-cooking sausage, so it only needs to simmer for a few minutes instead of a few hours.

Italian Grilled Cheese sandwiches are a delicious, dressed-up version of the traditional favorite. "The pocket of melted mozzarella or provolone cheese and a crisp crumb coating give these hot sandwiches a tasty twist," says Vera Ambroselli of Lehigh Acres, Florida. For added taste, use a combination of cheeses.

Pretty Cherry Parfaits are just the treat when you want to serve a dessert that's fast, lovely and scrumptious, assures Bernice Morris of Marshfield, Missouri.

Sausage Bean Soup

3/4 **pound bulk Italian sausage**
1/2 **cup chopped onion**
1 **garlic clove, minced**
1 **can (15-1/2 ounces) butter beans, rinsed and drained**
1 **can (15 ounces) black beans, rinsed and drained**
1 **can (14-1/2 ounces) beef broth**

✎ Working with Dry Beans

When you do have time and you'd like to prepare Sausage Bean Soup using dry beans, keep in mind this simple substitution: 1 cup packaged dry beans (uncooked) equals about two 15-1/2-ounce cans of beans (drained).

Before using the dry beans, sort and rinse them. Place in a soup kettle; add enough water to cover by 2 inches. Bring to a boil; boil for 2 minutes. Remove from the heat; cover and let stand for 1 hour. Drain and rinse; discard liquid.

1 **can (14-1/2 ounces) diced tomatoes, undrained**
1 **tablespoon minced fresh basil _or_ 1 teaspoon dried basil**
2 **tablespoons shredded Parmesan cheese**

In a large saucepan, cook sausage, onion and garlic until the sausage is browned; drain. Add beans, broth, tomatoes and basil. Cover and simmer for 10 minutes. Sprinkle each serving with Parmesan cheese. **Yield:** 4-6 servings.

Italian Grilled Cheese

4 **slices Italian bread (1 inch thick)**
4 **slices mozzarella _or_ provolone cheese**
3 **eggs**
1/2 **cup milk**
3/4 **teaspoon Italian seasoning**
1/2 **teaspoon garlic salt**
2/3 **cup Italian-seasoned bread crumbs**

Cut a 3-in. pocket in each slice of bread; place a slice of cheese in each pocket. In a bowl, beat eggs, milk, Italian seasoning and garlic salt; soak bread for 2 minutes on each side. Coat with the bread crumbs. Cook on a greased hot griddle until golden brown on both sides. **Yield:** 4 servings.

Pretty Cherry Parfaits

1 **can (21 ounces) cherry pie filling**
1/4 **teaspoon almond extract**
1 **cup (8 ounces) sour cream**
1 **cup cold milk**
1 **package (3.4 ounces) instant vanilla pudding mix**
Whipped topping, chopped almonds and fresh mint, optional

Combine pie filling and extract; set aside. In a mixing bowl, combine sour cream and milk. Stir in pudding mix; beat on low speed for 2 minutes. Spoon half into parfait glasses; top with half of the pie filling. Repeat layers. Garnish with whipped topping, almonds and mint if desired. Refrigerate until serving. **Yield:** 4-6 servings.

Spring Supper Bursting With Flavor

FOR THOSE who love to cook, spending time in the kitchen preparing an elaborate meal is a joy. Still, there are some days when you need to pull together a satisfying meal in just minutes.

The complete-meal menu here is made up of family favorites from three great cooks. You can have everything ready to serve in just 30 minutes.

A tempting and beautiful glaze makes Mustard-Apricot Pork Chops an impressive main dish that looks like you fussed over it. "This recipe is so easy and so good," says Sheila Townsend of West Des Moines, Iowa. These tender chops are nice to serve during the week as well as for company on weekends.

Asparagus with Almonds will please the palates of everyone—even those who generally don't care for asparagus, assures Eileen Bechtel of Wainwright, Alberta. "I look forward to spring each year so I can make this tasty side dish."

Fruit Parfaits are a refreshing fruity treat, and you can use whatever flavor of gelatin you like. Spring City, Tennessee cook Erlene Cornelius shares the recipe. And because it calls for canned fruit, you can rely on it as a tasty dessert anytime of year.

Mustard-Apricot Pork Chops

1/3 cup apricot preserves
2 tablespoons Dijon mustard
4 pork loin chops (1/2 to 3/4 inch thick)
3 green onions, chopped
Hot cooked rice

In a small saucepan over low heat, cook and stir preserves and mustard until preserves are melted; set aside. Place pork chops on a lightly greased broiler pan; broil 4 in. from the heat for 5 minutes. Brush with half of the glaze; turn pork chops. Broil 5 minutes longer; brush with the remaining glaze. Broil 2-4 minutes more or until meat juices run clear. Top with onions. Serve over rice. **Yield:** 4 servings.

Asparagus with Almonds

2 tablespoons sliced almonds
4 teaspoons olive *or* vegetable oil, *divided*

1 pound fresh asparagus, cut into 2-inch pieces
1/4 cup water
1 teaspoon sugar
1/4 teaspoon salt
Dash pepper
1 teaspoon lemon juice

In a skillet, saute almonds in 1 teaspoon of oil until lightly browned; remove and set aside. In the same skillet, saute asparagus in the remaining oil for 1 minute. Add water, sugar, salt and pepper; bring to a boil. Reduce heat; cover and simmer for 3-4 minutes or until asparagus is tender. Drain. Sprinkle with lemon juice; top with almonds. **Yield:** 3-4 servings.

Fruit Parfaits

☑ Nutritional Analysis included

1 can (15 ounces) fruit cocktail
1 package (3 ounces) lemon gelatin
8 ice cubes (1-1/2 cups crushed ice)

Drain fruit cocktail, reserving the syrup. Divide fruit among four parfait glasses and set aside. Add water to the syrup to measure 3/4 cup; pour into a saucepan. Bring to a boil. Place the gelatin in a blender; carefully add syrup. Cover and blend on low until gelatin is dissolved, about 30 seconds. Add ice; cover and blend until dissolved, about 1 minute. Pour over the fruit. Cover and refrigerate until set, about 15 minutes. **Yield:** 4 servings. **Nutritional Analysis:** One 1/2-cup serving (prepared with fruit cocktail in light syrup and sugar-free gelatin) equals 69 calories, 53 mg sodium, 0 cholesterol, 16 gm carbohydrate, 1 gm protein, trace fat. **Diabetic Exchange:** 1 fruit.

Asparagus Tips

You can store unwashed asparagus in a sealed plastic bag in the refrigerator for up to 4 days. Just before using, cut off the tough white portion on the stalk and soak in cold water to clean.

Reel in Raves on Warm Sunny Days

ARE YOU fishing for fast and fun foods to prepare for your famished family on hurried, hectic days? You'll love this quick and easy meal, while everyone will agree it's "reel"-y delicious!

The complete-meal menu here is made up of favorites from three great cooks and combined in our test kitchen.

Don't settle for ordinary hamburgers when you can serve Zesty Salmon Burgers. "They're quick and easy to make and are a regular summer main dish at our house," reports Melanie Dunn of Wilmore, Kansas. "Horseradish adds a tasty zip to convenient canned salmon." Even those people who normally don't care for salmon will likely be "hooked" after one bite of these specialty fish sandwiches.

With water chestnuts and celery, Crunchy Pea Salad is a refreshing side dish with a fun crunch. "Frozen peas are a handy base for this good-tasting salad," remarks Mary Reid Fisher of Brownwood, Texas. "It's also a great dish for a potluck because it can be made ahead. Everyone enjoys this when I serve it."

If you're watching your waistline, cut some of the calories and fat by simply substituting fat-free mayonnaise and nonfat sour cream.

Lemon Crisp Cookies are a snap to make using a boxed cake mix. Says Julia Livingston of Frostproof, Florida, "The sunny yellow color and big lemon flavor are sure to bring smiles." You'll likely prepare these tempting treats even when you do have time to bake.

If you have a yellow cake mix on your pantry shelf that you'd like to use up, feel free to use it in place of the lemon cake mix. The cookies won't have a strong lemon flavor, but they'll still be delicious!

Zesty Salmon Burgers

    1 can (14-3/4 ounces) salmon, drained, skin
      and bones removed
    2 eggs
1/2 cup dry bread crumbs
1/4 cup finely chopped onion
1/4 cup mayonnaise
    1 to 2 tablespoons prepared horseradish
    1 tablespoon diced pimientos, optional
1/4 teaspoon salt
1/8 teaspoon pepper
    2 tablespoons butter *or* margarine

    4 kaiser rolls, split
Lettuce leaves

Combine the first nine ingredients; mix well. Shape into four patties. In a skillet over medium heat, cook patties in butter until browned, about 6 minutes on each side. Serve on rolls with lettuce. **Yield:** 4 servings.

Crunchy Pea Salad

✓ Nutritional Analysis included

    1 package (10 ounces) frozen peas, thawed
    1 can (8 ounces) sliced water chestnuts,
      drained
    1 cup thinly sliced celery
1/2 cup sliced green onions
1/4 cup mayonnaise
1/4 cup sour cream
1/2 teaspoon seasoned salt, optional

In a bowl, combine the first four ingredients. In a small bowl, combine mayonnaise, sour cream and seasoned salt if desired; mix well. Add to the pea mixture; toss to coat. Chill until serving. **Yield:** 8 servings. **Nutritional Analysis:** One 1/2-cup serving (prepared with fat-free mayonnaise and nonfat sour cream and without seasoned salt) equals 60 calories, 116 mg sodium, 1 mg cholesterol, 12 gm carbohydrate, 3 gm protein, trace fat. **Diabetic Exchange:** 1 starch.

Lemon Crisp Cookies

    1 package (18-1/4 ounces) lemon cake mix
    1 cup crisp rice cereal
1/2 cup butter *or* margarine, melted
    1 egg, beaten
    1 teaspoon grated lemon peel

In a large bowl, combine all ingredients until well mixed (dough will be crumbly). Shape into 1-in. balls. Place 2 in. apart on ungreased baking sheets. Bake at 350° for 10-12 minutes or until set. Cool for 1 minute; remove from pan to a wire rack to cool completely. **Yield:** about 4 dozen.

Dig into Delicious Outdoor Dinner

WHETHER you're working in the garden or relaxing in the shade, summer tempts even avid cooks to spend more time outdoors and less in the kitchen.

Fresh air builds appetites, so you'll surely need a fast-to-fix, nutritious meal that satisfies.

The complete-meal menu here is made up of favorites from three terrific cooks, combined in our test kitchen. You can sit down to eat in about 30 minutes!

Broiled Beef Kabobs are a fun summer main dish seasoned in a snap with a tangy homemade marinade. "These kabobs are so simple to prepare," assures Margery Bryan of Royal City, Washington.

Apple-Nut Tossed Salad is a refreshing alternative to a plain lettuce salad. "We love the light dressing over crunchy apples, walnuts and lettuce sprinkled with blue cheese," remarks Maureen Reubelt of Gales Ferry, Connecticut.

Strawberry Lemon Parfaits make a cool, elegant dessert that's hardly any fuss to fix. The recipe for these pretty parfaits comes from Joy Beck of Cincinnati, Ohio.

Broiled Beef Kabobs

✓ Nutritional Analysis included

1 tablespoon olive *or* vegetable oil
1 tablespoon lemon juice
1 tablespoon water
2 teaspoons Dijon mustard
1 teaspoon honey
1/2 teaspoon dried oregano
1/4 teaspoon pepper
1 pound boneless top sirloin steak (1 inch thick), cut into 1-inch cubes
2 small green *and/or* sweet red peppers, cut into 1-inch pieces
12 large fresh mushrooms
Hot cooked rice

In a bowl, combine the first seven ingredients; mix well. Add beef, peppers and mushrooms; toss to coat. Thread meat and vegetables alternately on metal or soaked wooden skewers. Broil 3 in. from the heat, turning often, until meat reaches desired doneness and vegetables are tender, about 12-16 minutes. Serve over rice. **Yield:** 4 servings. **Nutritional Analysis:** One serving (calculated without rice) equals 231 calories, 122 mg sodium, 75 mg cholesterol, 8 gm carbohydrate, 28 gm protein, 10 gm fat. **Diabetic Exchanges:** 3-1/2 lean meat, 1-1/2 vegetable.

Apple-Nut Tossed Salad

3 tablespoons olive *or* vegetable oil
1 teaspoon Dijon mustard
3/4 teaspoon sugar
Salt and pepper to taste
1/2 cup chopped apple
1 tablespoon chopped green onion
3 cups torn Bibb lettuce
1 to 2 tablespoons chopped walnuts
1 to 2 tablespoons crumbled blue cheese

In a bowl, combine oil, mustard, sugar, salt and pepper. Add apple and onion; toss to coat. Add lettuce, walnuts and blue cheese; toss gently. Serve immediately. **Yield:** 4 servings.

Strawberry Lemon Parfaits

✓ Nutritional Analysis included

1 pint fresh strawberries
3 tablespoons sugar
3 cartons (8 ounces *each*) lemon yogurt

In a food processor, combine strawberries and sugar. Process for 20-30 seconds or until berries are coarsely chopped. Divide half of the mixture into four parfait glasses. Top with yogurt and remaining berries. **Yield:** 4 servings. **Nutritional Analysis:** One serving (prepared with nonfat yogurt) equals 109 calories, 40 mg sodium, 1 mg cholesterol, 24 gm carbohydrate, 3 gm protein, trace fat. **Diabetic Exchanges:** 1 fruit, 1/2 skim milk.

Berry Basics

Buy plump strawberries with bright green caps and nice red color. Store them in an uncovered colander or container in the refrigerator. Don't wash or hull the berries until you're ready to use them.

Rise and Shine with Bright Breakfast

WHEN your alarm clock rings, the hustle and bustle of your day begins. So, why not get your day off to a good start with a hearty, wholesome breakfast?

Ready to serve in just 30 minutes, the delightful breakfast or brunch menu here combines recipes from three super cooks. They were combined in our test kitchen for a mouth-watering morning meal.

Oven Denver Omelet is suggested by Ellen Bower of Taneytown, Maryland. "I like omelets but don't always have time to stand by the stove. That's why I favor this oven-baked variety that I can quickly pop into the oven at a moment's notice," she notes. "My family frequently requests this for Sunday brunch. They always empty the dish." Chopped fresh mushrooms would be a nice addition to this enticing omelet.

Raspberry Lemon Muffins are a tart treat to eat along with a meal or as a snack. Says Georgia Carruthers of Livonia, Michigan, "I collect bread and muffin recipes, and this is one of my favorites." You can easily substitute fresh or frozen blueberries for the raspberries if you prefer. Plus, these muffins freeze well, so they're easy to have on hand.

Golden Smoothies take no more effort to whip up than orange juice from concentrate, relates Nancy Schmidt of Delhi, California. "A tall glass of this rich, smooth eye-opener makes any morning special," she adds.

Oven Denver Omelet

- 8 eggs
- 1/2 cup half-and-half cream
- 1 cup (4 ounces) shredded cheddar cheese
- 1 cup finely chopped fully cooked ham
- 1/4 cup finely chopped green pepper
- 1/4 cup finely chopped onion

In a bowl, beat eggs and cream until light and fluffy. Stir in the cheese, ham, green pepper and onion. Pour into a greased 9-in. square baking dish. Bake at 400° for 25 minutes or until golden brown. **Yield:** 4-6 servings.

Raspberry Lemon Muffins

- 2 cups all-purpose flour
- 1/2 cup sugar

- 1 teaspoon baking powder
- 1 teaspoon baking soda
- 1/2 teaspoon salt
- 2 eggs, lightly beaten
- 1 cup (8 ounces) lemon yogurt
- 1/4 cup butter *or* margarine, melted and cooled
- 1 teaspoon grated lemon peel
- 1 teaspoon vanilla extract
- 1-1/2 cups fresh or frozen raspberries

In a bowl, combine flour, sugar, baking powder, baking soda and salt. Combine eggs, yogurt, butter, lemon peel and vanilla; mix well. Stir into dry ingredients just until moistened. Fold in raspberries. Fill greased or paper-lined muffin cups three-fourths full. Bake at 400° for 18-20 minutes or until muffins test done. **Yield:** 1 dozen.

Golden Smoothies

✓ Nutritional Analysis included

- 1-1/2 cups orange juice
- 1 carton (8 ounces) peach yogurt
- 1 can (5-1/2 ounces) apricot nectar
- 1 teaspoon honey
- Orange slices and maraschino cherries, optional

Place the first four ingredients in a blender; cover and process until smooth. Pour into glasses; garnish with oranges and cherries if desired. **Yield:** 3 cups. **Nutritional Analysis:** One 3/4-cup serving (prepared with fat-free yogurt; calculated without fruit garnish) equals 128 calories, 37 mg sodium, 2 mg cholesterol, 29 gm carbohydrate, 3 gm protein, trace fat. **Diabetic Exchanges:** 1 skim milk, 1 fruit.

Egg Basics

At the store, only purchase eggs stored in the refrigerator case and put them into your refrigerator as soon as you get home. To help prevent eggs from picking up odors and flavors from other foods in the refrigerator, it's best to store eggs in their original carton.

Meals on a Budget

With these six frugal yet flavorful menus, you can serve your family tasty home-style foods for just pennies a person.

🍽 🍽 🍽

ECONOMICAL ENTREES. Clockwise from upper left: Orange Chicken, Baked Rice Pilaf and Chocolate Chip Cake (p. 288); Pizza from Scratch, Italian Cucumber Salad and Chewy Peanut Butter Bars (p. 286); Chicken Veggie Casserole, Wheat Yeast Rolls and Moist Chocolate Cake (p. 282); Garlic Swiss Steak, Simple White Bread and Lemon-Glazed Carrots (p. 284).

Feed Your Family for $1.12 a Plate!

IF HOLIDAY SPENDING has stretched your family budget, you'll like this penny-pinching meal. It's from three great cooks who estimate the total cost at just $1.12 per setting.

Salisbury Steak with Onion Gravy gets high praise from Kim Kidd of New Freedom, Pennsylvania. "This hearty main dish is a favorite at our house," reports Kim. "It really warms you up."

Corn 'n' Broccoli Bake is a sweet, comforting corn side dish from Betty Sitzman of Wray, Colorado. It's a very creamy casserole that resembles corn pudding.

Coconut Pie is an old-fashioned dessert. "I sometimes top warm slices with a sprinkling of cinnamon or nutmeg," notes Virginia Krites from Cridersville, Ohio. "Best of all, it's easy to assemble when dinnertime is fast approaching."

Salisbury Steak with Onion Gravy

- 1 egg
- 1 can (10-1/2 ounces) condensed French onion soup, undiluted, *divided*
- 1/2 cup dry bread crumbs
- 1/4 teaspoon salt
- Pinch pepper
- 1-1/2 pounds ground beef
- 1 tablespoon all-purpose flour
- 1/4 cup water
- 1/4 cup ketchup
- 1 teaspoon Worcestershire sauce
- 1/2 teaspoon prepared mustard
- 6 cups hot cooked egg noodles
- Chopped fresh parsley, optional

In a large bowl, beat egg. Stir in 1/3 cup of soup, bread crumbs, salt and pepper. Add beef; mix gently. Shape into six oval patties. Brown in a skillet over medium heat for 3-4 minutes on each side. Remove and set aside; discard drippings. In the same skillet, combine flour and water until smooth; add ketchup, Worcestershire sauce, mustard and remaining soup; bring to a boil. Cook and stir for 2 minutes. Return patties to skillet. Cover and simmer for 15 minutes or until meat is no longer pink. Serve patties and gravy over noodles. Garnish with parsley if desired. **Yield:** 6 servings.

Corn 'n' Broccoli Bake

- 1 can (16 ounces) cream-style corn
- 1 package (10 ounces) frozen chopped broccoli, thawed
- 1/2 cup crushed saltines, *divided*
- 1 egg, beaten
- 1 tablespoon dried minced onion
- Dash pepper

2 tablespoons butter *or* margarine, melted

In a bowl, combine the corn, broccoli, 1/4 cup of saltines, egg, onion and pepper. Place in a greased 1-1/2-qt. baking dish. Combine the butter and remaining saltines; sprinkle over top. Cover and bake at 350° for 45 minutes. **Yield:** 6 servings.

Coconut Pie

2 cups milk
1 cup sugar

4 eggs
1/2 cup all-purpose flour
6 tablespoons butter *or* margarine
1 teaspoon vanilla extract
1/2 teaspoon salt
1 cup coconut

In a blender, combine first seven ingredients. Cover and blend for 10 seconds; scrape sides. Blend another 10 seconds. Add coconut; blend for 2 seconds. Pour into a greased 10-in. pie plate. Bake at 350° for 50-55 minutes or until a knife inserted near center comes out clean. Serve warm. **Yield:** 6 servings.

Feed Your Family for 81¢ a Plate!

EVEN at today's prices, you can feed your family for just pennies a person.

This time, we show how easy it is to assemble a low-budget menu to serve family and guests for just 81¢ per serving (including two rolls per person).

Chicken Veggie Casserole is a hot, satisfying complete meal in one dish. The recipe is shared by Martha Balser of Cincinnati, Ohio.

Wheat Yeast Rolls are light and have a delicate flavor. "They're inexpensive and delicious," says Peggy Starkweather of Gardiner, Montana.

The recipe for Moist Chocolate Cake comes from Gansevoort, New York cook Janice Arnold. "This cake is extra chocolaty," Janice assures. The recipe makes the perfect number of servings, so leftovers are never a problem.

Chicken Veggie Casserole

> **1 can (10-3/4 ounces) condensed cream of chicken soup, undiluted**
> **1/2 cup milk**
> **1/4 teaspoon dried thyme**
> **1/4 teaspoon salt**
> **1/4 teaspoon pepper**
> **2 cups diced cooked chicken**
> **1 can (16 ounces) whole kernel corn, drained**
> **2 cups frozen cut green beans, thawed**
> **2 cups sliced cooked potatoes**

In a large bowl, combine the soup, milk, thyme, salt and pepper. Stir in chicken, corn, beans and potatoes. Pour into a greased 1-1/2-qt. baking dish. Bake, uncovered, at 400° for 15 minutes or until heated through. **Yield:** 6 servings.

Wheat Yeast Rolls

✓ Nutritional Analysis included

> **1 package (1/4 ounce) active dry yeast**
> **1 cup warm water (110° to 115°)**
> **1/3 cup vegetable oil**
> **3 tablespoons sugar**
> **1 teaspoon salt**
> **1-1/2 cups whole wheat flour**
> **1-1/2 to 2 cups all-purpose flour**

In a mixing bowl, dissolve yeast in water. Add oil, sugar, salt and whole wheat flour; beat until smooth. Add enough all-purpose flour to form soft dough. Turn onto a floured surface; knead until smooth and elastic, about 6-8 minutes. Place in a greased bowl; turn once to grease top. Cover and let rise in a warm place until doubled, about 1 hour. Punch down; divide into 12 pieces. Shape into rolls; place 3 in.

apart on greased baking sheets. Cover; let rise until doubled, about 30 minutes. Bake at 375° for 15-20 minutes or until golden. Cool on wire racks. **Yield:** 1 dozen. **Nutritional Analysis:** One roll equals 175 calories, 195 mg sodium, 0 cholesterol, 26 gm carbohydrate, 4 gm protein, 7 gm fat. **Diabetic Exchanges:** 1-1/2 starch, 1-1/2 fat.

Moist Chocolate Cake

1 cup all-purpose flour
1 cup sugar
1 cup hot water
1/2 cup baking cocoa
1 teaspoon baking powder
1 teaspoon baking soda
1 egg
1/4 cup butter *or* margarine, melted
Confectioners' sugar

In a mixing bowl, combine the first six ingredients. Add egg and butter; mix well. Pour into a greased 8-in. square baking pan. Bake at 350° for 30-35 minutes or until a toothpick inserted near the center comes out clean. Cool. Dust with confectioners' sugar. **Yield:** 9 servings.

Feed Your Family for 92¢ a Plate!

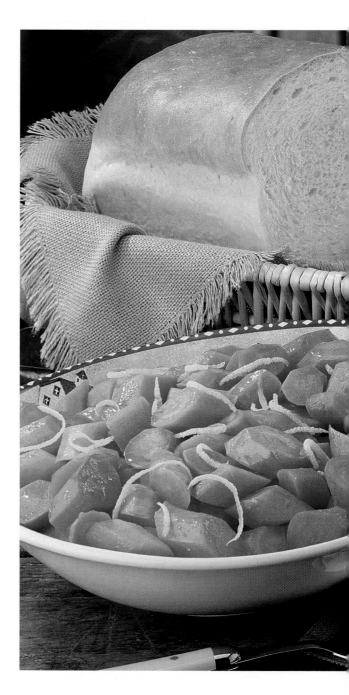

JUST because you're eating "cent-sibly" doesn't mean you have to forgo the tantalizing taste of steak.

The frugal, flavorful meal here is from three cooks who estimate the total cost at just 92¢ per setting.

Garlic Swiss Steak is a delicious main dish that looks as good as it tastes. "This favorite beef entree was perfect when our four children were at home," shares Patricia Craft of Greenville, Texas. "It was simple for me to fix this budget-stretcher, and the kids loved it." Cooking the round steak slowly in a tangy tomato sauce makes the meat turn out tender every time.

From Marengo, Iowa, Ruth Von Lienen shares the recipe for Simple White Bread. These tall golden loaves have wonderful homemade flavor and a texture that also makes this bread ideal for toast and sandwiches. It's a terrific way to round out a hearty penny-pinching meal. Serve one loaf and freeze one for later.

Lemon-Glazed Carrots are a super vegetable side dish suggested by Ruby Williams from Bogalusa, Louisiana. "These lovely tangy carrots are a special treat," Ruby relates.

—— 🝑 🝑 🝑 ——

Garlic Swiss Steak

1-1/2 **pounds bone-in round steak**
1/3 **cup all-purpose flour**
1 **teaspoon salt**
1/2 **teaspoon pepper**
2 **tablespoons vegetable oil**
1 **can (14-1/2 ounces) stewed tomatoes**
1 **small onion, chopped**
1/2 **medium green pepper, chopped**
2 **garlic cloves, minced**

Cut steak into serving-size pieces; discard bone. Combine flour, salt and pepper; sprinkle over steak and pound into both sides. In a large skillet over medium heat, brown steak on both sides in oil. Transfer to a greased 13-in. x 9-in. x 2-in. baking dish. Combine tomatoes, onion, green pepper and garlic; pour over steak. Cover and bake at 350° for 1-1/2 hours or until tender. **Yield:** 6 servings.

Simple White Bread

2 **packages (1/4 ounce *each*) active dry yeast**
2-1/2 **cups warm water (110° to 115°)**
1/2 **cup instant nonfat dry milk powder**
1/2 **cup vegetable oil**
2 **tablespoons sugar**
1 **tablespoon salt**
8-1/2 to 9 **cups all-purpose flour**
1 **tablespoon butter *or* margarine, melted**

In a mixing bowl, dissolve yeast in 1/2 cup of water. Add remaining water, dry milk, oil, sugar, salt and 3 cups of flour. Beat on medium speed for 3 minutes or until smooth. Stir in enough remaining flour to form a soft dough. Turn onto a floured surface and knead until smooth and elastic, about 6-

8 minutes. Place in a greased bowl, turning once to grease top. Cover and let rise in a warm place until doubled, about 1 hour. Punch the dough down. Divide in half; shape into loaves. Place in two greased 9-in. x 5-in. x 3-in. loaf pans. Cover and let rise until doubled, about 1 hour. Bake at 375° for 35 minutes or until golden brown. Remove from pans to cool on wire racks. Brush with butter. **Yield:** 2 loaves.

Lemon-Glazed Carrots

1-1/2 pounds medium carrots, cut into 1/2-inch diagonal slices
3 tablespoons butter *or* margarine
3 tablespoons brown sugar
3 tablespoons lemon juice
1/4 teaspoon salt
Grated lemon peel, optional

Place carrots in a saucepan; cover with water. Bring to a boil; reduce heat. Cover and simmer for 10-12 minutes or until crisp-tender. Meanwhile, in a small saucepan, melt butter. Add brown sugar, lemon juice and salt; bring to a boil, stirring constantly. Drain carrots; add butter mixture and toss gently. Garnish with lemon peel if desired. **Yield:** 6 servings.

Carrot Equivalents

Six or seven carrots make up 1 pound. One pound of carrots serves about four people.

Feed Your Family for 82¢ a Plate!

HOMEMADE MEALS are always more economical —and certainly more delicious—than foods prepared in a restaurant. That's especially true when it comes to pizza and all the fixin's!

Three terrific cooks show how easy it is to put together a tempting Italian-style menu for just 82¢ a setting.

Pizza from Scratch is a low-budget crowd-pleaser that tastes so good. This recipe comes from Audra Dee Collins of Hobbs, New Mexico, who asks, "Why pay for takeout or pop a frozen pizza in the oven?

"You can make this tasty pizza yourself with hardly any fuss. My sister shared the recipe with me years ago. It's now a staple in our home," says Audra Dee. "Have everyone pitch in when assembling the pizzas…it's a nice way to get the family together. Also, you can mix and match topping ingredients to suit your family's tastes."

Italian Cucumber Salad, shared by Jane Nichols of Houston, Texas, is a snap to prepare and a great use for your garden's bounty of vegetables. "Folks enjoy this tangy, refreshing side dish," Jane conveys. "I came up with the recipe after sampling a similar salad at a local cafeteria."

Chewy Peanut Butter Bars have been a favorite treat at the Milan, Ohio home of Deb DeChant for years. "With seven of us here, including two teenage boys, these bars never last long!" Deb admits. "It's hard to believe how simple they are to prepare."

Pizza from Scratch

    1 package (1/4 ounce) active dry yeast
    1 cup warm water (110° to 115°)
    2 tablespoons vegetable oil
    1 teaspoon salt
    1 teaspoon sugar
2-3/4 to 3-1/4 cups all-purpose flour
SAUCE:
    1 can (15 ounces) tomato sauce
1/2 cup chopped onion
3/4 teaspoon Italian seasoning
1/4 teaspoon garlic powder

1/4 teaspoon salt
1/8 teaspoon pepper
TOPPINGS:
1/2 pound bulk Italian sausage, cooked and drained
    1 can (4 ounces) mushroom stems and pieces, drained
    1 medium green pepper, sliced
1-1/2 cups (6 ounces) shredded mozzarella cheese

In a mixing bowl, dissolve yeast in water. Add oil, salt, sugar and 2 cups flour. Beat on medium speed for 3 minutes. Stir in enough remaining flour to form a soft dough. Turn onto a floured surface; knead until smooth and elastic, about 6-8 minutes. Place in a greased bowl, turning once to grease top. Cover and let rest in a warm place for 10 minutes. Meanwhile, combine sauce ingredients; set aside. Divide

dough in half. On a floured surface, roll each portion into a 13-in. circle. Transfer to greased 12-in. pizza pans; build up edges slightly. Bake at 375° for 15 minutes or until lightly browned. Spread sauce over hot crusts; sprinkle with sausage, mushrooms, green pepper and cheese. Bake for 20 minutes or until cheese is melted. **Yield:** 2 pizzas (8 servings).

—— 🍴 🍴 🍴 ——

Italian Cucumber Salad

- **2 medium cucumbers, peeled and sliced**
- **1 cup halved cherry tomatoes**
- **1 cup sliced red onion**
- **1/2 cup chopped green pepper**
- **1/2 cup Italian salad dressing**

In a large bowl, combine all of the ingredients; cov-

er and refrigerate until serving. Serve with a slotted spoon. **Yield:** 8 servings.

—— 🍴 🍴 🍴 ——

Chewy Peanut Butter Bars

- **1/2 cup butter *or* margarine**
- **1/2 cup creamy peanut butter**
- **1-1/2 cups sugar**
- **1 cup all-purpose flour**
- **2 eggs, beaten**
- **1 teaspoon vanilla extract**

In large saucepan, melt butter and peanut butter. Remove from heat; add sugar and flour. Stir in the eggs and vanilla. Spread into a greased and floured 13-in. x 9-in. x 2-in. baking pan. Bake at 350° for 28-32 minutes or until lightly browned and edges start to pull away from sides of pan. **Yield:** 2 dozen.

Feed Your Family for $1.31 a Plate!

CHICKEN and rice have always been economical mealtime mainstays. And with some additional everyday ingredients, you can serve up a flavorful meal fit for a king…without breaking the bank!

The frugal yet flavorful meal here is from three terrific cooks who estimate the total cost at just $1.31 per setting.

Orange Chicken is a tasty way to dress up chicken drumsticks and thighs. "These golden chicken pieces are nicely seasoned with a tangy citrus marinade," explains Rita Goshaw of South Milwaukee, Wisconsin. The ingredients are easy to have on hand, so you can whip up this special chicken for friends and family anytime.

From Golden, Colorado, Sheree Feero sends the recipe for Baked Rice Pilaf. "I'm always in search of inexpensive yet delicious dishes like this one to serve at potlucks," Sheree says. "This fluffy rice dish tastes as good as it looks." The recipe can easily be doubled.

Chocolate Chip Cake, suggested by Sue Reichenbach of Langhorne, Pennsylvania, delightfully combines the flavors of chocolate and cinnamon. Enjoy this dessert with dinner and use leftovers the next day as a handy snack.

Orange Chicken

- 4 **chicken legs with thighs (3-1/2 pounds), skin removed**
- 1 **teaspoon salt**
- 1/8 to 1/4 **teaspoon pepper**
- 3 **tablespoons orange juice concentrate**
- 1 **tablespoon honey**
- 1 **teaspoon prepared mustard**

Place chicken in a single layer in a greased 13-in. x 9-in. x 2-in. baking pan; sprinkle with salt and pepper. Bake, uncovered, at 375° for 25 minutes. Meanwhile, combine remaining ingredients. Brush over chicken; bake 15 minutes longer. Brush again; bake 10 minutes more or until the juices run clear. **Yield:** 4 servings.

Baked Rice Pilaf

✓ Nutritional Analysis included

- 1-3/4 **cups water**
- 1 **cup shredded carrot**
- 1 **cup chopped celery**
- 3/4 **cup uncooked long grain rice**
- 3 **tablespoons minced fresh parsley**
- 2 **tablespoons finely chopped onion**
- 2 **tablespoons butter *or* margarine, melted**
- 1 **tablespoon chicken bouillon granules**

Combine all ingredients in an ungreased 8-in. square baking dish. Cover and bake at 375° for 40-45 minutes or until rice is tender, stirring after 25 minutes. **Yield:** 4 servings. **Nutritional Analysis:**

One 1/2-cup serving (prepared with margarine and low-sodium bouillon) equals 212 calories, 108 mg sodium, 0 cholesterol, 35 gm carbohydrate, 4 gm protein, 6 gm fat. **Diabetic Exchanges:** 2 starch, 1 fat.

Chocolate Chip Cake

> 1/2 cup butter *or* margarine, softened
> 1-1/2 cups sugar, *divided*
> 2 eggs
> 1 teaspoon vanilla extract
> 2 cups all-purpose flour
> 1-1/2 teaspoons baking powder
> 1 teaspoon baking soda
> 1 cup (8 ounces) sour cream
> 3/4 cup semisweet chocolate chips
> 1 teaspoon ground cinnamon

In a mixing bowl, cream butter and 1 cup sugar. Add eggs, one at a time, beating well after each addition. Stir in vanilla. Combine flour, baking powder and baking soda; add to the creamed mixture alternately with sour cream. Spread half of the batter into a greased 9-in. square baking pan. Sprinkle with chocolate chips. Combine cinnamon and remaining sugar; sprinkle over chips. Spread with remaining batter. Bake at 350° for 45-50 minutes or until a toothpick inserted near the center comes out clean. **Yield:** 8 servings.

Feed Your Family for 95¢ a Plate!

WITH all the entertaining you do around the holidays, cutting corners isn't easy...especially when it comes to feeding the family. But this palate-pleasing meal deliciously proves you can enjoy the flavors of the season without breaking the bank.

The great cooks who shared their recipes for this festive supper estimate a total cost of just 95¢ per setting.

The recipe for Glazed Sprouts and Carrots uses simple seasonings to turn this vegetable duo into a special side dish. "It complements any dinner menu," relates Page Alexander of Baldwin City, Kansas.

Cranberry Turkey Loaf is a delightful alternative to traditional meat loaf, assures Paula Zsiray, a Logan, Utah cook. "It's very moist, and the cranberry sauce gives it a tasty twist," she adds.

Mock Apple Pie, suggested by Shirley Hunter of St. Paul, Minnesota, almost magically imitates a real apple pie. "My mother made this dessert often during the Depression, and our guests were always astounded that soda crackers could be such convincing 'apples'," chuckles Shirley.

Glazed Sprouts and Carrots

✓ Nutritional Analysis included

     1/2 **cup water**
       1 **cup halved fresh brussels sprouts**
       2 **medium carrots, sliced**
     1/3 **cup orange juice**
       1 **teaspoon cornstarch**
     1/2 **teaspoon sugar**
     1/4 **teaspoon salt, optional**
     1/8 **teaspoon ground nutmeg**

In a saucepan over medium heat, bring water to a boil. Add vegetables. Cover and simmer for 6-8 minutes or until almost tender; drain and return to pan. In a small bowl, combine orange juice, cornstarch, sugar, salt if desired and nutmeg; stir until smooth. Pour over vegetables. Bring to a boil over medium heat; cook and stir for 2 minutes. **Yield:** 4 servings. **Nutritional Analysis:** One 1/2-cup serving (prepared without salt) equals 39 calories, 18 mg sodium, 0 cholesterol, 9 gm carbohydrate, 1 gm protein, 0 fat. **Diabetic Exchange:** 2 vegetable.

Cranberry Turkey Loaf

       1 **egg**
     1/2 **cup herb-seasoned stuffing mix, crushed**
     3/4 **cup whole-berry cranberry sauce, *divided***
     1/4 **teaspoon salt**
     1/8 **teaspoon pepper**
       1 **pound ground turkey**

In a bowl, beat the egg; add stuffing mix, 1/4 cup

cranberry sauce, salt and pepper. Stir in turkey; mix well. Spoon into an ungreased 8-in. x 4-in. x 2-in. loaf pan. Bake, uncovered, at 350° for 55-65 minutes or until a meat thermometer reads 165°. Heat remaining cranberry sauce in a microwave on high for 1 minute or until heated through. Slice turkey loaf; top with cranberry sauce. **Yield:** 4 servings.

Mock Apple Pie

Pastry for double-crust pie
   18 saltines, halved
1-1/2 cups sugar

1-1/4 cups water
   2 tablespoons lemon juice
   1 teaspoon cream of tartar
1/2 to 1 teaspoon ground cinnamon
1/2 to 1 teaspoon ground nutmeg

Place the bottom pastry in a 9-in. pie plate. Layer crackers in shell; set aside. In a small saucepan, combine remaining ingredients; bring to a boil. Carefully pour over crackers (filling will be very thin). Cool for 10 minutes. Cut lattice strips from remaining pastry; place over filling. Seal and flute edges. Bake at 400° for 25-30 minutes or until golden brown. **Yield:** 8 servings.

Getting in the Theme of Things

**These fun and festive meals—
featuring theme-related menus,
decorating ideas and activities—
will make your parties
extra special.**

ENTERTAINING IDEAS. Clockwise from upper left: Spooky Supper for Hungry Goblins (p. 304), Step Up to the Plate for Ballpark Bash (p. 298), Make the Grade with Class Party (p. 302) and Snowy Breakfast Kicks Off Winter Fun (p. 294).

Snowy Breakfast Kicks Off Winter Fun

By Renae Moncur, Burley, Idaho

Our son, Spencer, loves to ski. When he brought his girlfriend home during the Christmas holidays, I planned a skiers' breakfast to welcome them.

Special theme breakfasts are a family tradition for us. As the children were growing and active in school, sports and jobs, it got difficult to sit down together for an evening meal. So occasionally I'd wake everyone a bit earlier than usual for an enjoyable theme breakfast.

Now that our children are grown and gone, I still do this whenever we are able to get together, whether it be at my home or theirs.

Planning this winter morning, I made a tablecloth of white batting, snipping the edges into jagged points to resemble icicles. Then I grouped three little artificial pine trees, a stuffed ski bear and several snowball candles into a centerpiece and sprinkled fake snow over everything.

I put stick-on snowflakes on the bottoms of my clear glass plates and set them atop royal blue ones. Red bandannas for napkins were tucked into glasses I'd later fill with frothy blended Fruity Milk Shakes.

A festive German Pancake highlighted the menu. As it puffs up high in the oven, the edges curl and bake to a golden brown. The homemade buttermilk syrup is deliciously smooth and easy to make. You'll appreciate the fact that no special cast-iron skillet is required for this recipe.

With the pancake, I served warm Sauteed Apples and Raisins, plus breakfast meats such as sausages and Canadian bacon. What fun we had before I sent the couple off to the slopes!

Planning theme meals is fun, too, and it needn't be expensive. I've bought some cute dishes at yard sales and store clearances. And I invested in an inexpensive set of clear glass dishes. They can be used with any color scheme and for any holiday. I often put a patterned paper plate underneath each glass plate or set them on colored napkins.

Felt fur-trimmed mittens held the silverware, and our tin coffee mugs were wrapped with miniature knitted mufflers. I also purchased some little tubes of lip balm, which made useful favors.

Centerpieces can be made from almost anything. I may start with a favorite decoration and see what else is on hand to go along with my theme.

Our skiers' breakfast surely brightened a wintry morning. Why not adopt my idea and treat your family or friends to a similar eye-opener?

German Pancake

Piping hot and puffy from the oven, this golden pancake made a pretty presentation for the skiers' theme breakfast. Served with my homemade buttermilk syrup, it's a tempting treat that folks will gladly get out of bed for on a chilly morning. That simple syrup tastes great on waffles and French toast, too.

    6 eggs
    1 cup milk
    1 cup all-purpose flour
  1/2 teaspoon salt
    2 tablespoons butter *or* margarine, melted
BUTTERMILK SYRUP:
1-1/2 cups sugar
  3/4 cup buttermilk
  1/2 cup butter *or* margarine
    2 tablespoons corn syrup
    1 teaspoon baking soda
    2 teaspoons vanilla extract
Confectioners' sugar

Place the eggs, milk, flour and salt in a blender; cover and process until smooth. Pour the butter into an ungreased 13-in. x 9-in. x 2-in. baking dish; add the batter. Bake, uncovered, at 400° for 20 minutes. Meanwhile, in a saucepan, combine the first five syrup ingredients; bring to a boil. Boil for 7 minutes. Remove from the heat; stir in vanilla.

Dust pancake with confectioners' sugar; serve immediately with the syrup. **Yield:** 8 servings (about 2 cups syrup).

Sauteed Apples and Raisins

On a chilly morning, this fruity side dish warms you up. It complements just about anything you'd choose to serve for breakfast or brunch, such as the German Pancake, an egg dish or slices of warmed Canadian bacon.

✓ Nutritional Analysis included

    4 large tart apples, peeled and cored
  1/4 cup butter *or* margarine
    2 teaspoons cornstarch
  1/2 cup water
  1/2 cup packed brown sugar
  1/4 cup golden raisins
    1 teaspoon lemon juice

Cut apples in half and then into 1/4-in.-thick slices. Melt butter in a large skillet; add apples. Cook and stir over medium heat for 6-7 minutes or until almost tender. Dissolve cornstarch in water; add to skillet. Add brown sugar and raisins; bring to a boil. Boil for 2 minutes, stirring constantly. Remove from the heat; stir in lemon juice. Serve warm. **Yield:** 4 cups. **Nutritional Analysis:** One 1/2-cup serving (prepared with margarine) equals 182 calories, 73 mg sodium, 0 cholesterol, 34 gm carbohydrate, trace protein, 6 gm fat. **Diabetic Exchanges:** 2 fruit, 1 fat.

Fruity Milk Shakes

Shake up your breakfast—and surprise the family—by pouring tall glasses of this tasty blend instead of plain fruit juice or milk.

    1 can (6 ounces) frozen apple juice
       concentrate, thawed
    1 carton (8 ounces) vanilla yogurt
    1 medium ripe banana, sliced
  1/2 cup instant nonfat dry milk powder
  1/4 teaspoon coconut extract
    1 to 3 teaspoons honey
  12 ice cubes

In a blender, combine the first five ingredients. Cover and blend until well mixed. Add honey and ice; cover and process on high until the ice is crushed and mixture is foamy. Pour into glasses. **Yield:** about 4 cups.

Presidents' Day Menu and Motif

By Mary Beth de Ribeaux, Gaithersburg, Maryland

For Presidents' Day, I decided to put aside political parties and celebrate *all* the Presidents with a dinner party instead.

I worked up an easy menu with connections to the Oval Office. Appetizers included Georgia peanuts (recognizing Jimmy Carter) and a Lincoln Log of cheese on a platter surrounded by assorted crackers.

To make the log, I molded a flavorful cheese spread into the shape of a log, rolled it in chopped walnuts for a rough, "woody" texture and used parsley sprigs (rosemary would also work) as little "branches".

As they were called to the table, guests were asked to find out where the "buck stopped" by looking under their plates. On the bottom of one plate, I had taped

an envelope labeled "The buck stops here" (recalling Harry Truman) with a crisp $1 bill inside. That person was asked to give the "State of the Union Address" (the meal blessing).

The table was decorated with tiny American flags on each place card, flag paper napkins and printed menus.

Of course, when most people think of Presidents' Day, George Washington and the cherry tree legend come to mind. For a centerpiece, I anchored branches in a basket, made "leaves" of green tissue paper and tied on "cherries"—a few red jelly beans (Ronald Reagan's Presidential Sweets) wrapped in small squares of plastic wrap. To complete the patriotic look, my husband, Eugene, hung our American flag.

For the main course, I used my mom's easy potpie recipe but titled it Chicken in Every Pot Pie, echoing Herbert Hoover's campaign slogan. Everyone enjoyed their single-serving, comforting casserole.

One of my favorite vegetables made a good accompaniment. I named it Kale to the Chief and hummed the tune while bringing it to the table!

At least one food is associated with a President because he *didn't* like it…so I did *not* serve broccoli to honor George Bush. I even put "No broccoli permitted" on the menu.

Wanting cherries to be part of the dessert, I made my own White House ice cream (remembering a flavor by that name when I was a child) by softening vanilla ice cream, stirring in some frozen red cherries and then refreezing it.

I served scoops in dessert cups with a maraschino cherry on top and two homemade First Lady Fingers tucked alongside.

The dinner was such fun that we'll do it again. (When winter seems to drag on, we *need* a fun celebration…how about you?)

Lincoln Log

As an appetizer for my Presidents' Day dinner, I reshaped a favorite cheese ball recipe into this log. Rolled in nuts and sprouting herb sprig "branches", it was a fun and flavorful way to honor one of our most famous leaders.

        1 package (8 ounces) cream cheese, softened
        1 cup (4 ounces) shredded cheddar cheese
    1/2 cup diced red onion
        1 tablespoon Worcestershire sauce
        1 teaspoon celery seed
    1/2 cup chopped walnuts
        2 to 3 fresh rosemary *or* parsley sprigs
Assorted crackers

In a mixing bowl, combine the cheeses, onion, Worcestershire sauce and celery seed; beat until fluffy. Cover and refrigerate for at least 2 hours. Shape into a 7-in. x 1-1/2-in. log; roll in walnuts. Insert rosemary or parsley sprigs for branches. Serve with crackers. **Yield:** 2 cups.

Chicken in Every Pot Pie

*I created a new title for my mom's potpie recipe while trying to come up with a clever menu for our Presidents' Day party. An old political slogan came to mind that fit the theme and my main dish just fine! These in-*dividual pies are chock-full of chicken and vegetables.

        4 cups cubed cooked chicken
    1-1/2 cups chicken broth
    1-1/2 cups frozen peas
        3 to 4 medium carrots, cut into 1/4-inch slices
        1 can (10-3/4 ounces) condensed cream of mushroom soup, undiluted
    1/4 teaspoon salt
    1/4 teaspoon pepper
        2 cups biscuit/baking mix
    1-1/4 cups milk
        1 teaspoon garlic powder
    1/2 teaspoon celery seed
Paprika

In a saucepan, combine chicken, broth, peas, carrots, soup, salt and pepper; bring to a boil, stirring occasionally. Meanwhile, combine biscuit mix, milk, garlic powder and celery seed (mixture will be thin). Pour the hot chicken mixture into eight greased ovenproof 10-oz. custard cups or casseroles. Immediately spoon 1/4 cup of biscuit mixture evenly on top of each. Sprinkle with paprika. Bake, uncovered, at 350° for 30-35 minutes or until topping is golden brown. **Yield:** 8 servings.

First Lady Fingers

I didn't want to forget the "partners" of our Presidents for this patriotic occasion! So I renamed these fancy light-textured cookies and served them with ice cream in pretty dessert dishes. A hint of almond flavors them nicely.

        3 eggs, *separated*
    1/3 cup sugar
        1 teaspoon almond extract
    1/3 cup all-purpose flour
Pinch salt
    1/2 cup confectioners' sugar
Ice cream, optional

Grease and lightly flour two baking sheets; set aside. In a mixing bowl, beat egg yolks on high speed for 3 minutes. Gradually add sugar and extract, beating until light in color and thickened. Gradually add flour and salt, beating until thick and lemon-colored. In another bowl, beat egg whites until soft peaks form. Fold into yolk mixture. Cut a 1/2-in. hole in a corner of a heavy-duty plastic bag, or use a pastry bag with plain pastry tip #808. Fill with batter. Form 4-in.-long finger shapes 1 in. apart on prepared baking sheets. Dust with confectioners' sugar. Bake at 350° for 12-15 minutes or until golden. Cool on a wire rack. Serve with ice cream if desired. **Yield:** about 2 dozen.

Step Up to the Plate for Ballpark Bash

By Sue Gronholz, Columbus, Wisconsin

Batter up! To celebrate the baseball season, I fielded a theme party that was a big hit with our sports-minded gang.

Dugout Hot Dogs are heated in a zesty homemade sauce. They taste terrific with a zucchini relish that both of my grandmas used to make. I served them with Ballpark Baked Beans, an "all-American" dish.

Hungry fans of all ages cheered for hearty help-ings of Grand Slam Salad.

Play Ball Cake was the table's focal point. Along-side it, I anchored helium-filled balloons with a real mitt and baseball.

Try this meal for a pregame tailgate or a Little Lea-guer's birthday and get rousing cheers of your own.

Dugout Hot Dogs

I jazzed hot dogs up with an easy barbecue sauce and tangy relish.

ZUCCHINI RELISH:
2-1/2 cups chopped zucchini
    1 medium onion, chopped
  1/2 cup chopped green pepper
1-1/4 teaspoons salt
    1 cup sugar
  1/2 cup plus 2 tablespoons vinegar
1-1/2 teaspoons celery seed
  1/4 teaspoon ground mustard
  1/8 teaspoon ground turmeric

1 teaspoon cornstarch
1 tablespoon water
HOT DOGS:
3/4 cup ketchup
2 to 4 tablespoons chopped onion
2 tablespoons brown sugar
2 tablespoons cider vinegar
10 hot dogs
10 hot dog buns, split

In a bowl, combine the zucchini, onion, green pepper and salt; cover and refrigerate overnight. Rinse and drain well; set aside. In a saucepan, combine sugar, vinegar, celery seed, mustard and turmeric; bring to a boil. Add zucchini mixture; return to a boil. Reduce heat and simmer, uncovered, for 15 minutes, stirring occasionally. Combine cornstarch and water until smooth; stir into zucchini mixture. Simmer 6-8 minutes longer, stirring often. Cool; store in the refrigerator. For hot dogs, combine ketchup, onion, sugar and vinegar in a saucepan; simmer 2-3 minutes. Add hot dogs; simmer 5-10 minutes longer or until heated through. Serve on buns topped with the relish. **Yield:** 10 servings (2 cups relish).

Ballpark Baked Beans

You'll taste a sweet hint of pineapple in every bite of this bean casserole.

2 cans (16 ounces *each*) baked beans
1/4 cup packed brown sugar
2 tablespoons ketchup
2 teaspoons prepared mustard
1 can (20 ounces) pineapple tidbits, drained

In a large bowl, combine the beans, brown sugar, ketchup and mustard. Transfer to a 2-qt. baking dish. Bake, uncovered, at 350° for 30 minutes. Stir in the pineapple; bake 30 minutes longer. **Yield:** 10 servings.

Grand Slam Salad

(Not pictured)

With fruit cocktail and whipped topping, this salad turned out to be a winner with everyone.

1 can (20 ounces) crushed pineapple, drained
1 can (15-1/4 ounces) fruit cocktail *or* tropical fruit salad, drained
1 can (14 ounces) sweetened condensed milk

1 can (6 ounces) frozen lemonade concentrate, thawed
1 carton (8 ounces) frozen whipped topping, thawed
2 cups pastel miniature marshmallows

In a large bowl, combine the pineapple, fruit cocktail, milk and lemonade concentrate. Fold in the whipped topping and marshmallows. Cover and refrigerate for at least 2 hours. **Yield:** 12-16 servings.

Play Ball Cake

Fresh, pliable licorice works the best for forming the laces on the curved ball cake.

1/2 cup shortening
1-1/2 cups sugar
2 eggs
1 teaspoon vanilla extract
2-1/2 cups cake flour
2 teaspoons baking powder
1/2 teaspoon salt
1 cup milk
FROSTING:
1/2 cup shortening
1/2 cup butter *or* margarine, softened
3 cups confectioners' sugar
4 tablespoons milk, *divided*
1/2 teaspoon vanilla extract
1/4 teaspoon almond extract
Dash salt
1/4 cup baking cocoa
Red shoestring licorice

In a mixing bowl, cream shortening and sugar. Add eggs, one at a time, beating well after each. Add vanilla. Combine flour, baking powder and salt; add alternately with milk to the creamed mixture. Pour 1-1/2 cups batter into a greased and floured 3-cup ovenproof bowl. Pour remaining batter into a greased and floured 9-in. round cake pan. Bake at 325° for 40-45 minutes or until cakes test done. Cool for 10 minutes; remove to a wire rack to cool completely. For frosting, beat shortening and butter in a mixing bowl. Add sugar, 3 tablespoons of milk, extracts and salt; beat until smooth. Set aside 1 cup. To remaining frosting, beat in cocoa and remaining milk. Cut a 3-in. x 1-in. oval for the thumb opening from an edge of the 9-in. cake. Place cake on an 11-in. covered board. Frost with chocolate frosting. With four pieces of licorice, form two crosses over thumb opening for laces in mitt. Frost the rounded cake with white frosting. Use licorice pieces to form laces of ball. Place on mitt cake opposite the thumb opening. **Yield:** 8-10 servings.

Bugs Are Buzzing About Baby's Arrival

By Kendra Barclay, De Kalb, Illinois

How exciting it was becoming an aunt for the first time! I could hardly wait to plan a party for my newborn nephew, Adam.

I wanted the gathering to be memorable, different from typical bootie and cradle events. Recalling the poem that says little boys are "made of snakes and snails and puppy dog tails", I picked a fun critter-filled theme, adding turtles, frogs, bugs and bees to the list. (Little girls love critters, too, so my ideas could be easily adapted for a girl's party as well.)

Invitations said to "buzz on over" for a meal of Tur-

tle Wiches, Flutter-by Buns and Ladybug Cookies. All of the recipes begin with handy convenience foods, making it easy on the cook.

Everyone loved how I formed the cute Turtle Wiches using biscuit dough. Olive slices and poppy seeds speckled the "shells" from which mushroom "heads" peeked out. The one-of-a-kind sandwiches were filled with a homemade flavorful ham, cheese and mushroom mixture.

Convenient refrigerated cinnamon rolls were easy to shape and trim into Flutter-by Buns. I dressed them up by giving them cherry spots and outlining their wings with icing. One of these sweet rolls lighted on each person's plate. Folks seem to gobble these up in a hurry, so you may want to double the recipe!

For a fitting side dish, I made Jell-O, added gummy worm candies to it and molded it in muffin cups for individual servings. (If time allows, you could layer different flavors of gelatin…be sure to let each layer set completely before adding another layer.)

The Ladybug Cookies were a sweet surprise! I frosted purchased chocolate-covered marshmallow cookies and decorated them with gumdrops and licorice. These benevolent "insects" were meant to bring good luck to little Adam.

The colorful cookies served double duty as dessert and as a centerpiece. I placed them on a large glass plate around a shallow dish filled with water, and I floated a toy frog and several frog and turtle candles in the water.

I found paper napkins with a ladybug motif, filled a leaf-shaped candy dish with more gummy worms and set ladybug books, toy bugs and a bug cage on the table. Also, each guest received a ladybug or bumblebee candle as a favor.

While the guest of honor dozed off for a nap, we adults laughed and buzzed like a bunch of kids. The theme put everyone in a festive mood—it'll likely have the same effect on your friends and family!

Turtle Wiches

Little children are usually fascinated with outdoor creatures and insects. So I served specialty sandwiches shaped and decorated to resemble turtles for the party. A delicious ham filling bakes right inside the flaky biscuit dough.

> 1 tube (12 ounces) refrigerated buttermilk biscuits
> 1 cup chopped fully cooked ham
> 2 tablespoons finely chopped onion
> 2 tablespoons butter *or* margarine, softened
> 1 to 2 teaspoons prepared mustard
> 1 teaspoon poppy seeds
> 5 slices process American cheese
> 2 tablespoons sliced ripe olives
> Additional poppy seeds
> 5 whole canned mushrooms

Pat five biscuits into 3-1/2-in. circles on a greased baking sheet. Combine ham, onion, butter, mustard and poppy seeds; spoon 2 tablespoonfuls onto each circle. Fold cheese slices into quarters and place over ham mixture. Top with the remaining ham mixture. Pat remaining biscuits into 4-in. circles; place over filling (do not seal edges). Arrange

olives on top. Sprinkle with poppy seeds. Insert one mushroom into the filling of each sandwich for the turtle's head. Bake at 375° for 15-20 minutes or until golden brown. **Yield:** 5 sandwiches.

Flutter-by Buns

Cinnamon rolls for my theme menu took flight—as butterflies, naturally! I formed the wings using convenient refrigerated rolls. An icing outline and cherry "spots" brought the yummy rolls to life.

> 1 tube (12.4 ounces) refrigerated cinnamon rolls with icing
> 8 maraschino cherries

Separate rolls and cut in half. Place on a greased baking sheet with cinnamon side up and curved edges touching to form wings. Cut the cherries into six wedges; place three on each wing. Bake at 400° for 13-17 minutes or until golden brown. Cool on a wire rack. Stir icing until smooth; place in a pastry bag with a round tip (or in a small heavy-duty resealable plastic bag with a small hole cut in the corner). Pipe icing to outline the wings. **Yield:** 8 servings.

Ladybug Cookies

These bright, sweet "ladybugs" brought me good luck when it came to pleasing guests. I frosted chocolate-covered marshmallow cookies to make the whimsical treats, and they turned out so cute I used them as part of my centerpiece.

> 1 cup vanilla frosting
> 1/2 cup vanilla baking chips
> Red liquid *or* paste food coloring
> 1 package (10-1/2 ounces) chocolate-covered marshmallow cookies
> 12 large black gumdrops
> 3 strips black shoestring licorice, cut into 1-inch pieces

In a microwave-safe bowl, melt frosting and vanilla chips; stir until smooth. Stir in food coloring. Spread over the rounded tops of cookies; place on a waxed paper-lined baking sheet. For head, insert two pieces of licorice into gumdrops for antennae. With a toothpick, attach a gumdrop onto the side of each cookie. Use a toothpick or knife to draw a line from the head down the center of each cookie. Insert six pieces of licorice into frosting of each ladybug for legs. Chop remaining licorice into small pieces; place on top for spots. **Yield:** 1 dozen.

Make the Grade with Class Party

By Leslie Miller, Butler, Pennsylvania

Our daughter, Kayla, could hardly wait for her fifth birthday so she could start kindergarten. When the big day finally came, we wanted it to be really special for her. We invited eight of her friends to help celebrate with a school days theme.

Each guest was asked to wear a school backpack, which was used to hold goodies during a candy hunt. The eager group of new students also used colorful stickers and markers to personalize brown lunch bags, which I filled with favors and set at their places.

The braided Pepperoni Stromboli, filled with pizza-type ingredients and baked to a golden brown, received high marks from children and adults alike. For occasions like birthdays, when there are so many things to

do, this stromboli is easy to make and fun to serve.

Sprinkle Fruit Dip is light, fluffy and not too sweet. Candy sprinkles fleck the yogurt mixture, and their colors run as you scoop the dip, creating a rainbow or tie-dyed effect.

We had strawberries, red and green grapes and, of course, apples. But you could use any of your special favorites or fruits in season.

Kayla was delighted with her School Bus Cake! The other moms were impressed with its vibrant color and design, and I was quick to tell them how easy it was to bake, shape and decorate.

Since it was a beautiful day, we ate lunch outside on the picnic table. I set it with a paper birthday tablecloth, red and yellow streamers and balloons. On a little schoolhouse with a chalkboard roof, we wrote, "Happy Birthday, Kayla."

At the place settings where a knife would normally be placed, each child found a plastic stencil to keep. Their drinking cups were lined with red napkins and held new pencils, candy dispensers and shiny metallic paper party horns.

With a send-off like this, what child wouldn't be excited to go to kindergarten?

If someone in your family is ready to enroll…or if you'd like to plan a unique meal to mark the beginning of a new school year, try this theme.

Pepperoni Stromboli

There's a surprise inside this impressive golden braided loaf—a flavorful pizza-like filling. The children at our daughter's special "going to school" birthday party loved it—and adults love it, too!

 2 loaves (1 pound *each*) frozen bread
   dough, thawed
1/2 cup spaghetti *or* pizza sauce
1/2 teaspoon dried oregano
 4 ounces sliced pepperoni
 2 cups (8 ounces) shredded mozzarella
   cheese
1/3 cup grated Parmesan cheese

Punch dough down. On a lightly floured surface, roll each loaf into a 20-in. x 8-in. rectangle. Place one rectangle on a greased baking sheet. Spread spaghetti sauce in an 18-in. x 4-in. strip down the center. Sprinkle with oregano, pepperoni and mozzarella cheese. Fold sides of dough over filling; set aside. Cut the remaining rectangle into three strips. Loosely braid strips; pinch ends to seal. Place braid on top of the cheese and dough; pinch dough to seal. Sprinkle with Parmesan cheese. Bake at 350° for 30 minutes or until golden brown. **Yield:** 8-10 servings.

Sprinkle Fruit Dip

Bright candy sprinkles make this creamy mixture even more festive. Served with an array of fresh fruit "dippers", it was fun for Kayla's party. Apple slices were especially appropriate to go with our school theme.

1-1/2 cups strawberry yogurt
1-1/2 cups whipped topping
  1/4 cup colored sprinkles, *divided*
    4 large green apples, sliced
    4 large red apples, sliced

 2 pints fresh strawberries
 4 cups red *and/or* green grapes

In a bowl, fold together yogurt, whipped topping and half of the sprinkles. Cover and refrigerate for 20 minutes. Just before serving, top with remaining sprinkles. Serve with fruit. **Yield:** 3 cups.

School Bus Cake

Kayla could hardly wait to board a real school bus to go to kindergarten, so I made her birthday cake to look like one. Everyone immediately recognized the sweet vehicle.

 1 package (18-1/4 ounces) yellow cake mix
 1 cup butter *or* margarine, softened
 1 cup shortening
 8 to 9 cups confectioners' sugar
1/4 cup milk
 1 teaspoon vanilla extract
1/4 teaspoon salt
 2 teaspoons black paste *or* gel food coloring
1/2 to 3/4 teaspoon yellow paste *or* liquid
   food coloring
 2 cream-filled chocolate sandwich cookies,
   cut in half
 2 yellow gumdrops
 6 red gumdrops

Prepare cake mix according to package directions. Pour batter into two greased 8-in. x 4-in. x 2-in. loaf pans. Bake at 350° for 40-45 minutes or until a toothpick inserted near the center comes out clean. Cool for 10 minutes; remove from pans to a wire rack to cool completely. Place cakes end to end on a 22-in. x 8-in. covered board. Level if needed. From the top of one end, form the front of the bus by cutting out a section 1 in. deep and 3 in. long. (Save the removed piece for another use.) For frosting, beat butter and shortening in a mixing bowl until fluffy. Beat in 6 cups sugar, milk, vanilla and salt. Beat in enough additional sugar until frosting reaches desired spreading consistency. Remove 3/4 cup of frosting; add black food coloring. Tint remaining frosting yellow. Frost entire cake yellow. Frost cut edge of cookies with yellow frosting to form wheel wells; place two cookie halves on each side of bus. Cut a hole in the corner of a plastic bag or insert a #5 round tip in a pastry bag; fill with black frosting. Outline windows on both sides of bus; pipe stripes under windows. Pipe windshield and back window; fill in with black frosting. Pipe lines on front for grille. Place yellow gumdrops on front of bus for headlights; place red gumdrops on front and back for lights. **Yield:** 12-16 servings.

Spooky Supper for Hungry Goblins

By Vicki Schlechter, Davis, California

As soon as our son and daughter were old enough for trick-or-treating, I began serving them a special Halloween meal. (My ulterior motive was to fill them up so they wouldn't eat too much candy!) Our spooky supper became a family tradition that outlived going door-to-door for treats.

No tricks—my menu is a treat! Jack-o'-Lantern Burgers are tasty patties with cheesy pumpkin-style "faces".

Broccoli Boo Salad, which can be made a day ahead, is a colorful accompaniment for the burgers. As a startling garnish, I placed a fake spider (available at craft stores) in the center of each serving. If your goblins are little, you may prefer to decorate the table with plastic spiders rather than set them on the salads.

Candy gummy worms hung over the bowl of Wormy Orange Punch inviting guests to sip some of this sparkling, frothy beverage. (I also dropped a worm into each person's cup.)

With its "cemetery topping", Graveyard Cake is always a hit! Cookie tombstones and whipped-topping ghosts set an eerie mood atop this haunted holiday dessert.

I made ghoulish-looking popcorn hands to set on each plate using disposable clear plastic gloves (found in a hardware store) and packed little treat bags with Halloween goodies such as fake teeth.

Years ago, my well-planned witchery to keep the kids filled up proved to be a trick on me—I caught my son sneaking out the door with a pillowcase to collect candy! Even so, the theme meal has become a time-honored treat…so try this ghostly grub on your gang!

Jack-o'-Lantern Burgers

It's fun to "carve" cheesy faces for these nicely seasoned burgers. Hungry trick-or-treaters welcome the hearty sandwiches. They're a can't-miss entree for a casual holiday get-together.

> 1 envelope onion soup mix
> 1/4 cup ketchup
> 2 tablespoons brown sugar
> 2 teaspoons prepared horseradish
> 2 teaspoons chili powder
> 2-1/2 pounds ground beef
> 10 slices process American cheese
> 10 hamburger buns, split

In a bowl, combine soup mix, ketchup, brown sugar, horseradish and chili powder. Add beef; mix well. Shape into 10 patties. Grill, broil or pan-fry until meat is no longer pink. Cut eyes, nose and mouth out of each cheese slice to create a jack-o'-lantern. Place cheese on burgers; cook until cheese is slightly melted, about 1 minute. Serve on buns. **Yield:** 10 servings.

Broccoli Boo Salad

There's nothing scary about the recipe for this popular salad—it's delightfully easy to put together. The mandarin oranges also look nice with the colors in other foods and decorations for my theme.

> 1 cup mayonnaise *or* salad dressing
> 1/4 cup sugar
> 2 tablespoons vinegar
> 8 cups broccoli florets
> 1 can (11 ounces) mandarin oranges, drained
> 1/2 cup chopped red onion
> 6 to 8 bacon strips, cooked and crumbled
> 1/2 cup raisins

In a small bowl, whisk mayonnaise, sugar and vinegar. Cover and refrigerate for at least 2 hours. In a large bowl, combine broccoli, oranges, onion, bacon and raisins. Add dressing and toss to coat. Cover and refrigerate for 1 hour. **Yield:** 10-12 servings.

Wormy Orange Punch

This simply delicious punch is great for any large gathering. No one can resist the sweet orange flavor.

> 1 gallon orange sherbet, softened
> 1 quart pineapple juice, chilled
> 1 liter lemon-lime soda, chilled
> Gummy worms

Combine sherbet and pineapple juice in a punch bowl; stir well. Add soda; stir until sherbet is almost dissolved. Decorate bowl with gummy worms. Serve immediately. **Yield:** 20 (1-cup) servings.

Graveyard Cake

Underneath the tasty "tombstones", ghosts, pumpkins, "worms" and "soil" that make this dessert a conversation piece, you'll find a delectable chocolate cake made from scratch in a few simple steps.

> 2 cups all-purpose flour
> 2 cups sugar
> 1 teaspoon baking soda
> 1/2 teaspoon salt
> 1 cup butter *or* margarine
> 1 cup water
> 1/4 cup baking cocoa
> 1/2 cup sour cream
> 2 eggs
> **FROSTING:**
> 1/4 cup butter *or* margarine
> 3 tablespoons milk
> 2 tablespoons baking cocoa
> 2 cups confectioners' sugar
> 1/2 teaspoon vanilla extract
> 18 cream-filled chocolate sandwich cookies
> 9 cream-filled oval vanilla sandwich cookies
> 1 cup whipped topping
> Green and brown decorator's icing *or* gel
> Pumpkin candies and gummy worms, optional

In a mixing bowl, combine flour, sugar, baking soda and salt; set aside. In a saucepan over medium heat, combine butter, water and cocoa; bring to a boil. Add to flour mixture; beat well. Beat in sour cream and eggs. Pour into a greased 13-in. x 9-in. x 2-in. baking pan. Bake at 350° for 35-38 minutes or until a toothpick inserted near the center comes out clean. Cool on a wire rack for 5 minutes. Meanwhile, in a saucepan, combine butter, milk and cocoa; bring to a boil. Remove from the heat; stir in sugar and vanilla. Pour over the warm cake. Crumble chocolate cookies; sprinkle over frosting while still warm. Cool completely. For tombstones, use icing to decorate vanilla cookies with words or faces; place on cake. For ghosts, make mounds of whipped topping; use icing to add eyes and mouths as desired. Refrigerate for at least 1 hour. Just before serving, add pumpkins and gummy worms if desired. **Yield:** 16 servings.

General Recipe Index

This handy index lists every recipe by food category and/or major ingredient, so you can easily locate recipes.

Issue-by-Issue Index

Do you have a favorite dish from a specific Taste of Home issue but can't recall the recipe's actual name? You'll easily find it in this categorized listing of recipes by issue.

Nutritional Analysis Recipes Index

Refer to this index when you're looking for a recipe that uses less sugar, salt and fat and includes Nutritional Analysis and Diabetic Exchanges. These good-for-you recipes are marked with a ✓ throughout the book.

The Cook's Quick Reference

From the *Taste of Home* Test Kitchens

Substitutions & Equivalents

— ▼ ▼ ▼ —

Cooking Terms

— ▼ ▼ ▼ —

Guide to Cooking with Popular Herbs

Substitutions & Equivalents

Equivalent Measures

3 teaspoons	=	1 tablespoon	16 tablespoons	=	1 cup
4 tablespoons	=	1/4 cup	2 cups	=	1 pint
5-1/3 tablespoons	=	1/3 cup	4 cups	=	1 quart
8 tablespoons	=	1/2 cup	4 quarts	=	1 gallon

Food Equivalents

Grains

Macaroni	1 cup (3-1/2 ounces) uncooked	=	2-1/2 cups cooked
Noodles, Medium	3 cups (4 ounces) uncooked	=	4 cups cooked
Popcorn	1/3 to 1/2 cup unpopped	=	8 cups popped
Rice, Long Grain	1 cup uncooked	=	3 cups cooked
Rice, Quick-Cooking	1 cup uncooked	=	2 cups cooked
Spaghetti	8 ounces uncooked	=	4 cups cooked

Crumbs

Bread	1 slice	=	3/4 cup soft crumbs, 1/4 cup fine dry crumbs
Graham Crackers	7 squares	=	1/2 cup finely crushed
Buttery Round Crackers	12 crackers	=	1/2 cup finely crushed
Saltine Crackers	14 crackers	=	1/2 cup finely crushed

Fruits

Bananas	1 medium	=	1/3 cup mashed
Lemons	1 medium	=	3 tablespoons juice, 2 teaspoons grated peel
Limes	1 medium	=	2 tablespoons juice, 1-1/2 teaspoons grated peel
Oranges	1 medium	=	1/4 to 1/3 cup juice, 4 teaspoons grated peel

Vegetables

Cabbage	1 head	=	5 cups shredded	Green Pepper	1 large	=	1 cup chopped
Carrots	1 pound	=	3 cups shredded	Mushrooms	1/2 pound	=	3 cups sliced
Celery	1 rib	=	1/2 cup chopped	Onions	1 medium	=	1/2 cup chopped
Corn	1 ear fresh	=	2/3 cup kernels	Potatoes	3 medium	=	2 cups cubed

Nuts

Almonds	1 pound	=	3 cups chopped	Pecan Halves	1 pound	=	4-1/2 cups chopped
Ground Nuts	3-3/4 ounces	=	1 cup	Walnuts	1 pound	=	3-3/4 cups chopped

Easy Substitutions

When you need...		Use...
Baking Powder	1 teaspoon	1/2 teaspoon cream of tartar + 1/4 teaspoon baking soda
Buttermilk	1 cup	1 tablespoon lemon juice *or* vinegar + enough milk to measure 1 cup (let stand 5 minutes before using)
Cornstarch	1 tablespoon	2 tablespoons all-purpose flour
Honey	1 cup	1-1/4 cups sugar + 1/4 cup water
Half-and-Half Cream	1 cup	1 tablespoon melted butter + enough whole milk to measure 1 cup
Onion	1 small, chopped (1/3 cup)	1 teaspoon onion powder *or* 1 tablespoon dried minced onion
Tomato Juice	1 cup	1/2 cup tomato sauce + 1/2 cup water
Tomato Sauce	2 cups	3/4 cup tomato paste + 1 cup water
Unsweetened Chocolate	1 square (1 ounce)	3 tablespoons baking cocoa + 1 tablespoon shortening *or* oil
Whole Milk	1 cup	1/2 cup evaporated milk + 1/2 cup water

Cooking Terms

HERE'S a quick reference for some of the cooking terms used in *Taste of Home* recipes:

Baste—To moisten food with melted butter, pan drippings, marinades or other liquid to add more flavor and juiciness.

Beat—A rapid movement to combine ingredients using a fork, spoon, wire whisk or electric mixer.

Blend—To combine ingredients until *just* mixed.

Boil—To heat liquids until bubbles form that cannot be "stirred down". In the case of water, the temperature will reach 212°.

Bone—To remove all meat from the bone before cooking.

Cream—To beat ingredients together to a smooth consistency, usually in the case of butter and sugar for baking.

Dash—A small amount of seasoning, less than 1/8 teaspoon. If using a shaker, a dash would comprise a quick flip of the container.

Dredge—To coat foods with flour or other dry ingredients. Most often done with pot roasts and stew meat before browning.

Fold—To incorporate several ingredients by careful and gentle turning with a spatula. Used generally with beaten egg whites or whipped cream when mixing into the rest of the ingredients to keep the batter light.

Julienne—To cut foods into long thin strips much like matchsticks. Used most often for salads and stir-fry dishes.

Mince—To cut into very fine pieces. Used often for garlic or fresh herbs.

Parboil—To cook partially, usually used in the case of chicken, sausages and vegetables.

Partially set—Describes the consistency of gelatin after it has been chilled for a small amount of time. Mixture should resemble the consistency of egg whites.

Puree—To process foods to a smooth mixture. Can be prepared in an electric blender, food processor, food mill or sieve.

Saute—To fry quickly in a small amount of fat, stirring almost constantly. Most often done with onions, mushrooms and other chopped vegetables.

Score—To cut slits partway through the outer surface of foods. Often used with ham or flank steak.

Stir-Fry—To cook meats and/or vegetables with a constant stirring motion in a small amount of oil in a wok or skillet over high heat.

Guide to Cooking with Popular Herbs

HERB	APPETIZERS SALADS	BREADS/EGGS SAUCES/CHEESE	VEGETABLES PASTA	MEAT POULTRY	FISH SHELLFISH
BASIL	Green, Potato & Tomato Salads, Salad Dressings, Stewed Fruit	Breads, Fondue & Egg Dishes, Dips, Marinades, Sauces	Mushrooms, Tomatoes, Squash, Pasta, Bland Vegetables	Broiled, Roast Meat & Poultry Pies, Stews, Stuffing	Baked, Broiled & Poached Fish, Shellfish
BAY LEAF	Seafood Cocktail, Seafood Salad, Tomato Aspic, Stewed Fruit	Egg Dishes, Gravies, Marinades, Sauces	Dried Bean Dishes, Beets, Carrots, Onions, Potatoes, Rice, Squash	Corned Beef, Tongue Meat & Poultry Stews	Poached Fish, Shellfish, Fish Stews
CHIVES	Mixed Vegetable, Green, Potato & Tomato Salads, Salad Dressings	Egg & Cheese Dishes, Cream Cheese, Cottage Cheese, Gravies, Sauces	Hot Vegetables, Potatoes	Broiled Poultry, Poultry & Meat Pies, Stews, Casseroles	Baked Fish, Fish Casseroles, Fish Stews, Shellfish
DILL	Seafood Cocktail, Green, Potato & Tomato Salads, Salad Dressings	Breads, Egg & Cheese Dishes, Cream Cheese, Fish & Meat Sauces	Beans, Beets, Cabbage, Carrots, Cauliflower, Peas, Squash, Tomatoes	Beef, Veal Roasts, Lamb, Steaks, Chops, Stews, Roast & Creamed Poultry	Baked, Broiled, Poached & Stuffed Fish, Shellfish
GARLIC	All Salads, Salad Dressings	Fondue, Poultry Sauces, Fish & Meat Marinades	Beans, Eggplant, Potatoes, Rice, Tomatoes	Roast Meats, Meat & Poultry Pies, Hamburgers, Casseroles, Stews	Broiled Fish, Shellfish, Fish Stews, Casseroles
MARJORAM	Seafood Cocktail, Green, Poultry & Seafood Salads	Breads, Cheese Spreads, Egg & Cheese Dishes, Gravies, Sauces	Carrots, Eggplant, Peas, Onions, Potatoes, Dried Bean Dishes, Spinach	Roast Meats & Poultry, Meat & Poultry Pies, Stews & Casseroles	Baked, Broiled & Stuffed Fish, Shellfish
MUSTARD	Fresh Green Salads, Prepared Meat, Macaroni & Potato Salads, Salad Dressings	Biscuits, Egg & Cheese Dishes, Sauces	Baked Beans, Cabbage, Eggplant, Squash, Dried Beans, Mushrooms, Pasta	Chops, Steaks, Ham, Pork, Poultry, Cold Meats	Shellfish
OREGANO	Green, Poultry & Seafood Salads	Breads, Egg & Cheese Dishes, Meat, Poultry & Vegetable Sauces	Artichokes, Cabbage, Eggplant, Squash, Dried Beans, Mushrooms, Pasta	Broiled, Roast Meats, Meat & Poultry Pies, Stews, Casseroles	Baked, Broiled & Poached Fish, Shellfish
PARSLEY	Green, Potato, Seafood & Vegetable Salads	Biscuits, Breads, Egg & Cheese Dishes, Gravies, Sauces	Asparagus, Beets, Eggplant, Squash, Dried Beans, Mushrooms, Pasta	Meat Loaf, Meat & Poultry Pies, Stews & Casseroles, Stuffing	Fish Stews, Stuffed Fish
ROSEMARY	Fruit Cocktail, Fruit & Green Salads	Biscuits, Egg Dishes, Herb Butter, Cream Cheese, Marinades, Sauces	Beans, Broccoli, Peas, Cauliflower, Mushrooms, Baked Potatoes, Parsnips	Roast Meat, Poultry & Meat Pies, Stews & Casseroles, Stuffing	Stuffed Fish, Shellfish
SAGE		Breads, Fondue, Egg & Cheese Dishes, Spreads, Gravies, Sauces	Beans, Beets, Onions, Peas, Spinach, Squash, Tomatoes	Roast Meat, Poultry, Meat Loaf, Stews, Stuffing	Baked, Poached & Stuffed Fish
TARRAGON	Seafood Cocktail, Avocado Salads, Salad Dressings	Cheese Spreads, Marinades, Sauces, Egg Dishes	Asparagus, Beans, Beets, Carrots, Mushrooms, Peas, Squash, Spinach	Steaks, Poultry, Roast Meats, Casseroles & Stews	Baked, Broiled & Poached Fish, Shellfish
THYME	Seafood Cocktail, Green, Poultry, Seafood & Vegetable Salads	Biscuits, Breads, Egg & Cheese Dishes, Sauces, Spreads	Beets, Carrots, Mushrooms, Onions, Peas, Eggplant, Spinach, Potatoes	Roast Meat, Poultry & Meat Loaf, Meat & Poultry Pies, Stews & Casseroles	Baked, Broiled & Stuffed Fish, Shellfish, Fish Stews